# Institutional Innovation and the Steering of Conflicts in Latin America

Edited by Jorge P. Gordin and Lucio Renno

ecpr PRESS

ROWMAN &
LITTLEFIELD
INTERNATIONAL
*London • New York*

Published by Rowman & Littlefield International Ltd
Unit A, Whitacre Mews, 26-34 Stannary Street, London SE11 4AB
www.rowmaninternational.com

Rowman & Littlefield International Ltd. is an affiliate of Rowman & Littlefield
4501 Forbes Boulevard, Suite 200, Lanham, Maryland 20706, USA
With additional offices in Boulder, New York, Toronto (Canada), and Plymouth (UK)
www.rowman.com

This work was carried out with the aid of a grant from the International Development
Research Centre, Ottawa, Canada. The views expressed herein do not necessarily
represent those of IDRC or its Board of Governors.

**British Library Cataloguing in Publication Data**
A catalogue record for this book is available from the British Library

**Library of Congress Cataloging-in-Publication Data**

HARDBACK ISBN: 978-1-78552-231-4
PAPERBACK ISBN: 978-1-78661-111-6

∞™ The paper used in this publication meets the minimum requirements of American
National Standard for Information Sciences—Permanence of Paper for Printed Library
Materials, ANSI/NISO Z39.48-1992.

Printed in the United States of America

**More from the ECPR Press Studies in Political Science series:**

**Global Tax Governance**
ISBN: 9781785521263
*Peter Dietsch and Thomas Rixen*
'Tax specialists may think they have little to learn from a book on global tax
governance, especially one that concludes that the best solution is to create
a new International Tax Organisation (ITO). They would be wrong. Anyone
concerned with international taxation will benefit from this excellent collection
of essays about the nature and possible resolutions of the conflicts within and
between states about fiscal sovereignty, tax competition, and domestic and
international equity that underlie the international tax discussion. The authors
do not always agree with each other and few readers are likely to agree with all
of them. But this book makes clear what is really at issue in this discussion and
shows why even the recent prodigious efforts of the OECD-G20 BEPS group are
most unlikely to produce any lasting solutions. For nation-states and economic
globalisation to coexist, something like an ITO may indeed prove necessary.'
**Richard Bird, University of Toronto**

**Decision-Making under Ambiguity and Time Constraints**
ISBN: 9781785521256
*Reimut Zohlnhöfer and Friedbert W. Rüb*
'Associated with the work of US political scientist John W Kingdon, for more
than three decades, the multiple-streams Framework has informed the work of
numerous policy scholars from all over the world. Featuring an excellent line-
up comprised of well-known and more junior contributors, this edited volume
offers a timely overview of key comparative, empirical-methodological, and
theoretical issues raised by the Multiple-Streams Framework. This coherent book
will interest the many policy scholars who draw on this now classic Framework.'
**Daniel Béland, Johnson-Shoyama Graduate School of Public Policy,
University of Saskatchewan**

Please visit www.ecpr.eu/ecprpress for up-to-date information about new
and forthcoming publications.

# Table of Contents

# List of Tables

# List of Figures

*Chapter One*

# Introduction: Institutional Innovation and the Steering of Conflicts in Latin America

*Jorge P. Gordin and Lucio R. Renno*

## Introduction

Few would dispute that conflict is a troubling constant in Latin America, with instances ranging from bloody civil wars in El Salvador and Guatemala to less violent yet persistent street protests in Argentina, Bolivia and, more puzzlingly and recently, Brazil and Chile. Tangible and pragmatic issues that affect living conditions – such as political freedoms, equal rights, the quality of public services and socioeconomic concerns – underlie the contentious actions in the region. Additionally, neoliberal economic adjustment (Brysk and Wise 1997; Yashar 1998), nongovernmental support for the concerns of indigenous people (Keck and Sikkink 1998) and parallel constitutional changes (Van Cott 2002) have triggered a sort of 'ethnic revival', opening up further the spectrum of conflict dimensions in the region. Hence, we can trace back conflicts to, at least, two roots: distributional and identity. The latter is clearly related to economic inequality: The former to rights recognition. Both are pervasive and durable and both relate to demands for inclusion.

It is undeniable that as democracy swept across most countries in Latin America in the 1980s, it has assuaged political demands by offering a variety of channels and instruments for citizens to participate in the political process. Still, the problems linger on. Therefore, distributional and identity conflicts pose a significant challenge to the architecture of political institutions in Latin America.

Furthermore, increasing disenchantment with politics (Lechner 1991; Munck 1993) and recurrent economic crises have shifted interest to the institutional origins of these troubles, calling attention to putative deficiencies in institutions. Consequently, how institutions are designed and redesigned to address conflicts has received little attention in Latin America. Hence, theoretical inquiry should not only consider how institutions present solutions for social and economic problems, but also how they are moulded, changed, reconstructed in face of conflicts.

This concern with the quality of institutions is not unique to Latin America (Acemouglu and Robinson 2012). It confronts political science research with the following dilemma about institutional causality: How can we disentangle institutional performance from the effects that policy problems and solutions (Kingdom 2003), crisis and failure (Carpenter 2010) as well as feedback effects (Pierson 1993) and critical junctures (Collier and Collier 1991) exert on institutions themselves? Relatedly, how to understand the resiliency of failed institutional designs, which consistently produce sub-optimal outcomes? Lock-in effects seem powerful and first moves decisive (Collier and Collier 1991; Pierson 1993), as both generate increasing returns to scale. The important role of veto players in constraining the set of alternatives also merits consideration (Tsebelis 1995). However, as both political dissatisfaction and economic crises, in turn, impair the motivational and material foundations of institutional arrangements, we are left in a sort of inextricable theoretical conundrum. This raises the question whether institutional adjustment and change is possible and, more broadly, if it is possible to isolate the independent role of institutional design to absorb and process conflict. Likewise, it urges us to ponder about the ontological nature of conflicts: conflicts may not necessarily entail a Hobbesian state of war, they are a dimension of diversity and pluralism in democracy and peace and thus institutional arrangements can be defined through conflict processes which are driven by unequal power relations. Institutions are solutions to original conflicts, but are also molded by divergence among institutional architects, as they are built, rebuilt and destroyed. This of course adds new layers of complexity and possibilities of a theoretical endogeneity trap. We argue that these analytical challenges merit further theoretical and empirical consideration.

This book seeks to open the institutional *Pandora box* of conflict management and trains its focus on two central questions. The first is: To what degree do Latin American political contexts create a viable space for institutional design – making design feasible and legitimate? The second, and concomitant, is: What kind of processes tend to make institutional *architects* able to exploit such available space to address conflict management innovatively? Our point of departure is that institutions are primarily conflict-solving entities and that they create greater regularity in individual and social behaviour than would be found without the existence of those institutions. Without denying the merits of the path-breaking Northian heuristic characterisation of institutions as rules of the game devised to reduce uncertainties in human interactions (North 1990), we argue that institutions are set to be much more than that: institutions do (and should) emerge and are eventually in time redesigned to meet human necessities. They are endogenous to human action and desire (Przeworski 2004). In light of the pending social and economic challenges in most of Latin America, institutional designers are confronted with the fact that nothing within the institutions inherently guarantees that conflict is processed in ways that tackle distributive and ethnic inequalities in the region.

In this vein, this book contributes to theorising about how institutions and conflicts are related. Our goal is to sketch pathways through which a constellation of factors aligns to generate a model linking institutional emergence, continuity and change with different types of conflicts in society. Ultimately, we advance a theoretical approach that maps how institutions affect and are affected by social and economic conflict, attempting to clarify the ambiguous and complex relationship between conflict and institutional design. Our emphasis, however, is on the institutional side of this complicated equation.

We start by defining institutions and distinguishing between distinct interpretations of what institutions mean and include. Overall, we see institutions as entities aimed at solving complex, collective problems. We then focus on two characteristics of institutions: strength and weakness. In general, the literature argues that strong institutions are desirable, as they are legitimate, durable, adaptable, complex, bounded. However, strong institutions can be seen as cages that lock-in perverse effects on society, controlling but not solving problems that originally generated social conflicts. We also argue that so-called weak institutions may be an opportunity for change. As weak institutions are less complex, less effective and less legitimate, they are easier to reform and more porous to channel changes proposed by new agendas or unresolved conflicts. Hence, our focus is on how institutions are designed (emergence and innovation), redesigned (change) or resilient (continuity) based on how they are affected by conflicts. Unresolved or new conflicts generate incentives for institution building and reform. Institutional resilience, on the other hand, may occur because some benefit from the existing architecture, be they the original institutional engineers or new beneficiaries.

Historically speaking, institutional design has not been kind to Latin American changing realities and resulting cleavages. Many Latin American countries deliberately modelled their political orders on that of the United States, mostly its constitution. In turn, the ensuing gap between doctrine and reality has revealed the limits of institutional import (Weyland 2009). Specifically, formal political institutions in the United States were purposefully designed to inhibit strong political action and to limit the power of the government to such an extent that they were dysfunctional to the levels of social conflict and increasing levels of structural inequality in Latin America. Likewise, both the Washington Consensus and the parallel decentralisation campaign advocated by international agencies rendered a legacy of institutional reforms that have been increasingly questioned (on democratic governance, see Gibson 2012; on corruption, see Treisman 2002). Overambitious institutional import thus underscores the frequent divergence between formal rules, on the one hand, and actual behaviour and the informal mechanisms guiding it, on the other. Herein lie some of the fundamental roots of the institutional weaknesses in the region in coping with conflict, leading to earlier democratic breakdowns and currently to increasing levels of political apathy and related crises of representation (Dominguez 1997; Hochstetler and Friedman 2008; Mainwaring, Bejarano and Leongomez 2006).

## Explaining Institutional Solutions to Conflicts

This book subscribes the fundamental spirit of the 'New Institutionalism' scholarship and its explanations of economic and political change in terms of how institutions interact with individual actors and the broader economic and social environment to reduce uncertainty and thus tackle conflicts inherent to institutional solutions and lack thereof. Still, it casts doubt on the validity and applicability of some tenets of this paradigmatic compass of institutional research. In a nutshell, the budding cottage industry on institutional research drawing on this scholarship shares the basic idea that the initial choices made early in the process of institution building will have a continuing, fairly determinant influence over subsequent choices, far into the future. The practical theoretical and empirical limitations of this rather disappointingly, simple analytical blueprint is compounded by the functionalist bias that underlies it.[1] Borrowing from Pierson (2000: 475), 'the explanation of institutional forms is to be found in their functional consequences for those who create them'.

The tautological potential of this understanding of institutions lies underneath Jack Knight's (1992) *Institutions and Social Conflict*. Amounting to perhaps the most seminal and systematic treatment on the institutional underpinnings of conflict dynamics, Knight's study sets out to reject unrealistic functionalist arguments, claiming that power asymmetries among actors beget institutional designs that are simply instruments of those in favourable bargaining positions. While sometimes collective benefits result from institutional innovation, the extension of bargaining asymmetries and, thus self-interested considerations, are of primary importance for understanding institutional design. Still, this apparently robust theory of spontaneous and decentralised emergence and functioning of institutions falls short of plotting how institutions, once established as enforceable rules, constrain individual choice. More worrisomely, from the vantage point of this volume, Knight's analysis overlooks the feedback mechanism through which institutions affect resource asymmetries, which is part and parcel of the obstacles to address conflicts in developing polities. Especially, if we consider that in Latin American countries, people's economic achievements, as well as their cultural and territorial rights, are significantly conditioned by their circumstances, not their choices.

The second school of thought on how institutional design affects conflict management relates to the ground-breaking contribution of Arend Lijphart. His theory of consociationalism offers concrete treads on how practices to bridge political, economic and ethnic elites may well become worthy instruments of governance in polities with multiple cleavages (Lijphart 1968). Yet, these top-down institutional arrangements have been questioned insofar as oftentimes they end up exacerbating ethnic and territorial grievances and putatively leading to instability and violence as well as inhibiting meaningful and substantive democratic progression. Useful as this theory is in taking for granted the existence of conflict and rivalry among distinct communities for cultural, economic and social goods, consociationalism has had limited explanatory power for conflict-ridden developing countries. On practical grounds, this arrangement predicates on the cooperation of elites representing conflicting interests, but plotting elite cooperation is precisely the problem of most divided societies. In normative democratic terms, it amounts to a sort of model of exclusionary democracy requiring a high degree of elite autonomy from their constituencies (Wilsford 2000: 2).

---

1.   The school of rational choice institutionalism intrinsically advocates a view of institutions as systems of rules and inducements in which the behaviour of utility-maximising individuals must be coordinated and /or restrained (Bates 1981).

Alternatively, the consociational option renders a non-territorial solution to political conflicts. In intensely divided societies that seek to avoid civil wars and political violence, the stakes are too high to conduct politics as a zero-sum game. Originally conceived as an institutional solution based on power-sharing for overcoming ethnic, religious and language divisions (Lijphart 1968), consociationalism has also been regarded as a viable instrument in Latin American countries such as Colombia and Uruguay where political power has been historically disputed by opposing partisan groups. In this vein, consociationalism advances cooperation between elites representing all segments of society, rendering a form of governance that encompasses executive, or at least collegial, power-sharing by means of a grand coalition for overcoming patronage concerns as well as distributive demands.

In Latin America, consociationalism has been used mainly to illustrate Colombia's coalition regime of 1958 after an extended period of political violence and military rule (Hartlyn 1988). Still, considering the subsequent guerrilla insurgency and drug trade challenge, it is hardly a poster child solution for sustainable conflict management. Similarly, Venezuela has incorporated consociational features as a result of the Punto Fijo agreement followed by four decades of institutional stability. The virtual collapse of its party systems and the beginning of the Chavez era cast doubt nonetheless on the long-term prospect of such cartel arrangement. Consequently, this begets the question whether there might be more legitimate and effective institutional arrangements at lower levels of the conflict dimensions pillars than the elite level in the Latin American context.

### The Notion of a Conflict

A variety of meanings can be found in the political science literature on conflict. In large part, its definition entails a Hobbesian-minded approach focused on the unrelenting incompatibility of actors' goals based on their interests and resources, leading to domestic political unrest and grievances or interstate, international, confrontation. An alternative approach sees conflict both as the origin and 'leitmotiv' of politics and as a powerful instrument of government that all regimes must resort to (Schattschneider 1957). Another possibility is to look at the evolutionary nature of conflicts, identifying their genesis, periods of escalation and thresholds of explosion. This study, however, takes a much simpler and thinner approach to conflicts. Our idea of conflict relates to the disagreement among individuals and social groups that obstructs the sorting out and tackling of the key developmental challenges in a political system, namely the challenges that entail distributive and ethnic/identity implications. More often than not, these conflicts operate in a zero-sum dynamics largely due to significant gaps among actors in their access to material and reputational resources. Herein, in its developmental consequences, lies the crux of such conflicts and their political corollaries. Likewise, we do not endorse normative positions on conflicts, whether they are part and parcel of politics itself or they rather lacerate human coexistence. In our approach to the subject, conflicts embody the visible and tangible dimensions of central developmental problems, whose solutions are disputed and contested by individuals, groups and organisations. In this regard, our understanding draws its basic insights from the classic literature on cleavages, insofar as said developmental problems may lead to conflict, but these problems need not always be attended by conflict. [2]

In this vein, we are primarily interested in two major types of conflict: distributional and ethnic/identity. Distributional conflicts refer basically to issues of resource allocation in society, mostly but not exclusively related to fiscal policy. The concern is with the dispute over the authoritative allocation of public, collective resources. Conflicts around ethnic and identity issues refer mostly to rights recognition and access to the law. Understood broadly, these two types of conflict can be seen as the predominant ones in Latin America. Both types of conflict are related to issues of inclusion and inequality, but not limited to them. Both also are deeply ingrained in Latin American history and neither of easy solution. What is more, these conflict scenarios are sometimes intertwined, hampering the drawing of precise conceptual boundaries, as can be seen in decentralisation debates in Bolivia and indigenous rights in Ecuador.

Based on our understanding of institutions as arrangements to solve social, political and economic dilemmas that spur conflicts, we must consider the potential impacts of distinct institutional traits and trajectories in solving or attenuating these conflicts. Thus, we claim that it is of essence to think about not only how institutions are moulded by conflict but also how they affect prevailing forms of conflict. That said, and considering that cooperation is necessary for crafting acceptable and legitimate agreements, what are the 'mechanics' of the institutional underpinnings of conflict solutions? At this stage, we opt for talking about the mechanisms rather than the underlying causes of institutional performance because of the putative reciprocal effects we have discussed above, hence the jury is still out on the issue of causality and institutional genesis of conflict management. In fact, we are sceptical that there will ever be decisive evidence about causal primacy on this matter. We will go back to the mechanics of the argument once we lay out the institutional parameters shaping conflict management.

### *Unpacking Institutional Blueprints: The Paradox of 'Strong' and 'Weak' Designs*

As mentioned before, we define institutions as human devised entities aimed at solving complex, collective problems and, consequently, addressing existing, latent or imminent conflicts that may arise in society. This definition is purposely broad as we wish to consider as political institutions the formal rules of the game, the official procedures in a political system, the organisations embedded in these rules and based on procedures (including political parties, legislatures,

---

2.    The seminal characterisation of cleavages by Rae and Taylor (1970: 1) is that 'cleavages are the criteria which divide members of a community or subcommunity into groups, and the relevant cleavages are those which divide members into groups with important political differences at specific times and places'. Thus, we see cleavages as dimensions of potential political conflict.

governmental agencies, bureaucracies), and the informal norms that steer behaviour. In this light, we look at how institutions originate, change, persist, and survive in the process of addressing distributive and identity conflicts. Hence, the focus is on two specific traits of institutions: weakness and strength. We define a weak institution as one that political actors and elites can unilaterally manipulate and modify its guiding principles and rules to their own strategic and material benefit. Conversely, a strong institution is one whose guiding principles and rules are entrenched in the terms in which such an institution was originally designed and survives in an equilibrium that cannot be unilaterally altered. That said, as we will explain thereafter, strong designs are not always desirable Pareto-optimising equilibriums, whereas weak designs may engender windows of opportunity for innovative institutional solutions.

The concept of institutional strength is widely used but often poorly defined in the literature on comparative politics and political economy. Characterisations range from a Weberian understanding of state institutions as the monopolist of legitimate violence and protectors of private property rights (Milgrom *et al.* 1990; Weingast 1995) to their ability to penetrate deeply into society and effectively regulate social, economic, or political behaviour of citizens (Evans 1995; Huntington 1968; Levi 1988). Institutional strength has been associated with ideational innovation (Weir 1992), 'veto points' or 'strategic openings' (Immergut 1990) and implementation capacity (Wildavsky 1980). While most of these perspectives share some tacit understanding about the significance and causal role of political institutions, they seldom refer explicitly to the notion of institutional strength nor identify its concrete and measurable indicators.

To fill this analytical vacuum, the concept of institutionalisation has been often employed as a proxy of institutional strength, mostly drawing on Samuel Huntington's definition of institutionalisation as 'the process by which organisations and procedures acquire value and stability' (Huntington 1968: 12). In the same vein, North (1990: 3) claims that institutions reassert themselves by 'providing a structure to everyday life', generating a scenario that is not easily modified. These heuristic characterisations have, however, translated into more rigorous and precise scrutiny in research on legislatures and political parties. First, building on the seminal study by Nelson Polsby (1968) on the US Congress, analysts have shown that legislatures institutionalise through professionalisation, namely when boundaries for roles, internal complexity and universalistic criteria are well established (Cooper and Brady 1981; Squire 1992). In addition, institutional constraints preclude cyclical majorities, generating stability and explaining different actors' power to influence choices, as the likes of Tullock, Shepsle and Weingast, among many others who focus on social choice and legislative politics, have consistently shown time and again. Second, party institutionalisation takes place when 'citizens and organised interests must perceive that parties and elections are the means of determining who governs, and that the electoral process and parties are accorded legitimacy' (Mainwaring and Scully 1995: 14). Institutionalisation then connotes the process of consolidating a democracy and presages responsible policymaking. Agreement among actors about the rules of the game as the only one in town become essential to the consolidation of an institutional arrangement and begets the question of legitimacy, or support. This strand of research marks the discussion on the problems of democratic transition and consolidation, a path breaking agenda that is too vast to cite here but includes a roster of scholars who actually moulded the practice of political science in Latin America, including Juan Linz, Guillermo O'Donnell, Alfred Stepan, Laurence Whitehead, Adam Przeworski, Fabio Wanderley Reis, among others. Put simply, while the scholarship on institutionalisation diverges in the object of study, there is one factor it agrees upon: insofar as institutionalisation amounts to ascertaining and entrenching the 'rules of the game', it is adjoined by positive developments and performance. The bottom line of this research strand (and the above is certainly a very limited list of it) is that the more institutionalised an organisation or set of rules are (be it Congress, political parties, the executive branch, the presidency, a political regime), the more likely these institutions are to impose order and to effectively influence policy decisions and political outcomes. They gain an aura of exogeneity: of causal primacy over outcomes.

Levitsky and Murillo (2009) provide perhaps the clearest characterisation of institutional strength. They identify enforcement and stability as two central dimensions to assess institutional strength. Accordingly, formal institutional arrangements that persist in substance and over time are deemed strong. In practice, this suggests that when said arrangements withstand adversity and endure, actors and groups become increasingly aware of the effect of institutional rules on their interest and, concomitantly, learn how to organise to cope with institutional effects, even the unintended ones. Thus, when institutional arrangements persist and they reasonably survive crises and changes of government, actors invest in skills and organisation thereby raising the cost of institutional replacement. This is the type of institutional dynamics that transpires when key actors, protected by institutional veto points, control the process of institutional adjustment. For instance, despite the results of the US Presidential election of 2000 having been publicly questioned because the candidate that received the most votes was not elected, no major institutional recalibration occurred. The underlying reason is that a constitutional revision would need the approval of the small states uninterested in such reform as a direct popular vote would eventually diminish their actual clout. Thus, enforceable and stable arrangements do not necessarily induce Pareto-optimal outcomes.

We argue that understanding the types of institutional changes, their likelihood, and the motivations that generate changes becomes key to understanding processes of institutionalisation. In fact, the process of change itself, how it takes place, who participates, what is kept and what is removed, tells us enormously about the evolution of an institution. If change is accompanied by improvements in the functioning of the institution in meeting its objectives, which is a clear definition of efficacy, and of doing so economically, then a clear definition of efficiency than just change means institutionalisation. If an institution changes to reduce conflict and becomes accepted, we can talk about a consolidated (institutionalised) institutional framework. If an institution lingers on, but always as a source of renewed conflict, always being criticised and change is rejected by a small number of powerful veto players, this is the type of perverse institutional design that does not attenuate conflict and insists in existing due to vested interests or a possible and legitimate concern of reformers with the unanticipated effects of institutional engineering.

Accordingly, we contrast two research agendas on institutional design that identify the context affecting how institutional arrangements emerge and survive to generate collective benefits, each led by some fundamental understanding of the consequences that path dependence has in institutional analysis. In so doing, this book inquires about the theoretical implications of a prevalent conventional wisdom on the deleterious consequences of institutional weakness in developing countries (Acemoglu and Robinson 2001; Bates 1981; Rodrik 1999). The main lesson of these works is that in institutionally weak societies, elites and politicians will find various ways of expropriating collective goods and rents of different sectors of the society, via different policies. We object to this characterisation and argue that seemingly strong institutional arrangements may 'lock-in' previous decisions in perverse and Pareto-suboptimal ways. By the same token, inchoate and ostensibly weak institutional designs may engender ideational innovations that foster conflict-solving patterns. Painting in broad strokes, we identify two institutional constellations:

1. *The dark side of 'strong' institutional designs*: This scenario draws attention to the pervasiveness of early choices and the ensuing perils of deadlocking malfunctioning institutions. The argument goes that institutions, be they weak or strong, can at times undermine the normative purposes for which they were created in the first place. What is more, strong, historically persistent, institutional arrangements have unintended distortionary distributional consequences that extant institutionalist research often fails to acknowledge. The main contention is that transaction costs and related public policy approaches overstate the merits of equilibrium models of institutional persistence. In fact, the aspects being praised by equilibrium models of institutional persistence may ultimately compound deadlocked and perennially malfunctioning political arrangements.

Arguably, the 'weak institutions cum policy decay' thesis actually overlooks instances of perverse institutionalisation of political power, namely when groups and entities holding political power at a certain point in time have strong incentives to manipulate institutional arrangements to protect their interests in the future. One prominent illustration of the above is the manipulation of territorial institutional design, which results from the political empowerment of particular subnational units, usually transpiring as legislative overrepresentation (malapportionment). Beyond the substantial and deleterious consequences of malapportionment on the quality of the political system (estrangement between executive and legislative branches, weakening of progressive forces and bolstering of patronage-dependent forces), it is thought to have distributive and welfare-detrimental consequences. As overrepresented, often economically poor and transfer-dependent, jurisdictions are aware of their strategic advantages as more affordable coalition partners than more-expensive-to-co-opt, they are institutionally endowed to extract resources from the national government with little concern for the potential impact of their economic decisions on the polity as a whole. This political empowerment of peripheral jurisdictions has also significantly funnelled the fate of fiscal decentralisation in some Latin American federations. For instance, while Argentina has one of the most fiscally decentralised system in terms of the spending powers of provinces, the revenue responsibility and authority lies mostly at the national government level. In such an institutional scenario, peripheral provinces, mostly unpopulated and hence overrepresented, have used their political clout to perpetuate revenue centralisation, releasing them from the political costs of revenue collection, which has encouraged soft-budget constraints of gargantuan proportions at the subnational level (Jones, Sanguinetti and Tommasi 2000). The fiscal correlate of this representational arrangement is the disjuncture between national-level fiscal priorities and subnational-level overspending, which contributed to Argentina's 2001 economic crisis, the worst since the Great Depression of the 1930s.

Worrisomely, this representational bias looms large as one of the most difficult-to-amend institutional arrangements because special majorities (or dictatorial decrees like in Argentina and Chile) are required to make the necessary statutory or, even worse, constitutional adjustments. The underlying reason is that such revisions would need the approval of the overrepresented states uninterested in such reform. A cursory look at Samuels and Snyder's (2001: 662) list of worldwide malapportionment in upper chambers hints at the entrenchment of this institutional arrangement in the region: among the first twenty-five countries listed, ten are Latin American cases. Let alone that Argentina, Brazil, Bolivia and Dominican Republic, respectively, rank highest in such a worldwide list.

Another example of strong institutional design relates to the adoption of electoral rules and reforms of electoral systems. Similarly, and based on their difficult-to-amend nature, electoral systems are not evolving independently from overriding conflicts. For instance, despite the adoption of proportional representation (PR) which is often regarded as a democratising exercise aimed at opening the political competition to partisan forces representing the poor and minorities, the literature has posited that strategical considerations were the decisive influence, as a response either to economic transformations or changes in the broader political environment as the source of political anxiety among right wing politicians (Boix 1999; Rokkan 1970). A cursory glimpse at the Latin American experience reveals that by 1900 most countries in the region resorted to majoritarian representation and that by the middle of twentieth century a considerable number of countries shifted to PR. Among these experiences, the Brazilian case deserves special attention. Since its inception in 1932, the adoption of the PR system, as Ricci and Zulini show in this book, had been justified by a discourse about protecting minorities but it has, nevertheless, increased the chances that traditional political forces gained representation in the Chamber of Deputies, thus bolstering the political representation of those forces opposed to the opening of political spaces to the weak sectors. When we consider the subsequent splintering and patronage-enhancing effects of PR and its open-list component (Ames 2001), it is possible to argue that overall PR prompted something of conservative sort of governance, which hampered the ability of the country's political leadership to transcend patronage politics and develop coherent policies suitable for addressing social inequality until the coming of the 1988 Constitution.

The above having been said, while institutional designs that are deemed strong often lock-in malfunctioning, conflict-ridden political interaction, it is necessary to consider some exceptions. If we accept the above-mentioned Levitsky and Murillo's (2009) typological characterisation of enforcement and stability to understand institutional strength, the Coparticipation in Uruguay, albeit informal in nature, has proven to be a fairly resilient arrangement that, because of its routinisation, has emerged as a sort of collegial co-government where the opposition is consulted and included in the most decisive critical decisions in the country.

2.  *The promise of 'weak' becoming institutions*: Drawing on an increasingly influential literature on ideational innovation (Grindle 2000; Hall 1992; Weir 1992), this perspective looks at institutional entrepreneurs, emphasising agency and the 'practical authority' capital (Abers and Keck 2013) that institution builders engender when starting from scratch to breathe life into new institutional design.

This perspective builds upon a two-pronged strategy to analyse institutional change and innovation. First, the political and institutional environment creates opportunities for institutional evolution. In particular and counter-intuitively, we advance the idea that prior institutional weakness promotes chances for change. Institutions that haven't gained legitimacy or deep roots or haven't become complex and specialised, are easier prey for change. Second, institutional evolution and rearrangements only occur when real-life political actors and stakeholders engage in practices and adopt strategies that lead to modifications in institutional designs, governmental agencies and policy programmes. For change to occur, individuals and groups must act, must be motivated and must acquire influence and power so as to modify institutions. Hence, the strategies institutional engineers and architects use to change rules and organisations from within are also vital for understanding how modifications in institutional frameworks actually occur.

James Mahoney and Kathleen Thelen pioneered the conceptualisation of types of institutional change and their driving forces. In 'A Theory of

Gradual Institutional Change', they propose an interpretation of institutions as distributional instruments that have a built-in dynamic component because they 'represent compromises or relatively durable but still contested settlements based on specific coalitional dynamics', making 'institutions vulnerable to shifts' (2010: 8). This theoretical definition of institutions is extremely important for the argument we develop here. First, it indicates that institutions are intrinsically built with specific motivations that can be related to an actor's preferences over outcomes on distributional issues. More specifically, distributional conflicts can be based on economic factors as well as the recognition of rights and access to the legal system. Second, it suggests that institutional change is associated with contextual factors, such as the traits of the actual institution targeted for reform.

Another theoretical avenue concerns the subjective orientations of political actors and how these catalyse opportunities for change. This transpires in James Stimson's discussion of political moods, emphasising the policy preferences identified by public opinion polls and their congruence with a government's policy choices. Stimson's argument clearly focuses on the macro-level aspect of public opinion, which is central to the understanding of how public opinion and general beliefs create structural opportunities for change. Stimson's argument thus relates to the aggregate ideational environment, as we call it here, leading to macro opportunities for change. In a nutshell, when there are broad agreements for the need of change, the likelihood of institutional evolution increases. An additional macro characteristic that deserves attention is the occurrence of some policy tragedy. Daniel Carpenter argues, in his discussion of food and drug regulation in the United States, that a triggering event for institutional innovation is the failure of a prior institutional arrangement (Carpenter 2010). In turn, policy tragedies are marked by the unquestionable failure of some existing policy programme, leading to frustration with existing outcomes. The inability of a past action to solve or mitigate a specific conflict or problem stimulates new thinking and opens the arena for new ideas. It also creates the opportunity for the construction of a new image of the institution, a reputation that may lead to its institutionalisation as was the case of the Food and Drug Administration in the US.

In sum, prior institutional weakness, an opinion environment prone to change, and policy tragedies compose a constellation of contextual ingredients that may open opportunities for innovation. However, these innovations only come about through the action of individuals and groups. The role of ideas and strategies to build authority and influence (Abers and Keck 2013) are fundamental. Motivations are also important. This perspective shifts the focus to the institutional architects and engineers. It is about how they develop capabilities, embody ideas, win recognition, build coalitions through networking, and are motivated to influence the behaviour of others who have disparate perspectives and are differently situated. For Abers and Keck, institution-building is a relational process that occurs through human action and involves: creating and disseminating ideas, struggling over legal design, experimenting with new solutions, accumulating organisational and technical capabilities and building networks (2013: 3). Clearly, institution-building is a result of conflict and realignments and as Carpenter had argued, there is no clear founding moment, no single designer; it is born from and moulded by conflict (2013: 118). Exploring the dynamics of conflict at the micro level is an important element of the institution-making equation.

In Latin America, and Brazil in particular, significant changes in social policy have become the mark of the left-wing turn in national and regional governments. The amply studied Participative Budget Process (PBP) is one of these innovations that aim at increasing popular participation in budgetary decisions, affecting governmental investment in directly combating inequality and poverty (Abers 1998; Avritzer 2002; Goldfrank and Schneider 2006; Renno and Ames 2010). Still, many innovations are yet to be explored. A much less studied case is the construction of a social welfare infrastructure that coordinates social policy programmes and distributive mechanisms in the State. The creation of the Ministry of Social Development, *Ministério do Desenvolvimento Social (MDS)* in Brazil, during the Workers' Party first Lula da Silva administration, is a special case to study under the approach above, which combines macro and micro level factors. It epitomises the dynamics of institution building triggered by a paradigmatic shift in social welfare policies in Brazil from a philanthropically driven '*assistencialismo*' to more genuine social inclusion prompted by the 1988 Brazilian Constitution. Narrating the trajectory that lead to the creation of this institution throws light on how a weak prior institutional architecture is remodelled, stimulated by a new consensus about the priority of social policies. The transformation of social policy programmes in Brazil, from state *assistencialismo* and philanthropy to an institutionalised bureaucratic agency that manages welfare programmes is fundamental to understanding important recent institutional reforms that spur from the left-wing turn in Latin America. We argue that this approach can be applied to many processes of institutional change.

## *Mechanics*

Even though the preceding discussion is broad and diverse, the focus of this book is narrower and examines the institutional development of conflict resolution instances in Latin America. That said, it places the theoretical emphasis on the two research agendas of institutional building and change outlined above and identifies the different processes of institutional design to assess their conflict-solving potential based on the empirical experience of a number of Latin American cases. Furthermore, as argued before, we opt for outlining the mechanics rather than the underlying institutional causes of conflict. This analytical strategy is chosen to identify the institutional scenarios whereby developmental problems turn into conflict arenas rather than providing a definitive causal explanation. This usage of mechanics does not imply that observed patterns are mechanical; on the contrary, a host of contextual macro (policy diffusion, crises) and micro (leadership, beliefs, motivations) parameters condition the impact of institutional designs on conflicts.

The mechanism consists in a framework that knits together institutional emergence, stability and change to identify the pathways through which strong and weak institutional designs tackle distributive and identity conflicts in Latin America. We begin by arguing that the emergence of institutional designs does not unfold in a vacuum but rather reflects the initial root conflict. Specifically, we identify boundary settlement and state organisation imperatives, on the one hand, and recognition rights, on the other hand. The former had been addressed through territorially decentralising solutions or partisan power-sharing agreements and the latter through the state's recognition of multicultural rights, customary law and indigenous autonomy. These root conflicts had not been addressed simultaneously or synchronically. While federal institutional solutions and regional empowering measures, on the one hand, and partisan power-sharing mechanisms, on the other hand, transpired from the mid-1800s and onset of 1900s, the constitutional and electoral recognition of indigenous people is of more recent, if not ongoing, nature. Thus state responses to territorial and distributive grievances engendered strong institutional designs in the sense that they entailed constitutional and statutory safeguards (i.e. federal arrangements and legislative representation rules in Argentina and Brazil) or either informal, yet resilient, co-governing pacts (i.e. the *Coparticipación* in Uruguay). Conversely, recognition claims have encountered feeble state institutional responses, basically consisting in the co-optation of indigenous voters in exchange for façade autonomy in the most multi-ethnic and ethnically divided Andean region countries (Bolivia, Ecuador and Peru) and Mexico, where the long governing Party of the Institutional Revolution (PRI) state had allowed indigenous administrators to rule their territories in exchange for the concomitant registration of these administrators as PRI members. This weak institutional setting persisted until new types of representation aimed at redressing recognition demands began to emerge, largely fuelled by the development of indigenous movements since the 1960s and the 1989 creation of the International Labour Organization's Proposition 169, which compels countries to uphold international standards for recognising indigenous rights.

However, weak and strong institutional responses have not intrinsically and uniformly given rise to desirable solutions for developmental problems and thus at times have failed to address conflict scenarios satisfactorily. Strong institutional responses can fall prey to entrenched interests wanting to preserve and deadlock a welfare-detrimental balance, as can be seen in the extremely malapportioned and fiscally centralised Argentine federation and its recurrent fiscal crises, but they can also moderate zero sum centrifugal political moves and generate an acceptable playing field to sort out distributive conflicts as shown in the Uruguayan co-governing arrangement. By the same token, weak institutional responses are related to electoral authoritarian manipulation of indigenous representation via indigenous customs (*usos y costumbres* or UC) in Mexican Oaxaca, yet such responses can breed electoral mechanisms such as prior consultation (*consulta previa*), namely the collective right of indigenous communities whose lands or environment could be potentially affected by resource extraction or mega-development projects to be consulted before projects begin. Albeit questioned because it does not fully impede manipulation by elites (Schilling-Vacaflor and Flemmer 2013), *consulta previa* may actively engage indigenous communities in staging their demands, provided certain institutional conditions such as the intervention of socially-minded constitutional courts in Colombia, as Pozas-Loyo and Rios-Figueroa show in this volume, are present.

Then, what makes strong institutional designs not only durable but also effective instruments to address conflicts? Equally, what infuses innovative breath into weak institutional designs, in spite of the shorter trajectory, to turn them into effective arenas to tackle such conflicts? Insofar as engineering cooperation lies at the core of any action or settlement of conflicts, we focus on two factors drawn from the seminal contributions of Knight and Lijphart outlined previously. One such dimension that is central to Knight's thesis is *power asymmetry* among organised and relevant bargaining agents. We lay emphasis on relevancy, as increasing the absolute, arithmetic number of powerful agents is not a necessary condition for conflict management. What is more, as Mancur Olson's thesis on institutional sclerosis avers, polities with a greater number of organised interests are less economically successful and more impaired in their conflict-solving capacities (Olson 1984). Hence, assuming that resource asymmetries precede the institutional arrangements under scrutiny in our volume, we take a structural look at the conflict-relevant bargaining agents. Namely, the territorial units in federal arrangements, political parties in co-governing arrangements, the triangle of state, business and indigenous elites for cases such as *consulta previa* and the relation between a hegemonic political party and indigenous leaders for instances such as UC. The second factor relates to the *cohesiveness* of the bargaining agents, which is the cornerstone of Lijphart's model of consociationalism. The functioning of the institutional response, in turn, depends on the internal consistency of each bargaining unit (i.e. elites), their political discipline and the degree of control respective units exercise over their groups or trustees. In this parameter, we look at the vertical distribution of powers and authority with each relevant unit, be it a political party, national business association, subnational unit and so on. The stylised argument reflecting the mechanism outlined above then is that issues of institutional strength and weakness have full, real-world, implications to the tackling of conflicts inasmuch as we give account of the internal consistency of the agents involved as well as the power asymmetries among them. Put simply, institutional designs are necessary but per se not sufficient conditions for addressing the more pressing developmental problems in Latin America. Only once we square the anatomy of the agents cooperation in the mechanism discussed heretofore, will it be possible to pinpoint the institutional origins (and solutions) of conflicts.

## A Note on Conceptualisation and Methodology

The cases analysed in this book do not lean towards comparative analysis at first glance. We are throwing together instances of electoral manipulation, power-sharing arrangements, bureaucratic agency building and grassroots democratic participation into the same analytical framework. While we risk morphological comparative inconsistency, it is important to emphasise that this volume analyses a spectrum of institutional designs that are canonical to understand the anatomy of conflicts and institutional design in the region. Despite obvious differences among the distinct institutional options, there are striking similarities in the evolution of their conflict-solving potential. To our credit, while the instances of institutional design have attracted rigorous scholarly attention, this is one of the first attempts to offer an account of institutional dynamics that gives justice to the changing social, economic and political realities of Latin America. With this regional focus, we engage in midlevel theorising, hoping that scholars studying other regions of the world are inspired to review our findings and juxtapose them to the rest of the world. While analysing the promise and limitation of institutional solutions to conflict in the region, the book also seeks to engage itself in the broader debate on whether success in economic and political development depends primarily on improving institutions.

Therefore, the chapters that ensue adopt the same rationale about institutional transformation and resilience outlined above, in light of specific distributive and identity conflicts in Latin America, but also innovate theoretically as they attempt to explain various distinct cases. Hence, the approach we discuss is not a theoretical straightjacket to which all must abide. Instead, it's an attempt to illustrate the theoretical challenges that a systematic discussion about conflicts and institutions entail and that cut across the distinct cases explored in the subsequent chapters. In fact, each chapter has a life of its own and can be read juxtaposed to the other chapters or as a stand-alone piece.

We should also add that the theoretical approach spelled out above is adjustable to various distinct research designs and analytical strategies. In particular, the study of institutional change must be one that includes both history and current context in the specification of a model that explains changes in the processing of social, political and economic conflicts. Several chapters adopt a historical narrative to explain foundational choices and processes of continuity. Others adopt cross-sectional statistical models to understand the determinants of institutional change. Others still focus on shorter process-tracing strategies to uncover specific decisions and decision-making processes. The types of variables also vary: from individual level survey data to aggregate level historical data at the macro-level. Hence, the book is a testament for methodological plurality, without abandoning epistemological canons of rigor and systematic research.

## Book Plan

While the topics addressed in this book are not unknown, it ventures into new theoretical territory. The contributions in this volume seek to identify the limits and opportunities of stagnant and innovative institutional designs, reflecting the increased interest in the conflict-solving potential of such arrangements. Regardless of their substantive foci, these chapters discuss contrasting experiences of conflict management with the explicit challenge of elucidating the institutional sources of distributive and ethnic tensions in Latin America with two theoretical goals in mind. First, the strongly-context dependent effect of institutional designs implies that issues of reciprocal causality merit careful attention in light of the mutually conditioning effects of institutional options and the severity and scope of the conflict scenario. Second, the chapters share the assumption that, beyond the normative plea for an inclusive polity, the accommodating effects of institutional designs should be assessed empirically in terms of how such designs address deep-seated problems of inequality in the region.

The focus of the book, therefore, is on institutional dynamics in its relationship with social, political, and economic conflict. The book division reflects this logic and the eight substantive chapters that follow fall into three parts that focus on distinct moments of institutional dynamics: foundational stories, resiliency and innovation. The founding moments of institutions are important to understand how institutions came to be and which conflicts they intended to address. Narratives of resiliency focus on how institutions linger on, how some institutions have ingrained lock-in mechanisms that resist change, albeit there would be reasons for change. Finally, the cases of innovation build on the environmental and individual conditions that create opportunities for remodelling or re-creating institutions. The last chapters of the book focus on cases of institutional reconstruction to address specific, paramount conflicts.

Part One discusses the founding moments of institutional creation, especially of institutions that have lingered on in Latin America in spite of the lack of consensus about their positive outcomes to society. Hence, the emphasis is on the historical dimension of the foundational stages as well as how recent institutional innovations in the region reflect enduring patterns of unsettled fundamental conflicts. These fundamental conflicts around the creation of formal institutions have decisive consequences both for the political order and hegemonic actors steering the political process. Alternatively, the consociational option renders an informal institutional solution to political conflicts. In intensely divided societies that seek to avoid civil wars and political violence, the stakes are too high to conduct politics as a zero-sum game. In this vein, consociationalism embodied in the so called *Copaticipación* has also been regarded as a long-standing, viable instrument in Latin American countries such as Uruguay where political power has been historically disputed by opposing partisan groups.

In Chapter Two, Sergio Toro-Maureira and Juan Arellano-Gonzalez examine the reasons for the excessive concentration of executive power in Latin America by identifying the root causes that have influenced the continent's general institutional fragility. Specifically, they seek to determine how the original formation of representative institutions – predicated upon a high concentration of power – reproduced an initial root conflict which has remained latent down to the present day in the rupture and breakdown of representative institutions. Accordingly, Toro and Arellano identify three fundamental types of root conflicts: Emancipation, Boundary Settlement and State Organisation, which amount to critical junctures that shape the nature and dynamics of institutional approaches to conflicts in the region. Of essence, these three root conflicts ensue synchronically and diachronically, determining the likelihood a given country will be institutionally equipped to meet future challenges. While a wide sample of countries is analysed, the case of Uruguay epitomises the effect of the configuration of such root conflicts on the relative outstanding performance of this country in tackling distributive conflicts that have lead other countries in the region to massive disaffection and violence.

Chapter Three is authored by Paolo Ricci and Jacqueline Porto Zulini and focuses on the adoption of proportional representation (PR) in Brazil, a country that has historically experienced widespread electoral fraud and restricted access to ballots. This process crystallised through the approval of the 1932 Electoral Code. Like any change in the institutional rules, the adoption of electoral rules begets the central question on who wins and who loses from such reform. Paradoxically, and challenging the conventional wisdom of 'cleavage theory', the 1932 reforms did not aim at protecting European national minorities in pre-First World War or were a response from the elites to contain the impending socialist threat. Rather, the adoption of PR principles intended to protect the old oligarchies that had been defeated during the 1930 revolution. In turn, and as Ricci and Porto Zulini show, the reform ended up increasing the top-down control of the electoral process and minimising risks of defeat. Amounting to a sort of 'reactionary' institutional arrangement, the 1932 Electoral Code set Brazil apart from the British and American cases where the reforms to fight electoral corruption enhanced programmatic appeals, prompting the control of voters and of the electoral bureaucracy, not the choice of the electoral system. Hence, PR reforms institutionalised distributive conflicts under the umbrella of an exclusionary political regime.

In Chapter Four, Daniel Chasquetti explores the role of the Coparticipación (Coparticipation) in the solving-capacity of democracy in Uruguay. Amounting to perhaps one of the most successful cases of consociational politics in the developing world, the Coparticipación consists of an informal nearly tacit understanding among the major political parties, the Blancos and Colorados, that because of its routinisation has emerged as an institutional arrangement leading to a sort of co-government whereby the opposition is accommodated in the most decisive critical decisions in Uruguay. This arrangement has evolved from some form of some basic type of watchdog role for minority forces to the sweeping, almost radical, decision in 1967 of incorporating representatives of the opposition in the director's boards of state-owned enterprises as well as in decentralised bodies. Resembling the *Proporz* system in Austria, the Coparticipación has been largely extolled for having avoided the patronage manipulation that lurks underneath the crisis of representation in Austria that lead to the emergence of xenophobic populists leaders like Jörg Haider. Still, while this Uruguayan institutional innovation has significantly moderated the *zero-sum game* nature that afflicted its neighbouring countries, it was gradually collapsing to similar pitfalls as those experienced in Austria. Chasquetti claims that although these issues are still evolving, the Coparticipación epitomises how inclusive institutional mechanisms by means of both their tangible and symbolic significance have feedback and contagion effects that bolster the conflict-solving armour of developing countries facing redistributive demands parallel to those of Uruguay.

The first section of the book, therefore, focuses on macro explanations of why and how institutions come into existence and were first put into place.

Part Two takes a closer look at the resiliency of institutional designs that, nonetheless, generate suboptimal results. It is, therefore, on the 'dark' side of strong institutions and how they have lock-in effects that explain their longevity. This part starts with the assumption that democracy is not a homogeneous political entity and that the founding pacts upon which most democracies rest entail some consciously-induced biased political representation (Pitkin 1967; Young 2002). In this vein, the adoption of federalism in some parts of Latin America, as the evidence from federal nations in other regions also attest (Samuels and Snyder 2001), amounted to a constitutional built-in bias to weigh the interests of some regions more than proportionally in the policy process by granting equal legislative representation to territorial units with contrasting demographic and developmental characteristics. Added to these cases of the so called federal malapportionment, several unitary Latin American countries have also adopted electoral reforms to enhance disproportional representation, mostly Bolivia and Chile, the latter analysed in detail in Montecino Zúñiga and Navia's chapter. To be clear, this historical legacy of nation-building raises the question whether institutionally-engineered inequalities of representation could have similar integrative effects in the future. What is more, despite its ostensible violation of an arithmetic conception of representation (Dahl 2002), malapportionment might serve as an important tool for helping contemporary democracies cope with explosive problems ranging from ethnic conflicts, urban–rural inequity, and most notably, wealth gaps, thus becoming an appealing option for unitary countries as well.

In Chapter Five, Carlos Gervasoni looks at a little-noticed aspect in which federations across the world differ: the extent to which their populations are unevenly distributed among their constituent units. At an extreme, several important federations (e.g., Argentina, Brazil and Canada) contain a few provinces/states/regions with very large populations and many that are much smaller. This 'dissymmetry' often occurs in constitutionally 'symmetrical' federal nations, i.e., those in which all subnational units (at the same level) possess equal powers. Under typical institutional arrangements, smaller units are strongly overrepresented in the legislature, and typically command several other political and fiscal advantages that make them dominant vis-à-vis the larger districts. Evidence from Argentina and Brazil shows that situations in which demographically and economically larger units are politically subordinated can be surprisingly stable. Such equilibrium, however, is normatively undesirable, as political rights and often public spending are distributed unfairly among the citizens depending on their place of residence. This chapter describes this type of federation, analyses the reasons for its apparent success at avoiding (expected) territorial conflicts, and assesses its practical and normative virtues and pitfalls.

In Chapter Six, Olivia Montecino Zúñiga and Patricio Navia examine the experience of Chile, a country that had not experienced striking regional conflicts throughout its nation-building period but nonetheless ranks among the ten most malapportioned polities worldwide (Samuels and Snyder 2001). They draw attention to the backward-looking, illiberal dimension of malapportionment, that is to say, cases in which military outgoing elites redistributed seats in the lower house just before the transition to democracy. The rationale is that, by manipulating legislative apportionment to overrepresented districts where the conservative elite is dominant, the military regime secures the political and economic interests of its strategic allies once democratic elections take place. Both Argentina and Brazil have witnessed this kind of *garrison* reapportionment in the early 1980s but perhaps the most salient case is that of Chile. That having been said, after presenting longitudinal evidence to show that forces identified with Pinochet's conservative and neoliberal economic legacy were dominant in the deliberately overrepresented districts, the authors identify something of a paradox: that is, that said conservative districts are not only been increasingly seized by opposite forces but also the local authorities of these districts can be singled out as the most contentious and aggressive in debating redistributive and equity-enhancing programmes. In so doing, Montecino Zúñiga and Navia's study underscores the unintended (in this case, welfare-improving) consequences of deadlocked institutional designs and offers a nuanced account of institutional engineering that puts some of the conventional wisdom on malapportionment to question.

Part Two of the book, therefore, keeps an eye on the resiliency of institutions, through lock-in effects and how they continue to exist in spite of lagging, unsolved conflicts. The emphasis, hence, is on the dark side of strong institutions.

Part Three examines institutional modification, remodelling and re-creation to address ethnic and redistributive conflicts. This section is about institutional innovation focusing on the construction of an architecture of inclusion in the region. This section has two sets of chapters. First, the focus is on identity issues. The last decades of the past century have seen a remarkable surge of activism by and on behalf of indigenous people in Latin America. Concretely, this means that at least formally significant steps were taken to recognise the pluriethnic composition of the population (Assies 2005; Van Cott 2001). In this way indigenous demands and responses to these demands got under way in the context of democratisation processes and have raised a spectrum of institutional solutions, ranging from formal consultative mechanisms for natural resources exploitation to partial, ad hoc self-government and territorial autonomy.

The second section of Part Three addresses particular issues in institutional design affecting distributive concerns in Latin America. This is a remarkably central concern in the region because institutional arrangements have locked into place structural inequality, underscoring extreme levels of socioeconomic unfairness. By the same token, pre-existing levels of inequality set the boundaries of institutional innovations, especially of a fiscal nature. Thus institutional choice and distributive conflicts are intertwined or, put differently, endogenously co-determined (Beramendi 2012; Iversen and Soskice 2009). That said, structural inequality in Latin America has been generally tackled through political and social means. First, as argued before in this chapter, 'strong' political arrangements such as legislative overrepresentation, that despite having originally been devised for compensating economically vulnerable territorial units (thus addressing structural inequality adjacently), has proved to confer wrong fiscal incentives that ended up squeezing state financial capacities to ultimately address socioeconomic gaps. This representational bias can be further aggravated by fiscal arrangements where powerful subnational actors have electoral incentives to tilt the public purse, as Gonzáles and Lodola illustrate in the Argentina case. Social institutional arrangements, deemed oftentimes as 'weaker' based on their non-constitutional malleable nature, have prompted income redistribution and precluded social discontent and unrest in periods of significant institutional transformation such as during the Lula era in Brazil. Participatory budgeting and the creation of the Ministry of Social Development and its *Bolsa Família* had effectively reduced violent, innovation-inhibiting reactions from the economic agents threatened by socioeconomic change. Relatedly, beliefs of social inclusion held by political elites, and reasonably accepted by powerful economic actors, appear to have a decisive impact on institutional choice for tackling redistributive concerns. As much as in the recent past when Latin American 'technopols' embraced neoliberal and free-market principles for economic policy making (Dominguez 1996), overlapping concerns on redistribution by political and social groups help explain the significance of the ideas and preference of decision makers in fulfilling expectations of equity-enhancing institutional designs in the region. Contrastingly, as Rhodes-Purdy shows in his chapter on Venezuela, institutional innovations may encounter and coexist with extremely polarised political contexts, leading to a more sombre perception on the promise of institutional design. In particular, the expansion of communal councils and other forms of local organisation embody probably the most controversial and contested attempt at institutional innovation aimed at changing the mechanism of distribution, chiefly of natural resource rents.

In Chapter Seven, Andrea Pozas-Loyo and Julio Rios-Figueroa discuss the historical conditions leading to the creation and expansion of the constitutional courts, which is one of the institutional innovations of the last round of transitions to democracy in Latin America. Constitutional courts are, their argument goes, independent, accessible, and have ample judicial review powers which can play the role of third-party mediators in conflict-resolution: they can obtain and effectively transmit, to the actors in conflict, relevant information to reduce the uncertainty that causes their conflict. Acknowledging that constitutional courts are among the most politicised and probably unbalanced legal institutions in Latin America, notably in Peru, the authors offer arguments and evidence on the problem-solving potential of such courts. They apply these theoretical arguments to the conflicts related to natural resources management and with resource exploitation and infrastructure projects. Said conflicts revolve around two seemingly good and legitimate claims: the encouragement of private investment for developmental purposes and the autonomy of indigenous people to decide how to administer their ancestral lands. This tension is what brings the recourse of *consulta previa* to reconcile private entrepreneurship with ethnic and cultural imperatives. Using the experiences of Colombia, Mexico and Peru as the putative scenarios, Pozas-Loyo and Rios-Figueroa show that the Colombian Court has actually helped businesses and indigenous communities to clarify the object of their conflict and to find solutions to them. In essence, the Colombian court, based on its erstwhile experience in dealing with indigenous communities' claims, has produced innovative and forward-looking jurisprudence, facilitating dialogue and assisting the parties in identifying and articulating their own interests, priorities, and needs to each other, helping them reach mutually satisfactory agreements. This contrasts with the role of the Mexican and Peruvian Supreme Courts. In the former, the noticeable lack of access to the courts stands out as the main predicament, aggravated by the indifference of the courts to indigenous leaders' pleas in the scarce occasions that *consulta previa* cases were handled. In Peru, a clear top-down, arbitrator-rather-than-mediator style has dampened any hint of optimism in the futility of the consultative process. One would hope that these chapter's findings are too pessimistic, since they suggest a clear path-dependent effect of previous expertise and interest of the judges dealing with *consulta previa*, suggesting a sort of vicious circle may be at play. Future research would also require the inclusion of other cases, probably Bolivia, where the politicisation of the judiciary may nonetheless work in favour of the increasing institutionalisation of this institutional innovation within the framework of democratic governance in the region.

Chapter Eight contrastingly backtracks to the pre-democratisation phase and shows how weak illegitimate institutional settings can further the ethnic cause out of strategic considerations. Allyson Benton claims that the scholarly research on institutional design and the management of ethnic conflict has tended to focus almost exclusively on the strategies used by national governments in democratic systems. However, national democrats are not the only ones that face ethnically diverse populations whose tendency toward conflict can undermine political stability. National authoritarian regimes also often rule over ethnically diverse populations, whose inter-group conflict can easily turn into regime opposition, thereby undermining national authoritarian rule. Accordingly, she examines whether and how national autocrats use some of the same political institutional arrangements as national democrats to manage ethnically diverse populations. Specifically, Benton argues that, when national autocrats face ethnic conflict that is being directly channelled against the regime, they grant ethnic populations greater political autonomy via UC to manage their political affairs, in the hope that a reduction of inter-ethnic conflict will dampen opposition to the regime. In contrast, when national autocrats face ethnic conflict that is not being directly channelled against the regime, they will maintain centralised authoritarian political institutional configurations, with the hopes that they will be able to root out ethnic conflict and manage political control. Although national autocrats may wish to grant political autonomy to all ethnically diverse groups in order to dampen their opposition to the regime, they are unable to do so out of their need to maintain aggregate political support and territorial control.

In Chapter Nine, Lucas Gonzáles and Germán Lodola draw on an extensive literature examining the redistributive dimension of fiscal federalism, albeit on the doling out side of the decentralisation equation. Using Argentina as central case study, the authors claim that government spending is a powerful tool subnational incumbents can utilise to favour different social groups in a federation. In this fiscally decentralised country, provincial governments undertake a large share of the total spending at the same time they collect only a small fraction of taxes. Thus, provincial politicians enjoy a large share of the political benefit of spending, yet pay only a small fraction of the political cost of taxation. Strategically positioned within this seemingly swayed common pool of federal resources are the provincial governors who stand out as perhaps the most critical nexus linking the institutional dimension of Argentine federalism and fiscal favours. In Gonzáalez and Lodola's view, this complex political game is best understood by focusing on the influence that governors' office ambitions have on their strategic decisions to allocate the public money, prioritising either patronage or universalistic spending. Specifically, they show that subnational executives' office ambitions – whether they are national-centred or state-centred – affect their decisions to strategically allocate social infrastructure (collective) and civil administration (particularistic) expenditures by delineating different electoral linkages between politicians and citizens. These findings undercut the hitherto overly electoral and partisan credentials of redistributive spending choices present in the mainstream literature and provide substance to the micro-foundations of subnational government spending. In summary, this contribution prompts us to ponder about the limits to redistribution when the structure of incentives of powerful political actors does not align in a direction of universalistic, collective spending priorities within the parameters of less than optimal fiscal institutional designs.

Chapter Ten presents a case of institution building for dealing with problems of social and economic exclusion. Lucio Renno claims that the combination of a pre-existing weak institutional order and the emergence of agents committed to addressing a specific collective problem increase the probability for the emergence of new institutions. Drawing on the literature on policy entrepreneurship, he stresses the central role of voluntarism, namely the forceful commitment of policy makers and bureaucrats to solve unsettled yet significant collective, social conflicts. Such voluntarism looms large as the micro foundation of institution building, thus epitomising the genesis of the so called 'weak' institutional designs. This is the ideational and agency context whereby *Bolsa Família*, the world's largest anti-poverty scheme, compounded a public policy domain from which the Ministry of Social Development unfolded. Renno goes as far as to argue that this ministry, probably the most significant institutional innovation of the then incumbent Worker's Party PT at the national level, is inextricably contingent on the ideational legacies that bold policy actors left behind. In short, considering that almost a quarter of Brazil's population benefits from *Bolsa Família*'s aid and that programmes such New York's Opportunities NYC partly replicated the Brazilian experience, this chapter illustrates one of the most impressive laboratories of institutional design aimed at addressing social inequality through conditional cash transfers.

In Chapter Eleven, Carlos Pereira and Frederico Bertholini largely concur with Renno's claim that social inclusion has come to be something of a keyword in Brazilian politics since the introduction of the 1988 Constitution, which has explicitly endorsed a doctrine of social rights and extended universal health coverage to all Brazilian citizens. Yet they focus on two seeming paradoxes of contemporary Brazilian political economy; the first, how is it possible to sustain a consensually desirable social spending without encumbering further an already high tax burden; the second, what accounts for the congressional support for a very inclusive social agenda beyond the ideological division between left and right. Both paradoxes are predicated on a belief consensus that, while macroeconomic stability has a decisive impact on incumbent approval and re-election, neither voters nor congressmen seem to accept such stability if it comes at the cost of setbacks in the provision of public policies that maintain or expand the path of social inclusion. That is, whenever social inclusion policies are at stake, legislators will consistently proclaim being in favour of greater expenditure despite their own ideological preferences. The ensuing effect of this belief in a fiscally sound social inclusion lurks underneath some of the most significant institutional innovations of Cardoso's period, subsequently kept in place by Lula, such as the Fiscal Responsibility Law of 1999, which penalised patronage-ridden subnational indebtedness and hence increased the treasury's disposable resources for social assistance purposes.

Chapter Twelve looks at the experience of Bolivarian Venezuela and the ever-present legacy of Hugo Chávez in the contemporary politics of this country. Matthew Rhodes-Purdy offers original and compelling evidence on the counter-intuitive effect of participatory governance in Venezuela. While in other countries, such as Brazil and Uruguay, deepening local participation has diminished social and distributive conflicts, Venezuela has conversely witnessed its aggravation. What is more, political conflict between supporters of Chávez and his opponents has only grown more acrimonious as the Bolivarian regime has sought to reinvent Venezuelan democracy. Inasmuch as the impact of participatory democracy is contingent on its political context, top-down Bolivarian governance, the argument goes, aimed at legitimating populist hegemony at the national level by allowing confined spaces for participatory governance at the local level. Contrary to the equalitarian spirit of the so called Chavista revolution, the incumbent regime pursued a deliberate battle against any flare of dissent, even from its own loyalist ranks, compounding something of a sort of deceptive decentralised governance. In fact, the government, as Rhodes-Purdy shows in his study, has discriminated communal councils from the opposition and recruited loyal councils for campaigning on behalf of the Chavista side in the referendum. Far from alleviating conflict, institutional experimentation in Venezuela has polarised the population into two incompatible camps: Elitist, *Punto Fijo* supporters and 'the people'. What is more, the natural resources rent, largely the most relevant source of state income, has been used to redistribute resources only to those previously economically disenfranchised sectors aligned with Chávez's administration. It should be reminded, though, that this analysis is not a normative plea against conflict as a manifestation of dissent, nor does it cast any normative objection to the opening of a political system marred by paramount access and distributive gaps throughout the pre-Chávez era. Despite the ostensible sombre conclusions offered by this chapter, Rhodes-Purdy offers a prime example of contemporary institutionalist research that is empirically driven, which suggests that the implications of participatory democracy for redistributive conflicts should be studied analytically on a case-by-case basis, especially since the interaction of mass political participation with other politico-institutional factors is highly context dependent.

Hence, Part Three of the book focuses on institutional innovation and remodelling, examining the promises of prior institutional weakness and other contextual factors that germinate opportunities for change, as well as the novelties brought on by institutional architects and concomitant limitations.

## Concluding Remarks

This book is an exercise in mixing and bridging, since it sets out to bring together hitherto separate research on institutional design and conflict management, respectively. With the deliberate conviction that the whole is more than the sum of the parts, we venture into new theoretical territory. Hopefully, this volume will deliver many inspiring ideas about how the complex methodological, theoretical and analytical problems raised by the phenomenon of innovating institutional repertoires might be successfully tackled in future research. We approached the research project from which this book was conceived with something of a *deja vu* feeling about extant theories of institutional design and change. Especially when said theories advance views on the nature of institutions as rules of the game for constraining self-interested human behaviour, which may not encapsulate the complexity of the challenges Latin American institutional architects face for managing the conflicts of the region with the world's most unequal wealth distribution amid increasing grievances on recognition and ethnic representation.

The contributors to this volume share the sense that our work is only beginning to scratch the surface of possibilities for the field of institutional research on conflicts. We identified several paradoxes and inconsistencies related to the nature of institutional strength and weakness and the apparent dialectical relationship between both ends of the institutional continuum. We raise issues for consideration by pundits and academics and offer suggestions informed by comparative experience. In this spirit, this book analyses the design of institutions that allow disenfranchised actors and groups more access to distributional decision making and institutional design more supportive of cultural autonomy. Albeit with substantive diverse foci, the chapters raise the question as to what extent institutions are forged out of conflict and history and, concomitantly, how such institutions are effective in steering longstanding ethnic and distributional conflicts.

This book project and its constituent chapters grew out of a workshop organised by the research project, 'The Architecture of Diversity: Institutional Design and the Management of Conflicts in the Americas', financed by the International Development Research Centre, Canada, that took place at the Universidad Diego

Portales, Santiago, Chile, in July 2014. Special thanks are due to Fernando Rosenblatt for contributing to the organisation of the workshop and valuable feedback in the planning of this volume. We wish to thank each of the participants of the workshop and each of the contributors to this book for their efforts in helping us construct what we feel sure will be a worthy addition to the genre and a catalyst for future discussions and iterations on the subject matter of this volume.

## References

Abers, R. (1998) 'From clientelism to cooperation: local government, participatory policy, and civic organizing in Porto Alegre, Brazil', *Politics and Society* 26(4): 511–537.

Abers, R. and Keck, M. (2013) *Practical Authority: Agency and institutional change in Brazilian water politics*, New York: Oxford University Press.

Acemoglu, D. and Robinson, J. (2001) 'A theory of political transitions', *American Economic Review* 91: 938–963.

—— (2006) *Economic Origins of Dictatorship and Democracy*, Cambridge: Cambridge University Press.

—— (2012) *Why Nations Fail: The origins of power, prosperity and power*, New York: Crown Publishing Group.

Ames, B. (2001) *The Deadlock of Democracy in Brazil*, Ann Arbor: The University of Michigan Press.

Assies, W. (2005) 'Two Steps Forward, One Step Back: Indigenous peoples and autonomies in Latin America', in M. Weller and S. Wolff, (eds) *Autonomy, Self-Governance and Conflict Resolution: Innovative approaches to institutional design in divided societies*, New York: Routledge, pp. 180–212.

Avritzer, L. (2002) *Democracy and the Public Space in Latin America*, Princeton: Princeton University Press.

Bates, R. (1981) *Markets and States in Tropical Africa*, Berkeley: University of California Press.

Beramendi, P. (2012) *The Political Geography of Inequality: Regions and redistribution*, New York: Cambridge University Press.

Boix, C. (1999) 'Setting the rules of the game: the choice of electoral systems in advanced democracies', *American Political Science Review* 93(3): 609–624.

Brysk, A. and Wise, C. (1997) 'Liberalization and ethnic conflict in Latin America', *Studies in Comparative International Development* 32: 76–104.

Carpenter, D. (2010) *Reputation and Power: Organizational image and pharmaceutical regulations at the FDA*, Princeton: Princeton University Press.

Collier, R. and Collier, D. (1991) *Shaping the Political Arena: Critical junctures, the Labor movement, and regime dynamics in Latin America*, Princeton: Princeton University Press.

Cooper, J. and Brady, H. (1981) 'Toward a diachronic analysis of Congress', *American Political Science Review* 75(4): 988–1006.

Dahl, R. (2002) *How Democratic is the American Constitution?*, New Haven: Yale University Press.

Dominguez, J. (1996) *Technopols: Freeing politics and markets in Latin America in the 1990s*, University Park, PA: The Pennsylvania State University Press.

—— (1997) 'Latin America's crisis of representation', *Foreign Affairs* 76(1): 100–113.

Evans, P. (1995) *Embedded Autonomy: States and industrial transformation*, Princeton: Princeton University Press.

Gibson, E. (2012) *Boundary Control: Subnational authoritarianism in federal democracies*, New York: Cambridge University Press.

Goldfank, B. and Schneider, A. (2006) 'Competitive institution building: the PT and participatory budgeting in Rio Grande do Sul', *Latin American Politics and Society* 48(3): 1–31.

Grindle, M. (2000) *Audacious Reforms: Institutional invention and democracy in Latin America*, Baltimore: The Johns Hopkins University Press.

Hall, P. (1992) 'The Movement from Keynesianism to Monetarism: Institutional analysis and British economic policy on the 1970s', in S. Steinmo, K. Thelen and F. Longstreth (eds) *Structuring Politics: Historical institutionalism in comparative politics*, Cambridge: Cambridge University Press, pp. 90–113.

Hartlyn, J. (1988) *The Politics of Coalition Rule in Colombia*, Cambridge: Cambridge University Press.

Helmke, G. and Levitsky, S. (eds) (2006) *Informal Institutions and Democracy: Lessons from Latin America*, Baltimore: Johns Hopkins University Press.

Hochstetler, K. and Friedman, E. (2008) 'Can civil society organizations solve the crisis of partisan representation in Latin America?', *Latin American Politics and Society* 50(2): 1–32.

Horowitz, D. (1985) *Ethnic Groups in Conflict*, Berkeley: University of California Press.

Huntington, S. (1968) *Political Order in Changing Societies*, New Haven: Yale University Press.

Immergut, E. (1992) 'The Rules of the Game: The logic of health policy-making in France, Switzerland and Sweden', in S. Steinmo, K. Thelen and F. Longstreth (eds) *Structuring Politics: Historical institutionalism in comparative politics*, Cambridge: Cambridge University Press, pp. 57–89.

Iversen, T. and Soskice, D. (2009) 'Distribution and redistribution: the shadow of the XIX Century', *World Politics* 61(3): 438–486.

Jones, M., Sanguinetti, P. and Tommasi, M. (2000) 'Politics, institutions and fiscal performance in a federal system: an analysis of the Argentine provinces', *Journal of Development Economics* 61: 305–333.

Keck, M. and Sikkink, K. (eds) (1998) *Activists beyond Borders: Transnational advocacy networks in international politics*, Ithaca: Cornell University Press.

Kingdon, J. (2003) *Agendas, Alternatives, and Public Policy*, New York: Longman.
Knight, J. (1992) *Institutions and Social Conflict*, New York: Cambridge University Press.
Lechner, N. (1991) 'The search for lost community: challenges to democracy in Latin America', *International Social Science Journal* 129: 541–553.
Levi, M. (1988) *Of Rule and Revenue*, Berkeley: University of California Press.
Levitsky, S. and Murillo, M. (2009) 'Variation in institutional strength', *Annual Review of Political Science* 12: 115–133.
Lijphart, A. (1968) *The Politics of Accommodation: Pluralism and democracy in the Netherlands*, Berkeley: University of California Press.
Mahoney, J. and Thelen, K. (2010) *Explaining Institutional Change: Ambiguity, agency, and power*, New York: Cambridge University Press.
Mainwaring, S. and Scully, T. R. (1995) 'Introduction: Party systems in Latin America', in S. Mainwaring and T. R. Scully (eds) *Building Democratic Institutions: Party systems in Latin America*, Stanford: Stanford University Press.
Mainwaring, S., Bejarano, A. and Leongomez, E. (eds) (2006) *The Crisis of Democratic Representation in the Andes*, Stanford: Stanford University Press.
Milgrom, P., North, D. C. and Weingast, B. (1990) 'The role of institutions in the revival of trade: the law merchants, private judges, and the champagne fairs', *Economics and Politics* 2(1): 1–23.
Morgan, J. (2012) *Bankrupt Representation and Party System Collapse*, University Park: The Pennsylvannia State University Press.
Munck, R. (1993) 'After the transition: democratic disenchantment in Latin America', *European Review of Latin American and Caribbean Studies* 55: 7–19.
Neri, M. (2013) *The Macroeconomic Effects of Government Transfers: A Social Accounting Matrix approach*, Brasilia: International Policy Centre for Inclusive Growth.
Norris, P. (2008) *Driving Democracy: Do power-sharing institutions work?*, New York: Cambridge University Press.
North, D. (1990) *Institutions, Institutional Change and Economic Performance*, New York: Cambridge University Press.
North, D., Wallis, J. and Weingast, B. (2009) *Violence and Social Orders: A conceptual framework for interpreting recorded human history*, New York: Cambridge University Press.
Olson, M. (1984) *The Rise and Decline of Nations*, New Haven: Yale University Press.
Pierson, P. (1993) 'When effects become cause: policy feedback and policy change', *World Politics* 45(4): 595–628.
—— (2000) 'The limits of design: explaining institutional origins and change', *Governance* 13(4): 475–499.
Pitkin, H. (1967) *The Concept of Representation*, Berkeley: University of California Press.

Polsby, N. (1968) 'The institutionalization of the U.S. House of Representatives', *American Political Science Review* 62: 14–68.

Przeworski, A. (2004) 'The last instance: are institutions the primary cause of economic development?', *European Journal of Sociology* 45(2): 165–188.

Rae, D. and Tayoy, M. (1970) *The Analysis of Political Cleavages*, New Haven: Yale University Press.

Renno, L. and Ames, B. (2010) 'Participatory Budgeting, Discussion Networks and Political Information in Two Brazilian Cities', in M. Wolf, K. Ikeda and L. Morales (eds) *Political Discussion in Modern Democracies: A Comparative Perspective*, London: Routledge.

Rodrik, D. (1999) 'Where did all the growth go? External shocks, social conflict and growth collapses', *Journal of Economic Growth* 4: 385–412.

Rokkan, S. (1970) *Citizens, Elections and Parties*, New York: David McKay Co.

Samuels, D. and Snyder, R. (2001) 'The value of a vote: malapportionment in comparative perspective', *British Journal of Political Science* 31: 651–671.

Schattschneider, E. (1957) 'Intensity, visibility, direction, and scope', *American Journal of Political Science* 4: 933–42.

Schilling-Vacaflor, A. and Flemmer, R. (2013) 'Why is Prior Consultation Not Yet an Effective Tool for Conflict Resolution? The case of Peru', GIGA working Papers, Hamburg.

Soares, F., Ribas, R. and Osorio, R. (2010) 'Evaluations of the impact of Brazil's Bolsa Família: cash transfer programs in comparative perspective', *Latin American Research Review* 45(2): 174–90.

Treisman, D. (2002) 'The causes of corruption: a cross-national study', *Journal of Public Economics* 76(3): 399–457.

Tsebelis, G. (1995) 'Decision making in political systems: veto players in presidentialism, parliamentarism, multicameralism and multipartyism', *British Journal of Political Science* 25(3): 289–325.

Van Cott, D. (2001) 'Explaining ethnic autonomy regimes in Latin America', *Studies in Comparative International Development* 35(4): 30–58.

—— (2002) 'Constitutional Reform in the Andes: Redefining indigenous-state relations', in R. Sieder (ed.) *Multiculturalism in Latin America: Indigenous rights, diversity and democracy*, London: Palgrave, pp. 45–73.

Wampler, B. (2007) *Participatory Budgeting in Brazil: Contestation, cooperation and accountability*, University Park: The Pennsylvannia State University Press.

Weingast, B. (1995) 'The economic role of political institutions: market-preserving federalism and economic development', *The Journal of Law, Economics & Organization* 11(1): 1–31.

Weir, M. (1992) 'Ideas and the Politics of Bounded Innovation', in S. Steinmo, K. Thelen and F. Longstreth (eds) *Structuring Politics: Historical institutionalism in comparative politics*, Cambridge: Cambridge University Press, pp. 188–216.

Weyland, K. (2009) 'Institutional change in Latin America: external models and their unintended consequences', *Journal of Politics in Latin America* 1(1): 37–66.

Wildavsky, H. (1980) 'Policy as its Own Cause', in H. Wildavsky (ed.) *The Art and Craft of Policy Analysis*, New York: Macmillan, pp. 34–67.

Wilsford, D. (2000) 'Studying Democracy and Putting it into Practice: The contributions of Arend Lijpahrt to democratic theory and to actual democracy', in M. Crepaz, T. Koelble and D. Wilsford (eds) (2000) *Democracy and Institutions: The life and work of Arend Lijphart*, Ann Arbor, The University of Michigan Press, pp. 1–7.

Yashar, D. (1998) 'Contesting citizenship: indigenous movements and democracy in Latin America', *Comparative Politics* 31(1): 23–42.

Young, I. (2002) *Inclusion and Democracy*, Oxford: Oxford University Press.

PART ONE

FOUNDING MOMENTS OF INSTITUTIONAL
CREATION IN LATIN AMERICA

Chapter Two

# The Architecture of Governments in Conflict Environments: The Origin and Crystallisation of Presidentialism in Latin America[1]

*Sergio Toro Maureira and Juan Carlos Arellano González*

## Introduction

When Alberto Fujimori dissolved the Peruvian Congress in 1992, his reasoning called for a strong presidential style that 'was capable of solving the problems of the country's political class'. In his message to the nation, the President alleged that the conflict with Congress was exacerbated to the point of becoming an 'obstacle to government action aimed at achieving the objectives of national reconstruction and development' (Fujimori 1992). After the government-led coup, the idea of presidential strength and legislative obstructionism caused the structure of Congress to be reformed from a bicameral design to a unicameral design. However, this highly exclusionary change was not resolved after Fujimori's tumultuous exit. Despite the political class's distinct questioning of Fujimori's decisions, the option of reverting Congress's structure vis à vis the executive has never been changed by subsequent Peruvian governments.

This example of presidents who demand great power is not a unique phenomenon within Latin America. In the majority of Latin American countries – and in any historical period – presidents modify institutions without considering the styles, forms, and results of these actions. The imprint of a strong presidentialism[2] can be considered to be a routine policy in the economic, social, and political duties of these countries. In Latin America, presidential styles comprise not only a form of government that is codified in the Constitution but also a framework of formal and informal dynamics that was originally ingrained in these countries' political games. At what point did this particular form of exercising power crystallise?

---

1.   This research is framed within the FONDECYT's Project No. 1140564 and the Millennium Nucleus for the Study of Stateness and Democracy in Latin America, Project (RS130002). All caveats apply.

2.   We refer to presidentialism not only as a form of government that is codified in various constitutions but as a formal and informal exercise of power that demands increased power.

Few answers to this empirically transcendent question have been developed in political science. Although numerous scholars agree that presidential styles have varied in form and substance over the years, with constitutional variety among Latin American presidentialism (Cheibub, Elkins and Ginsburg 2010; Gargarella 2013; Negretto 2013a), the literature suggests that a dynamic of concentrated exercise of power has persisted from the creation of the republics until the present day, which has permanently strained the political stability of Latin American countries.

This paper attempts to close this theoretical gap and explains the causes – and subsequent reinforcement – of a concentrated form of exercising power in Latin America. Using a historical narrative, we investigate the historical conditions that served a role in the selection and reinforcement of this option. We believe that an analysis of the construction of institutional order can offer answers to a series of paradoxes about the persistence of this phenomenon. We trace the process of the construction of the State and explain how preferences were consolidated towards the dynamics of the power concentration in Latin America.

We hypothesise that the haste of the actors in organising the State and separating the territories after the Hispano-American revolution reinforced the personalised dynamics in the institutional organisation of the countries. These dynamics were reinforced by a series of conflicts over the placement of borders and State organisation, which were addressed by the dominant elites via a series of formal and informal mechanisms for the control of territory and state power.

To test this hypothesis, we develop a temporal analysis to observe the sequence of contexts, actors and entities that crystallised a dynamic that constantly seeks the concentration of power in Latin America. We aim to develop a historical analysis and identify the causal mechanisms that favoured the acceptance of this particular form of exercising power.

Three sources of information are included in this chapter. The first source is an exhaustive collection of historiographical studies of Latin America and its individual countries, we obtained a map of conflicts and outcomes that helped to generalise certain conclusions. The second source is a series of interviews with academics who have investigated the history of the nineteenth century in Latin America. The third source – which has less intensity – is the historical material of the countries and actors involved in the process of State formation. These three types of information enabled us to delimit our hypotheses and detect the causal mechanisms that contributed to the crystallisation of presidentialism in Latin America.

The chapter is divided into three parts. The first part retraces the rationales of conflict, order, and institutional trajectory. The second part (the longest part) includes the theoretical proposal of this study and demonstrates a causal chain that reinforces the normative preferences of agents towards postures of power concentration. In this section, we analyse how the conflict of emancipation, border definition and State organisation conditioned the construction of the rules of the game (registered in formal and informal actions), which involve a high concentration of power in Latin America. By analysing the dynamics of the actors within these conflicts, we observe how these conflicts strengthen centralising ideas with less capacity for reversal. We conclude this paper by analysing the future implications of this proposal to advance knowledge about institutions in Latin America.

## Conflict, Order and Institutional Reinforcement in Latin America

The literature on State construction in Latin America presents two relevant axioms. The first axiom states that the characteristics of the emancipatory process conditioned centralised forms of exercising power combined with strong-man leadership (Crespo 2013a; 2013b). The second axiom states that subsequent conflicts maintained a sequence that prevented the formation of strong and capable states in the majority of the continent after this formula was established (Centeno 2002).

Both axioms prompt a question that has not been addressed in the literature: Is it possible that the conflicts reinforced concentrated power over other alternatives? The literature on conflict and institutional order has signalled that the former is a moment that disturbs the balance and accelerates the processes of change or institutional foundation (Kalyvas *et al.* 2008). These perspectives, however, do not permit us to observe how these conflicts can become features that reinforce and maintain certain institutions, that is, conflict can be considered to be a feature of continuity for the agents instead of an element of change.

For rational choice institutionalism, for example, institutions are formal and informal arrangements that seek to resolve – or at least to restrict – social conflicts by establishing conventions and rules of the game that aid in maintaining equilibrium over time. The texts in of North *et al.* (2013) maintain that violence is a feature that is prevalent in societies and these societies endorse the production of order that ensures the containment of conflicts. In this manner, the institutional order would be the consequence of crises and conflicts that can be resolved by specific arrangements between the actors and the survival of these arrangements is a determining factor for reducing conflict (Huntington 1968).

Conflict is also addressed in studies of the rise of the State and state power. Scholars who analyse the rise of the European state (Tilly 1992; Cohen, Brown and Organski 1981) incorporate violence and conflict as a central feature in the process of accumulating power in nation states. This focus suggests that wars were a necessary condition for the formation of states, as they encouraged state actors to organise forms of concentration and the accumulation of capital and coercion. The idea that 'wars make a state' is one of the main sources of inspiration for scholars who analyse the origin of institutions in various places.

In Latin America, the idea of conflict and the formation of a state was problematised from a different perspective from the idea of conflict and the formation of a State in Europe. The classic text of López-Alves (2003) defines that the types of wars in combination with the types of rural mobilisation defined the type of state and the regimes that emerged. Specifically, this author suggests that war and the collective action of rural people were the primary engines of the processes of institutionalisation. Centeno (2002) refers to the capacity of Latin American states to absorb conflicts. The fundamental argument is that conflicts and wars may not generate state structures – but may generate chaos – especially in zones without any type of structure and political organisation. These obstacles were detailed by Centeno and Ferraro (2014), who state that Latin American countries experienced threats to state capacity when encountering obstacles such as external pressure, intra-elite conflicts and social conflicts.

The rationale of conflict as a mechanism that reinforces certain practices and institutions has not been analysed by theory. The text of Kling (1956) suggests that violence served as a feedback mechanism that was perpetuated and legitimated in the organisation and maintenance of Latin American governments. We believe that this reinforcement of conflict is directly related to the form and trajectory of the type of institutional order in Latin America. Specifically, conflicts in the continent condition the construction of leadership styles and institutions that are capable of simultaneously enduring security challenges, warfare, State organisation and recognition of internal and external sovereignty (refer to Crespo 2013a). These challenges tipped the balance towards strong-man leadership formulas, with a high concentration of power, strong personality politics and a low tolerance for other powers. Many of the original leaders gained titles such as 'Protector,' 'Supreme Director,' 'Supreme Dictator' or 'Dictator.'

However, the historiographical and contemporary interpretations of Latin America have demonstrated the presence of these characteristics in the Latin American political system in a piecemeal manner. History, for example, has developed an extensive range of literature on the foundational moment after the dismembering of the Ancien Régime (Lynch 1989; Guerra 2010; Bethell 1991; Drake 2009). These studies suggest that these countries enabled regimes with a high concentration of power and poorly defined powers (Negretto and Aguilar Rivera 2000; Gargarella, 2003; Crespo 2013a). For example, in many countries, conflicts occurred with processes of political belligerence, military influence (Vogel 2001; Loveman 1999) and caudillo-style governments (Chapman 1932; Vallenilla Lanz 1991; Lynch 1993; Basadre 2002; Aljovín 2000).

Similarly, civil and international wars legitimised centralised regimes that privileged states of siege or exception (Loveman 1993, 1999; Posada-Carbó 1995; Earle 2000). In this context, an institutional construction emerged that had to negotiate adverse situations while lacking legitimacy in political environments that were reluctant to reconcile interests and tending towards confrontation. In this arena, figures emerged that demanded a personality-based institutional order using the label 'saviours' with 'redemptive' and 'regenerative' tasks.

These initial conditions began to establish a path for the exercise of power in Latin America. This path was subsequently reinforced by conditions that interacted in moments of conflict and required the concentration of power.

## Reinforcement of a Presidentialist Architecture

How does the type of exercise of power that demands the concentration of decision-making power in the President crystallise? This proposal analyses the causal mechanisms that influenced the reinforcement of the presidentialist option in Latin

America. We assume the presence of a causal chain of three fundamental conflicts in the beginning of the nineteenth century (emancipation, border definition and organisation of the State) and the application of four causal mechanisms that helped reinforce these conflicts (formal and informal control of powers of the State and territories). This chain and these mechanisms would have led to the crystallisation of the forms of concentration of the exercise of power.

Via a historical analysis, we observe the actions and preferences of the actors and entities to maintain certain political rationales in institutional practice. Specifically, this analysis aims to complement the theory of historical institutionalism from two starting points. First, we suggest the reinforcement and fight to maintain the normative preferences of the actors[3] to maintain certain political practices instead of the existence of an institutional inertial block. We differentiate between the idea of persistent institutional inertia that was proposed by Pierson (2004), which highlights the important role of the articulation of the actors to maintain certain arrangements and institutional practices. Specifically, we integrate actors within the reinforcement processes of practices and institutions.

Second, our analysis does not focus on institutional change; it focuses on the role of actors to maintain certain formal and informal practices. The focus on the gradual change of Thelen (2004) and Mahoney and Thelen (2009) includes the role of the agency in the processes of institutional transformation. The authors suggest a dynamic rationale in which distribution is the central incentive for institutional change. Specifically, institutional change occurs without the need for exogenous changes but with conflicts of interest of the agents according to existing institutions (Mahoney and Thelen 2009). We complement this viewpoint with the idea that the actors perform actions that are aimed not only at institutional change but also at maintaining institutions. Specifically, the perpetuation of certain practices is the product of agents who seek not only to change but also to maintain – and frequently recuperate – political practices and institutional designs.

This proposal, which is based on agents (rather than institutional inertia) and on maintenance (rather than change) enables an understanding of the persistence of certain political practices in Latin America despite the historical variations of institutional design. Specifically, it helps us to understand how presidentialism has endured not only based on institutional design but also on specific forms of hierarchical exercise of power, which formally and informally broaden the discretional power held by presidents. According to Latin American academics, this idea is reinforced in a pyramidal structure in Latin American institutional designs.[4]

The line of argument develops as a causal chain that includes the following conditions and effects:

---

3.  For a study that focuses on the normative preferences of participants based on the analysis of process tracing, refer to (Mainwaring and Perez Liñán 2013)

4.  The analogy of the construction and institutional trajectory of Peru as noted by José Chaupis is interesting. In an interview with the authors, he noted that presidentialism in Peru is a 'pyramid without a foundation'.

1. The actors' haste in organising the State and dividing up territories after the Hispano-American revolution prompted the establishment of concentrated power exercise by the dominant elites.
2. This concentrated exercise of power was reinforced in Latin American countries by a long succession of border-defining and state organisation conflicts.
3. This concentration was crystallised via four mechanisms that were employed by the dominant elites to maintain the concentrated exercise of power: a) formal mechanisms to defend against other powers, b) formal mechanisms to defend territories, c) informal mechanisms to defend power and d) informal mechanisms to defend territories.
4. The form of using these mechanisms determined the level of permanence or replacement of the dominant elites and success in maintaining a dynamic of concentration of power.

The first significant conflict was emancipation. Compared with other revolutions, such as the revolutions of the United States of America and France, the emancipation conflict in Latin America faces two conditions that influenced the preference for a concentration of power: a) the separation and territorial disintegration prior to the colonial breakdown and b) the temporal and territorial extension of the context of war. Although this revolution appears to have been one great undertaking, institutional designs were dispersed with a minimal amount of debate and consensus from national actors. Simón Bolívar (1815) is emphatic in his Letter from Jamaica, in which he compares Latin America with the fall of the Roman Empire: '...each dismemberment produced a political system according to its interests and situation....' (Bolívar 1815).

In addition to the emancipation conflict, the conflict around border definition across the continent existed among the emerging states that were formed after independence. The dismemberment of the territories and the rise of territorial powers collaborated to maintain formulas of concentration of power. A neighbouring threat enables a concentration of power without significant opposition. In some cases, this formula determined the definition of isolated borders with centralised and lifelong governments with no interest in being part of confederations (Paraguay); in other cases, the search for concentrating power developed a rationale of caudillo-style leadership that was interlaced with civil wars and internationalised factions (Uruguay).

Both conflicts presented a sufficient condition for reinforcing the normative preferences of rulers that experience conflicts of State organisation. Given their previous experience, the actors adopted preferences that were consistent with concentrating power to address emerging territorial conflicts, party factions and powers of the State. In this stage, Latin American countries bifurcated in their forms of action while maintaining the idea of concentrating power. Thus, the majority of cases favoured the delegation of power in the hands of the executive and only differed in the way in which the States constructed their mechanisms to protect the presidentialist-style architecture that employs formal and informal mechanisms.

The first conflict was related to codified rules that empowered the executive, such as the centralist constitutions that assigned a hegemonic role to the President or the frequent use of emergency decrees. Conversely, the second conflict represented *de facto* actions to subordinate the remaining powers to the decisions of the President. These actions occurred extra-legally via privileges or informal agreements.

The formal and informal actions of the concentration of power were also presented to limit challengers at the grassroots level (the territory). For the first case, rules and regulations codified the supremacy of central power over the provinces. Actions that were related to the administrative division of the territory, the designation of provincial authorities, the allocation of resources and the control over military enlistment are important in this aspect. Among the informal actions, patronage and favouritism by Presidents contained the rise of local leaders as a way of maintaining national control over the leaders.

The causal flux of presidentialist reinforcement is shown in the following figure.

*Figure 2.1: Causal path of presidentialist regimes*

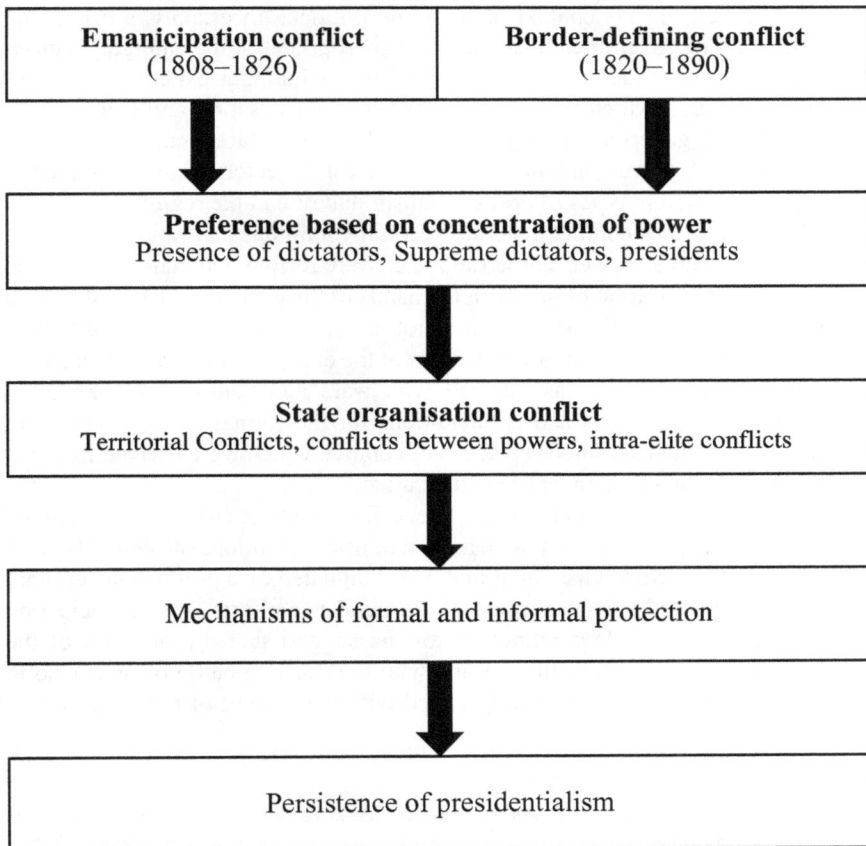

The origin and consolidation of presidentialism in Latin America is explained by the concatenation of conflicts that support the normative preferences. Although this chain of events is present in all emerging states of Latin America, certain bifurcations are established in the territorial conflicts and the organisation of states. These bifurcations are generated not only by the existence or lack of conflict but also by the intensity of the actors who participate in the conflict or the balances of their forces, which render it impossible for one to impose itself above the other. The manner in which these stages reinforce the presidentialist architecture with a high concentration of power is described as follows:

## a) Emancipatory conflict: emphasis on the concentration of power

The breakup of the monarchic Spanish *Ancien Régime* in 1808 with the abdication of Bayona began a process of territorial dismemberment and atomisation of political power in a large part of Latin America. The old structures and institutional hierarchies were dissolved, and new political experiments that precisely sought to provide form and solution to the emerging conflicts after the fall of the monarchy were established. In this context of wars and political uncertainty, a discussion about the form of government that was most appropriate for the emerging nations of Latin America ensued. After an exercise in institutional experimentation or 'political learning', which was characterised by improvisation and contingency, a new form of government began to prevail, which placed emphasis on the concentration of power and defined a historical trajectory that subsequently prompted the different types of presidentialism that rule in the region.

The emancipatory conflict generated certain conditions and rationales for the exercise of executive power. These rationales were re-foundational in nature and invoked the concentration of power in the hands of the executive. The installation of the new order in Latin America was not an easy task. The improvisation of institutional architects, which was a product of the events of the Iberian Peninsula, prompted a process that was plagued with wars and conflicts. Unlike other revolutions, the conditions and preconditions for the formation of a state were marked by long and continuous episodes of conflict, which were derived from the separation and dismemberment of emancipation.

The emancipation conflict was the scene for the emergence of new national states and, consequently, the implementation of new institutional designs.[5] Both of these processes emerge in a context that was dominated by a political uncertainty that initially required a concentration of independence efforts. The emancipation conflict was long and devastating. Historians suggest that the duration of the conflict was approximately fifteen years, with the decisive battle of Ayacucho in Peru (1824); however, it definitively ended with the seizure of the royal fort of

---

5.    The objective of this paper does not approach the causal variables that explain the fall of the monarchy, as literature on this topic exists (refer to Guerra 2010; Lynch 1989; Halperín Donghi 1985).

Callay and San Juan de Alúa in Mexico in 1826.[6] In this environment, nascent and improvised political organisations that are marked by militarism and caudillo-style leadership emerge because of a belligerent context.

The concentrated exercise of power emerged due to the territorial dispersion that was caused by the fall of the monarchy. The fall of the crown immediately generated the problem of 'who will govern and in whose name?' (Guerra 2010: 122–123). Returning sovereignty to the hands of the people or the 'peoples' prompted the installation of a series of juntas and improvised governments in Latin America that invoked a pact-based tradition to legitimise the importance of corporations and territories over individuals (2010: 48).

The first governments of the Junta in Latin America were established in Mexico (1808), and the first government of the Junta of Cuzco was established in Peru (1814).[7] With this event, a process of political fragmentation was generated (referred to as 'multiple sovereignties') that tumultuously caused the formation of States. The war, which was led by military caudillos, gradually began installing provisional governments in locations where royal forces were expelled. This process varied as the periods of emancipation differed. In accordance with Crespo's assertion, the transition to strong, centralised executives responded to the need to create a power that was internally and externally capable of waging war, ensuring peace and implementing the processes of state organisation and recognition (2013a: 386). During the emancipatory process, all emerging political entities activated centralised governments that were headed by a political figure with broad military and political powers.[8]

During the emancipatory conflict and justified by the belligerent context of the period, the first political orders that were established in the continent were very protective of centralisation. For half a century, at different time and places in Latin America, executive powers were invoked with plenipotentiary powers that claimed to restore political order and safeguard the processes of independence.

Beyond the assigned names of the institutional orders and their durations, the creation of institutional orders is highlighted to show a concentration of civil and military prerogatives that operate under the control of small groups or provisional regulations that enabled governance with diffuse limits of power. These prerogatives were adopted under the following forms of government: monarchic or pseudo-monarchic governments, dictatorships, supreme directorships and protectorates, lifelong presidentialism or presidents with broad powers.

However, these institutional constructs were not the first and only forms of government to circulate during this time. The initial forms of government included the Government Juntas (Crespo 2013a: 69). In the decade of the 1810s, for example, institutional orders were implemented that installed a figure of plural

---

6.   The process of prolonged wars of independence with a declaration of war to the death by Bolívar was broader than the revolution of the United States of America (refer to Bushnell 2010: 28).

7.   A total of sixteen juntas existed during this period.

8.   Peru, Mexico and Uruguay were the most recent juntas.

*Table 2.1: Conflicts of emancipation*

| Outcomes of the conflict | Temporary concentration with military emphasis: extraordinary (Congress, assemblies)/De facto (imposed) | Generalisimo, Dictator, Protector, Supreme Director, Emperor | Powers |
|---|---|---|---|
| Emancipation (1808–1828) | Valencia Congress (1812), extraordinary-delegation-based outcome | Francisco de Miranda, 'Generalisimo dictatorial powers' (Venezuela, 1812) | Military |
| | Chilpancingo Congress, extraordinary-delegation-based outcome | José María Morelos, 'Generalisimo' (New Spain, 1813) | Military |
| | Caracas De facto-Assembly, extraordinary-delegation-based outcome | Simón Bolívar 'General Captain of the Militaries' (Venezuela, 1813) 'Supreme Chief of the Republic' (Venezuela, 1816) | Military-legislative-judicial |
| | Congress (1814), extraordinary-delegation-based outcome | José Gaspar Francia, 'Supreme Dictator of the Republic' (Paraguay 1814) | Military-legislative |
| | Assembly (1814), extraordinary-delegation-based outcome | Gervasio Antonio Posadas, 'Supreme Director' (United Provinces of Río de la Plata, 1814) | Military |
| | Assembly (1815), extraordinary-delegation-based outcome | Carlos María de Alvear, 'Supreme Director' (U.P. Río de la Plata, 1815) | Military-legislative-judicial |
| | Tucuman Congress (1816), extraordinary-delegation-based outcome | Juan Martín Pueyrredón, 'Supreme Director' (U.P. Río de la Plata, 1816) | Military-legislative |
| | Union of free peoples (1815), extraordinary-delegation-based outcome | José Gervasio Artigas, 'Protector' (Seacoast Río de la Plata, 1815) | Military-legislative |
| | Santiago Junta (1817), extraordinary-delegation-based outcome | Bernardo O'Higgins 'Supreme Director' (Chile, 1817–1823) | Military-legislative |
| | De facto, self-delegated outcome (1821) | José de San Martín, 'Protector' (Peru, 1821–1822) | Military-legislative |
| | De facto, self-delegated outcome (1821) | Agustín de Iturbide, 'Emperor' (Mexico, 1822) | Military-legislative-judicial |
| | 'Popular assemblies – electoral juntas', extraordinary-delegation-based outcome (1828) | Simón Bolívar, 'Dictator' (Great Colombia, 1828) | Military-legislative-judicial |

Source: Elaborated by the authors based on works cited.

executive powers, which was suspicious of the concentration of power in only one person (Crespo 2013a: 83–84). An example of this institutional architecture was the Venezuelan case with the Constitution of 1811. This institutional order suggested the popular election of three representatives of executive power, with strong control by the legislature. The same case was observed in the provinces of Río de la Plata in 1813 and Mexico with the Constitution of Apatzingán in 1814; these constitutions instituted chartered executive power. In addition, the Constitutional Regulation of 1811 in Chile was composed of three members and established strong congressional control.

However, in all Latin American countries, the option of a plural executive was quickly discarded as the independence processes were confronted with the contingency of war. This contingency opened the door to forms of government that were characterised by the concentration and expansion of executive powers. Note that this type of institutional order, which granted broad powers to the executive, did not disappear after the end of the wars of independence but transformed into a legacy of border-defining conflicts (our second category of conflict) between two independent countries.

### b) Conflict between Latin American states: the definition of borders

Despite the long process of emancipatory revolutions, the territories did not experience any rest. In parallel with or immediately after the independence conflicts, other conflicts regarding borders occurred. These conflicts newly conditioned the emerging institutional bodies to continue and reinforce the rationales of the concentration of power to overcome external threats. Loveman (1999), for example, notes that the international post-independence wars were stimulated by the interests of nation states in consolidating their borders (1999: 29). Some of these international wars even unfolded during the second half of the nineteenth century.[9] These conflicts left a mark of blood and debt in Latin America (Centeno 2002) that did not always influence the strengthening of the nation-state and caused repercussions in the preferences of actors in favour of the institutional designs and practices that led to concentrated power.

Border-defining conflict contributed to the militarisation of politics in a large part of the continent. Military leaders continued to monopolise the political-institutional scene. Thus, political caudillos maintained their power and legitimacy, which was supported by arms and military prestige gained during wartime. The fragile institutional order was incapable of counterbalancing the weight of the figure of the military caudillo, which entailed a reinforcement of executive power in the institutional order in which the will of the all-powerful military caudillo ruled via 'emergency powers' (extraordinary powers) or the discretional use of power. Because of the length of their mandates, the most representative cases were José Gaspar

---

9. The most significant cases were the War between Mexico and France (1862–67), the War between Ecuador and Colombia (1863), the War of the Triple Alliance (1864–70), and the War of the Pacific (1879–84).

Rodríguez de Francia in Paraguay (1816–1840), José Antonio Páez in Venezuela (1830–48), José Manuel de Rosas in Argentina (1829–52) and Antonio López de Santa Anna in México (1831–1853). Other cases that governed with caudillo-like characteristics and with a discretional use of power but with the bad luck of being overthrown by internal civil wars are Agustín Gamarra (Peru), Andrés Santa Cruz (Bolivia-Peru), José Ballivián (Bolivia), Juan José Flores (Ecuador), Francisco de Paula Santander (New Granada), and Tomás Cipriano de Mosquera (New Granada).

The conflict supported the dynamics of the concentration of power in the hands of the presidential figure. This feedback was produced via the activation of formal emergency powers mechanisms or improvised extra-constitutional delegation of powers. Armed conflict not only called for the State to intensify its abilities to mobilise resources and men but also made demands on the entire political system due to the urgency of decision-making. In the first half of the nineteenth century, the wars between the states became an extension of the emancipation conflict. The extension of war implied the implementation of measures that necessitated a concentration of power. In this manner, the actors drew upon figures and actions, such as a) provisional presidencies or *de facto* presidentialism, b) militarisation of the presidency, c) activation of extraordinary powers, and d) suspension of Congresses and tribunals. Table 2.2 details the most significant wars in Latin America.

In the case of the Confederation of the United Provinces of Río de la Plata, the border conflict influenced actors' preferences for a concentration of power. The imminent war with Brazil in 1826 intensified the discussion to establish a national and permanent executive, who was referred to as the 'President of the Republic' (Crespo 2013a: 375). The creation of the presidency of the republic can be considered to be a curiosity given its brief period of existence. Executive power was reinforced by this war. The chaos and anarchy among different political factions (a product of the negative impacts of the war for the Cisplatina Province) prompted the rise to power of Juan Manuel de Rosas, who imposed a strong informal executive from the government of the province of Buenos Aires and who governed with ordinary and extraordinary powers for more than twenty years.

The war between Chile and the Peruvian-Bolivian Confederation demonstrates how the wars between the states in Latin America influenced the reinforcement of an executive who claimed broad powers. This war can be interpreted as a Peruvian civil war with the intervention of neighbouring countries (Contreras and Cueto 2007:108). The Peruvian civil war (in which Bolivia finally intervened) created a political entity that consisted of three states (North Peruvian State, South Peruvian State and Bolivia) under the rule of Andrés Santa Cruz – a Bolivian military official who was declared its 'Protector'. Vast powers were established for the executive, which enabled the control of the entire bureaucratic and military apparatus with a role in the naming of judges to the Supreme Court and the ability to dissolve the General Congress.[10]

---

10. Fundamental Law of the Peruvian-Bolivian Confederation (1837) Available: http://www4. congreso.gob.pe/dgp/constitucion/constituciones-peru.htm (accessed 9 November 2016).

*Table 2.2: Conflicts of border definition*

| Border conflicts first half of 19th century | Provisional delegation-based regulation (directors, dictators, protectors, presidents) | Military presence in the executive | De jure Constitutionalism (power imbalance) | De facto Presidentialism (imposed, patronage networks) | Emergency powers |
|---|---|---|---|---|---|
| **Cisplantina Province (1825–28)** | Fundamental Law, (Presidency, Provisional executive with military powers and foreign affairs 1824–1826) (Río de la Plata) | Military predominance in the Cabinet (Río de la Plata) Rosas begins his control over the militia | Argentina, Constitution 1826, Río de la Plata (failed) | Rivadavia, President of the Republic, 1826 → López y Planes Provisional President, 1827 → Juan Manuel de Rosas, Governor of Buenos Aires,[11] 1829 (Río de la Plata). | **Extraordinary military, legislative, judicial powers (Río de la Plata)** |
| **La Plata War/ Uruguayan Civil War (1836–51)** | Federal Pact, 1831. Legislature assigns extraordinary powers to J. M. de Rosas | Military predominance in the Cabinet (Río de la Plata) Rosas begins his control over the militia | Federal Pact. Confederation U.P.Río de la Plata | Juan Manuel de Rosas, Governor of the Province of Buenos Aires. Military power, patronage networks with the governors of the provinces. | **Extraordinary military, legislative, judicial powers** |
| | Extension of the presidency of Manuel Oribe.Interim presidency of Fructuoso Rivera (1839–1843) Interim presidency of José Suarez (1843–1851) | Military predominance in the exercise of power | Centralist Constitution, operative 1830–1839 (Uruguay) | Extra-constitutional and imposed Presidency, Fructuoso Rivera (1839–1843), later take up the defence of the 'Government of the Defence.'Manuel Oribe (1839–1843), extra-constitutionally extended to 'The government of Cerrito' | **Extraordinary military, legislative powers (call an Extraordinary Session of the General Assembly)** |

(Continued)

11. The figure of the President is eliminated. During the civil wars there was no central power; the Governor of Buenos Aires managed foreign relations.

*Table 2.2: Continued*

| Border conflicts first half of 19th century | Provisional delegation-based regulation (directors, dictators, protectors, presidents) | Military presence in the executive | De jure Constitutionalism (power imbalance) | De facto Presidentialism (imposed, patronage networks) | Emergency powers |
|---|---|---|---|---|---|
| **War of the Peruvian-Bolivian Confederacy (1836–1839)** | Constitution of the North and South Peruvian, Andrés Santa Cruz 'Protector,' Confederation (1836–1839). Provisional president Agustín Gamarra | Military predominance (Peru-Bolivia) | Confederation, Executive predominance, re-election (1837–1839) | Andrés Santa Cruz, military imposition (1836) Agustín Gamarra, military imposition (1838) | Extraordinary powers, Confederation (1836–1839) |
| | Absence | Civic-military coexistence (Chile) | Constitution (1833) Executive Predominance, and re-election (Chile) | | Congress-extraordinary powers, Chile (1837–1839) |
| **Independence of Texas (1836)** | Centralist provisional Constitution (1835) | Military predominance, military caudilloism (Mexico) | Constitution, The Seven Laws (1836) | | Military powers |
| **Pastry War (1838)** | Interim Presidency Antonio López de Santa Anna (1839) | Military predominance, military caudilloism (Mexico) | Constitution, The Seven Laws (1836) | | Military powers |
| **Peruvian-Bolivian War (1841)** | Provisional President Agustín Gamarra (1839) | Military predominance, military caudilloism (Peru) | Constitution Huancayo (1839) | Agustín Gamarra, military imposition (1839) | Extraordinary powers |
| **Mexican-American War (1846–48)** | Provisional Presidency Mariano Paredes, Valentín Gómez Farías, Antonio López de Santa Anna | Military Predominance | Constitution (1843) Constitution (1824) | Mariano Paredes military imposition (1846) Antonio López Santa Anna, military imposition (1847) | Military, legislative |

*Source:* Elaborated by the authors based on works cited

Although the Confederation was a brief political project, the presidentialist logic of the expansion of executive powers endured in Peru. After the war, Agustín Gamarra, who was recognised as the restorer, was named Provisional President by the allied Congress in 1839. The caudillo installed a new Constitution that granted extensive powers to the executive over other powers in preparation to launch a subsequent war against Bolivia.

Chile had a Constitution (1833) that was distinguished by the ability to assign great powers to the executive. Declared in the conflict with the Peruvian-Bolivian Confederation, President José Joaquín Pérez asked Congress for extraordinary powers in accordance with the Constitution. The extraordinary powers remained valid during the war, which had a considerable impact on Chilean political institutionalism and became one of the decisive factors in its stability (Valenzuela and Valenzuela 1983; Collier 2005: 59).

Border-defining conflicts were a constant occurrence in Mexican politics. After the emancipation conflict at the end of the 1830s, Mexico had to contend with the secession of the State of Texas, the fleeting war with the French and the traumatic conflict with the United States. In this stage, the presidential figure of the caudillo Antonio López de Santa Anna was prominent in each of these conflicts. Santa Anna was thrice elected president (1833, 1843 and 1847), was named provisional president (1839) and was twice designated dictator (1841–43 and 1853–55) (Vázquez 2001). Many of these designations were attributed to his role in the border conflicts.

The overlapping relationship between the emancipation conflicts and the border-defining conflicts in the nascent states became a transcendent variable in the design and practice of the exercise of presidential power. Monarchies and dictatorships were replaced by presidentialism, which was a normative preference in accordance with the republican and liberal concepts of the time. The violence that was inherited from the emancipation conflicts, transposed with the need to territorially delimit the emerging political entities, are the causes that influenced the exercise of a particular type of presidentialism that constantly assumes a re-foundational character to regain stability and order. Similarly, internal conflicts, such as the civil wars and the challenges to the governments, also provided feedback for a presidentialism that is resurrected as a political device to overcome situations of chaos and anarchy despite its permanent questioning and resistance.

## c) The blockade of normative preferences: organisational conflict

The third conflict was the conflict for the organisation of the State (the third conflict). In this period, countries noted similarities and differences in the construction of institutional order, and bifurcating institutional outcomes occurred during the nineteenth century. Among their similarities, we observe the pre-eminence of institutional presidential architectures. Among their differences, we observe the different mechanisms for protecting and reinforcing this presidentialist architecture.

For many of the countries in Latin America, the main concern of rulers was the search for survival mechanisms in a context of strong belligerence and opposition. This belligerent condition contributed to the feedback of an institutional trajectory that was notable for its concentration of power. This exercise of power caused the installation of hierarchical regimes that were crowned by the figure of the president in an attempt to substitute – in the words of Colomer – weak states with strong governments (Colomer 2013: 82).

Presidentialism was imposed on post-emancipation institutional designs. Its implementation, however, led to strong conflicts due to the level of opposition to the established order. The dispute between federal or centralist parties, party factionalisation and military caudillism are conflicts that contributed to the formation of the institutional architecture of presidentialism.

The conflicts constituted highly concentrated presidential rule to sustain the series of military interventions, the production of patronage networks, and the creation of constitutions with a re-foundational spirit. Consequently, the idea of a hierarchical one-person presidential structure was an effective institutional architecture to overcome these conflicts.

In the process of the organisation of States, this formula was highly contested by opposition groups. In some cases, the conflicts ended in the construction of a highly unstable presidentialism without institutional coherence. The exercise of

*Table 2.3: Conflicts related with the organisation of the States*

| 1820–1900 | Number of conflicts | Years | Type of conflict | Outcomes of conflict. Second half of 19th century |
|---|---|---|---|---|
| Argentina | 8 | 19 | Federal-Unitarian | Federal, centralised Presidentialism |
| Chile | 4 | 4 | Liberal-conservative | Reformist Presidentialism |
| Mexico | 4 | 55 | Federal/Centralist/ liberal-conservative/ indigenous | 'Porfiriato', centralised, patronage Presidentialism (1876–1911) |
| Uruguay | 2 | 18 | Partisan | Contested, negotiated Presidentialism (failed) |
| Colombia | 7 | 19 | Partisan, federal/ centralist | Contested and negotiated Presidentialism (imposed) |
| Ecuador | 3 | 17 | Military caudillos | Military Presidentialism |
| Paraguay | – | – | – | Supreme Presidentialism |
| Venezuela | 3 | 8 | Regional-military caudillos | Military Presidentialism |
| Peru | 4 | 22 | Military caudillos, coast, mountain, partisan | Military, patronage, centralised Presidentialism |

*Source:* Adapted from Centano (2002: 45, 144).

presidential power constantly sought to reinforce its political power in formal and informal ways using constitutional or *de facto* mechanisms.

Thus, presidentialism crystallised with formal and informal mechanisms and operated in a central and territorial dimension: a) formal mechanisms to defend against other powers, b) formal mechanisms to defend territories, c) informal mechanisms to defend power and d) informal mechanisms to defend territories. The installation of presidentialism was a consequence of the original conflicts; however, its crystallisation was a result of its correlation with the conflict around state organisation. The coherent implementation of the mechanisms and the conflict of state organisation explain the degrees of presidentialism in the different countries in Latin America.

With regard to a formal institutional architecture, the literature has recognised the existence of constitutional instruments that sought to establish the predominance of the Executive over other powers, such as Congress (Loveman 1993; Negretto and Aguilar Rivera 2000; Gargarella 2003; Cheibub, Elkins and Ginsburg 2010; Crespo 2013a). The following components of its design have been highlighted: a) the ability to designate and evaluate ministers without consulting the legislature, b) legislative initiative, the creation of decrees and the capacity to veto and c) the existence of 'emergency powers', which are characterised by their ambiguity in limits on the assigned powers.[12]

An example of the formal logic of the containment of other powers was observed in Peru when observing the predominance of the Executive in the Constitution of 1839, which was implemented by Agustín Gamarra. This constitution installed great powers in the legislative, judicial and administrative spheres. The same situation was observed in Bolivia with the Constitution of 1843, which enabled the President of the Republic to dissolve the chambers with prior approval of the State Council and the Supreme Court.

The nineteenth century was characterised by the proliferation of constitutional designs that established the predominance of the executive over the legislative. The need to contain conflict and the finalisation of a government agenda for establishing the desired order arose as the principal justifications for its incorporation and implementation.

Similarly, underlying the formation of emerging states was a need for the formal control of territories. The installation of presidentialist systems in a context of political disorder and state precarity introduced the need to control territories via structures that are capable of supporting executive power. The definition of a presidential system and its conciliation with the demands of the territories became a difficult problem, and the centralised, federated or confederated institutional designs became an engine of conflict throughout the entire nineteenth century. The resolution of this conflict implied a distribution of power and resources between the central apparatus and the different regional and local actors. Consequently, the

---

12. The following constitutions have some of these features: Chile (1833), Peru (1826, 1839, 1860), Colombia (1821, 1886), Venezuela (1857), Bolivia (1831, 1834, 1851), Argentina (1853), Paraguay (1844), Mexico (1857).

institutional architects employed different constitutional experiments to reconcile or impose formal exits from the territorial conflict.

The Peruvian constitutions, for example, left the definition of local authorities, such as the Prefect and Sub-Prefect and the control of the departmental militias and public employees that depended on the State in the hands of the executive (Constitutions of 1828, 1839, 1860, 1867). In Argentina, the Constitution of 1853, and its subsequent reforms in 1860, established a presidential power with certain powers for controlling local governments; with emergency powers, it established the predominance of the president during internal conflicts (Negretto 2013b: 164). Federalist and centralist conflict was also present in Mexico, as demonstrated by the tension that exists in Mexico's constitutions of 1824, 1836 and 1843. The war of 1836 (that ended with the separation of the state of Texas) was a reaction to the Mexican centralism, which always sought control over its extensive territory via formal mechanisms. In Colombia, a Constitution was established in 1886 that defined the country as a unitary Republic that concentrated great powers in the Executive and granted the power to name department governors and absolute military control (Duque-Daza 2011: 192).

Presidential styles in Latin America were also created using informal mechanisms. The main problem of the rulers in the first half of the nineteenth century was the fragility of formal institutions. The abundance of constitutional experiments showed the institutional precarity with which the rulers had to lead. Because of the weakness of the formal institutionalism of Latin America, the use of informal mechanisms such as patronage networks, bribery and eliminating the opposition was common. These mechanisms offered greater support for the formal institutional order in some cases.

For the case of informal mechanisms in the containment of powers, we observe the configuration of servile congresses via the election of candidates that were allied with the government. Some of the main mechanisms were as follows: a) the creation of parliamentary lists with candidates who were close to the current administration at the time and b) bribery and electoral fraud controlled by the Executive. This informal mechanism was conflictive due to the levels of violence that it generated and the complaints of corruption by opposition forces (Posada-Carbó 2000; Annino 1995), which does not negate the existence of competition in the electoral processes of the nineteenth century, as the opposing factions also employed these informal mechanisms, with differences in behaviour between different nations and regions. Note that electoral fraud was a widespread instrument in Latin America (Posada-Carbó 2000).

Extreme cases of the manner in which governments managed the electoral processes include the cases of Juan Manuel de Rosas and Porfirio Díaz, who were defined as 'government electors' (Posada-Carbó 2000: 631). The creation of a sole list of candidates, such as in the Argentine case, or the list of 'non-contested candidates' in Mexico are examples. In the Chilean case, J. S. Valenzuela (1985, 1987) highlights that the executive power resorted to a series of contraptions in the process of qualifying electors, in the composition of electoral juntas, and in the electoral mobilisation of the civic police. The pre-eminence of buying votes is also observed among other patronage mechanisms. The 'government electors' did not always employ informal mechanisms. For the Colombian case, Posada-Carbó suggests that being an officialist candidate indicated more responsibility than advantages; the use of informal mechanisms was not exclusively associated with governments (2000: 635, 637).

The need to maintain servile congresses prompted the creation of informal strategies to control territories (our fourth strategy), which were aimed at the articulation of patronage relationships with local caudillos. In a weak State, patronage systems were organised using a structure forged in large estates, in which the 'patron' provided the resources and security in exchange for services from his peons or tenants in times of war and peace (Lynch 1993; Pfoh 2005: 136–37). Simultaneously, the prestige and resources that were provided by the patron enabled him to join the territory with the regional ruling class through family or social relations. The central government sought to incorporate these networks via co-action or the joining of networks with the local caudillos to construct a base for the presidentialist power structure. These patronage networks were conflicting elements within the process of State organisation, as they were interpreted as vestiges of a traditional society that reproduced nuances of this type of relationship in different regions.

An example is the case of the provinces of Río de la Plata after the independence process. Patronage networks were dominated by family alliances and interests that overtook the region, and only Juan Manuel de Rosas (1829–52) was able to control them and offer a certain level of stability in this highly precarious institutional architecture (Halperín Dongui 2005: 380–404). Presidentialism benefited from these patronage networks that settled into their power structure. However, the existing patronage networks in the provinces also served as a challenging barrier for executives who sought to root their power in the territory.

Territorial control via informal networks was common in many of the countries in Latin America. In Peru, for example, caudillo-ism was considered to be a series of broad traditional coalitions on the local and national level rather than a power vacuum left by the State (Walker 1999: 280). Consequently, the formation of the State should not be considered to be the impossibility of establishing a formal institution. Associated with the absence of this type of order was a hidden series of conflicts and power networks that informally or traditionally operated. In the case of Peru, strengthening the State by increasing tax assets during the first government of Ramón Castilla enhanced the state apparatus and its ability to compensate the patrons of the local governments that were distributed throughout the regions and localities (McEvoy 1997: 25).

The predominance of informal mechanisms was also evident in Mexico during the Porfiriato after a turbulent history that was marked by international conflicts and military 'pronouncements' (Fowler 2011: 102). For example, General Porfirio Díaz managed to impose all of his presidential power on the territory using government machinery, coercion and patronage networks with local governors and political chiefs to be re-elected (Ponce 2011; Bravo 2011). Using these mechanisms, a coherent power structure that enabled Díaz to establish a solid base in the territory that conformed with the formal institutional architecture was constructed.

The use of informal mechanisms was more difficult in countries such as Uruguay, Colombia and Venezuela, as the political entities in these countries were to be imposed by strengthening the military of the State. The conflicts between centralist and federalist factions, which were assumed by the parties, were evident in the national governments' inability to impose their control over the territory.

In Uruguay, the parties divided the control of the territory that was rooted in their patronage networks in both urban and rural zones, which prevented any possibility of control from a central government. Thus, the Uruguayan political order was formed amid a balanced correlation of forces that were supported by informal mechanisms and alliances with neighbouring powers. Consequently, the conflict endured based on fragile pacts of power distribution or via the rationale of obliterating the opposition.

In the case of Colombia, the political parties co-opted patronage networks, as the treasury became a supplier of militias (López-Alves 2003: 186). At the end of the century, President Rafael Núñez was able to break and partly curtail this system and establish a strong alliance between the conservative factions and the military, which facilitated in the growth of the latter.

We observe the same path in Venezuela, which highlights the inability of the central government to root its power in territory. This path is evident in the eleven constitutions and the eight 'Constitutional Acts' in the nineteenth century – acts that represent a revolution in the established order (Brewer-Carías 1985). Informal mechanisms and the rationale of obliterating the opposition – known as 'historical praetorianism' – were established (Irwin and Micett 2008). In return, the federal versus centralist struggle was not as intense, as it disguised the interest in maintaining power quotas for some landowners in the regions (Guardia and Olivieri 2005: 17). The conflict for the organisation of the state was determined by the resolution of the war and the personality of the caudillos in exercising power. Local bosses managed the military, and leaders who dominated the regions and the informal links with local elites controlled the distribution of resources, which established a disconnection between the State and the territory (López-Alvez 2003: 266). The impossibility of accessing these informal mechanisms forced the State to wait for the gradual strengthening of the central military, which could not be consolidated until the beginning of the twentieth century (López-Alvez 2003: 266).

## Conclusion

The objective of this chapter was to investigate the reasons for the trajectory of presidential styles in Latin America via observation of the mechanisms that reinforce the preferences for concentration of power. Specifically, we sought to establish how the conflicts from the beginning of the nineteenth century reinforced the characteristics – formal and informal – of presidentialism in Latin America. The primary hypothesis of this investigation is that the reinforcement of one type of presidential style that demands concentration of power is attributed to the option at the beginning of the rules of the game, which was reinforced by the conflicts of emancipation, border definition, and organisation of the State during the nineteenth century.

The proposal entailed a far-reaching investigation that would encompass the origins of representative institutions and examine institutional- and political-type variables in the context of the variables forged in the institutional order of Latin America. We attempted to reactivate the discussion about presidential styles and applied it to the origin of the republics and integrated the dynamics that would have composed its trajectory in Latin America.

This investigation focused on the causal mechanisms that explain the paths of institutional persistence. Fundamentally, we centred on the variables of conflict, analysed formulas and recontextualised seminal studies of the origin and evolution of institutions. The relevance of this investigation is that it centres on the origin variables of the phenomena of power concentration that are currently maintained in Latin America. Using diachronic observation of the institutional construction of Latin America, the reasons that reinforce the actors' preferences for the concentration of power were observed.

The results of this analysis will facilitate the creation of new questions for political science in general and historical comparativism in particular. For example, this paper revealed a causal chain from the beginning that enabled us to articulate the institutional designs in Latin America. This causal chain began with the emancipatory conflict and the presence of authorities with high power concentration. This order was maintained to solve internal conflicts and was subsequently codified in centralist Constitutions that were personified in the figure of the President. This codification obscured the inheritance of previous conflicts and finally impeded the actors' preferences for this type of solution.

Substantial effort is needed to advance the comprehension of the political order of Latin America. We believe that the scope of the concepts and causalities that have existed in Latin America should be expanded. The origin of the institutions is central to understanding presidentialism and the persistence of the struggle to concentrate power in Latin America.

## References

Aljovín, C. (2000) *Caudillos y Constituciones: Perú: 1821–1845*, Lima: Pontificia Universidad Católica del Perú, Fondo de Cultura Económica.

Annino, A. (ed.) (1995) *Historia de las elecciones en Iberoamérica, siglo XIX: de la formación del espacio político nacional*, Buenos Aires: Fondo Cultura Económica.

Basadre, J. (2002) *La iniciación de la república: contribución al estudio de la evolución política y social del Perú*, Vol. 1, Lima: UNMSM, Fondo Editorial.

—— (1981) *Sultanismo, corrupción y dependencia en el Perú republicano*, Lima: Editorial Milla Batres.

Bethell, L. (ed.) (1991) *Historia de América Latina*, Vol. 6, Barcelona: Editorial Crítica.

Bolívar, S. (1815) Carta de Jamaica.

Bravo, C. (2011) 'Elecciones de gobernadores durante el Porfiriato', in J. A. Aguilar Rivera (ed.) *Las elecciones y el gobierno representativo en México (1810–1910)*, México: Fondo de Cultura Económica, Instituto Federal Electoral, pp. 257–81.

Brewer-Carías, A. (1985) *Las Constituciones de Venezuela*, Madrid: Ediciones de la Universidad Católica de Tachira, Instituto de Estudios de la Administración Local, Centro de Estudios Constitucionales.

Bushnell, D. (2010) 'Las independencias comparadas: las Américas del Norte y del Sur', *Historia Crítica* 41: 20–37.

Centeno, M. A. (2002) *Blood and Debt: War and the nation-state in Latin America*, Pennsylvania: Pennsylvania State University Press.

Centeno, M. A. and Ferraro, A. (eds) (2014) *State and Nation Making in Latin America and Spain: Republics of the possible*, Cambridge and New York: Cambridge University Press.

Chapman, C. (1932) 'The Age of the Caudillos', *Hispanic American Historical Review* 12(3): 23–31.

Cheibub, J. A., Elkins, Z. and Ginsburg, T. (2010) 'Latin American presidentialism in comparative and historical perspective', *Texas Law Review* 89(7): 1707.

Cohen, Y., Brown, B. R. and Organski, A. F. (1981) 'The paradoxical nature of state making: the violent creation of order', *American Political Science Review* 75(4): 901–910.

Collier, S. (2005) *Chile: la construcción de una república 1830–1865, política e ideas*, Santiago: Ediciones Universidad Católica.

Colomer, J. M. (2013) 'Elected kings with the name of presidents: on the origins of presidentialism in the United States and Latin America', *Revista Latinoamericana de Política Comparada* 7: 79–97.

Contreras, C. and Cueto, M. (2007) *Historia del Perú contemporáneo: Desde las luchas por la Independencia hasta el presente*, 4th edn, Lima: Instituto de Estudios Peruanos.

Crespo, M. V. (2013a) *Del Rey al presidente. Poder Ejecutivo, formación del Estado y soberanía en la Hispanoamérica revolucionaria 1810–1826*, México D.F.: El Colegio de México.

—— (2013b) 'Del republicanismo clásico a la modernidad liberal: La gran mutación conceptual de la dictadura en el contexto de las revoluciones hispanoamericanas (1810 político 1830)', *Prismas* 17(1): 67–87.

Drake, P. (2009) *Between Tyranny and Anarchy: A history of democracy in Latin America, 1800–2006*, Stanford: Stanford University Press.

Duque Daza, J. (2011) 'La reforma constitucional de 1910: Constantes institucionales, consensos y nuevas reglas', *Papel Político* 16(1): 185–212.

Earle, R. (ed.) (2000) *Rumours of Wars: Civil conflict Nineteenth-Century Latin America*, London: Institute of Latin American Studies, University of London.

Fowler, W. (2011) 'Entre la legalidad y la legitimidad: elecciones, pronunciamientos y la voluntad general de la nación, 1821–1857', in J. A. Aguilar Rivera (ed.) *Las elecciones y el gobierno representativo en México (1810–1910)*, México: Fondo de Cultura Económica, Instituto Federal Electoral, pp. 95–122.

Fujimori, A. (1992) 'Mensaje a la Nación del Presidente del Perú, ingeniero Alberto Fujimori el 5 de abril de 1992', in Congreso Nacional del Perú, Available: http://www4.congreso.gob.pe/museo/mensajes/Mensaje-1992-1.pdf (accessed 8 October 2015).

Gargarella, R. (2003) 'El período fundacional del constitucionalismo sudamericano', *Desarrollo Económico* 43(170): 305–328.

—— (2013) *Latin American Constitutionalism, 1810–2010: The Engine Room of the Constitution*, Oxford: Oxford University Press.

Guardia, M. and Olivieri, L. (2005) *Estudio de las relaciones civiles militares en Venezuela desde el siglo XIX hasta nuestros días*, Caracas: Fundación Centro Gumilla, Universidad Católica Andrés Bello.

Guerra, F.-X. (2010) *Modernidad e independencias: Ensayo sobre las revoluciones hispánicas*, México: Fondo de Cultura Económica.

Halperín-Dongui, T. (1985) *Reforma y disolución de los imperios ibéricos 1750–1850*, Madrid: Alianza Editorial.

—— (2005) *Revolución y guerra: Formación de una elite dirigente en la Argentina criolla*, Siglo Veintiuno.

Huntington, S. P. (1968) *Political order in changing societies*, New Haven, CT: Yale University Press.

Irwin, D. and Micett, I. (2008) *Caudillos, militares y poder: Una historia del pretorianismo en Venezuela*, Caracas: Universidad Católica Andrés Bello.

Kalyvas, S. N., Shapiro, I. and Masoud, T. E. (eds) (2008) *Order, Conflict, and Violence*, Cambridge: Cambridge University Press.

Kling, M. (1956) 'Towards a theory of power and political instability in Latin America', *The Western Political Quarterly* 9(1): 21–35.

López-Alves, F. (2003) *La formación del Estado y la democracia en América Latina*, Bogotá: Editorial Norma.

Loveman, B. (1993) *The Constitution of Tyranny: Regimen of exception in Spanish America*, Pittsburgh: University of Pittsburgh Press.

—— (1999) *Por la Patria: Politics and armed forces in Latin America*, Wilmintong: DE: SR Books.

Lynch, J. (1989) *Las revoluciones Hispanoamérica 1808–1826*, Barcelona: Ariel.

—— (1993) *Caudillos en Hispanoamérica, 1800–1850*, Madrid: Editorial Mapfre.

Mahoney, J. and Thelen, K. (eds) (2009) *Explaining Institutional Change: Ambiguity, agency, and power*, New York: Cambridge University Press.

Mainwaring, S. and Pérez-Liñán, A. S. (2013) *Democracies and Dictatorships in Latin America: Emergence, survival, and fall*, Cambridge: Cambridge University Press.

McEvoy, C. (1997) *La utopía republicana: Ideales y realidades en la formación de la cultura política peruana (1871–1919)*, Lima: Fondo Editorial de la Pontificia Universidad Católica del Perú.

Negretto, G. (2013a) *Making Constitutions: Presidents, parties, and institutional choice in Latin America*, New York: Cambridge University Press.

—— (2013b) 'Los orígenes del presidencialismo en América Latina: un estudio sobre el proceso constituyente argentino (1853–1860)', *Revista Latinoamericana de Política Comparada* 7: 127–168.

Negretto, G. L. and Aguilar Rivera, J. A. (2000) 'Rethinking the legacy of the liberal state in Latin America: the cases of Argentina (1853–1916) and Mexico (1857–1910)', *Journal of Latin American Studies* 32(2): 361–397.

North, D. C., Wallis, J. J., Webb, S. B. and Weingast, B. R. (eds) (2013) *In the Shadow of Violence: Politics, economics, and the problems of development*, Cambridge: Cambridge University Press.

Pfoh, E. (2005) 'La formación del Estado Nacional en América Latina y la cuestión del clientelismo político', *Revista de Historia de América* 136: 129–148.

Pierson P. (2004) *Politics in Time: History, institutions, and social analysis*, Princeton: Princeton University Press.

Ponce, M. E. (2011) 'Las elecciones presidenciales de 1877 a 1888: modalidades y tendencias', in J. A. Aguilar Rivera (ed.) *Las elecciones y el gobierno representativo en México (1810–1910)*, México: Fondo de Cultura Económica, Instituto Federal Electoral, pp. 282–307.

Posada-Carbó, E. (1995) *Wars, Parties and Nationalism: Essays on the politics and society of Nineteenth-Century Latin America*, London: Institute of Latin American Studies, University of London.

—— (2000) 'Electoral juggling: a comparative history of the corruption of suffrage in Latin America, 1830–1930', *Journal of Latin American Studies* 32(3): 611–644.

Thelen, K. (2004) *How Institutions Evolve: The political economy of skills in Germany, Britain, the United States, and Japan*, New York: Cambridge University Press.

Tilly, C. (1992) *Coerción, capital y los estados europeos*, Barcelona: Alianza Editorial.

Valenzuela, A. and Valenzuela, J. S. (1983) 'Los orígenes de la democracia: reflexiones teóricas sobre el caso de Chile', *Estudios Públicos* 12: 7–39.

Valenzuela, J. S. (1985) *Democratización vía reforma: la expansión del sufragio en Chile*, Buenos Aires: Ediciones IDES.

—— (1987) 'Hacia la formación de instituciones democráticas: prácticas electorales en Chile durante el siglo XIX', *Estudios Públicos* 66: 215–257.

Vallenilla Lanz, L. (1991) *Cesarismo democrático y otros textos*, Caracas: Biblioteca Ayacucho.

Vázquez, J. (2001) 'Santa Anna: El Villano', *Nexos* (Sept.): 76–77.

Vogel, H. (2001) 'War, Society and the State in South America, 1800-70', in P. Silva (ed.) *The Soldier and the State in South America: Essays in civil-military relations*, New York: Latin American Studies Series.

Walker, C. (1999) *De Túpac Amaru a Gamarra: Cusco y la formación del Perú republicano, 1780–1840*, Cuzco: CBC.

Chapter Three

# The Politics of Electoral Reforms: The Origins of Proportional Representation in Brazil and the Electoral Code of 1932[1]

*Paolo Ricci and Jaqueline Porto Zulini*

## Introduction

Electoral systems are institutions created to process political conflict. In this chapter we focus on the causes leading to proportional representation (PR) adoption in the Brazilian 1932 Electoral Code. Since the seminal work by Stein Rokkan (1970), political science literature has produced several studies aimed at disentangling the reasons behind the adoption of different electoral formulas and estimating the effects of each formula on both the behaviour of legislators and the party system (Benoit 2004; Colomer 2005; Hazan and Leyenaar 2011). We know that proportional representation is associated with higher levels of participation and with a multi-party system whereas majority systems tend to reduce the number of political parties and the representation of distinct groups. After the 1930 coup d'état in Brazil, the public and political debate was centred on the necessity to permit the entrance of opposition parties into parliament. Clearly, the adoption of proportional representation created opportunities for opposition parties to hold seats in Congress. Hence, at first sight, PR follows conventional wisdom behind the incentives distinct electoral systems produce.

The Brazilian case is interesting because it has important theoretical implications for our understanding of how conflict is solved by institutional arrangements. We argue that exclusive focus on the necessity to provide more effective representation of opposition parties is insufficient to understand the adoption of PR. The change in electoral system must be understood as one of the components in a package of electoral reforms delineated by the 1932 Electoral Code. The adoption of the PR system, therefore, might have a very different reason to come to existence. It is this perspective we adopt here. To uncover the real motivations of the creation of new institutions, an approach based on the micro foundations of institutional change where new institutions are created or redesigned in accordance with pre-existing institutional mechanisms and contextual factors is called for. We will show that the Electoral Code emerged in 1932 as an answer to how elections were held during

---

1.    We thank Ângela de Castro Gomes, Fernando Bizzarro, and Fernando Limongi for their comments on earlier versions of this paper. We are also grateful for the financial support from FAPESP to this research project (Projects 2013/25053-0 and 2015/19455-3).

the previous regime and reflected the tension between old and new political elites for the control of power.

Currently, there are no disputing interpretations about the nature of the PR innovation of 1932 in the literature. After the Empire (1822–1899), Brazil experienced its first republican regime between 1889 and 1930. The new regime was characterised by high levels of decentralisation in which each state holds considerable power and autonomy from the centre. Focusing on how the president was to be selected is the key element for understanding how the institutional equilibrium was established until 1930. For some decades, the President's candidates (and the Vice) were selected in accordance with the preferences of important states. Before the election year, political elites negotiated the name for the succession during the preceding months. Consequently, the election became only a stage confirming this intra-elite agreement. However, in the twenties, the succession process was driven by São Paulo and Minas Gerais, excluding others states and new political actors (Viscardi 2012). The hegemonic concentration of power in two states created the conditions to contest the regime itself. In 1930 São Paulo broke the alliance with Minas and monopolised the succession process. Clearly, the situation leads to claiming a new institutional equilibrium. In October 1930, an armed revolutionary movement prevented a newly elected president from taking office, and this event culminated in a coup d'état that brought down the First Republic. A provisional government headed by Getúlio Vargas (who led the 1930 coup d'état) and supported by military groups was then entrusted with the task of calling elections for a Constituent Assembly, which would draft a new Constitution and set the stage for a liberal restoration. As a first step, the provisional government unilaterally approved a package of electoral reforms, embodied in the *Electoral Code of 1932*. Besides the PR system, the new legislation introduced the universal and mandatory suffrage,[2] the secret ballot, as well as the Electoral Justice, an independent bureau responsible for overseeing the electoral process; from voters' registration to the counting of votes and the certification of winning candidates. Even today, scholars associate the Code only with the struggle for political freedoms, against fraudulent practices commonly observed in the previous republican regime (Cabral 2004[1932]; Diniz 1999; Lamounier and Steinbach 1992). This interpretation follows classic views about the adoption of the PR system in 1932 (Porto 1995; Weffort 2009). The general understanding is that the PR system strengthened the representation of the opposition, which had been constrained by election rigging during the previous political regime.

The problem with this interpretation is that it takes institutional changes as 'democratic conquests' (Bethell 2008) and considers elections at that time to be 'reasonably democratic' (Conniff 1991). Following insights from recent studies

---

2.  The 'universal' suffrage was limited to citizens older than twenty-one, independently of sex. However, the illiterate, the homeless, and the military were still not allowed to vote (Electoral Code, article 4). The legal obligation to vote among women had also exceptions. It was mandatory only among those who were public employees. Other women voted only if authorised by their husbands, whereas widows and single women voted only if presenting proof of income.

about electoral reforms (Benoit 2004; Colomer 2005; Hazan and Leyenaar 2011), we assess the instrumental logic leading the new regime to adopt the PR system. Our analysis focuses on the quest for controlling electoral results. We claim that the electoral reforms enacted in 1932 aimed at legitimising the revolution, institutionalising conflict, controlling its achievements, and reducing uncertainties created by electoral disputes. In practice, it means that the provisional government needed to prevent the widespread use of electoral fraud and the interference of opposition parties during elections. In the First Republic (1889–1930), political parties fought for controlling the electoral process from voters' registration to certifying winning candidates in the National Congress. Two institutional mechanisms provided by the Code were particularly important to this end: the secret ballot and the creation of the Electoral Justice, both assuring a higher level of predictability in electoral results. Once old instruments used by parties to win elections had been weakened, the electoral success of the new political regime would be guaranteed by an element external to the Code: the better territorial organisation of ruling parties. Levels of party organisation, therefore, entered the calculus of institutional architects to adopt rules that favoured their own camps. The PR system was not an isolated choice of electoral engineering, nor could it be reduced to the moralising discourse of that time; it was rather a component of a complex structure of norms creating conditions for the strengthening of the new political regime. Therefore, the Electoral Code was an opportunity to introduce new rules in line with the debate around political freedom as well as to reduce the influences of old republican elites.

This chapter contains three sections. The next one focuses on the study of electoral fraud during the Brazilian First Republic (1894–1930), the regime that preceded the revolution that inspired the Electoral Code of 1932. Our intention is to go beyond the rhetorical discourse on the necessity of eliminating electoral fraud. We show that constraints on the representation of minorities through vote rigging were actually the result of a tight struggle for controlling voters and the several stages of the electoral process. That is, any electoral reform aimed at effectively changing the dynamics of elections would have to tackle the deep roots of party conflicts. In the second section, we analyse the introduction of the PR system. We claim that its viability was due to two complementary measures that limited the influence of parties over elections: the secret ballot and the Electoral Justice. In order to demonstrate this, we present data on the first elections conducted after the enactment of the Code: those for the Constituent Assembly in May 1933 and for the Chamber of Deputies in October 1934. Our analysis suggests that the effects of the introduction of the PR system were limited. Our conclusion is that the rationale behind the adoption of the PR system depends on other provisions introduced by the Electoral Code. The electoral reform was justified as a means of protecting minorities, but, ironically, constituents' main concern was to suppress opponents of the regime. The Electoral Justice was crucial to achieve this goal. Since the introduction of an administrative bureau responsible for overseeing the electoral process tended to guarantee more transparency for elections, opposition parties were now incapable of perpetuating frauds in all stages of the electoral process.

## Elections in Brazil before the introduction of the PR system

During the Brazilian First Republic, elections were a regular instrument for selecting representatives for the Chamber of Deputies carried out every three years in multi-member districts by majority rule.[3] The law 35 of 26 January 1892 regulated every step of the electoral process in the earlier years of the new regime. It established sixty-three electoral districts where 212 representatives were elected to the Chamber of Deputies. In ten small states, forty-one deputies (19.3 per cent of the total) were elected in single districts corresponding to the state territory; the remaining 171 deputies were elected in states divided in two to twelve districts. A few years later, the law 1269 of 15 November 1904, also known as the Rosa e Silva law, reduced the number of districts to forty-one, without changing the number of seats in the Chamber (212). Following this reform, sixty-one deputies (28.8 per cent) became representatives of single-district states, whereas the remaining ones (151) were elected in states divided among two to seven districts.[4]

On election days, voters could express several simultaneous preferences. Electoral laws established the limited and cumulative vote in reference to article 28 of the 1891 Constitution, which explicitly secured the representation of minorities.[5] The law of 1892 (article 36, paragraphs 3 and 4) allowed each voter to cast votes for two thirds of the seats under dispute in the district, although voters were also allowed to indicate only one candidate in the ballot. The reform of 1904, due to changes in the number of districts, also changed the number of votes each voter was allowed to cast[6] and introduced the cumulative vote. According to the law,

> when the number of seats to be filled in the district is five or more, the voter could accumulate all of his votes or part of them in only one candidate, writing the name of the same candidate as many times as is the number of votes to be cast for him.
>
> (Law 1269/1904, article 59)

Candidates with the highest vote shares were elected.

Below we analyse two aspects of an election's modus operandi. We discuss how political parties used some legal mechanisms to control voters and, at the same

---

3.  This was a common combination in the nineteenth century. The classic distinction between majority rule and proportional representation not only tends to disregard numerous combinations between multi-member districts and several electoral formulas adopted in majority systems, but also has generated some confusion regarding the way these systems work. The study by Wills-Otero (2009), for example, classifies the electoral system used in Brazil between 1900 and 1944 as semi-proportional. For an informative review of these systems, see Colomer (2004; 2007).

4.  This arrangement was upheld by law 3208 of 27 December 1916. During the Republican regime, other electoral laws were enacted to regulate some specific aspects of the process, without altering it substantially.

5.  The limited and cumulative vote is described by the literature as increasing the chances of victory of minorities (Horowitz 2003; Lijphart 2004).

6.  According to article 58, paragraph 3, 'each voter will cast three votes in states represented by four deputies; four votes in districts represented by five; five votes in those represented by six, and six votes in districts of seven deputies'.

time, circumvented the legislation to manipulate electoral results. In this sense, our approach to the problem is legalist, that is, based only on the study of the electoral legislation.[7] Such an approach is the most appropriate for understanding the reason why some specific measures were included in the Electoral Code of 1932.

## Mechanisms for controlling voters

The control over voters is directly related to the secret ballot. The legislation in the First Republic made such control relatively easy. Voting took place in polling stations comprised of, at most, 250 voters. They voted as the polling station committee called them. During the process, voters were subject to the oversight of politicians standing only a few steps from the ballot box and capable of watching everything happening inside the polling station. The ballots dropped by voters in the box were handed out directly by politicians or canvassers. There was not a standard official ballot at that time, and candidates were responsible for producing and distributing ballots to voters. This distribution was made a few days before Election Day, or even on that very day – a practice known as *boca de urna*. The electoral reform enacted in 1904 institutionalised the unconcealed vote. Article 57 established that 'the election will have a secret suffrage, but voters are allowed to cast unconcealed votes'. According to the same law, the voter should carry two ballots: one to be dropped in the box and another to be kept with him 'after both had been dated and signed by members of the polling station committee'. At that time, this practice was glorified as a way of expressing the freedom to vote. Some candidates claimed that those who cast unconcealed votes 'felt the moral obligation of eloquently manifesting their opinion in favor of the one who advocated interests of the homeland and its traditions of honesty and honor'.[8] However, the second ballot clearly helped local bosses to control voters, as it was proof of their electoral choices. It was, in the words of a contemporary politician, a means of ensuring 'the plain duty, before local bosses, of the voting behavior'.[9] In this sense, the unconcealed vote solved problems of coordination created by cumulative voting, making it possible for parties to better control the distribution of electoral preferences.[10] Hence, the vote during the First Republic was public.

7. Following a sociological approach, most authors have assessed voters' dependency on local *coronéis*, who in practice constrained their freedom to vote. There is evidence of violence and voter intimidation, as well as of forms of bargaining, especially in urban centres, such as bribery and vote buying. Examples are Carvalho (2007), Leal (1977), Porto (2004), and Telarolli (1982). Recent studies show that the vote worked as an instrument of bargaining for material benefits, which raise questions against the classic view that voters were totally dependent on the local coronel. One classic study to make this claim is Queiroz' (1975). New considerations about the complex relation between these actors can be found in Ricci and Zulini (2014, 2017a).

8. Annals of the Chamber of Deputies (ACD), 04/26/1927, p. 60.

9. ACD, 05/08/1921, p. 194.

10. Only a few studies discuss the use of cumulative voting during the First Republic. For similar approaches dealing with the coordination between parties and voters, refer to Bowler *et al.*'s (1999) study on the British case.

## Control over electoral results

Controlling voters, however, was not enough to ensure victory. This brings us to the issue of electoral fraud. Within a legalist perspective, fraud is different from coercion of voters and refers to an action that 'breaks the law' (Lehoucq 2003: 235). In the case of the Brazilian First Republic, it was manifested in practices such as the manipulation of voters' registration, elections decided by the *bico de pena* ('pen-nib' in literal translation), intentional biases during the counting of votes, and even the non-recognition of winning candidates by the National Congress. Indeed, the 'menu of electoral manipulation' was diverse.[11]

Reports of fraud are well known. Still, most of the authors endorse normative analyses of elections, which, keeping the democratic paradigm in mind, tend to focus on critiques related to the unfairness of the electoral process. In our view, it is necessary that we overcome such a perspective. It is important that we understand the 'rationale' behind fraud, that is, the reasons leading to the massive use of vote manipulation by political parties. In general, studies of other countries point towards a positive association between electoral fraud and political competition (Dardé 1996; Lehoucq 2003; Lehoucq and Molina 2002; Molina and Lehoucq 1999; Ziblatt 2009). Still, there is a problem in this interpretation. Because fraud is hard to identify (Birch 2009), authors use formal complaints presented by defeated candidates as a proxy. The common scholarly practice does not differentiate between fraud and the act of denouncing it: both are misleadingly taken as the same thing. However, a potential empirical association between political competition and formal complaints does not imply that fraud did not happen in environments with low levels of party competition. The data collected for the Brazilian case demonstrates the validity of this critique. The figure below shows cases of fraud complaints during the Brazilian First Republic aggregated by state, but collected at the level of electoral districts.[12]

Let us consider only states with better-defined situations. Bahia, Pernambuco, the Federal District, and Rio de Janeiro are characterised by high rates of political competition and a stark prevalence of districts with fraud complaints. In these cases, due to difficulties regarding the consolidation of stable party systems (Ferreira 1994; Levine 1980; Pinto 2011; Pang 1979), the political forces used fraud to win most of the elections. The common use of formal complaints attests to the tight dispute among political parties during elections. On the other hand, other states deemed more central to the Republican political dynamics (e.g., Minas Gerais, São Paulo, and Rio Grande do Sul) are characterised by a much lower rate of electoral fraud complaints. This does not mean lack of fraud. In these states, the

---

11. The expression is used by Schedler (2002: 104) to describe numerous strategies for controlling elections.

12. During the First Republic, the Brazilian territory was divided among the Federal District (DF) and other twenty states: Alagoas (AL), Amazonas (AM), Bahia (BA), Ceará (CE), Espírito Santo (ES), Goiás (GO), Maranhão (MA), Minas Gerais (MG), Mato Grosso (MT), Pará (PA), Paraíba (PB), Paraná (PR), Pernambuco (PE), Piauí (PI), Rio de Janeiro (RJ), Rio Grande do Norte (RN), Rio Grande do Sul (RS), Santa Catarina (SC), São Paulo (SP), and Sergipe (SE).

*Figure 3.1: Distribution of fraud complaints by Brazilian states (1900–1930)*

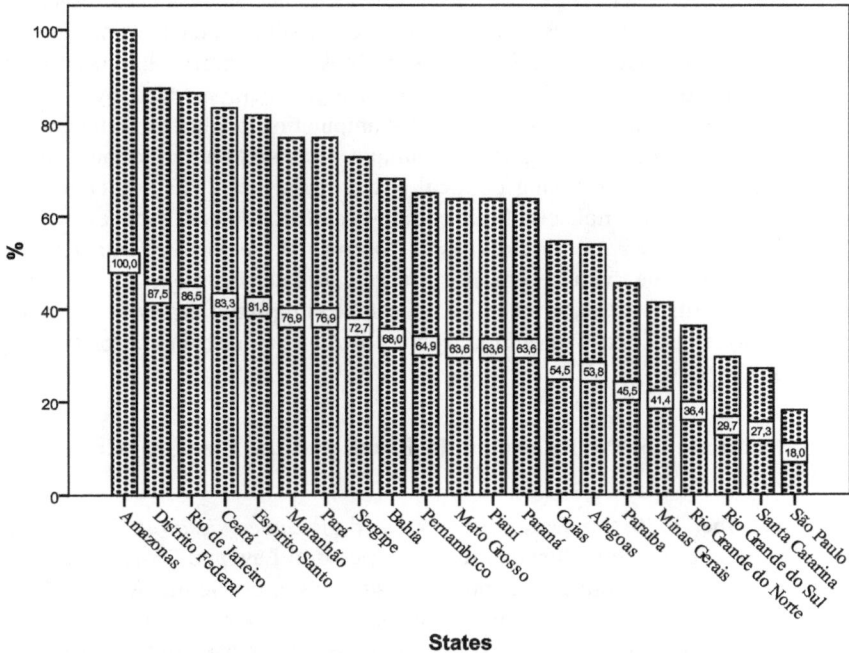

**States**

*Source:* Annals of the Chamber of Deputies and *Official Gazette* of the National Congress.

control over the electoral process was monopolised by only one party (Rezende 1982; Love 1975). Despite the existence of opposition parties, the ruling party managed to organise elections and hold control over the several electoral stages. It was hard for the opposition to register voters, and, if they succeeded, all the further stages in the electoral process would be full of difficulties.

It means that fraud and its denunciation are two completely different phenomena. Our study of the Brazilian First Republic confirmed the association between electoral competition and fraud complaints only partially (Ricci and Zulini 2014).[13] In some sense, fraud complaints were indeed associated with high levels of political competition. The large amount of denunciations indicated the struggle of politicians for controlling the electoral machine, that is, the electoral bureaucracy.[14] To be more specific, parties fought for controlling voters' registration,

---

13. In this work political competition is operationalised as the ratio between total votes for the candidate with highest vote share among the defeated and total votes for the least voted candidate among the elected. Therefore, the level of competition ranged from zero to one, with higher scores indicating more electoral competition. According to the authors, the level of political competition in districts with and without complaints was, respectively, 0.69 and 0.39.

14. For an exhaustive analysis of parties' domination over the several electoral stages, refer to Ricci and Zulini (2017a).

the composition of polling station committees, the counting of votes, and the process of certifying winning candidates in the National Congress.[15] However, the same rationale is valid for cases with no fraud complaints, such as Minas Gerais, São Paulo, and Rio Grande do Sul. In these states, ruling parties had been more efficient in controlling the electoral bureaucracy. As demonstrated by a recent study on authoritarian regimes, 'electoral manipulation ought to be understood not merely as a marginal vote-getting technique, but also as an important tool for consolidating and monopolising political power' (Simpser 2013: 4). This is the argument we want to emphasise here: complaints of fraudulent practices indicate the *inability of local elites and parties to control the electoral bureaucracy*. In general, and in line with recent historiographic interpretations of the Latin American and European experiences, fraud can be interpreted as a symptom of the tension between political forces fighting for power; as an instrument for assuring victory in the polls.[16]

## The introduction of the PR system in Brazil and the Electoral Code of 1932

On 6 December 1930, the decree 19549 created the *Subcomissão de Reforma da Lei e Processo Eleitorais* (Subcommittee on Electoral Law and Process Reform). The work of this committee was constantly supervised by Getúlio Vargas, Chief of the Provisional Government, and his Minister of Interior, with no interference of parties or oppositions groups. The committee was composed of three members and its main task was to set the rules for the election of the Constituent Assembly. Their efforts resulted in the elaboration of the Electoral Code, enacted by the decree 21076 of 24 February 1932.[17] The PR system was established by article 58. Deputies would now be elected by means of a simultaneous two-round system, the first one allocating seats in accordance with electoral and party quotas, and the second one allocating seats to the most voted for remaining candidates.[18] How can this change be explained? Why have legislators decided to adopt a PR electoral system?

---

15. In a previous work, we show that the last electoral stages (the counting of votes and the formal certification of winning candidates in the National Congress) were not as decisive as the previous ones (see Ricci and Zulini 2012).

16. For a review of the literature on this topic, refer to Posada-Carbó (2000), Sabato (2001), and Morelli (2004).

17. For a detailed description of the elaboration of the Code, refer to Pires (2009).

18. The complexity of the system has generated some confusion among scholars. Some classify the formula adopted in 1932 as proportional, while others consider it to be hybrid (Kinzo 1980) or mixed (Nicolau 2012) due to the way seats were allocated. Our interpretation is that the electoral system of 1932 was formally mixed, but the PR component was prevalent in practice. Some evidence can be presented to support our view. In 1933, 65.4 per cent of deputies were elected in the first round, most of them through party quotas. Moreover, the Electoral Code required, for the first time, that candidates be endorsed by party nominations, which also indicates an emphasis on the system's PR component.

The literature is consensual in answers to both questions. Even today, scholars explain the introduction of the PR system through contextual analyses of that period, when critiques were frequently directed to the way elections had functioned in the Brazilian First Republic. In general, authors underscore that one of the goals of the 1930 Revolution was to defend political freedoms and protect the representation of different opinions about the Republican regime, which was then deemed inaccessible to the opposition (Kinzo 1980; Pandolfi 1999; Weffort 2009; Holanda 2008). Bolivar Lamounier, for example, interprets the introduction of the PR system as resulting from the recognition of the regime's pluralist and consociational component. According to the author, legislators wanted to avoid the '*governismo* and the single-party regimes of the Old Republic, which turned the electoral reform necessary' (Lamounier 1992: 35). In the years preceding the debates about the PR system, newspapers usually glorified such a reform and its potential to 'endorse minority rights',[19] making it a true 'synonym of democracy',[20] based on a 'criterion of fairness'.[21] Most of the parties did not hesitate in taking a stance in favour of the PR system. The Social Party of Pernambuco declared that,

> the proportional system assures, in the composition of the parliament, the representation of all parties in which are deposited national aspirations. It achieves as much as possible the democratic ideology – the government of the people, comprehending all classes and cultural elements of the Nation.[22]

We can assert that scholars have endorsed official justifications for the electoral reform, and that, to use the words of a member of the committee responsible for drafting the Code, the central issue was the protection 'of the opinions, measured in numbers, from citizens who wanted to express their stances about political issues' (Cabral 1932: 16).

However, the reality is more complex and the thesis of protecting minorities is, to say the least, oversimplifying, if not unrealistic. The main mistake is to ignore the political dynamics of that time. As Przeworski (1991) claims, one of the central issues in regime transitions is the conflict between opponents and defenders of the new regime. The main problem for the revolutionary elites was that the upcoming elections for the 1933 Constituent Assembly would be disputed by Brazilian old oligarchies, who had been defeated during the 1930 Revolution. Added to that was the fact that there were no nationally organised parties: their influence remained limited to the state level as it was in the First Republic. Elections brought about the risk that revolutionaries would lose control over the process of political liberalisation. It was clear that they had 'to make an effort of

---

19. *Diário da Manhã*, 08/15/1931, p. 1.

20. *A Republica*, 09/13/1931, p. 1.

21. *A Batalha*, 01/22/1932, p. 1.

22. *Diario Carioca*, 12/01/1932, p. 6. Newspapers of that time commonly published declarations of parties in favour of the PR system.

mobilisation and organisation capable of guaranteeing the victory of a political-ideological orientation' (Gomes 1980: 29). From this standpoint, the PR system could be an element of risk for parties supporting the coup d'état, leading to the success of old oligarchies.

In practice, the electoral victory depended on two factors not related to the electoral system. The first one was the control over the process of political restoration in each state (Gomes 1996). The *interventores* who replaced state governors deposed by the coup had a central role. They brought new political elements to their respective states and also had influence in the elaboration of new party programs (Gomes 1980). Despite difficulties in some states, especially the need to negotiate with non-aligned political actors, it is clear that ruling parties were already well entrenched in state governments at the eve of the 1933 elections.[23] Nonetheless, it is also possible to assert that the political mobilisation of the oppositions succeeded in some situations. By the end of 1932, many parties supporting the revolution were still not organised in every state, favouring the fast resurgence of old Republican parties, who intended to dispute the upcoming election. It means that the process of party reorganisation in the states and the efforts of political mobilisation by the *interventores* were not a sufficient condition for securing the success of the revolution.

For this reason, it is particularly interesting that we reflect about the second factor potentially capable of affecting electoral results: the array of practices aimed at controlling (1) voters and (2) the different electoral stages, from voters' registration to the certification of winning candidates in the National Congress. The fact that the electoral reform may lack effectiveness can be illustrated by the case of the state of Rio Grande do Sul, where the PR system had been introduced already in 1913, in elections for state deputies. The idea behind the law 153 of 14 July 1913, to use the words of state Governor Borges de Medeiros, was to 'turn the constitutional promise of minorities' representation a reality'.[24] It established that in elections for the State Assembly of Rio Grande do Sul, the whole state would function as a single district, and ballots or lists would be prepared and delivered by parties. This system was employed for the first time in the election of 20 August 1913, when the opposition Federalist Party managed to elect one representative for the first time.[25] Although the Federalists succeeded in electing other state representatives in the following elections, the domination of the governor's party was never threatened. The literature emphasises that this was the result of electoral fraud and the use of a very effective party machine for controlling instruments of voters' mobilisation at the municipal level (Love 1975; Rouston 2012; Trindade 1980; Wasserman 2004). At the stage of formally recognising and certifying winning candidates

---

23. Since its inauguration, the provisional government participated directly in the process of party reorganisation in the states and favoured the formation of aligned parties with the support of *interventores*.

24. Citation extracted from Rouston (2014: 228).

25. See Trindade (1980) for an explanation of the political dynamics in Rio Grande do Sul.

at the State Assembly, a Federalist deputy denounced the rigging of the 1992 election using these words: 'From you, who are apologists of the proportional representation, came the duty of reserving a place for the minority, so that you could say later that votes were counted under the watch of the opposition'.[26] This case indicates how the success of political forces loyal to the government depended less on the electoral method and much more on the adoption of concrete measures for reducing or dissipating the influence of old oligarchies on electoral results.

This was also the perception among drafters of the Code of 1932. As Nicolau (2012) points out, only a few Brazilians defended the PR system before 1932. Among them were Assis Brasil and João Cabral, both members of the committee in charge of drafting the Electoral Code. Still, the system proposed by Assis Brasil was designed to ensure both the representation of minorities and the control of the government by the majority (Kinzo 1980). Moreover, Cabral and Assis Brasil advocated the adoption of the PR system only in combination with other measures. They were both convinced that the representation of different opinions and political forces in the parliament depended less on the format of the electoral system and more on the introduction of mechanisms for reducing electoral fraud, especially those affecting voters' behaviour and the administration of elections.

We claim that the PR system must be understood in association with two other measures introduced by the Electoral Code: the secret ballot and the creation of the Electoral Justice. Regarding the former, rules were established to guarantee that voters would be free of coercion. It was determined that they would vote within an inviolable voting booth capable of securing their isolation (article 57). At the same time, it was forbidden to distribute ballots next to the place where the polling station committee was seated (article 77), curbing, therefore, attempts of influencing vote choices at polling stations. Although the Code did not arrange for the production of official ballots[27] and maintained the parties' prerogative to produce and distribute ballots to voters, it set a standard for ballot size and design. They should be typewritten in a white background and have dimensions corresponding to the *sobrecartas* – the official envelopes where ballots were placed to assure secrecy before they were dropped in the ballot box (articles 71 and 91, paragraph 3). On the other hand, a substantial portion of the Code was devoted to preventing practices aimed at rigging the polls. It created the Electoral Justice, an independent administrative bureau in charge of organising voters' registration, distributing voter ID cards, making decisions on candidates' registrations and locations of polling stations, nominating members of polling station committees, counting votes, announcing the results and deliberating about

---

26. Citation extracted from Rouston (2012: 175).

27. The first official ballot was used in the 1955 presidential election.

electoral complaints.[28] This was an innovative mechanism for preventing fraud in all stages of the electoral process.

Similarly to what we noticed about the introduction of the PR system, the common wisdom about those two measures endorses the thesis of the moralisation of elections and justifies their employment as a way of '"guaranteeing the right to vote", reducing the violence in electoral disputes and revealing the "electoral truth"' (Sadek 2010: 27).[29] For our purposes, it is important to unravel the rationale behind these measures and the real political payoffs generated by their introduction. The question, then, can be tackled from the viewpoint of the actors involved in the electoral game, that is, the political parties themselves. Regarding the secret ballot, the aim was to reduce the ability of party agents to control voters. As reported in the editorial of an issue of the *Diario Carioca*, 'the secret ballot virtually dissipates the appearance of cohesiveness among parties [...] The inviolable booth turns commitments into ashes, destroy agreements, and, in summary, makes the party discipline a myth'.[30] This way, 'a party does not know a priori, with mathematical certainty, how many of its candidates will be elected'.[31] The jurist Pinto Serva, one of the members of the subcommittee that drafted the Electoral Code, stated that the secret ballot 'abolishes the *cabala* [i.e., the practice of canvassing votes for a party's candidate], the influence of authorities, practices of vote buying and vote selling, and shameless negotiations in front of the ballot box'.[32] Regarding the Electoral Justice, the delegation of responsibility to an independent bureau for voters' registration, the organisation of elections, and the counting of votes meant that politicians lost the ability to manipulate electoral results in all electoral phases. In some way, from that time forward, the political dispute became limited to the struggle for controlling voters.

If we take the ambitions of political actors into account, it becomes clear that the electoral reforms of 1932 were aimed at reducing the ability of old Republican oligarchies to succeed in the 1933 election for the Constituent Assembly. It is true that those were universal measures that affected all political parties, including those

---

28. At the federal level, the electoral judicial system was composed of a Superior Court (TSJE) with eight effective members whose decisions were made by majority rule. Each of the twenty states and the federal district had a Regional Court (TRJE) with six members. For the purpose of counting votes, the article 88 of the Electoral Code of 1932 established that employees of each TRJE would be assigned to election scrutiny boards (*Turmas Apuradoras*, or TAs). One could appeal to the TRJE against decisions made by presidents of TAs, with no suspensive effect. If the TRJE retained TAs' decisions, however, one could not appeal to the TSJE unless through a legal action against the certification of winning candidates (Electoral Code of 1932, article 89).

29. The idea that the Electoral Justice was created to repel the previous fraudulent system is disseminated in the literature (Kinzo 1980; Lamounier and Amorim Neto 2005; Nicolau 2012; Skidmore 1988; Vale 2009 – to cite only a few). For a broad analysis about the ideal of a judicial system that is impartial and free of political influence, from the Imperial era to current days, *see* Fleischer and Verge Barreto (2009) and Sadek (2010).

30. *Diario Carioca*, 05/06/1933, p. 6.

31. *A Republica*, 06/15/1933, p. 2. Similar statements can be found in several news articles published in the months preceding the elections.

32. *Diario de Notícias*, 05/17/1933, p. 3.

aligned with the government. Nonetheless, the latter ones benefitted remarkably from the process of party organisation led by the *inteventores*. The secret ballot and especially the Electoral Justice were yet more obstacles against actions by old Republican oligarchies.

## The election of 1933 and voting practices

The Code of 1932 regulated the 1933 election for the Constituent Assembly and the subsequent elections for the National Congress and state Legislative Assemblies, which were restored after the approval of the new constitution in 1934. We have argued that the adoption of the PR system in Brazil must be interpreted as a component of a whole package of electoral reforms implemented in 1932, also including the secret ballot and the Electoral Justice. To elucidate this point, we present data on those elections below. Our first endeavour was to analyse the effects of proportional representation on the party system.

Figure 3.2 presents boxplots for the proportion of seats won by the most voted party in each state during the Brazilian First Republic (1900–1930) and the two elections for the Chamber of Deputies carried out right after the revolution, already under the PR system (1933–1934).

The data show that the adoption of a new electoral formula did not produce significant effects on the party system.[33] Although the medians for the 1933 and 1934 elections are comparatively lower, note that values for some other elections (1912, 1915, and 1921) are similar. The effective number of legislative parties indicates one important aspect of the electoral trend in the 1930s: 1.4 in 1933 and 1.7 after the 1934 election for the Chamber of Deputies. In general, opposition parties remained barely represented.

As a matter of fact, the main difference between the Brazilian First Republic and the 1930s was the way the opposition attained representation. In the earlier period, opposition groups managed to win some seats after negotiating with the ruling party. In other instances, the government itself ceded representation to independent candidates by including the name of the 'opposition' contender in the list of nominees presented by the ruling party. At that time, politicians who truly opposed the government were incapable of achieving representation (Ricci and Zulini 2017b).[34] Diversely, opposition candidates who were elected in 1933 and 1934 really belonged to political parties with alternative programmes. Most of the time, they were old politicians and Republican oligarchs who had been mobilised after the revolution to defend Republican ideals. Therefore, the distinctiveness

---

33. We thoroughly discuss electoral results during the Brazilian First Republic in another work (Ricci and Zulini 2014). Here, we concentrate on a broader analysis of the main differences between the two periods, with an emphasis on the 1933 and 1934 elections.

34. There are some notable exceptions, however. Electoral disputes were tight, especially as a result of splits in the ruling party, or because of difficulties in the consolidation of a dominant state party. The most complex party dynamics was observed, at different times, in the Federal District (Pinto 2011), Rio de Janeiro (Ferreira 1994), Bahia (Pang 1979), and Pernambuco (Levine 1980).

*Figure 3.2: Proportion of seats won by the most voted party in each state (1900–1934)*

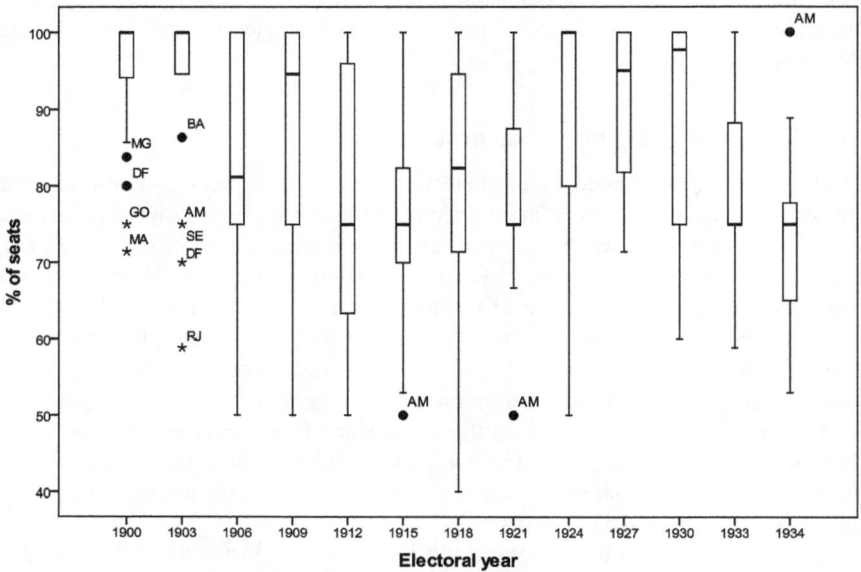

*Source:* Data for the 1933 and 1934 elections were extracted from Electoral Bulletins of the Superior Court of Electoral Justice (1933 and 1934). Data for the First Republic were collected from major contemporary newspapers and from the Annals of the Chamber of Deputies.

of the electoral arena in the 1930s stemmed from the ability of the opposition to effectively attain representation.[35] Still, opposition groups remained a minority.

The weak association between district magnitude and number of parties also indicates the limited impact of the PR system.[36] It is well established that the higher the district magnitude is, the higher the number of parties tends to be (Cox 1997; Sartori 1976; Taagepera and Shugart 1989). In 1931, Assis Brasil defended the adoption of large districts (or 'stretched' districts, as he used to say), because 'only large numbers can lead to a fair representation of the various organised opinions or parties' (Brasil 1931, 1993). Hence, the Brazilian case is interesting because it exhibits considerable variation in the number of seats allocated for each state, allowing us to observe the effect of district magnitude on party systems in one single country. The figure below shows the cross-state association between district magnitude and the effective number of parties for the 1933 and 1934 legislative elections.

---

35. We make this claim based on electoral data for the Chamber of Deputies. Opposition parties were comparatively more successful during the 1934 elections for state assemblies: on average, the winning party gained 64.7 per cent of the seats and the effective number of legislative parties was 1.9.

36. At that time, each state was a single electoral district.

*Figure 3.3: District magnitude and effective number of legislative parties, by state (1933 and 1934)*

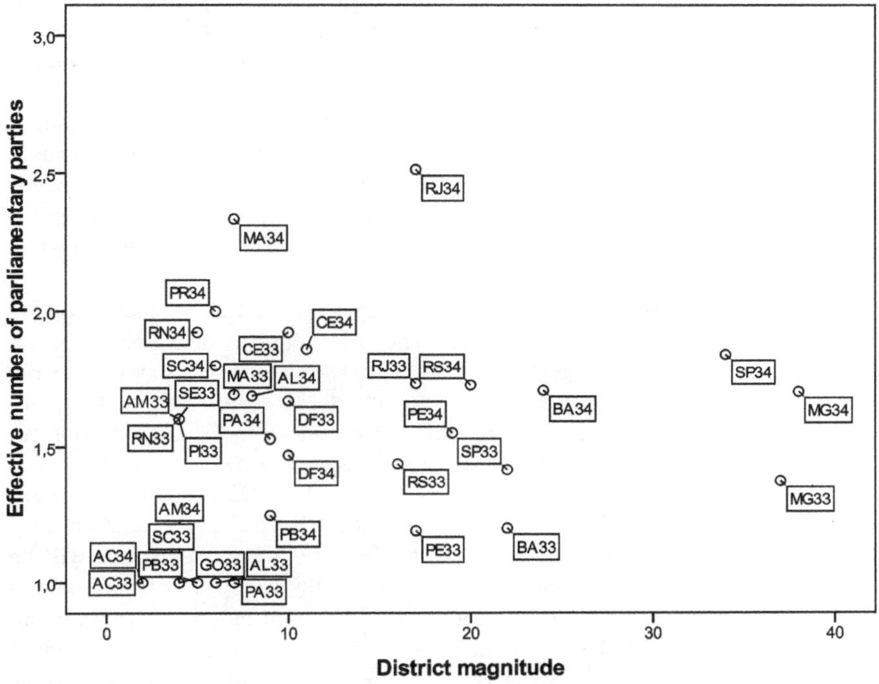

*Source:* The effective number of parliamentary parties (ENPP) was calculated using data extracted from Electoral Bulletins of the Superior Court of Electoral Justice (1933 and 1934). We applied the Laakso-Taagepera (1979) formula to parliamentary seats. *Note*: 33 and 34 refers to respectively 1933 and 1934 elections. References to States are by abbreviation: Acre (AC), Alagoas (AL), Amazonas (AM), Bahia (BA), Ceará (CE), Distrito Federal (DF), Goiás (GO), Maranhão (MA), Minas Gerais (MG), Pará (PA), Paraíba (PB), Pernambuco (PE), Piauí (PI), Rio de Janeiro, (RJ), Rio Grande do Norte (RN), Rio Grande do Sul (RS), São Paulo (SP), Santa Catarina (SC), Sergipe (SE).

The interpretation of the graph is straightforward: the introduction of proportional representation *did not produce visible effects on the party system*. In general, variations in the effective number of parties resulted from the internal dynamics of political disputes within each state.

How can we explain the adoption of the PR system in Brazil? In the previous section, we insisted that its adoption should be analysed in combination with other innovations brought about by the Code of 1932. Our argument is that the electoral reform was aimed at maximising the electoral chances of loyalist parties, to the detriment of the opposition. Two other provisions introduced by the Code played a more important role than the PR system: the secret ballot and the Electoral Justice. Below, we analyse information extracted from formal fraud complaints presented by parties to the Electoral Justice in order to estimate the effects of those two measures on results of the 1933 election. Politicians who felt harmed by electoral irregularities could formally appeal against electoral results by means of a legal action.[37] As a supplementary source of information, we resorted to news articles published before and after the 1933 election. Even during the First Republic, party newspapers had been a systematic source of information and an outlet for the promotion of party propaganda. Throughout these periods, the opposition expressed its discontentment towards the electoral process and denounced cases of fraud. Information published in these newspapers allows us to have a better understanding of the electoral environment in 1933.[38] The figure below displays the relative proportion of each type of allegation presented to the Electoral Justice after the dispute for the Constituent Assembly in 1933.

Three topics are prevalent among formal complaints of fraud, and they comprise together more than 80 per cent of the total. The most frequent one was secret ballot violations (39 per cent). It referred to different machinations directed towards the identification of *sobrecartas*, as well as attempts to associate their content with individual voters – such practices certainly corresponded to the negative portrait depicted by some contemporary newspapers about electoral events. At the eve of the election, there was a hesitant sentiment towards the effectiveness of the norm establishing the secret ballot.[39] A reporter of *Diario de Noticias* wrote at the very day of the election: 'Surprises about the secret ballot? No doubt there will be novelties. At least in this regard political matters really changed in Brazil. Wait a minute. It is about time...'.[40] In the following days, both optimistic views about the success of the secret ballot and statements that the polls' secrecy was 'small talk' were often reported.[41] News articles about the elections reported diverse manoeuvres employed by parties to watch voters' behaviour at the polls.[42] Even issues related to the format and printing of ballots, allegedly not matching legal provisions, had been raised.[43] Finally, there were also reports of politicians using transparent *sobrecartas* to identify enclosed ballots.[44]

---

37. During the First Republic, legislators had the last say on appeals against electoral results. Following the creation of courts of Electoral Justice in 1932, this prerogative was transferred to magistrates.

38. The amount of fraud taking place at that time may be underestimated if we focus only on formal complaints, because potential claimants had to deal with their own subjective perception of the facts before deciding to file a formal appeal. According to Green (2007), potential claimants needed to weigh the costs related to such actions and their odds of success.

39. We analysed news articles published between 3 May, the day of the election for the Constituent Assembly, and 26 March 1934, the day in which the list of winning candidates was published by the TSJE.

40. *Diario de Noticias*, 05/03/1933, p. 3.

41. *Correio de São Paulo*, 10/19/1933, p. 2.

42. *A Batalha*, 05/09/1933, p. 3.

43. *A Batalha*, 06/01/1933, p. 1.

44. *Diario Carioca*, 05/13/1933, p. 3.

*Figure 3.4: Types of fraud complaints in the 1933 election as a proportion of the total*[45]

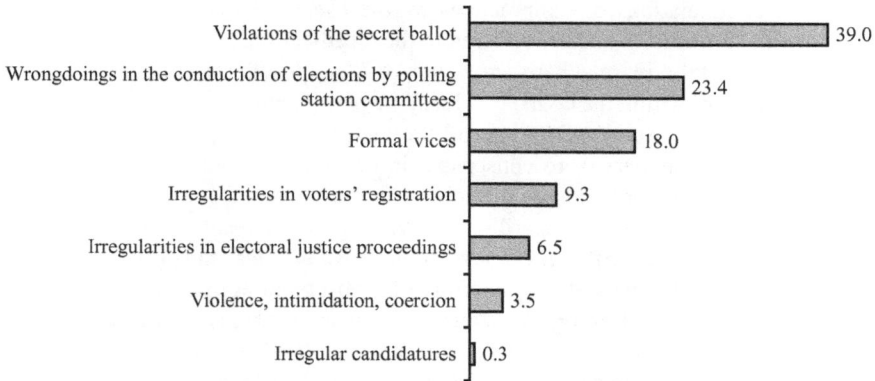

|  |  |
|---|---|
| Violations of the secret ballot | 39.0 |
| Wrongdoings in the conduction of elections by polling station committees | 23.4 |
| Formal vices | 18.0 |
| Irregularities in voters' registration | 9.3 |
| Irregularities in electoral justice proceedings | 6.5 |
| Violence, intimidation, coercion | 3.5 |
| Irregular candidatures | 0.3 |

*Source:* Electoral Bulletins and authors' calculation.

The second most cited problem in appeals against electoral results in 1933 was electoral misconduct by polling station committees (23.4 per cent), including irregularities in its composition, frequently in disagreement with legal provisions. According to article 65 of the Code, committees should be appointed by regional electoral courts (TRJEs) and chaired by a voter, preferably a magistrate, a member of the *Ministério Público* (Public Prosecutor's Office), a professor, a professional with college degree, a court clerk with a law degree, or a taxpayer. The chairmanship should not be assigned to workers lacking job stability or to Electoral Justice magistrates. However, the Superior Court of Electoral Justice (TSJE) allowed mayors, justices of the peace, and their surrogates to chair poll station committees, potentially increasing the amount of local interference in the electoral process.[46] It is worth noticing that mayors were appointed by the *interventor*, who enjoyed the autonomy to make replacements if those appointed by him did not follow his desired political orientation. Following this logic, *interventores* could easily hold control over local politics and, by extension, electoral results. This leads us to believe that the category of irregularities perpetrated by polling station committees is related to electoral problems at the municipal level.

Complaints about formal vices (18 per cent) were the third most frequent type of fraud allegation. Besides the lack of signatures required by law, this category also refers to problems during the dispatch of electoral documents, such as delays or failed deliveries in higher instances. Finally, it also accounts for the use of irregular ballots, such as those produced by parties not registered in the TSJE or displaying candidates' personal information (e.g., their profession or address).

45. Refer to the appendix for details on data sources, criteria of classification, and missing data.

46. This decision was made during analyses of elections for the Constituent Assembly in Minas Gerais. See article 65 on page 138 of the *Código Eleitoral de 1932 comentado por Cabral*.

None of the remaining categories reaches 10 per cent of the total.[47] Among them are denunciations of malpractices by the Electoral Justice (6.5 per cent). Complaints of this kind usually referred to the nullification or improper validation of elections. Only in one case, however, the supposed misconduct involved magistrates from within the court.[48] Indeed, the periodicals we examined converge in describing the well-functioning of the recently created bureau. Accounts published in newspapers were consensual in this regard.[49] As we can see, there is no evidence that local bosses influenced the judicial system during the 1933 election, which could have jeopardised the validity of the results.

The data lead us to the theme of the relation between voters and politicians. They show something that was already admitted by observers at that time. According to those observers, instituting the secret ballot was worthless if voters remained conditioned by a multitude of social mechanisms that kept them dependent on a local politician. Analysing the 1933 election, a *Diario de Noticias'* reporter stated 'such a mentality would [hardly] be transformed overnight, especially with superficial measures such as the institution of the secret ballot'.[50] The gazette *A Batalha* was even more emphatic in this regard, stating 'people with average culture like ours elect whoever the government nominates'.[51] Other explicit reports about the preservation of previous patterns of electoral behaviour can be found in speeches by Domingos Velasco in the Constituent Assembly: 'while the economic conditions of our rural masses remain as they are, I deem ineffective the efforts of political propaganda and legal provisions for assuring the electoral truth, which are intended to solve the problem of Brazil'.[52] Azevedo Amaral, an intellectual supporter of the *Estado Novo* (i.e., the dictatorial regime launched by a coup d'état in 1937), shares this view.

> The secret ballot corresponded to what enthusiasts theoretically expected from it only in the most advanced populous cities, and, in general, only among electoral groups displaying higher levels of culture. The electoral masses kept voting in the same inconsistent conditions as they have always done (Amaral 1938: 183–184).[53]

---

47. In general, the geographic distribution of types of fraud complaints corresponds to the frequency of such formal complaints, which varies across states. Pará is the leader with 124 irregularities recorded in the TSJE. At the lowest extreme is Paraná with only four. Knowing the reasons for this wide variation would require further research on the political situation of each state, which is not among our goals in this chapter.

48. A claimant in Pará registered this case. *Electoral Bulletin*, 08/19/1933, p. 2563.

49. Our research covered news articles published between 05/03/1933 and 12/31/1933.

50. *Diario de Noticias*, 08/10/1933, p. 1.

51. *A Batalha*, 05/23/1933, p. 2. References to the political culture of the electorate can be found in other news articles: *Correio de São Paulo*, 05/10/1933, p. 2; *Correio de São Paulo*, 11/16/1933, p. 1; *Jornal de Recife*, 05/16/1933, p. 1; *Jornal de Recife*, 07/05/1933; *O Dia*, 04/23/1933, p. 4.

52. Annals of the Constituent Assembly 02/02/1934, p. 325.

53. Regarding the control over voters as a function of the 'environment', see *Diario da Noite*, 05/10/1933, p. 2; *O Dia*, 05/29/1933, p. 3. For an example of a news article describing how much harder it was to secure the secret ballot in the countryside, see *Jornal de Recife*, 05/04/1933, p. 1. It reports even stories of masses of voters being transported to the polls.

We will not deal with the classic theme of Brazilian voters' socioeconomic conditions here. For our purposes in this chapter, where we propose an interpretation of the adoption of the PR system in Brazil as an electoral reform aimed at favouring the electoral victory of loyalist parties, the issue is framed differently: the winner is the one who organises the electoral process most effectively. When we look at the numbers, the importance of the process of voters' registration and, more generally, their mobilisation, stands out.

Likewise in the previous political experience, parties were responsible for registering voters. They assembled all the paperwork required for proving their eligibility and for applying for electoral ID cards. Parties announced, in their own newspapers, the addresses where their agents stood ready to file applications for registration on behalf of voters. In the Federal District, for example, the Brazilian Socialist Party required from their voters that they 'promoted the party's propaganda and showed up at the party's headquarters to fulfil some required formalities, including taking a photo'.[54] Also there, the Economist Party published, a few days before the deadline for voters' registration, an official note requesting 'the urgent presence of registered voters who have been notified about the need to complete or revise their respective registrations'.[55] Efforts to produce voters went beyond the capitals. In São Paulo, the Democratic Party had distributed a memo four months before the election, where they exhorted their supporters living in the countryside to apply for registration with these words: 'We mobilise for the constructive peace. We count on your effort and sacrifice. We must be *'Paulistas'* also as voters: voting is victory'.[56]

Indeed, the number of registered voters increased in 1933 following the expansion of party activity outside the capitals. There were also more requirements to be met in applications for voters' registration, and the costs of mobilisation rose. Periodicals published critiques about these new requirements, including costs related to photos for electoral ID cards.[57] In Rio Grande do Sul, for example, complaints about the high costs of voters' registration among parties dependent on private sponsors were common.[58] In order to produce voters, party bureaus had to overcome obstacles and push 'this heavy mechanism capable of manufacturing only one voter every three other days'.[59] Not surprisingly, politicians used to say: 'we know each one of our voters'.[60]

The Electoral Code of 1932 granted to unions the right to register voters, but only among the professionals they represented. This practice became known as

54. *Diario de Noticias*, 01/28/1933, p. 3
55. *Diario de Noticias*, 03/12/1933, p. 3.
56. *Diario de Noticias*, 01.21.1933, p. 1.
57. *Correio da Manhã*, 12/07/1932, p. 4.
58. *A Federação*, 03/08/1933, p. 1.
59. *A Batalha*, 12/02/1933, p. 2.
60. *A Federação*, 05/10/1933, p. 2.

*ex-officio* registration and was widely publicised. In Rio Grande do Sul, the *Centro Operário de Pelotas* (Labor Centre of Pelotas) expressed their intention to register their members from both sexes *ex-officio*, whereas the non-registered ones should 'remain highly independent, waiting for instructions to be delivered by their leaders in the greatest interests of the labor class'.[61] In general, the literature infers that the role played by unions in filing *ex-officio* applications was determinant for controlling voters, particularly in urban centres (Kinzo 1980). According to the *Diario Nacional*, the Federation of Volunteers produced, for example, no less than 70 per cent of the electorate in the state of São Paulo by means of this instrument.[62] Only in Pará, complaints about irregular or fraudulent *ex-officio* registrations were formally filed.[63] Being a strategic stage in the electoral cycle, voters' registration was relatively less contested in appeals presented to the Electoral Justice during the 1933 election. The highest number of complaints in this category was related to supposedly fraudulent *ex-officio* registrations made in Pará.

In light of this whole situation, the adoption of the PR system in Brazil seems less consequential. Our study shows that electoral results were conditioned primarily by parties' domination over the organisation of voters. The arbitrary violence, *coronéis'* ruffianism, or the *voto de cabestro* (popular expression denoting electoral behaviour controlled by local bosses) would stop being associated with the success of parties after the end of the First Republic.

The end of the story is well known. Critiques of the electoral legislation and the Federal Constitution of 1934 were invoked as justifications for the elaboration of a new Constitution in 1937, when a new coup d'état took place in Brazil. Elections were suspended until 1945, after which liberal freedoms were restored and the Brazilian first democratic experience began.

## Conclusion

It is common knowledge that parties want to win elections. During the Brazilian First Republic, politicians used systematically two mechanisms to this end: control over voters and control over the electoral bureaucracy. The use of these mechanisms was still important during the 1933 election. The adoption of the PR system had been justified by the rhetoric about protecting minorities, and it indeed increased the chances that traditional political forces gained representation in the Chamber of Deputies. However, new strategies for assuring the victory of loyalist parties were also devised. Instruments that reduced the amount of resources controlled by opposition parties, particularly the secret ballot and the Electoral Justice, guaranteed their continuation in power. The former instrument made it harder for oligarchs to control voters, and the latter one weakened their influence

---

61. *A Noite*, 01/31/1933, p. 2.

62. *Diario de Noticias*, 04/02/1932, p. 2.

63. Even in this case, these complaints represented 8.5 per cent (13 out of 153) of formal denunciations against elections in the state.

over the electoral bureaucracy. Our argument does not deny the importance of the discourse about elections moralisation, but reduces its centrality relative to classic interpretations. Put differently, the rhetoric about protecting minorities might have been a necessary condition for the approval of electoral reforms, but such an achievement also depended on supplementary legal provisions diminishing the level of political interference on electoral results.

The historic re-evaluation proposed by this chapter compels us to (re) think the breakthrough of Brazilian democracy within the theoretical framework of institutional innovations. Consider the introduction of the Electoral Justice. We claimed that its creation in 1932 was aimed at controlling electoral results, rather than moralising elections. In this sense, the Brazilian case is similar to other Latin American experiences, and far from the British and American cases. In Britain and in the US, efforts to fight electoral corruption are commonly linked to processes of industrialisation and economic growth, which enhanced the importance of programmatic appeals in elections (Stokes *et al*. 2013). The creation of the Brazilian Electoral Justice, on the other hand, may be explained without any resort to the modernisation theory. As stated by Fabrice Lehoucq, electoral governance 'does not emerge as a simple by-product of economic modernisation' (Lehoucq 2002: 30), but as an attempt to eliminate party influences on elections.

Regarding the second institutional innovation (the PR system), Brazil is a hard case to explain. The 1932 reforms do not conform to the classic thesis that the adoption of this electoral system is an attempt of elites to respond to the socialist threat (Ahmed 2013; Rokkan 1970; Boix 1999), nor to recent theoretical models centred on the structure of economic interests (Cusack *et al*. 2007). At the same time, neither does it conform to analyses placing its origin on the pre-First World War stage of 'protection of minorities' in some European countries (Rokkan 1970; Calvo 2009). As we explained, the Brazilian minorities were old oligarchies that now opposed the new regime. After we assessed the 1933 electoral context, based on systematic readings of party newspapers and on the codification of irregularities pointed out in complaints filed to the TSJE, our impression is that the PR system was a secondary issue. After the breakdown of the previous regime, revolutionaries enhanced their electoral support through the actions of *interventores* that were pivotal in organising ruling parties (Gomes 1980; 1996). In this sense, the Brazilian case is consistent with studies about the role of elections in authoritarian regimes. As pointed out by Andreas Schedler, 'authoritarian incumbents contaminate electoral contests. Since they stand for election not to lose power but to legitimate their continuity in office, they commonly try to distort and control the electoral process in order to minimise the risk of defeat' (Schedler 2002: 103). According to this view, the proportional representation was just a matter of electoral engineering. The main challenge was the control of voters and of the electoral bureaucracy, not the choice of the electoral system. This fact, as we see it, is the starting point for understanding other reforms introduced by the Code, including the universal suffrage.

## Appendix: methodological note

We coded potential irregularities taking place during the election for the Constituent Assembly in May 1933 using information from decisions made by the TSJE – the last judicial instance to analyse and validate elections in Brazil after the approval of the Code of 1932. Decisions published in *Electoral Bulletins* were comprised of a) a summary about how elections unfolded in the state; b) reports from election scrutiny boards (*Turmas Apuradoras* – TAs) and complaints filed at this stage; c) appeals presented to TRJEs against vote counts and the court's decision about these appeals; d) appeals presented to the TSJE against the certification of winning candidates and the court's decision about these appeals (including the court's opinion about decisions made at lower instances). In order to map the electoral dynamics in 1933, we considered all of the problems observed at the level of polling stations, independently of the instance where they were first analysed. We assembled a total of 706 irregularities and disregarded thirty-nine cases lacking the precise geographic location of polling stations, fifty-three cases of general complaints about polling station proceedings in the whole state, and twenty-eight cases without clear substantiation. Out of the thirty-nine cases of unknown location, ten referred to misconduct by polling station committees, nine to violations of the secret ballot, eight to irregularities in voters' registrations, five to violence, intimidation, and coercion, five to misconduct by the Electoral Justice, and two to formal vices. Out of the fifty-three cases with general complains at the state level, nineteen were related to the use of the PR system for the allocation of seats, which indicated confusion in law interpretations and in calculations of party and electoral quotas. The other sixteen cases dealt with irregularities in the conduct of the Electoral Justice at the state level, particularly in decisions made by TAs. Considering that the Electoral Justice was hardly criticised in party newspapers, we believe that these critiques targeted the autonomy and impartiality recently achieved by these boards, especially at the local level. These denunciations are certainly worth being better investigated. The remaining cases in the category of general complaints at the state level can be properly classified in those predetermined categories: four referred to violations of the secret ballot, two to irregularities in voters' registration, three to violence, intimidation, and coercion, two to formal vices, and one to another case.

For unknown reasons, *Electoral Bulletins* did not publish decisions about elections carried out in the state of Paraíba, and we coded them as missing. Below, we indicate in parentheses the dates to which our data on formal appeals (extracted from decisions published in those bulletins) refer in each state: AC (10/18/1933), AL (09/02/1933), AM (07/17/1933), BA (10/18/1933), CE (08/12/1933), DF (08/05/1933), ES (08/19/1933), GO (07/22/1933), MA (07/29/1933), MG (08/30/1933), MT (07/17/1933), PA (08/19/1933), PE (07/26/1933), PI (08/02/1933), PR (08/23/1933), RJ (08/26/1933), RN (08/30/1933), RS (10/11/1933), SC (10/07/1933), SE (07/08/1933) e SP (09/09/1933), and DF (08/05/1933).

# References

Ahmed, A. (2013) 'The existential threat: varieties of socialism and the origins of electoral systems in early democracies', *Studies in Comparative International Development* 48(2): 141–171.

Azevedo Amaral, A. (1938) *O Estado autoritário e a realidade nacional*, Rio de Janeiro: José Olympio.

Benoit, K. (2004) 'Models of electoral system change', *Electoral Studies*, 23(3): 363–389.

Bethell, L. (2008) 'Politics in Brazil under Vargas, 1930–1945', in L. Bethell (ed.) *The Cambridge History of Latin America*, Vol IX, *Brazil since 1930*, Cambridge: Cambridge University Press, pp. 3–86.

Birch, S. (2009) 'Electoral Corruption', in T. Landman and N. Robinson (eds) *The Sage Handbook of Comparative Politics*, Thousand Oaks, CA & London: Sage, pp. 395–409.

Boix, C. (1999) 'Setting the rules of the game: the choice of electoral systems in advanced democracies', *American Political Science Review* 93(3): 609–624.

Bowler, S., Donovan, T. and Farrel, D. (1999) 'Party strategy and voter organization under cumulative voting in Victorian England', *Political Studies* 47(5): 906–917.

Brasil, A. (1931) *Democracia representativa do voto e do modo de votar*, 4th edn, Rio de Janeiro: Imprensa Oficial.

Cabral, J. C. da Rocha (2004[1932]) *Código Eleitoral da República dos Estados Unidos do Brasil*, Brasília: TSE.

Calvo, E. (2009) 'The competitive road to proportional representation: partisan biases and electoral regime change under increasing party competition', *World Politics* 61(2): 254–295.

Carvalho, J. (2007) 'Os três povos da República', in A. Carvalho Homem, A. Malheiro da Silva and A. Cesar Isaia (eds) *Progresso e religião: A Republica no Brasil e no Portugal (1889–1910)*, Coimbra: Imprensa da Universidade de Coimbra, pp. 131–64.

Colomer, J. (ed.) (2004) *Handbook of Electoral System Choice*, London: Palgrave-Macmillan.

—— (2005) 'It's parties that choose electoral systems (or Duverger's Laws upside down)', *Political Studies* 53(1): 1–21.

—— (2007) 'On the origins of electoral systems and political parties: the role of elections in multi-member districts', *Electoral Studies* 26: 262–273.

Conniff, M. (1991) 'The National Elite', in M. Conniff and F. Mccann (eds) *Modern Brazil: Elites and masses in historical perspective*, Nebraska: University of Nebraska Press, pp. 23–46.

Cox, G. (1997) *Making Votes Count: Strategic coordination in the world's electoral systems*, New York: Cambridge University Press.

Cusack, T., Iversen, T. and Soskice, D. (2007) 'Economic interests and the origins of electoral systems', *American Political Science Review* 101(3): 373–391.

Dardé, C. (1996) 'Fraud and passivity of the electorate in Spain, 1875–1923', in E. Posada-Carbó (ed.) *Elections Before Democracy: The history of elections in Europe and Latin America*, New York: St. Martin's, pp. 201–23.

Diniz, E. (1999) 'Engenharia institucional e políticas públicas: dos conselhos técnicos às câmaras setoriais', in D. Pandolfi (ed.) *Repensando o Estado Novo*, Rio de Janeiro: Ed. Fundação Getúlio Vargas, pp. 21–38.

Ferreira, M. de Moraes (1994) *Em Busca da Idade de Ouro: As Elites Políticas Fluminenses na Primeira República (1889–1930)*, Rio de Janeiro: Editora UFRJ.

Fleischer, D. and Verge Barreto, L. (2009) 'El impacto de la justicia electoral sobre el sistema político brasileño', *América Latina Hoy* 51: 117–138.

Gomes, Â. (1980) *Regionalismo e Centralização Política, Partidos e Constituinte nos Anos 30*, Rio de Janeiro: Nova Fronteira.

—— (1996) 'Confronto e compromisso no processo de constitucionalização (1930–1935)', in B. Fausto (ed.) *História geral da civilização brasileira: O Brasil republicano*, 6th edn, São Paulo: Difel, pp. 9–75.

Green, M. (2007) 'Race, party, and contested elections to the U.S. House of Representatives', *Polity* 39(2): 155–178.

Hazan, R. and Leyenaar, M. (eds) (2011) *Understanding Electoral Reform*, London: Routledge.

Holanda, C. (2008) 'A questão da representação política na Primeira República', *Caderno CRH* 21(52): 25–35.

Horowitz, D. (2003) 'Electoral systems: a primer for decision makers', *Journal of Democracy* 14(4): 115–127.

Kinzo, M. (1980) *Representação Política e Sistema Eleitoral no Brasil*, São Paulo: Edições Símbol.

Laakso, M. and Taagepera, R. (1979) 'Effective number of parties: a measure with application to West Europe', *Comparative Political Studies* 12(1): 3–27.

Lamounier, B. (1992) 'Estrutura institucional e governabilidade na década do 1990', in J. dos Reis Velloso (ed.) *O Brasil e as reformas políticas*, Rio de Janeiro: José Olympio, pp. 24–47.

Lamounier, B. and Amorim Neto, O. (2005) 'Brazil', in D. Nohlen (ed.) *Elections in the Americas: A data handbook: Volume 2 South America*, Oxford: Oxford University Press, pp. 163–252.

Lamounier, B. and Steinbach, G. (1992) 'El modelo institucional de los años treinta y la presente crisis brasileña', *Desarrollo económico* 32(126): 185–198.

Leal, V. (1977) *Coronelismo: The municipality and representative government in Brazil*, trans. J. Henfrey, New York: Cambridge University Press.

Lehoucq, F. (2002) 'Can parties police themselves? Electoral governance and democratization', *International Political Science Review* 23(1): 29–46.

——— (2003) 'Electoral fraud: causes, types, and consequences', *Annual Review of Political Science* 6: 233–256.

Lehoucq, F. and Molina, I. (2002) *Stuffing the Ballot Box: Fraud, reform, and democratization in Costa Rica*, New York: Cambridge University Press.

Levine, R. (1980) *A Velha Usina: Pernambuco na Federação Brasileira (1989–1937)*, Rio de Janeiro: Paz e Terra.

Lijphart, A. (2004) 'Constitutional design for divided societies', *Journal of Democracy* 15(2): 96–109.

Love, J. (1975) *O Regionalismo Gaúcho e as Origens da Revolução de 1930*, São Paulo: Perspectiva.

Molina, I. and Lehoucq, F. (1999) 'Political competition and electoral fraud: a Latin American case study', *Journal of Interdisciplinary History* 30(2): 199–234.

Morelli, F. (2004) 'Entre ancien et nouveau regime', *Annales: Histoire, Sciences Sociales* 5(4): 759–781.

Nicolau, J. (2012) *Eleições no Brasil: Do Império aos Dias Atuais*, Rio de Janeiro: Zahar.

Pandolfi, D. (1999) *Repensando o Estado Novo*, Rio de Janeiro: Ed. Fundação Getúlio Vargas.

Pang, E. (1979) *Coronelismo e Oligarquias, 1889–1943: A Bahia na Primeira República Brasileira*, Rio de Janeiro: Civilização Brasileira.

Pinto, S. Conde Sá (2011) *Só para Iniciados... O Jogo Político na Antiga Capital Federal*, Rio de Janeiro: Mauad.

Pires, J. (2009) 'A invenção da lista aberta: o processo de implementação da representação proporcional no Brasil', 2009, 150 f. (Master's Thesis in Political Science) – Iuperj, Universidade Cândido Mendes, Rio de Janeiro.

Porto, W. (2004) *A Mentirosa Urna*, São Paulo, Martins Fontes.

——— (1995) *Dicionário do Voto*, São Paulo: Editora Giordano.

Posada-Carbó, E. (2000) 'Electoral juggling: a comparative history of the corruption of suffrage in Latin America, 1830–1930', *Journal of Latin American Studies* 32(3): 611–644.

Przeworski, A. (1991) *Democracy and the Market: Political and economic reforms in Eastern Europe and Latin America*, New York: Cambridge University Press.

Queiroz, M. (1975) 'O coronelismo numa interpretação sociológica', in B. Fausto (ed.) *História geral da civilização brasileira: O Brasil republicano*, São Paulo: Difel, pp. 155–90.

Rezende, M. (1982) *Formação da Estrutura de Dominação em Minas Gerais: O Novo PRM (1889–1906)*, Belo Horizonte: UFMG Editora.

Ricci, P. and Porto Zulini, J. (2012) '"Beheading", rule manipulation and fraud: the approval of Election Results in Brazil, 1894–1930', *Journal of Latin American Studies* 44(3): 495–521.

——— (2014) 'Partidos, Competição Política e Fraude Eleitoral: A Tônica das Eleições na Primeira República', *Dados – Revista de Ciências Sociais* 57(2): 443–479.

—— (2017a) 'The meaning of electoral fraud in oligarchic regimes: lessons from the Brazilian case (1900–1930)', *Journal of Latin American Studies* 49(2) DOI: https://doi.org/10.1017/S0022216X16001371 (accessed 9 February 2017).

—— (2017b) – 'The Election of 1899', in E. Posada-Carbó and A. Robertson (eds) *The Oxford Handbook of Revolutionary Elections in the Americas, 1800–1910*, Oxford: Oxford University Press (forthcoming).

Rokkan, S. (1970) *Citizens Elections Parties*, New York: David McKay Co.

Rouston Jr., E. (2012) 'Não só do pão do corpo precisa e vive o homem, mas também do pão do espírito': a atuação federalista na Assembléia dos Representantes (1913–1924), 2012, 339 f., (Master's Thesis in History) – Faculdade de Filosofia e Ciências Humanas, Pontifícia Universidade Católica do Rio Grande do Sul, Rio Grande do Sul.

—— (2014) *O Rio Grande do Sul republicano sob a ótica parlamentar da oposição federalista (1913–1924)*, Porto Alegre: EDIPUCRS.

Sabato, H. (2001) 'On political citizenship in nineteenth-century Latin America', *The American Historical Review* 106(4): 1290–1315.

Sadek, M. (2010) *A Justiça Eleitoral e a consolidação da democracia no Brasil*, 2nd edn, São Paulo: Konrad Adenauer.

Sartori, G. (1976) *Parties and Party Systems: A framework for analysis*, Cambridge: Cambridge University Press.

Schedler, A. (2002) 'The nested game of democratization by elections', *International Political Science Review* 23(1): 103–122.

Simpser, A. (2013) *Why Governments and Parties Manipulate Elections: Theory, practice, and implications*, Cambridge: Cambridge University Press.

Skidmore, T. (1988) *Uma história do Brasil*, São Paulo: Paz e Terra.

Stokes, S., Dunning, T., Nazareno, M. and Brusco, V. (2013) *Brokers, Voters, and Clientelism: The puzzle of distributive politics*, Cambridge: Cambridge University Press.

Taagepera, R. and Shugart, M. Soberg (1989) *Seats and Votes: The effects and determinants of electoral systems*, Yale University Press, New Haven and London.

Telarolli, R. (1982) *Eleições e Fraudes Eleitorais na República Velha*, São Paulo: Brasiliense.

Trindade, H. (1980) *Poder legislativo e autoritarismo no Rio Grande do Sul (1891–1937)*, Porto Alegre: Sulina.

Vale, T. (2014) 'Aspectos históricos da Justiça Eleitoral Brasileira', *Cadernos Adenauer* 1: 11–26.

—— (2009) 'A justiça eleitoral e judicialização da política: um estudo através de sua história', 233 f. (Doctoral Thesis in Political Science) – Iuperj, Universidade Cândido Mendes, Rio de Janeiro.

Viscardi, C. (2012) *O teatro das oligarquias: uma revisão da 'política do café com leite'*, 2nd edn, Belo Horizonte: Fino Traço.

Wasserman, C. (2004) 'O Rio Grande do Sul e as elites gaúchas na Primeira República: guerra civil e crise no bloco do poder', in L. Grijó, F. Kuhn, C. Guazzelli, and E. Newmann (eds) *Capítulos de História do Rio Grande do Sul*, Porto Alegre: Editora da UFRGS, pp. 273–89.

Weffort, F. (2009) 'Which political reform?', *Estudos Avançados* 23(67): 37–45.

Wills-Otero, L. (2009) 'Electoral systems in Latin America: explaining the adoption of proportional representation systems during the Twentieth Century', *Latin American Politics and Society* 51(3): 33–58.

Ziblatt, D. (2009) 'Shaping democratic practice and the causes of electoral fraud: the case of Nineteenth-Century Germany Harvard University', *American Political Science Review* 103(1): 1–21.

*Chapter Four*

# Copartnership and Competition in the Building of Uruguayan Democracy

*Daniel Chasquetti*

*The concept 'copartnership' is translated in dictionaries without any warning about its use in Uruguay. Actually, it is a word used in various senses that overlap.*

Göran Lindahl, 1971

## Introduction

Uruguayan democracy is recognised in the world by the strength of its institutions and the legitimacy of its electoral procedures. Most international rankings place it among the select core of consolidated democracies that ensure the observance of full political rights and civil liberties. However, this was not always the case. There was a time when Uruguay was an unstable and violent country. We refer to the first forty years of independent life, in which Uruguay, besides being a poor and sparsely populated nation, recorded more than twenty revolts, revolutions and coups. Additionally, an international civil war for more than a decade territorially divided the country. During those forty years, twenty-three individuals occupied the Presidency of the Republic, but only eight had been elected by the procedures provided by the Constitution. The rest were Presidents of the Senate, who completed the mandate of the deposed Presidents, or leaders of triumphant revolts against the government. In this period, instability also reached Parliament that remained closed for nearly a quarter of the time (24 per cent), and the High Court whose members often were deposed from office, persecuted or simply deported (Pivel Devoto and Ranieri 1966).

Scholars have indicated that the reasons for the instability of the Uruguayan nineteenth century must be sought in the inadequacy of the first Constitution to the political, economic and social reality of the new country (Gros Espiell and Arteaga 1991; Pérez Antón 1988; Pivel Devoto 1994). The first Constitution was a typical presidential text of the time, where citizenship was restricted in terms of sex, education and occupation. The president was elected by the General Assembly (session of both chambers, Senate and Representatives) for a period of four years. The legislature was bicameral and its members were elected by a majority system (one senator per department for a period of six years and one representative per district composed for three thousand citizens, for a period of three years). Some aspects of the Constitution favoured the political instability, such as the majority system to elect legislators, the absence of electoral warranties (no secret vote or permanent voter registration), the parliamentary election of the President, or the discretionary prerogative allowing the Executive to designate local authorities (Political Chiefs of Department).These institutional structures developed a perverse dynamic where presidents designated the departmental political chiefs from his own party, that could later have influence on the election of representatives. Thus, the ruling party could have a comfortable majority in parliament and ensure continuity in power. The opposition lacked the institutional spaces to have influence on decision making because the elections were not clean and the majority rules systematically prevented their fair representation. The army uprising was transformed into the only viable option for those who did not belong to the government party.

The Civil War that started in 1870, known as the war of the spears, was just that, an uprising of the *Partido Blanco*[1] against a government controlled by the Partido Colorado (PC). The *'Paz de Abril'* of 1872, established a para-constitutional mechanism that generated a new equilibrium point: the copartnership.[2] This unwritten arrangement meant a commitment by the president to deliver, for the opposition party, four out of the thirteen departmental chiefs of the country.

In the following decades, the conflict between the government and the opposition would weaken the respect for the institution of copartnership. However, in 1903, the Colorado President, José Batlle y Ordóñez, rebelled against that agreement (he did not appoint political leaders established by the unwritten mechanism) which triggered the last civil war in Uruguayan history. The victory of the government forced the Partido Nacional (PN) to modify the strategy, focusing since then in peaceful participation and the requirement of revision of the electoral system. The constitutional reform came in 1917 and included a Parliament elected by proportional representation, secret vote, and the direct election of local authorities. The copartnership, conceived as territorial distribution of political power, lost its usefulness. However, the constituents of 1917 used the mechanism to define the integration of the *Consejo Nacional de Administración* (collective body that integrated the executive branch, by the Presidency of the Republic) and the Directories of the Autonomous Entities of the State.

In the twentieth century the copartnership remained an institutional key of the democracy. It was present in the experiments of collegial government (1918–1933 and 1952–1967) and was the preferred mechanism for integrating the directories of autonomous entities of the state. In some cases, the copartnership implied a joint government of the presidential party and the opposition party, and in others,

---

1. *Partido Blanco* was renamed *Partido Nacional* in 1872, after the party approved a doctrinal reform (Real de Azúa 1971).

2. The term used in Uruguay *coparticipación* is translated from Spanish as *coparticipation* in some articles (Altman *et. al.* 2011). I prefer to use the term *copartnership* because I believe it captures better the sense it was given in Uruguay. This practice is an act in which two actors share power in a same institutional environment.

it was simply supervision of the administration by the opposition delegates. Also, the copartnership was the mechanism preferred by the two main parties to conduct the development of the state, fostered by the import substitution industrialisation model (ISI), which allowed the sharing of public resources for electoral purposes.

This chapter examines the creation and evolution of the institution of copartnership in two variants. On the one hand, we focused on the origin and effectiveness of the territorial copartnership to build political and institutional equilibrium, which allowed the elimination of the zero-sum game involved in the presidential dispute during the nineteenth century. On the other hand, we analyse the use of copartnership as an institutional tool to manage the statewide expansion of the twentieth century, where political parties appealed to patronage to resolve electoral races. The chapter argues that copartnership in the Uruguayan case approaches the consociational model of democracy proposed by Lijphart (1969) forty years ago, since this institutional mechanism allowed the stability of political competition and provided significant levels of political legitimacy to democracy.

## The Copartnership as an Equilibrium Solution

Since its independence, Uruguayan politics was marked by the competition between proto-parties, parties and factions. The first legislative election, held two weeks after the adoption of the Constitution of 1830, is a good example of this, due to the fact that elite members were quickly grouped around the two main independence leaders who competed for the vote of the electorate.[3] However, the most important episode in shaping party competition, occurred in September 1836 when Gral. Fructuoso Rivera (president between 1830 and 1834) took up arms against the government headed by President Manuel Oribe. The *Batalla de Carpintería* was the birth of Uruguayan political parties as armies in the battlefield.[4] This division will be at the origin of the so called *Guerra Grande*, the longest and most traumatic war in the Uruguayan nineteenth century, which would include the Uruguayan and Argentinian proto-parties and the governments of Brazil, France and Great Britain. For twelve years (1839–1851), the troops of Oribe and Argentinian *federales* besieged Montevideo where the government of the PC and the Argentinian *unitarios* took refuge. Although the desired peace brought a spirit of unity (under the slogan 'neither winners nor losers'), and years

---

3. In the election of 1 August 1830, Fructuoso Rivera had a single list of candidates, while Juan Antonio Lavalleja presented two. The majority system favored the strategy of the former, who was elected at the Asamblea General, a few weeks after, as the first President of the Uruguayan history (Pivel Devoto 1994: 33).

4. In the *Batalla de Carpintería*, government troops took the slogan, 'Defenders of the laws', carrying a white badge in their hats. Hence Oribe's followers took the name of White Party. The revolutionaries adopted the blue color of the national flag to identify themselves. However, this color was fading with the inclement weather; therefore they began to use the red, which was more firm and easily accessible for anyone (because it was often used in the linings of clothing). Since then, the followers of Rivera took the name of Colorado Party (Pivel Devoto 1994: 78).

later the ruling elite developed an anti-partisan impulse known as *política de fusion*,[5] the passion for political parties remain present in the heart of Uruguayans.

The parties were born in 1836 but their development, organisation and consolidation took half a century. From the beginning, the parties were coalitions of groups led by urban politicians (*doctores*) and rural politicians (*caudillos*). Both parties longitudinally cut the Uruguayan society, but their factions tended to represent specific interests. Doctors were a homogeneous group originated in patrician families whose economic power had declined (Real de Azúa 1981). They had influence on public opinion through newspapers and proclamations based on liberal doctrines. The leaders, however, resided in the countryside and were usually landowners. They exerted influence on the rural population thanks to their charisma and to the ties of dependence developed with the inhabitants of their areas. In wartime, recruited and mobilised armies of subordinates and in peacetime followers were organised to participate in the electoral causes that needed their commitment. Doctors tended to be more programmatic and ideological, while caudillos were more pragmatic and intuitive.

The internal organisation of parties in the nineteenth century was stressed by two axes: the kind of historical tradition (*colorado* or *blanco*) and the type of policy that was intended (ideological or traditional). The prevalence of one or the other axis depended on factors such as the specific political circumstances, the rules of the political game and the immediate political backgrounds. The triumph of historical tradition was due to the impact of certain political, economic and social circumstances. Given the changing scenarios, historical-party tradition was more flexible than ideological politics to add sector interests and maintain control of the course of events. Political parties were able to overcome dramatic challenges thanks to its enormous adaptability. Combination of change with continuity was the most common pattern to adjust to new political realities (Caetano and Rilla 1984). In the words of Barrán and Nahum (1983), they were *'new wine in old wineskin'*.

## From Institutional Exclusion to the Copartnership solution

In early 1868, Uruguay was on a critical juncture. On the same day the last two Presidents of the Republic,[6] Bernardo Berro, head of the Blanco Party and

---

5. The *Merger Policy* originates from a manifesto written by former Foreign Minister, Andrés Lamas in July 1855. In that text, he called for his compatriots to leave the old parties in pursuit of the development of a stable country. These ideas had great receptivity among the educated urban class, who quickly understood it as a patriotic expression of unity ('orientalism') and at the same time, as a brake on the ever latent impulses of rural 'caudillos'. The *Merger Policy* lived to its peak during the presidency of Gabriel Pereira (1856–1860) and began to weaken during the government of Bernardo Berro (1860–1864), under the political thrust of the caudillos, who acted on behalf of the badges that the government precisely wanted to nullify (see Barrán 1988).

6. This episode is known as the 'Night of the Long Knives' in reference to the murder of the head of the *Partido Blanco*, Bernardo P. Berro (constitutional president between 1860 and 1864) and the leader of the Partido Colorado, Venancio Flores (constitutional president between 1854 and 1855 and *de facto* president between 1865 and 1868). See Real de Azúa (1964 and 1997).

*Figure 4.1: Political segmentation and political parties in the nineteenth century*

**Political Orientation**

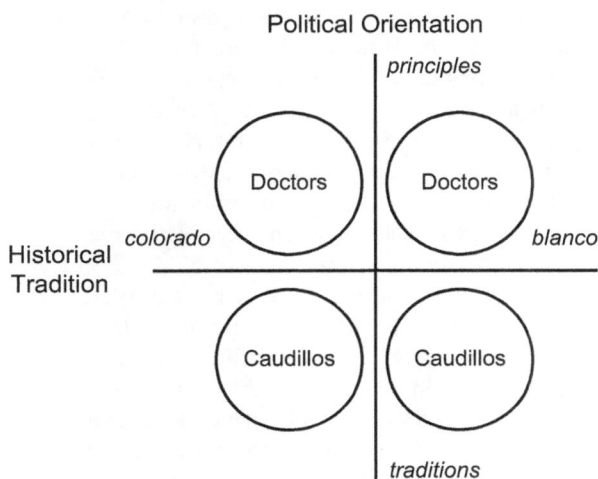

Venancio Flores, head of one of the factions of the Colorado Party, were murdered. The country faced an economic and financial crisis that required immediate decisions from the government (Pivel Devoto and Ranieri 1966: 318; Barrán and Nahum 1971: 110). On March 1, a General Assembly dominated by the colorado legislators appointed Lorenzo Batlle as President, who had promised to govern 'with his own party'. Thus, cabinet and departmental political headquarters were occupied by leaders and caudillos from different factions of the Colorado Party. The policy of exclusion developed by the President, together with the discomfort caused by the murder of the main opposition leader, created conditions for the armed uprising in 1870 that would become quickly a civil war.

The conflict between government and the revolutionaries—led by General Timoteo Aparicio—spread throughout the country for nearly two years. Although the national army had begun a process of professionalisation, the *Revolución de las Lanzas* (name under which the conflict was known) resembled the battles of independence because the riders equipped with lances dominated the scene. Historians point out 16,000 individuals as taking part in the conflict and estimate the number of victims as really high (Pivel Devoto and Ranieri 1966: 327). The absolute stagnation of war[7] encouraged the start of peace talks. In March 1872, President Lorenzo Batlle concluded his mandate and, as the war had prevented the holding of legislative elections, the General Assembly resolved to appoint Tomás Gomensoro—who was the president of the Senate—as President of the Republic. On 6 April the negotiators finally reached peace based on an agreement

---

7.  At that time, the coercive power of the state was very weak. The weapons used by the army were old and the revolutionaries could easily balance any battle. The civil war was basically a fight between chivalries, very similar to the struggles for independence. As none of the forces were able to destroy the enemy, the war became a chronic conflict (Barrán y Nahúm 1971: 88).

which established the disarming of the revolutionary army, preemption of political judgments, the return of military ranks for the uprising leaders, and the calling for elections in the coming months. However, the agreement also included an unwritten clause forcing the President to designate four Departmental Political Chiefs (Cerro Largo, Florida, Canelones and San Jose) from the *Partido Blanco*. The pact was not documented because the new institution was contrary to Articles 118 and 119 of the Constitution, which reserved to the President the discretionary power to designate those positions. Thus, the precept of copartnership was born, the institution that would change forever the way that competence between parties would be achieved.

\* \* \*

The Constitution of 1830 had three problems that affected dramatically the stability of party competition. First, the Constitution established restrictions on the exercise of citizenship and ordered the Parliament to create a civil register of voters. Different laws adopted over time established criteria for the development of the electoral register, but they were all unable to create a comprehensive and coherent regime. Second, the Constitution determined a majority electoral system for the election of senators and deputies. Third, the Departmental Political Chief was the main local authority and was not elected directly by the voters, but appointed by the President.

The state was extremely weak (had not yet fully exercised the legitimate monopoly of physical violence) and the existence of strong regional leaders determined the fragmentation of power. Those who wanted to be president and were not national leaders had to make commitments with local caudillos since they guaranteed peace and social order, organised the elections, appointed local judges and acted as civil police. Then, the local caudillos had the key of the legislative election.

When a presidential election was called in the General Assembly, local caudillos always had a chance to force presidential candidates to commit with a future appointment as departmental political chief in exchange for the votes of members they controlled. Only when the president was a national leader (e.g., Fructuoso Rivera or Venancio Flores from the Colorado Party) did they manage to impose their own preferences for appointments. When presidents were weak politicians, governance depended on the relationship with regional leaders.[8] Pérez Antón (1988) states that, at that time, 'the President could be considered as a peer primus of the department political chiefs'. If the president appointed the correct political leaders, the ruling party could stay indefinitely in power. If he did not, his government would be unstable.

Under these conditions, the opposition party lacked opportunities to have influence on government decisions. Usually, it only reached parliamentary representation in departments where their leaders were department chiefs. For different circumstances (linked to the political actions and decisions of national

---

8. Barran and Nahum (1971: 87) argue that 'until 1876, Uruguay did not have presidents who governed the whole country. Montevideo was merely the capital of a federation of regions constituted by the authorities of the departments, who sometimes did not fully control their own jurisdiction, because they had to share power with other local leaders'.

*Figure 4.2: Local power, parliament and president in the 1830 Constitution*

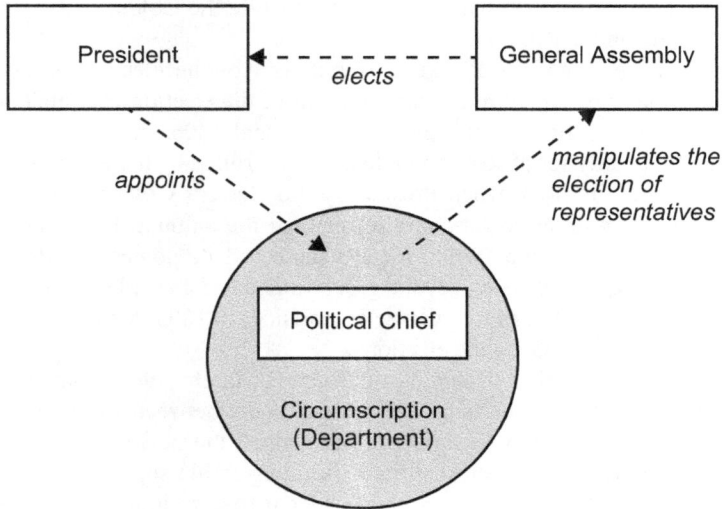

leaders like Fructuoso Rivera or Venancio Flores), the local caudillos of the PC were better distributed in the territory than the PN ones. When in 1868 President Batlle decided to govern with his own party, and designated departmental political leaders belonging to the PC, the induced equilibrium of the system snapped. The opposition had no choice. They organised his army and went to war. The result of the long conflict brought forward a new institutional balance: the copartnership.

Pérez Antón (1988) notes that copartnership allowed the pacification of the country. Since then, the political parties abandoned the idea of destroying the opponent and began to accept each other as subjects of government. In the absence of free elections, the copartnership pluralised the Parliament since departmental political chiefs ensured the election of members from their own parties. The agreement established a pattern of distribution of power with a majority party that controlled two-thirds of the influential positions (nine political departmental chiefs, nine senators and twenty-nine deputies) and a minority party which controlled one third (four political chiefs, four senators and twelve deputies).

## The End of Territorial Copartnership

In the following decade, presidents respected the unwritten clause agreed in the '*Paz de Abril*'. However, between 1880 and 1885, Parliament passed a series of laws that created six new departments, increasing thus the number of departments up to nineteen. These changes were motivated by disputes within the PC because its promoters sought advantages in the presidential elections (every new district involved the appointment of a new political chief that guaranteed one seat in the Senate and two or more deputies in the lower house). This situation changed the structure of distribution of power between parties. At the end of the day, the opposition became smaller and less influential while the Colorado Party became more powerful and hegemonic.

During those years, the PN kept its criticism of the electoral system. The registration was carried out in the early months of the election year under control of departmental political chiefs. Between 1872 and 1896, the *Directorio of the PN* called frequently for abstention in districts controlled by the PC. The situation began to worsen in 1890, when President Julio Herrera y Obes appointed only three nationalist political chiefs, one fewer than the amount determined by the status of the copartnership. While the PC increased its power, the PN became weaker. In these circumstances, several groups mandated by the Directory, based in Argentina and Brazil, began to organise an uprising. In 1893, nationalist caudillos promoted a revolt to impede the elections.

The election of President Juan Idiarte Borda in March 1894, elevated to power a politician with scarce charisma and little support between the groups of the PC.[9] As expected, the new government maintained the policy of excluding the opposition but with greater difficulties in building stable support in Parliament. In the legislative elections of 1896, the President tried to improve their political support but ended up being accused of manipulating the electoral results. This climate of tension and discredit accelerated the nationalist revolution.

When the year ended, the fight between the government army and the nationalist troops began. The conflict spread during the first half of 1897, and in August, when the combat operations had stalled, the unexpected assassination of the President occurred in Montevideo.[10] Immediately, the General Assembly elected, as successor, the Senate President, Juan Lindolfo Cuestas, who initiated efforts to reach an agreement with the nationalist revolutionaries. The *Pacto de La Cruz* ended the war and established the commitment of the government to pass a law to favour the representation of the minority in Parliament. As in 1872, the agreement established an unwritten clause which guaranteed the PN six departmental political chiefs. The result implied a defeat of those Colorado politicians that had opposed the policy of copartnership during the last decade. For them, the territorial distribution of power kept the feudalisation and the control of the opposition party over a portion of the country.

President Cuestas' period (1897–1903) showed a different political framework: the National Party had acquired a formidable veto after the civil war of 1897. In order to make decisions the government had to consult the Directory of PN and its military chief, the caudillo Aparicio Saravia. In 1898, Parliament passed a law

---

9. The presidential election was extremely complicated due to the division of the PC. Borda was elected after twenty-one unsuccessful voting procedures in the General Assembly (Vanger 1991).

10. Juan Idiarte Borda was a proactive president but shortly, showed affection for negotiation. A few months after taking office, Borda faced severe conflicts with the opposition and some members of his own Partido Colorado. The assassination took place on 25 August 1897, when the President was attending a Te Deum at the Cathedral of Montevideo, commemorating the anniversary of the country's independence. The origin of the tragedy can be found in the high level of political polarisation the country reached during civil war (Vanger 1991: 39).

*Figure 4.3: Territorial copartnership: distribution of departmental political chiefs*

| 1872-1897 | 1897-1904 |
|:---:|:---:|
| 13 departments | 19 departments |

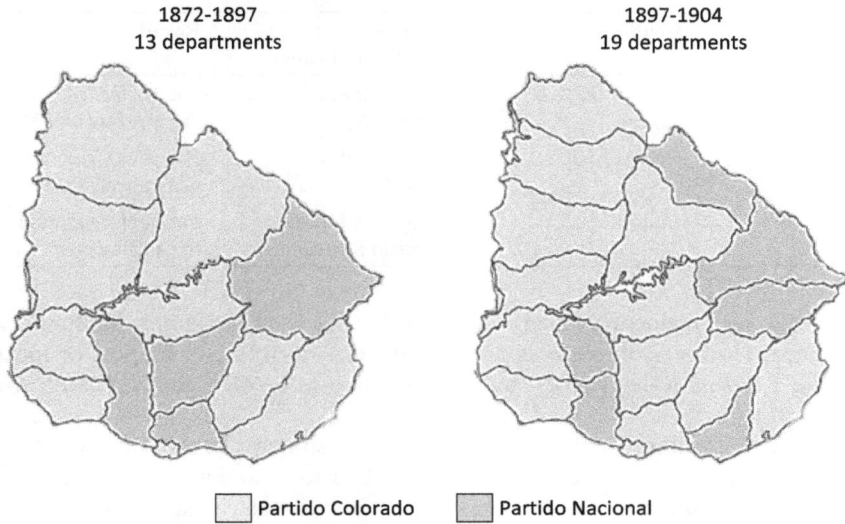

☐ Partido Colorado    ■ Partido Nacional

creating a permanent electoral register that weakened the power of departmental political chiefs. In October of that year, Parliament voted for an electoral reform which modified the districts of the lower chamber in order to increase minority representation. The PN could win a third of the seats in the lower house, if it reached a quarter of the votes in each district. As the new rules created a big uncertainty about the legislative election of that year, the government offered for the opposition to design joint lists with candidates of both parties. This agreement lasted until the legislative election of 1901 and implied that the Parliament map was frozen for six long years. The PC had eleven senators and forty deputies (58 per cent of the General Assembly) and the PN had eight senators and twenty-nine deputies (42 per cent).

In 1903, the General Assembly had to elect a new chief of state and given the internal division of the PC, the Presidency could end up in the hands of the PN. However, the Colorado candidate José Batlle y Ordóñez contrived to build alliances and to achieve enough votes to be elected in March. His rise to power would represent a breaking-point in the precarious institutional balance left by the war of 1897. The new President wanted to end the copartnership regime, and like his father, he believed in the need to establish a party government.[11] With the goal of gaining the confidence of the opposition and preserving his chance, Batlle promised to continue with the guidelines of the last administration: fiscal prudence and respect for the agreements of 1897. The presidential election at the General Assembly was not easy because there were several candidates, and

---

11.  José Batlle y Ordóñez was the first son of Lorenzo Batlle, President of the Republic between 1868 and 1872. His public service began in 1886 as *Jefe Político* of the Department of Minas.

*Table 4.1: Copartnership and armed conflicts*

| During | Conflicts | President / Revolution Leader | Result |
|---|---|---|---|
| 1870–1872 | *Revolución de las Lanzas* | Lorenzo Batlle / Timoteo Aparicio | *Paz de Abril*: 4 departments for PN |
| 1896–1897 | *Guerra Civil* | Idiarte Borda / Aparicio Saravia | *Paz de la Cruz*: 6 departments for PN |
| 1903–1904 | *Guerra Civil* | Batlle y Ordóñez / Aparicio Saravia | *Paz de Aceguá*: End of Copartnership |

the outgoing President as well as the PN did not want a triumph for Batlle y Ordóñez. However, through smart manoeuvers, he won the support of most of the *Colorados* legislators and the decisive vote of eight *Nacionalistas* legislators.[12]

After taking office, Batlle began to develop his strategy: he awarded two of the six departmental political chiefs (Rivera and San Jose) to the nationalist faction which supported him in the presidential election. That decision was rejected by the Directory of National Party, who wanted to maintain control of nominations in their departments. Immediately, the nationalist military leader, Aparicio Saravia ordered that power would not be delivered to the new political chief of Rivera and mobilised 15,000 troops ready to start the fight. A last-minute deal avoided civil war. However, at the end of the year, after a fortuitous incident on the Brazilian border, two regiments of the army invaded the department of Rivera in the northeast of the country. That was how the last civil war in Uruguayan history began. The government army mobilised 36,000 soldiers in addition to the police in towns and villages. The conflict lasted for eight months until in one of the decisive battles Aparicio Saravia was wounded, dying a few days later. This fact demobilised much of the Nationalist army, so its directory had to negotiate a new peace agreement similar to an unconditional surrender. The 'Paz de Aceguá' marked the end of the era of revolutions and the territorial division of power in Uruguay. The rebels were disarmed and, this time, there was no unwritten clause of copartnership between parties. The balance in deaths was the highest of all civil wars in Uruguay and its outcome shaped the politics of the next three decades.

---

12. The two leading candidates to become President were Eduardo Mac Eachen and José Batlle y Ordóñez. Although the nationalist caudillo, Aparicio Saravia, preferred the candidacy of the former, he initially ordered his legislators not to make quick commitments with the goal of getting an optimal agreement. After several weeks without results, Mac Eachen declined his candidacy, which surprised Nationalist legislators that still waited for Saravia's guidelines. In this situation, the faction led by Eduardo Acevedo Díaz -prestigious writer and journalist- announced that they supported Batlle y Ordóñez. This decision allowed the election of the President and accelerated the expelling of Acevedo Díaz and his group from the Partido Nacional (Vanger 1991: 100).

## The Reinvention of the Copartnership in the Twentieth Century

As well as the copartnership serving to pacify the country in 1872, paradoxically, its suppression in 1904 led to the same result. The dramatic defeat of the PN forced a change to its political strategy. Uruguay in the early twentieth century was a very different country than that of the decade of 1870. Vanger (1991) explains that the population had exceeded one million people; agricultural production was modernised and the early meat-processing factories – called saladeros because they used salt to preserve meat – were replaced by modern plants; a network of railways had linked the capital with the main towns of the country; the natural port of Montevideo was modernised to allow the entry of large ships; and the urban centres began to enjoy electricity, telephone, gas, etc.

Batlle y Ordóñez was a modern politician who adapted successfully to changing times. In the 1880s he founded the newspaper El Día and from that tribune developed an intense political campaign that led to a preeminent position inside the PC. His faction established a network of civic clubs all over the country, in order to engage citizens in public affairs. His opposition to President Borda put him on the side of those demanding guarantees for the vote. His opposition to the copartnership was based on the idea of restoring the state authority, which was achieved with the victory in the civil war of 1904. Since that time, Batlle y Ordóñez was in the centre of the new historical stage in which the country had entered.[13]

With the death of its main leader, the PN's fortune began to decline. The growing popularity of Batlle and the cancellation of war as a way to access power, forced the Nationalists to become a civic political party. The new orientation defined by its Directorio was centred in amending the electoral law, adopted in 1904, known by the name of '*mal tercio*' law. They also wanted to amend the Constitution including the secret ballot and proportional representation.[14]

### *The Slow Road to Constitutional Reform*

The idea of amending the constitution won support inside all parties. The legislature elected in 1907 stated interest in reviewing methods of reform, and the next one, elected in 1910 proposed possible mechanisms to formalise this change. Finally, the 25th legislature elected in 1912, selected the specific way in which

---

13. The two presidencies of Batlle y Ordóñez (1903–1907 and 1911–1915), and the mandate of President José Williman (1907–1911), were a period characterised by the approval of structural reforms that transformed the economy and society, establishing an early welfare state (Barrán and Nahum 1983).

14. The 'law of the third wrong' adopted in November 1904, was proposed with the aim of improving the minority representation in Parliament. As the electoral law of 1898, the new rule required 25 per cent of the votes in each district to reach one third of the seats. The membership of the Chamber of Deputies was also modified (increased from sixty-nine to eighty-one members) as well as the number of seats allocated in each district. This law severely hurt the interests of the minority because in several departments the achieved number of seats represented a smaller proportion than a third of seats scheduled.

the amendment would be made: election of a Constituent National Convention.[15] During this process, the parties agreed that the constitution should be changed but the motivations were naturally different. While the PN wished to modify the electoral system, Batlle y Ordóñez proposed to change the presidential system of government by a collegial system, composed of nine members.[16] This initiative encouraged the strong opposition of the PN and a few *colorados* senators led by Pedro Manini Ríos (this group took later the name of *Riverismo*). In September 1915, Parliament passed an electoral law for electing members of the National Constituent Assembly, that guaranteed – for first time in history – universal male suffrage, the secret ballot, and a quasi-proportional formula for allocating seats. The election was held on 30 July 1916, and threw an unexpected triumph to the *anti-colegialistas* coalition. The polarisation of the campaign debate transformed the election into a referendum around the figure of Batlle y Ordóñez. The electoral defeat forced *colorado* President Viera, to stop the reforms that Batlle's followers in government had projected.

Nationalist members of the Convention proposed the introduction of proportional representation together with rules to ensure fair elections; members who supported Batlle insisted on approving the *colegiado* regime; and dissident members of the PC defended the maintenance of the one-man presidency. In January 1917, legislative elections were held; they had been suspended the previous year due to the installation of the Convention, but using the old electoral system without PR or secret ballot. The results showed a wide triumph of Batllists' lists, which was interpreted as public support for the positions taken by Batlle. Therefore, the political scene was characterised by a tie between a Constitutional Convention dominated by *anti-colegialistas* and a Parliament dominated by *colegialistas*. The impasse was resolved by negotiation between both groups which resulted in the 'Pact of eight senators'. The agreement was voted for in the Convention in October 1917 and was ratified by a plebiscite a month later.

The new constitution created an original executive with a President of the Republic and the so called Consejo Nacional de Administración (CNA) composed of nine members. The President assumed the state representation, the preservation of order, and the command of the Armed Forces. The CNA was responsible for education policy, industry, agriculture, labour policies, etc. (Chasquetti 2003). The two-headed formula of government was satisfactory for the two groups in dispute, because it maintained the one-man presidency and introduced a collegiate body with the minority participation of the opposition.

---

15. The constitution was reformed through the longer path (art. 152–159), which was to declare the desirability of amending the Constitution by a vote of two-thirds of the chambers over three consecutive terms (1907–1910; 1910–1913; and 1913–1916). Once this goal was completed, the Executive called elections for a Convención Nacional Constituyente (July 1916) composed of twice as many members of the General Assembly. The project voted in the Convention was ratified by the citizens in a referendum held in January 1917 (Nahum 1975).

16. Batlle y Ordóñez had advanced in his ideas on reform when he published his 'Apuntes' on 4 March 1913 in the newspaper El Día (Nahum 1975).

The text also introduced a number of provisions guaranteeing the fairness of the vote: permanent electoral register, mandatory registration, secret ballot, proportional representation and the prohibition of political activity but not the vote – for soldiers and police. Furthermore, the constitutional amendment separated church from state, established the direct election of local authorities and created the institutional design that the state would have in industrial, educational and welfare policies. The tool would be the *Entes Autónomos*, Autonomous Councils whose directories would be proposed by the Executive and elected by the vote of three-fifths of the members of the Senate. These innovations allowed the return of the copartnership after fourteen years of ostracism, but now as a rule prescribed by the Constitution.

## The New Copartnership

The first level of partnership was the CNA, composed of nine members elected directly by the public body. Each member had a six-year term and the body should be renewed by two-thirds of votes every two years. In the election of members of the ANC, the winning party obtained two-thirds of the charges and the second, one-third. In accordance with the transitional provisions of the Constitution, the first CNA, and the President would be voted for by the General Assembly. From 1920 the ANC began being renewed by thirds in direct elections and from 1922 the President would be elected in the same way.

During the fourteen years of existence of the second Constitution, four presidents from the PC were elected. Moreover, this party controlled a majority of members in the CNA, although the party was deeply divided into three or four factions. The presidency of the CNA, elected directly every two years, was also

*Table 4.2: Consejo Nacional de Administración (CNA) – Composition[1]*

| Election | PC | PN | CNA Presidency | Total |
|----------|----|----|----------------|-------|
| 1919[2] | 6 | 3 | PC | 9 |
| 1920 | 6 | 3 | PC | 9 |
| 1922 | 6 | 3 | PC | 9 |
| 1924 | 5 | 4 | PN | 9 |
| 1926 | 5 | 4 | PC | 9 |
| 1928 | 5 | 4 | PC | 9 |
| 1930 | 6 | 3 | PC | 9 |
| 1932 | 6 | 3 | PC | 9 |

1. Every election renews one-third members. The winner also had the Presidency. The mandate of each *consejero* lasted six years.
2. Elected by General Assembly on 03.01.1919.
   PC = Colorado Party; PN = National Party

controlled by the PC, except in the period from 1925 to 1927, when it was occupied by the nationalist leader, Luis Alberto de Herrera.

The functioning of the CNA was determined by the level of factionalisation in the political parties during this decade. The high number of partisan actors became heavy and slowed the decision-making process, while the presence of prominent figures such as Batlle y Ordóñez, Feliciano Viera and Luis Alberto de Herrera, delivered speeches that often aroused the interest of the public but had little relation to specific issues that the CNA had to solve. In this scheme, the minority party increased its benefits given that it was able to influence the Executive agenda (something unthinkable a decade earlier) without having the Presidency of the Republic. The opposition also had the possibility to propose their own politicians to occupy charges in the high levels of the ministries or in the state enterprises directories (Lindahl 1977).

The second area of copartnership consisted of the directories of the state entities. The strengthening of the Uruguayan State started half century ago, in the so-called Militarist period (1876–1885), when the army was professionalised and the judicial system was extended to the entire country. In the last decades of the nineteenth century, the state began to develop a public education system and a network of health centres throughout the country, and started other activities such as railways, ports and electricity. From the arrival of Batlle and his group to the Presidency, the state's influence gained greater force due to the fact that the activity of the state replaced the absence of private investment (Nahum 1993). Since then, the *Banco República* and the *Banco Hipotecario* were nationalised (1911 and 1912), the *Banco de Seguros* was nationalised (1912) and state monopoly of electric energy (1912), port services (1912) and railways (1915) was established.

In 1918, each autonomous entity had a directory composed of five members. Given the factionalisation of the parties, nominations had to include names of politicians from various factions of different parties so the copartnership in these organisms was assured from the beginning. Solari and Franco (1983) estimate that in 1932 the country had nearly a dozen autonomous entities, which supports the conclusion that almost a hundred directors of both parties assumed positions in these agencies. While during the first years of the new regime, the PN had few charges and a single faction of the PC had a majority which allowed the monopoly of nominations, as time passed by, their relative position improved (Lindahl 1971). Before the end of 1931, the *batllista* faction of the PC and a faction of the PN opposing Herrera, agreed a set of laws aiming to expand state activity (regulation of foreign exchange operations, creation of the state oil company, reorganisation of the autonomous entities and establishment of the public monopoly on the telephone service), and to increase the copartnership agencies and the number of public employees in these areas.

Therefore, the expansion of the state in the twentieth century was processed with the agreement of the two major parties which used the copartnership as a perfect tool to develop partisan patronage using public employment. In 1920, the autonomous entities had 5,000 employees; in 1930 that number rose to 9,000; in 1940, to 13,000; and in 1950, to 36,000 (Nahum 2005: 228).

In the years following the adoption of the 1917 Constitution, Parliament passed a series of laws that completed the institutional design of the nascent polyarchy.[17] In 1924, a law created the *Corte Electoral*, an agency specialised in the organisation and arbitration of all elections. Furthermore, in 1934, the *Tribunal de Cuentas* was created, a body with similar status as the *Corte Electoral*, but oriented to the external control of budgetary policy of the state. The five ministers of this agency were elected in the General Assembly by two-thirds of members. These organisms have survived until the present and are a substantive part of the institutional design of the Uruguayan polyarchy.

*The Copartnership in the Twentieth Century*

After the 1933 coup led by President Gabriel Terra (ex *batllista*), the copartnership in the executive branch was transformed. Terra's government approved a new constitution (1934) that established an executive branch with a President and a Council of Ministers composed by the partisan factions that promoted the coup (half of members for *terristas*, and the other half for *herreristas*). With the return to democracy in 1942, a new constitutional amendment eliminated the mechanism of distribution of positions between the coup sectors[18] and reduced the copartnership to the directories of autonomous entities. In the early fifties, the *batllista* faction of the PC promoted the fourth constitutional reform that established the *Colegiado* regime. The executive branch was composed of nine members (six by the majority party and three by the second game), directly elected by citizens for a period of four years. This institutional design lasted until 1967, when a new reform restored the present formula of a presidency plus a council of ministers.

As shown in Figure 4.4, in the twentieth century the most stable organism, where copartnership has been developed, are the directories of the autonomous entities. With minor changes, the features of this institutional arrangement have survived to the present. The number of members of directorates has been declining (currently most directories only have three members), but the way of appointment is almost the same: the Executive proposes and the Senate votes by three-fifths of members. Only between 1952 and 1967, the Constitution mandated the Executive to propose lists that included three members of the major party and two members of the second one.

Political practice on appointments of directories of autonomous entities remained unchanged until the decade of the nineties. The big news was generated by President Sanguinetti in 1985, when he included the *Frente Amplio* into these

---

17. Since the constitutional reform, the members of the Supreme Court would be voted by two-thirds of members of the General Assembly, so the integration of the main level of Judiciary would be always subjected to an agreement between the two biggest parties.

18. In addition to the equal distribution of the cabinet between the factions which supported the coup, the Constitution of 1934 established a high chamber composed of fifteen seats for the largest faction of the winning party, and another fifteen seats to the largest faction of the second party. The Uruguayan folk wisdom called this chamber as the Senate of 'half and half', in direct reference to a popular drink, which mixed in equal parts, vermouth and cane.

*Figure 4.4: Copartnership within the executive branch in the 20th century*

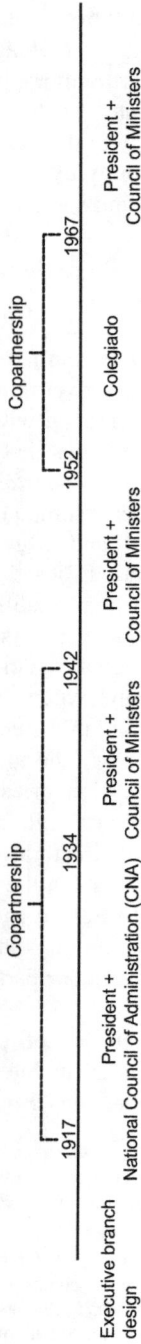

*Figure 4.5: Copartnership in directories of autonomous entities post-1985*

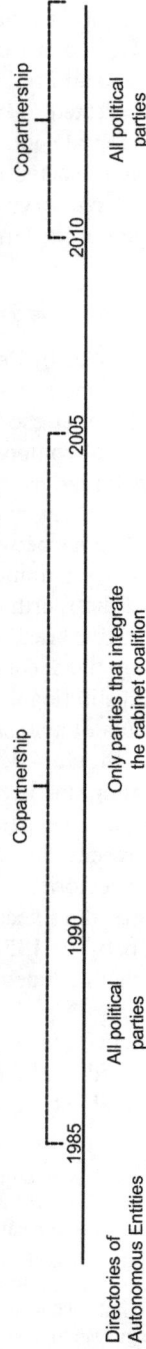

copartnership agencies. However, President Lacalle modified the allocation criteria because he used directories' positions to negotiate a coalition government with the PC. Any political group wishing to have directors should accept ministries and provide legislative support for his package of bills. The *colorado* factions accepted these conditions to join the coalition but the *Frente Amplio* remained in opposition and lost its access to the copartnership positions. The next two *colorado* Presidents (Julio Maria Sanguinetti and Jorge Batlle) also used the positions of copartnership with the purpose of building cabinet coalitions.

Success of coalitional governments prompted traditional parties to introduce some constitutional amendments in 1997 that allowed the Executive to use the autonomous entities positions as resources to negotiate legislative support for the new governments (Chasquetti 2008). When the Frente Amplio accessed government for first time in 2005, President Vazquez tried to return to the classic model of copartnership, but the new opposition of traditional parties did not accept the offer as they didn't share many of the programmatic guidelines of government. However, when the Frente Amplio won their second term in 2010, traditional parties changed their attitude and returned to the copartnership directories.

## Copartnership, a tool flexible and stable over time

The copartnership has been a crucial key in the building of Uruguayan democracy. The Swedish historian Göran Lindal (1971) has written: 'The word copartnership is translated in dictionaries without any warning about its use in Uruguay. Actually, it is a term used in a very special, or rather, in several overlapping senses'. These several senses have to do with the different empirical functions that this institutional arrangement has fulfilled throughout the years, but are also linked to various theoretical interpretations that the academy has provided.

As shown in this chapter, copartnership emerged in the nineteenth century as a way of territorial distribution of political power between the two major parties. Faced with a government party with a hegemonic vocation and a set of rules that facilitated this predominance, the copartnership served as a compensatory mechanism for the opposition party. The mechanism assured the minor party control of four departments and its representation in both chambers. However, over time, the point of balance was put in doubt by the same actors. While the government sought to reduce the relative weight of the opposition (creating new departments or appointing less political chiefs than it had been agreed), the opposition never failed to propose rules that would ensure fair elections and proportional representation in Parliament. Thus, both approaches undermined the effectiveness of the territorial copartnership to ensure stability. While in 1897 the model was redesigned, increasing to six the departments under control of the opposition, the institutional preferences of the majority of the actors had changed and required a new point of balance. The territorial partnership was useful while the development of the country allowed it. When the country changed, both political competition and representation demanded a new set of rules.

Goran Lindal (1977) noted that 'many scholars have referred to the contradictions that the term copartnership has in itself, without analysing the way it has changed its meaning'. That can be seen when the mechanism returns to the institutional design with the constitutional reform in 1917. The new copartnership has at least three new variants.

The first was the copartnership in the executive branch although that outcome was not intended by the political actors. We should remember that Batlle was inspired by the Swiss system and that is why he proposed the elimination of the presidency and the setting up of a *Junta Nacional de Gobierno* composed of nine members, two appointed by Parliament and seven elected by citizens at the rate of one per year (Manini Ríos 1973). This design would hardly admit copartnership, because the PC could impose its preferences in Parliament with its legislative majority, and also win the annual election of a single member ($M = 1$). Even losing a yearly election, Batlle thought that his majority could impose its conditions on the collegial body. However, the result of the reform was another design and the executive branch assumed a two-heads model: a collective body very similar to the *Junta Nacional* that Batlle wanted (nine members elected by two-thirds every two years), and a presidency, that all others actors wished to keep. Paradoxically, the collective body (CNA) opened the door to the opposition within the executive branch, something that Batlle never imagined. The seven elections of *consejeros* held between 1920 and 1932, showed that the winning party never won the three offices; therefore the copartnership of parties in the executive branch was determined by the number of positions in dispute ($M = 3$) and the preferences of the electorate.

When nationalist senators agreed with the *Batllismo*, it was not clear what the benefits of the new institutional design would be. They knew that they would never win the Presidency of the Republic in open elections but with the CNA, the opportunity to obtain advantages was open for three reasons. First, this organism allowed them to have influence in the general direction of government. Second, this organism led them to be part of the allocation process of authorities in high levels of public office. Third, after the victory in 1925 CNA elections, the nationalist leader occupied the presidency of this organism and this situation transformed the PN into a real alternative of government.

In the following decades, the copartnership in the executive branch acquired two new modes. During the quasi-democratic regime of the thirties, copartnership was implemented in cabinet, dividing its composition in two-thirds and one-third between factions which supported the coup of 1933 (a very similar resource to the one used by the National Front in Colombia since 1958 to 1974). Later, in the fifties and sixties, the copartnership was developed in the *Consejo Nacional de Gobierno*, another collective body composed by nine members who replaced the Presidency of the Republic during the period 1952–1967. In both situations, copartnership in the executive branch gave the opposition the opportunity to exert political influence and especially, to obtain positions in the state structure.

The second variant has been the copartnership in organs of control, as the *Corte Electoral* and the *Tribunal de Cuentas*, whose legal nature gives them independence from other government branches. In these cases, the copartnership was determined by the constitutional rules for appointment: two-thirds of members of the General Assembly, which required an agreement between the two major parties.

The third variant was the copartnership in directories of the state entities. This mechanism has been the most stable and efficient of the four methods tested during the twentieth century. Note that in this case the copartnership does not hinder the activity of the executive branch as had occurred in the *colegiados* experiences. In addition, the copartnership promoted cooperation of the opposition with government, stimulated the monitoring and control of public policies, and allowed the promotion of opposition politicians to higher levels of the state, which is very important if an alternation in government occurs.

While in the upswing of the state (during the thirties and forties) the copartnership served to develop patronage in public employment, in the phase of state reform in the nineties, however, the copartnership became useful to stimulate the formation of coalition governments.

Regarding the question on whether there was a joint government or merely deliberate political control, the nineteenth-century copartnership involved the territorial distribution of power and its optimal version supposed cooperation and co-government. The copartnership in the twentieth century, however, had greater versatility. When copartnership was implemented in the executive branch, leaders from both parties believed that its main function would be the political supervision of the administration. However, soon, political practice began to show that the copartnership could also involve cooperation in government. The most convincing proof of this is provided by the agreement within the NCA in 1931 between *batllistas* and independent nationalists. Therefore, the copartnership in the executive branch could allow political control, but also co-government and the choice depended on the preferences of the actors.

The copartnership in autonomous entities allowed the exercise of any of these functions. There are remarkable examples of cooperation in conducting those agencies, real co-government practices that summarise the views of the government and the opposition. But political practice also shows a permanent exercise of political supervision over the decisions of the government's majority. The factor that explains the predominance of one or the other function is the participants' preferences. The more aligned the preferences, the more inclined to cooperation and co-government, and vice versa, the less of a match, the more likely towards supervision.

Finally, we must ask whether the copartnership transforms the Uruguayan case into a consociational regime. Lijphart (1969) would respond affirmatively, saying that while Uruguay had a Swiss-style of government – with a *colegiado* – there is no doubt it had a consociational democracy. Lanzaro (2012) goes one step further and considers that Uruguay has historically been a consociational case (with or without *colegiado*) because, like Colombia, its institutional arrangements helped it overcome the political conflict. As Hartlyn (1993) used the concept 'party subcultures' to illustrate the depth of conflict in Colombia, Lanzaro (2012) rescued

*Table 4.3: Patterns of copartnership in Uruguay*

| Patterns | Period | Joint Government | Supervision of the Executive |
|---|---|---|---|
| 1. Territorial | 1872–1904 | Yes | No |
| 2.1. Executive Branch | 1919–1942; 1952–1967 | Yes | Yes |
| 2.2. Control Agencies | 1925 (1934) to present | Yes | No |
| 2.3. Directories Autonomous Entities | 1919–1990; 2010 to present | Yes | Yes |

the concept 'subjective fatherlands', proposed by the economist Julio Martínez Lamas in 1930, when he argued about cultural disagreements between *colorados* and *nacionalistas*. One way or another, it seems undeniable that the Uruguayan democracy has a strong dose of what Lijphart (1969: 225) calls 'consociational components', that favour the balance of competition and ensure a strong stability of the system.

According to Lijphart (1977: 25) the two characteristics of a consociational regime are (i) the existence of a plural society and (ii) cooperation among the elites. The deal usually results in an institutional design that integrates the conflicting segments. For that reason, the consociational democracy guarantees veto power to the parts, proportionality in the distribution of bureaucratic positions, and autonomy for the parties to resolve their internal affairs. This set of institutional features is an empirical model that is present in many modern democracies.

In analysing the Uruguayan case in depth, we could see that there is such a plural society as the one Lijphart has described. If we accept the argument of Hartlyn and Lanzaro, that equates political conflict between parties with the cleavages of plural societies, a discussion about the nature of agreement among elites is open. In Uruguay, none of the institutional arrangements gave the opposition a veto power over the general decisions. It could be argued that the *Partido Nacional* had autonomy to take decisions in the nineteenth century when it ruled four and then six departments, but its veto power resided in its own army and not in an institutional rule. In the nineteenth century there was no proportionality to allocate patronage, since the distribution of positions was the result of war. Proportionality did exist in the twentieth century, before the first reform of the Constitution, thanks to the different arrangements of copartnership, but the opposition lacked the power of veto and the autonomy. Therefore, if we strictly stick to the theoretical model of Lijphart, we can say that the Uruguayan case could not be classified as a consociational regime. However, there were consociational components based on the copartnership of parties.

## Final Remarks

This study makes clear two conclusions. First, the members of the Uruguayan political elite were ingenious institutional architects in finding solutions to the problem of political competition. The experiment required the making of rules that allowed the setting of a satisfactory balance point for different actors. Changes of context inevitably led to further amendments to the break-even. Second, different variants of copartnership were a superlative institutional finding that introduced consociational patterns in the political system. The copartnership favoured democratisation by providing a mechanism to share power and provided guarantees. Also, this constitutional provision has been flexible and stable over time. The copartnership was used in different historical conjunctures in order to solve different demands (to achieve representation in parliament, influence in government's agenda, develop patronage, and monitor the policies of government, etc.). But it also served to incorporate new actors that wished to participate in the political game on an equal basis (mainly the *Frente Amplio*) and, functionally, it contributed to the formation of many politicians who later hold important positions in the state structure. Copartnership, in short, has a privileged place within the institutional tools of Uruguayan democracy and without it many things would be different.

## References

Altman, D., Buquet, D. and Luna, J. (2011) 'Constitutional Reforms and Political Turnover in Uruguay: Winning a Battle, Losing the War', Document on Line 02/2011. http://cienciassociales.edu.uy/institutodecienciapolitica/wp-content/uploads/sites/4/2015/04/DOL_11_02_AltmanEtAl.pdf (accessed 29 June 2015).

Barrán, J. (1974) *Apogeo y crisis del Uruguay pastoril y caudillesco, 1839–1875*, Montevideo: Ediciones de la Banda Oriental.

Barrán, J. and Nahum, B. (1971) *Historia rural del Uruguay modern, Vol. 1, 1855–1885*, Montevideo: Ediciones de la Banda Oriental.

—— (1983) *Batlle, los estancieros y el Imperio Británico, Vol. IV, Las primeras reformas*, 1911–1913, Montevideo: Ediciones de la Banda Oriental.

Caetano, G. and Rilla, J. (1984) 'El sistema de partidos: raíces y permanencias', *Cuadernos del Claeh* 9(31): 81–98.

Chasquetti, D. (2003) 'El proceso constitucional uruguayo', in B. Nahum y G. Caetano (ed.) *El Uruguay del siglo XX: La Política*, Montevideo: Ediciones de la Banda Oriental, pp. 65–93.

—— (2008) *Democracia, presidencialismo y partidos políticos en América Latina: Evaluando la 'difícil combinación'*, Montevideo: Ediciones Trilce.

Diez de Medina, Á. (1994) *El voto que el alma pronuncia: Historia electoral del Uruguay*, Montevideo: Fundación de Cultura Universitaria.

Gros Espiell, H. and Arteaga, J. (1991) *Esquema de la evolución constitucional del Uruguay*, Montevideo: Fundación de Cultura Universitaria.

Hartlyn, J. (1993) *La Política del Régimen de Coalición: La experiencia del Frente Nacional en Colombia*, Bogotá: Tercer Mundo Editores.

Lanzaro, J. (2012) 'Continuidad y cambios de una vieja democracia de partidos', *Cuadernos del Claeh*, Vol. 100, Montevideo, pp. 37–77.

Lindahl, G. (1971) *Batlle: Fundador de la democracia*, Montevideo: Editorial Arca.

—— (1977) *Batlle: La segunda constitución*, Montevideo: Editorial Arca.

Lijphart, A. (1969) 'Consociational democracy', *World Politics* 21(2): 207–225.

—— (1977) *Democracy in Plural Societies: A comparative exploration*, New Heaven: Yale University Press.

Manini Ríos, C. (1973) *Anoche me llamó Batlle: Ocho años que condicionaron medio siglo, 1911–1919*, Montevideo: Letras S.A.

Méndez Vives, E. (1975) *El Uruguay de la modernización (1876–1904)*, Montevideo: Ediciones de la Banda Oriental.

Nahum, B. (1975) *La época batllista (1905–1920)*, Montevideo: Ediciones de la Banda Oriental.

—— (1993) *Empresas públicas uruguayas: Origen y gestión*, Montevideo: Ediciones de la Banda Oriental.

—— (2005) *Series estadísticas*, Montevideo: Facultad de Ciencias Económicas.

Pérez Antón, R. (1988) 'Cuatro antagonismos sucesivos: La concreta instauración de la democracia uruguaya', *Revista Uruguaya de Ciencia Política*, 2, Montevideo, pp. 41–59.

—— (1989) 'El parlamentarismo en la tradición constitucional uruguaya', *Cuadernos del Claeh* 49, Montevideo, pp. 107–133.

Pivel Devoto, J. (1994) *Historia de los partidos políticos en Uruguay*, Vol. 2, Montevideo: Cámara de Representantes.

Pivel Devoto, J. and Ranieri, A. (1966) *Historia de la República Oriental del Uruguay*, Montevideo: Editorial Medina.

Real de Azúa, C. (1964) *El impulso y su freno. Tres décadas de Batllismo*, Montevideo: Ediciones de la Banda Oriental.

—— (1971) *Política, poder y partidos en el Uruguay de hoy*, Buenos Aires: Siglo XXI.

—— (1981) *El Patriciado uruguayo*, Montevideo: Editorial Banda Oriental.

—— (1997) 'El centenario de Berro y Flores: El día de los cuchillos largos', in C. Real de Azúa, *Historia y Política en el Uruguay*, Montevideo: Editorial Cal y Canto.

Solari, A. and Franco, R. (1983) *Las empresas públicas en el Uruguay: ideología y política*, Montevideo: Fundación de Cultura Universitaria.

Vanger, M. (1991) *José Batlle y Ordóñez: El creador de su época (1902–1907)*, Montevideo: Ediciones de la Banda Oriental.

PART TWO

INSTITUTIONAL RESILIENCY IN LATIN
AMERICA: LOCK-IN AND SUBOPTIMAL
EFFECTS

*Chapter Five*

# Incongruent Federalism as a Solution to Territorial Conflict: (Political) Virtues and (Normative) Pitfalls

*Carlos Gervasoni*

## Introduction: The Puzzle of Incongruent Federalism

A little-noticed aspect in which federations across the world differ is the extent to which their populations are unevenly distributed among their constituent units. At an extreme, several important federations (e.g., Argentina, Brazil and Canada) contain one or two provinces/states/regions with very large populations and many that are much smaller. This demographic 'dissymmetry' often occurs in constitutionally 'symmetrical' federal nations, i.e., those in which all subnational units (at the same level) possess equal powers. Under typical institutional arrangements, smaller units are strongly overrepresented in the national legislature, and often command several other political and fiscal advantages vis-à-vis the larger districts. Evidence from countries such as Argentina and Brazil shows that situations in which the demographically and economically larger units (Buenos Aires and São Paulo) are politically disadvantaged (i.e., incongruent federalism) are, counterintuitively, likely to occur, and that they can be surprisingly stable. At the same time, such equilibrium is normatively undesirable, as political rights and often public spending are distributed unfairly among the citizens depending on their place of residence. This chapter describes this type of federation, analyses the reasons for its apparent success at avoiding (expected) territorial conflicts, and assesses its practical and normative virtues and pitfalls.

It is politically surprising that the most powerful subnational units in several federations accept disadvantageous institutional and fiscal arrangements. Malapportionment is a clear example. States such as São Paulo – which accounts for around 22 per cent of Brazil's population and 34 per cent of its GDP – not only are grossly under-represented in the national Senate (where all states elect the same number of legislators) but also in the lower house, where the state should have about 112 legislators but has only seventy. The situation of the Argentine province of Buenos Aires – described in more detail below – is even worse in this respect, and it is aggravated by fiscal federalism arrangements that are very unfavourable to it. This is 'incongruent federalism': the demographically (and economically) weightier subnational units are the least favoured by the federation's rules.

Both Argentina and Brazil were born as independent states in the midst of intense and often bloody regional conflict. The dispute between 'Buenos Aires' and '*el interior*' (the rest of the provinces) was at the heart of the politics of Argentina from its independence in 1810–16 until the consolidation of a national state in 1880. In spite of this legacy, Buenos Aires (or, more properly, its inhabitants and its elected rulers) seems comfortable with the current state of affairs, never bringing to the agenda the issue of malapportionment, and only timidly complaining about its very disadvantaged fiscal status. Why?

The more general question is the following: Why does territorial/regional conflict not arise in federations in which demographically and economically dominant subnational units are, at the same time, politically and/or fiscally discriminated against? Why don't these provinces and states use their obvious clout to try to redress the rules that hurt them? Why don't they even try to put these issues on the national agenda, as the Argentine case I analyse below shows?

As puzzling as this acquiescence might seem, it is in a sense a blessing. As history and comparative evidence remind us, regional conflicts within nations can be very disruptive and violent. Civil wars among subnational units have been common in federations, including Argentina, Brazil, Nigeria, Switzerland and the USA. Even in today's consolidated democracies, territorial conflict is notoriously difficult to process institutionally, as illustrated by the cases of Belgium, Canada (Quebec), Spain (Catalonia), and Ukraine (Russian-speaking territories). Since World War II, however, Latin America has been the only region in the world that has not witnessed a single secessionist civil war (Ross 2014). Of course, the region has suffered many internal conflicts in the period (thirty-six in nineteen countries according to Ross), 'yet none of them involved a separatist movement' (2014: 128).

It seems that, as it is often the case in politics, the ethics of principles and the ethics of responsibility are in tension: an unfair situation (in which the citizens of some subnational units are given more rights and resources than the citizens of others) may be better from the point of view of consequences than a situation in which territorial conflict to end discrimination destabilises a polity and, in the worst case, leads to civil war.

The considerations above bring up several interrelated descriptive and causal claims bearing upon the topic of 'Institutional Innovation and the Steering of Conflicts in Latin America', particularly with respect to the dimension of distributive-territorial conflicts. I briefly list these claims here and elaborate on them in the rest of the chapter:

1. *Demographic dissymmetry*: Some institutionally symmetrical federations are highly dissymmetrical demographically: they are made up of one (or a couple of) very large unit(s) and many very small ones.

2. *Pro-small units' bias*: the demographically small units are overrepresented in the national legislature and in intergovernmental decision-making institutions, and they are often favoured by fiscal federalism rules

(i.e., they are subsidised by tax revenues collected elsewhere). These advantages enjoyed by small districts are at the expense of the larger (and especially the largest) districts.

3. *Demo-institutional incongruence*: points 1 and 2 above logically imply a lack of congruence (or negative correlation) between demographic (and typically also economic) size and institutional advantages: the small districts are advantaged while the large ones are disadvantaged.

4. *Objective basis for cleavage:* large districts are treated unfairly, have demographic and economic resources to challenge the unfair status quo, have a local government that can organise political action, and have a history of conflicts with the rest of the country (that is, with the smaller units). In sum, there are 'objective' grounds for territorial conflict.

5. *Lack of politicisation of cleavage:* in spite of 4, ruling elites in the large and disadvantaged districts refrain from politically activating the potential cleavage.

6. *Pragmatically convenient but normatively problematic equilibrium*: Incongruence seems to be a stable equilibrium, at least in Argentina (and, less analysed in this chapter, Brazil). Therefore, it is desirable in terms of (at least some) consequences (territorial conflict is avoided) but undesirable in terms of principles (subnational units and citizens of different subnational units are treated differently).

## *Demographic dissymmetry*

Extreme levels of demographic dissymmetry are common in federal countries. Table 5.1 shows that in some important federations the largest subnational unit can contain close to 40 per cent of the total population (Argentina's Buenos Aires; Canada's Ontario), while the smallest always contains far less than 1 per cent. The ratios of largest to smallest districts yield remarkable high numbers: 123 to one in Argentina and ninety-two to one in Canada and Brazil. Even in countries in which the population is more evenly distributed across a number regions (like the USA, with significant concentration of inhabitants in the Northeast, the Midwest, the South and the West), the demographically largest states are far larger than the smallest ones (in the USA the ratio is sixty-six to one).

There are some clear historic, geographical and political reasons for these high levels of unevenness in the territorial distribution of the population, among them the difficulty to settle in some inhospitable areas (such as Patagonia, Amazonia or the Arctic), the positive feedback between large population centres and immigration, and the central government's drive to create new federal units in remote (and typically sparsely-populated) areas to reaffirm sovereign rights over those territories. A more even distribution of the population across subnational units is possible but rare in the real world: very significant differences between demographically large and small states are ubiquitous, from Germany to India and from Nigeria to Switzerland.

*Table 5.1: Largest and smallest subnational units by population for selected countries; Percentage of total population and ratio of largest to smallest units*

| Country | Largest unit | Population (% of total population) | Smallest unit | Population (% of total population) | Ratio of largest to smallest unit |
|---------|--------------|-----------------------------------|---------------|-----------------------------------|-----------------------------------|
| *Highly Dissymmetrical Federations* | | | | | |
| Argentina | Buenos Aires | 15,625,084 (38.9%) | Tierra del Fuego | 127,205 (0.32%) | 122.8 |
| Canada | Ontario | 12,851,821 (38.4%) | Prince Edward Island | 140,204 (0.42%) | 91.7 |
| *Dissymmetrical Federations* | | | | | |
| Brazil | São Paulo | 41,262,199 (21.6%) | Roraima | 450,479 (0.24%) | 91.6 |
| *Moderately Dissymmetrical Federations* | | | | | |
| USA | California | 37,253,956 (12.1%) | Wyoming | 563,626 (0.18%) | 66.1 |
| Mexico | Estado de México | 15,175,862 (13.5%) | Baja California Sur | 637,026 (0.57%) | 23.8 |

*Source:* 2010 national censuses (2011 for Canada). The table does not consider 'territories' (such as Nunavut in Canada or Guam in the USA).

## Pro-small units' bias

Many federal institutions are symmetrical (give equal powers and jurisdictions to all units) and disregard population size as a criteria for the distribution of power in several national decision-making bodies. Constitutions and legislation often give equal representation to each state in the Senate (regardless of their population), create one governor and one legislature per subnational unit (effectively producing over-representation in a myriad of inter-governmental agencies in which each state has one seat) and, in countries like Argentina and Brazil, sanction legislative over-representation for small units *also in the lower chamber* (Samuels and Snyder 2001). The other side of this coin is the under-representation of the most heavily populated districts. In fact, Buenos Aires is by far the most underrepresented province in Argentina, and Argentina the most malapportioned country in the world when both the upper and lower chambers are averaged out (Samuels and Snyder 2001; Reynoso 2004). Tierra del Fuego – with only 0.8 per cent of the population of the province of Buenos Aires – controls three senators (just as Buenos Aires), seats one provincial representative in many *consejos federales* (just as Buenos Aires), and sends five deputies to the national lower chamber, six times more than it should in the absence of malapportionment (Buenos Aires sends 30 per cent fewer than it should under proportional territorial representation).

In Argentina and other federations, small districts are not only political winners, but fiscal winners as well. Fiscal federalism rules tend to favour (and in the case of Argentina very strongly favour, see Gervasoni 2010) the demographically small units. This phenomenon has been called 'reallocative federalism' and it happens in other federations such as Brazil, Mexico and the USA, both for discretionary and nondiscretionary federal transfers (Gibson, Calvo and Falleti 2004). In Argentina Tierra del Fuego receives 1.28 per cent of nondiscretionary, automatic funds (*fondos coparticipables*) while Buenos Aires receives 20.3 per cent. Given the difference in their shares of the country's population (0.32 per cent and 38.9 per cent, respectively), these figures mean that if a *bonaerense* gets an average of $1,000 per capita per year, a *fuegino* obtains $7,700. This huge difference – unparalleled to my knowledge in other federations – cannot be justified in terms of relative development (Tierra del Fuego is the richest province in the country and has better social indicators than Buenos Aires) or differences in geographic scale and dispersion (Tierra del Fuego is much smaller geographically than Buenos Aires, and its population far less dispersed: it is almost entirely concentrated in just two cities).

These facts mean that both the voters and the political elites of Tierra del Fuego are hugely advantaged in terms of their representation in national decision-making and in terms of their economic welfare, especially when compared to the very disadvantaged politicians and voters of Buenos Aires.

This two-province comparison is useful to make the point, but it should be emphasised that the argument does not depend on an especially small outlying province. The twelve smallest provinces of Argentina have three senators and one governor each, are significantly over-represented in the lower house, and receive generous net fiscal transfers from the largest provinces (especially Buenos Aires). These twelve provinces include only 13.6 per cent of the country's population, but receive 27.8 per cent of non-discretionary federal transfers[1] and control 24.1 per cent of the deputies, 50 per cent of the senators and 50 per cent of the governors. Buenos Aires almost triples the population of these twelve provinces combined, but receives only 20.3 per cent of transfers and controls just 27.2 per cent of deputies, and 4.2 per cent of senators and governors.

Maybe Buenos Aires is compensated through other means? Far from it. Special tax treatments that the federal government has created to promote certain areas of the country have typically favoured small provinces. The so-called '*promoción industrial*' (a set of tax reductions and exemptions for industrial investment and production) has benefited, over the last decades, mainly the very small provinces of Catamarca, La Rioja, San Juan, San Luis and Tierra del Fuego. Reduction in

---

1. Some of these small provinces are also the largest oil and gas producers in the country (Chubut, Neuquén, Santa Cruz and Tierra del Fuego). The royalties paid by the companies that exploit these resources go entirely to those provinces' coffers. Even though these funds significantly increase the fiscal advantages of small districts, I do not include them in my analysis because they are not systematic features of the fiscal rules, but largely function of a random factor: the so-called 'geological lottery'.

payroll taxes instituted during the free-market reforms of the 1990s were larger for remote, sparsely populated provinces than for Buenos Aires and other provinces in the Pampas region. Likewise, taxes on agricultural exports (which are rare in other countries but have been recurrently used in Argentina since the nineteenth century, with especially high rates during most of the last five decades)[2] are mostly levied in the large agro-industrial provinces of Santa Fe, Buenos Aires and Córdoba. Surely, there have been specific instances in which Buenos Aires has been able to obtain some kind of benefit. For example, in the 1990s Governor Eduardo Duhalde negotiated the Fondo del Conurbano Bonaerense[3] and, more recently, Governor Scioli (2007–2015) received some special transfers when the province's finances were under strain. It is clear, however, that this type of assistance has been far from making up for the fiscal disadvantages described above.

### Demo-institutional incongruence

The interaction of the previous two points, demographic dissymmetry and an institutional and fiscal bias in favour of small provinces, leads by necessity to an incongruous situation: federations such as Argentina and Brazil are made up of a) several units that are demographically and economically tiny, but politically (and fiscally) advantaged (and therefore disproportionally relevant) and b) one or a couple of large units that are clearly dominant in terms of population and GDP, but whose political weight (and fiscal capacity) is strongly attenuated by the federal institutions in place. (Subnational units in between these extremes are more congruous).

This situation is somewhat counterintuitive, given that the most powerful units in some sense (demography, economics) are the losers of the federal bargain, while the weak (and often new: small population size tends to be correlated with recent creation) are the winners. History points to some reasons for this state of affairs, in particular the need to compromise among small and large pre-existing states/ provinces to achieve national unity, a compromise that resulted in 'undemocratic' (in the sense of violating the principle of 'one person one vote') institutions such as senates with equal representation by state (Stepan 2004: 53–57).

Notice also that incongruence results from the interaction between institutional rules and demographic tendencies. Should Argentines decide to relocate roughly evenly across the territory, incongruence would quickly and sharply diminish. But demographic imbalances have characterised Argentina (and many other countries, including all the federations in Table 5.1) for a long time, and are unlikely to disappear any time soon.

---

2.  Including the current scheme created by President Duhalde in 2002 and significantly expanded by President Kirchner in 2003–2007.

3.  A special federal transfer to the province of Buenos Aires to address special problems in the large surrounding metropolitan area of the city of Buenos Aires, which belongs to the province of Buenos Aires.

## Objective basis for cleavage

There is little justification for incongruence. True, one aspect of it is defensible on the basis of normative arguments and constitutional provisions (i.e., malapportionment by design in the Senate, which was part of the process of national unification in Stepan's (2004) 'coming-together' federations such as the USA and Argentina). Other aspects of incongruence, however, have no normative or legal basis. Why would deputies – the representatives of 'the people' – be allocated in favour of some citizens (those living in small provinces)? Why should some subnational governments receive eight times more federal transfers per capita than others?

In fact, the overrepresentation of small provinces in the lower chamber is undoubtedly unconstitutional in Argentina (and probably in most democracies; Snyder and Samuels 2004: 132). It is based on a decree of the last military government and runs clearly against the proportional intentions of the Argentine constitution in articles 45 and 47 (for details see Reynoso 2012). The fiscal privileges accorded to small provinces at the expense of Buenos Aires are the product of a long, convoluted and haphazard history of negotiations and renegotiations among the national and provincial governments that, as of today, has largely lost connection to objective criteria such as level of development, as the aforementioned disparities in transfers per capita between small but rich Tierra del Fuego and large but poorer Buenos Aires show (for historical, legal and technical details on Argentina's fiscal federalism, see Eaton 2001; Porto 2004 and Cetrángolo and Jiménez 2004).

It is clear, then, that large districts – especially Buenos Aires – are treated unfairly and in one aspect unconstitutionally. This means that there are objective bases for the (re)emergence of a territorial cleavage and, eventually, for distributive conflict. Those on the losing side of unfair situations, however, do not necessarily politicise them. Insights from social movements theory suggests that grievance-motivated political action needs some level of awareness, some way to resolve collective action problems, adequate resources, and favourable political opportunities (Tarrow 1998; McAdam, Tarrow and Tilly 2001). Notice, however, that the obstacles to convert objective deprivation into subjective grievances and, ultimately, into political action, do not appear to be especially daunting when the afflicted party is an organised polity (as opposed to a social movement). Subnational units have clear boundaries, members and leaders, significant bureaucratic, fiscal and political resources, and usually a shared identity. Take Buenos Aires (or São Paulo or California). It is a large polity that accounts for almost 40 per cent of the country's population and one third of its GDP and exports; it is ruled by a democratically elected government endowed with considerable resources; its rulers are well aware of the institutional and fiscal discrimination suffered by the province, and is harmed by them. Moreover, the province has a history of conflicts with the rest of the country (that is, with the smaller units). The conditions seem ripe for the birth (or revival) of a Buenos Aires vs. interior territorial cleavage.

*Lack of politicisation of cleavage*

In spite of the seemingly favourable conditions just described, people in the disadvantaged districts are often unaware of their situation, and leaders – who are aware – do little to politicise the matter. Malapportionment is far from the public agenda. Voters do not know about it, politicians do not speak about it, and no other politically relevant actor is especially concerned with it (only a few academics seem to care). Fiscal discrimination does sometimes find a place in the agenda, but hardly ever a central one.

The case of the province of Buenos Aires is paradigmatic. As explained above, its underrepresentation in the lower house is unconstitutional and especially illegitimate given that it is based on a decree of the utterly discredited 1976–1983 military government. In spite of this and of its extreme underrepresentation in the Senate, not a single provincial politician has brought up this issue since the redemocratisation of the country in 1983 (that the leaders of the other provinces – almost all of them overrepresented – do not talk about the matter either is, of course, to be expected).

The fiscal exploitation of Buenos Aires by the other provinces is also blatant – the 39 per cent of Argentines who live in the province receive only a 20 per cent share of all federal transfers – and has clear negative consequences. The provincial government is systematically underfunded, provincial hospitals, schools and policemen cannot keep up with demand, and some of the largest and most persistent pockets of extreme poverty are located in the province, even though it has a very productive agricultural sector, is home to some of the largest and most dynamic manufacturing clusters in the country, and enjoys some positive spillover effects from the far richer city of Buenos Aires. On this front *bonaerense* politicians are somewhat active. Governors and other leaders do periodically stress the fiscal discrimination faced by their province and timidly suggest something should be done about it. But neither the incumbent governor and party, nor the provincial opposition has put this matter at the centre of their agendas. Politics in the province has revolved around issues such as crime, public education, poverty, and local taxes, but never around a distributive conflict with the national government or the rest of the provinces. In spite of its many conflicts (including wars) with the 'interior' and of its 'autonomist' tendencies in the nineteenth century,[4] there has not been on the part of its most recent leaders even a hint of trying to create a territorial cleavage or frame.

There are several reasons for this acquiescent attitude. Argentina has been a solid nation-state for well over a century and has forged a national identity that cuts across provincial and regional boundaries. Buenos Aires has historically enjoyed many economic blessings (its privileged position as the main port for

---

4.   Buenos Aires' main political party in the second half of the nineteenth century was the 'Partido Autonomista', and in fact the province constituted a separate state between 1853 (when it seceded from the rest of the country) and 1859 (when, after losing the battle of Cepeda, rejoined the federation).

the country, its fertile and plentiful land, the arrival of large numbers of working-age immigrants), which made the aforementioned disadvantages seem 'fair'. The many military administrations that ruled the country between 1930 and 1983 sharply centralised power in the national executive, thus subordinating provincial interests to national authorities. In a similar vein, in twenty-eight of the thirty-two years of democracy between 1983 and 2015 the governor of the province has been of the same party as the president (a situation that will continue until 2019 with the election, in late 2015, of Mauricio Macri as president and María Eugenia Vidal as governor), which likely diminished the chances of a rebellious behaviour on the part of the former. Not less importantly, some of the disadvantages explained above are hard to perceive. Fiscal federalism in Argentina has repeatedly been described as a 'labyrinth' (because of its complexity), a fact that coupled with the low quality of provincial macroeconomic and fiscal statistics makes it difficult to see clearly who wins and who loses in the federal fiscal bargain. Likewise, underrepresentation in the lower chamber is obfuscated by the fact that Buenos Aires' delegation is by far the largest (even if, at the same time, by far the smallest relative to its population). In addition, timing has probably been important too: the fiscal and legislative disadvantages analysed here did not develop fully until the current democratic period. In a complex world, important facts and significant pieces of information may well go unnoticed – and therefore un-politicised:

> it is sometimes surprising in retrospect how important elements of policy debate can be virtually ignored for very long periods of time. While specialists are often aware of them, they simply do not gain attention compared to other dimensions of the debate.
>
> (Jones and Baumgartner 2005: 6)

It is in fact perfectly possible that the current state of acquiesce will be disrupted as time goes by and makes the situation clearer and ever more costly, or as a new political context with new political opportunities arises. One can imagine an opposition governor who launches a challenge against the national incumbent, or a provincial political entrepreneur who decides to resort to the current anti-Buenos Aires biases as a campaign theme. Thus, the long period of stasis in which the elites and voters of the province of Buenos Aires accepted an unfavourable status quo may well be suddenly disrupted if the issues described in this chapter became part of the public agenda. Baumgartner and Jones (1993) use the evolutionary metaphor of a 'punctuated equilibrium' to describe how 'iron triangles' in the USA typically persist for decades but are sometimes destroyed when their issue area becomes a central part of the public agenda and a new, and typically less favourable, 'policy image' is developed. It may then be the case that the declining historical trajectory of the province of Buenos Aires is not a deterministic outcome, but an admittedly lasting equilibrium that may be eventually disrupted or 'punctuated'.

The fact, however, is that so far political elites have not activated this potentially conflictive issue. Even the most obvious 'objective cleavages' such as class or ethnic differences need to be politicised to become the basis for political conflict. As Sartori aptly summarised it, from this point of view 'class' (or any other supposedly objective grounds for conflict) 'is an ideology' (1969: 85). In other words, far from early (and sometimes crass) Marxist and other structuralist views of conflict, modern political science sees cleavages largely as political constructions. In this view, elites have considerable room for defining the agenda and, therefore, for deciding what issues are politically important. Expressed more systematically, the traditional structural view on cleavages implies four unrealistic assumptions 1) that citizens' critical interests depend on their class, ethnicity, region or other 'objective' trait, 2) that they are conscious of those interests, 3) that they base their political behaviour on such conscious interests, and 4) that there are parties and other political forces that represent those interests in the political system (these assumptions are taken and slightly adapted from Mainwaring 1999: 52). It is not difficult to find clear objective grounds for political conflict that nevertheless are not politically expressed. One prominent example comes from Brazil, where some of the highest levels of socioeconomic inequality in the world – that largely overlapped with ethnic differences – did not give rise to a class or race cleavage in its political system (Mainwaring 1999: 46–54). However unfairly the province of Buenos Aires (or the state of São Paulo) is treated in their respective federations, the 'objective grievances' they suffer will be politically inconsequential until some significant sector of the political elite decides to put them at the centre of the agenda.

*Pragmatically convenient but normatively problematic equilibrium*

Incongruence has been a lasting equilibrium, at least in Argentina (and Brazil). However hurt the interests of the citizens and the elites of the largest subnational units are, there has been little or no political reaction. If in 1874 and in 1880 Buenos Aires, and in 1932 São Paulo, engaged in military resistance against the central government dominated by leaders from other provinces/states, in the last decades these national powerhouses have peacefully accepted to be one more among many peer units. In fact, Argentine politics has been dominated mostly by politicians from the 'interior' and the city of Buenos Aires since 1983, with only one former Buenos Aires governor (Eduardo Duhalde) achieving the (interim) presidency briefly between 2002 and 2003 (Paulista politicians have often been successful contenders for the presidency, but even so São Paulo's former governors have not been elected to the highest office since re-democratisation in 1985). In both countries, the regional dimension is at best a minor consideration in the electoral decision of voters, and the largest subnational units have not claimed any special right to have a representative in the main presidential tickets.

Compared with the serious conflicts of the past or with the present-day tensions in countries such as Belgium, Canada and Spain, this state of affairs seems desirable. Regional conflicts can be specially disruptive and difficult to process institutionally. Bringing together a set of pre-existing political units with their own local elites and cultural identities into a stable federation is a complex political endeavour. That Jujuy and Buenos Aires, Alagoas and São Paulo, or Louisiana and New York coexist harmoniously is a remarkable political achievement that should not be taken for granted (as the independence of Uruguay from Argentina illustrates).

The political situation that underlies this coexistence, however, is one of injustice, in which a large subnational unit, its citizens and its leaders are clearly worse off than their counterparts in rest of the country. From the point of view of an ethics of principles, the unfair treatment of Buenos Aires or São Paulo is immoral because it means that political rights and fiscal resources are distributed unevenly among the citizens depending on their place of residence: by just moving from Buenos Aires to Tierra del Fuego, a person automatically gains enormously both in terms of her legislative voting power and of the share of public spending she benefits from. Likewise, a politician who moves from one district to the other increases her chances of being elected to national or provincial offices and, if elected governor, can rule in a much more comfortable fiscal situation.

## Explaining Incongruence: A Path-Dependent Model

How is it that in a federal country the powerful units come to be weak while the weak become powerful? I propose a path-dependent model. The critical juncture in this model is the original 'coming-together' federal bargain (Stepan 2004), that is, the moment at which political units that were separate or loosely united in a confederation come to an agreement to create a common state with both a strong central government and local autonomies. This act has two relevant effects: 1) *uniform power distribution*, or the creation of an institutional structure in which to some extent political power is not distributed proportionally according to population (as in the 'one person one vote' principle) but allocated uniformly among the negotiating parties (as in the 'one state/region/province, one vote' principle), and 2) *central power delegation*, or the creation of a new actor, the national state, which is (or quickly becomes) in many ways more powerful than any of the contracting states, including the largest one.

Notice that both effects of national unification have in turn the consequence of weakening the largest polity. When Buenos Aires, or São Paulo or Virginia entered in a federation with, say, San Luis, or Maranhão or Rhode Island, they accepted a status of peers with polities that were demographically and economically much smaller. Likewise, delegating power to a national government brought in one more key actor into the scene, which following Schattschneider's (1960) famous argument about the scope of conflict, would favour the weakest party. Moreover, the new actor was not just one more of the same kind, but also one with legal authority and (eventually) with material resources that exceeded those of Buenos Aires, São Paulo or Virginia.

Of course, at this critical juncture the largest units can decide not to join, or to use their superior de facto power to alter the federal bargain (as illustrated by the 1852–1861 civil war period, when Buenos Aires and the interior clashed in the battles of Caseros, Cepeda and Pavón). But once a stable federal arrangement is in place, the consequences of 1 and 2 above (uniform power distribution and central power delegation, respectively) start to make themselves felt. The largest subnational unit loses power in relative terms, and it becomes vulnerable to an alliance between the new national government and the smaller units. As the national government expands its bureaucratic, military and fiscal capacities, it becomes stronger vis-à-vis the subnational units, reducing the potential of the largest unit to rebel. Rebellions may occur (they did in Buenos Aires, in 1874 and 1880) but they are less likely to be successful (both attempts, led by Bartolomé Mitre and Carlos Tejedor, failed).

The national government-small unit's alliance makes political sense in many ways, as the allies share a common rival. In fact, such insight has already been developed by international relations scholars (Huntington 1999; Wohlforth 1999). Their argument is that aspiring regional powers (say China or Brazil) are likely to be counterbalanced by an alliance of the global superpower (the US) and smaller regional powers (say India or Argentina), as the 'superpower and the secondary regional powers will thus often, although not always, share converging interests against major regional powers' (Huntington 1999: 42). It should not come as a surprise, then, that provinces such as Jujuy, La Rioja or San Luis joined forces with the new national government in the second half of the nineteenth century to counterbalance the previous dominance of the province of Buenos Aires, which was demographically, economically and fiscally much weightier than the (then) thirteen other provinces.

Moreover, once some kind of uniform power distribution is institutionalised (in the form of a Senate, for example), the so called logic of 'low-maintenance constituencies' (Gibson and Calvo 2000) kicks in: it is easy for the national government to make relatively inexpensive payments to small provinces (for example in terms of federal transfers or legislative overrepresentation in the lower chamber) in exchange for valuable (and overrepresented) political support from their governors and senators (Gordin 2006; Porto and Sanguinetti 2001). Thus these provinces gain at the expense of the largest one. These positive feedbacks set the latter on a path of progressive legislative and fiscal weakening. At this point it has neither enough institutional resources for challenging the status quo, nor the fiscal and/or military resources to rebel.

The current thirty-three year-long democratic period in Argentina, by far the longest in the country's history, shows significant evidence for the logic of 'low-maintenance constituencies' even before and after the period analysed by Gibson and Calvo. The authors documented that the politics of economic reform in the 1990s made the ruling Partido Justicialista (PJ) vote more peripheral in that decade: President Menem rewarded the small provinces' support for his agenda with discretionary fiscal transfers, and the governors and citizens of these provinces paid back in votes and legislative support.

Figure 5.1 shows boxplots of the PJ presidential vote for each election since 1983 divided by region, that is, the 'centre' (province of Buenos Aires plus the next four largest districts of the country – the federal capital, Córdoba, Mendoza and Santa Fe – plus the sixth largest district, Entre Ríos) and the 'interior' (the other eighteen smaller provinces). The boxplots indicate that the 'peripheralisation' of the vote in fact went much further during the Kirchners' years. The PJ starts in 1983 with a moderate peripheral bias, which actually disappears in the election of 1989 (when the PJ wins with Menem as its candidate). By Menem's re-election in 1995, the graph shows an increased peripheral bias in the PJ vote, which is maintained in 1999 (when Duhalde loses to De la Rúa) and 2003 (considering Kirchner as the PJ candidate, given that he was the only of the three Peronist candidates who was sponsored by President Duhalde). The most remarkable aspect of the graph is that the regional gap widens sharply in the 2007, 2011 and 2015 elections. If the 1983 difference between the median PJ vote in the centre and the median PJ vote in the interior was 3 per cent in the first democratic election of 1983, and 6 per cent in the election analysed by Gibson and Calvo, it was 7 per cent when Kirchner was elected in 2003, 17 per cent when Cristina Kirchner was elected in 2007, 19 per cent when she was re-elected in 2011 and again 19 per cent when Daniel Scioli, lost the 2015 election. In other words, during the Kirchner's years the PJ became much more peripheral than it had been in the past. This evidence is consistent with a positive feedback in which more political and legislative support from the small provinces to the centre results in more central fiscal support for these provinces, which in turn results in more votes for the national incumbent, which in turn produces a more peripheral ruling coalition in congress, and so forth.

Idiosyncratic analyses of Argentina tend to interpret this increasing peripheralisation of the vote as a characteristic of the PJ. This trend, however, might have been characteristic of any incumbent. That is, it is possible that another party (say the UCR) would have also become more peripheral if it had controlled the presidency almost continuously since 1989 as the PJ did. Evidence from earlier years shed light on the issue. Figure 5.2 below reproduces the analysis for the UCR in 1983 (when Alfonsín was elected at the end of the military government) and in 1989, when as the incumbent party it fielded Eduardo Angeloz as its candidate.

*Figure 5.1: Boxplots of PJ vote in presidential elections by region (1983–2015)*

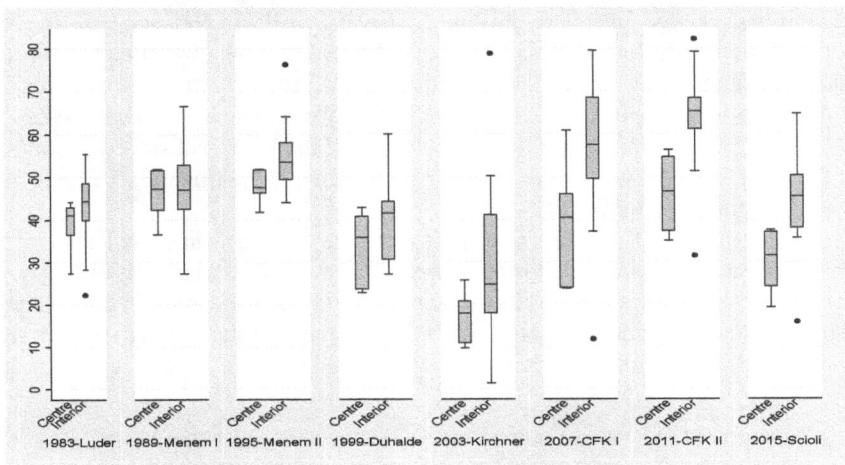

*Figure 5.2: Boxplots of UCR vote in presidential elections by region (1983–1989)*

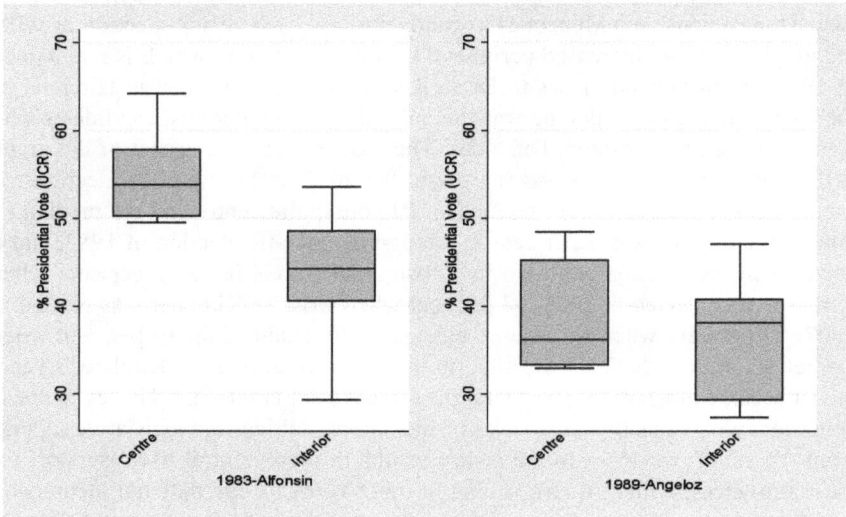

Although the UCR did significantly worse in both areas of the country in 1989 and lost the election to the PJ candidate Carlos Menem, its electoral geography changed substantially: if as a non-incumbent party in 1983 it did significantly better in the large districts (its median vote was approximately 10 per cent higher in those provinces), in 1989 it did marginally better in the smaller districts (the median vote was 2 per cent higher there than in the large provinces). This evidence is, again, consistent with a 'low-maintenance logic', which appears to operate both under PJ and UCR administrations.

In sum, the data seem to support a general application of a causal logic in which the small districts give the central government 'cheap' political and legislative support in exchange for (relatively modest) fiscal payoffs. In fact, some of Buenos Aires's worst fiscal losses happened during Alfonsín's years, when he negotiated increased funding for the provinces of the interior (mostly ruled by PJ governors) at the expense of Buenos Aires (incidentally, his own province) ruled until 1987 by UCR's Alejandro Armendáriz. In all likelihood, if the UCR had stayed in control of the presidency, its vote would have become even more peripheral, as Figure 5.1 shows was the case for the PJ.

Notice that similar patterns seems to have taken place in Brazil under the presidency of Lula, who came to power based on votes from the large cities and most populous states of the more developed Southeast and South, but once in government were able to reconfigure their electoral bases in favour of the smaller states or the poorer North and Northeast (Hunter and Power 2007; Zucco 2008).[5] Although the

---

5.  The tendency for presidential candidates of the incumbent party to do better in Brazil's poorer regions was also present in previous presidential elections (Zucco 2008).

literature tends to explain the shift in Lula's electoral support between 2002 and 2006 on the grounds of the effects of *Bolsa Família* and other pro-poor policies, there is evidence of a 'low-maintenance' logic at work concerning the distribution of discretionary federal spending in Brazil (Turgeon and Calvacante 2014).

Thus, political, institutional and fiscal pro-small unit biases tend to get entrenched. As these units have a firm control of the Senate and are (in Argentina and Brazil) also overrepresented in the lower chamber, any institutional attempt to diminish the bias is likely to fail. The largest unit seems to have three basic options in this context: acquiescence, extra-institutional pressures, or exit (secession). Acquiescence seems to be the norm regarding malapportionment: neither Buenos Aires nor São Paulo have so far articulated any demands to redress their sharp legislative underrepresentation. By extra-institutional pressures I mean inter-governmental negotiations based on some kind of credible threat on the part of the largest provinces. For example, governors of Buenos Aires often obtain some discretionary fiscal assistance from the central government by arguing that lack of funds will result in strikes or riots in the strategic Buenos Aires metropolitan area (most of which is located in the province of Buenos Aires, the rest is the Federal District). This is basically the logic of Gimpelson and Treisman's (2002) 'fiscal games', in which 'local and regional officials may deliberately set their employment levels beyond their fiscal capacity, prompting bailouts from the central government, which fears the political cost to it if wage arrears accumulate and provoke strikes'. Finally, there is the option of secession, which is usually too costly given the strong national identities that countries like Argentina and Brazil have built since their independence, the very high level of social and economic interdependence among provinces, and the centralisation of all military (and significant police) forces in the national government. To my knowledge, no political or social actor in Buenos Aires or São Paulo has ever even mentioned (in recent decades) secession as a solution to the discrimination against their states.

## Historical Evidence: National Building in Argentina and the Decline of Buenos Aires

In this section I offer historical evidence from the Argentine case that buttresses the plausibility of the path-dependent model outlined above. It is not an empirical 'test of the theory', as the model I propose was in part derived inductively from the Argentine case. A proper test would have to be based on evidence from other cases, such as São Paulo in Brazil or Ontario in Canada.

The organisation of the current Argentine national state started off in the 1860s under the leadership of Buenos Aires, by far the most economically and politically dominant province. This process quickly gave rise to a national government – with its own army, bureaucracy and revenue system – that was largely independent from Buenos Aires or any other province (Oszlak 2012 [1997]). A recent book on the political history of the province of Buenos Aires (Ollier 2010) offers a stylised periodisation that is very much consistent with the causal story proposed here. The first stage – from national independence in 1810–16 to the consolidation of the

Argentine national state in 1880 – is marked by Buenos Aires' hegemony over the rest of the country. The second stage spans from 1880 to 1916 (the year of the first competitive presidential election under universal male suffrage) and shows the 'resistance of Buenos Aires' in the face of its eroding power within the federation. Finally, the third stage (1916–present) includes the political defeat and 'surrender' of Buenos Aires (Ollier 2010: 26).

Consistent with the theoretical considerations above, the 'construction of a central power, in 1880, can be attributed to a coalition of subnational states whose goals was to subdue Buenos Aires [...]'[6] (Ollier 2010: 25). Oszlak (2012 [1997]: 169–173) also highlights the gradual transition from a national state built and led by Buenos Aires (in the figure of Bartolomé Mitre, president between 1862 and 1868) to an autonomous national state that grew progressively more detached from the main province and ended up defeating it militarily in the rebellions of 1874 (led by Mitre himself) and 1880 (led by Buenos Aires' governor Carlos Tejedor). The year 1880 was also critical because the national congress decided to convert the city of Buenos Aires – at that point the capital of the province of Buenos Aires – into the nation's capital. This 'federalisation' of the city of Buenos Aires deprived the province of its main urban, economic and political centre, and was the reason for the last attempt by provincial leaders to rebel against the national government, Tejedor's 'Revolución de 1880'. The conflict is very consistent with the path-dependent process I proposed above: the national government was controlled after 1868 by an alliance of governors of the interior provinces (which eventually became the dominant Partido Autonomista Nacional, or PAN). This 'league of governors' was able to elect presidents Domingo F. Sarmiento (from the province of San Juan; 1868–1874) and Nicolás Avellaneda (from the province of Tucumán; 1874–1880). In 1880 the incumbent's candidate was Julio Argentino Roca (born in Tucumán), Avellaneda's war minister. Governor Tejedor launched his own candidacy. Roca – supported by Avellaneda (national government) and by almost all the governors of the interior (smaller provinces) – won the election. Tejedor challenged the results and opposed the impending federalisation of the city of Buenos Aires. The ensuing bloody conflict between national forces and Buenos Aires militias ended in the defeat of the latter. Roca assumed the presidency, consolidated the national government, and launched a long period of peace and stability dominated by the 'league of governors'. Buenos Aires lost its main city and saw its political influence greatly diminished. After 1880 the province never rebelled or even hinted such action again. In sum, during this period of national unification 'the State consolidated its institutional apparatus and widened its social bases of support, detaching itself little by little from Buenos Aires's tutelage'[7] (Oszlak 2012 [1997]: 274).

During Ollier's second stage, Buenos Aires (or, more properly, its elites) expresses its dissent through institutional channels. It sided several times with the losing presidential candidate against the candidate of the

6. My translation.
7. My translation.

national-government-cum-smaller provinces alliance. By the beginning of the twentieth century, Buenos Aires' party system was dominated by the *Partido Conservador*, which tended to support the Partido Autonomista Nacional but remained autonomous from it. Its most significant leader, Marcelino Ugarte, aspired to jump from the governorship of the province (to which he was elected for the second time in 1914) to the presidency. The opposition party UCR, however, won the 1916 presidential election. Soon after President Hipólito Yrigoyen was sworn in, he used his constitutional powers to 'intervene'[8] the province of Buenos Aires and to call new elections. His UCR won and went on to dominate provincial politics until the 1930 coup. With this strike Yrigoyen not only deprived the opposition of the country's most important province, but it also replaced a local force of *autonomista* inclinations (namely, the Partido Conservador of the province of Buenos Aires) by a nationally organised party (namely, the UCR). Since then there have not been any significant provincial parties in Buenos Aires (even though such parties exist or have existed in several provinces).[9]

The third stage in the history of the province is marked by this intervention, which destroyed the last traces of autonomy. In the century that has passed since then, Buenos Aires was almost always politically aligned with the national government, during democratic periods because the president and the governor belonged to the same party (except, briefly, in 1987–1989 and 1999–2001), and during military regimes because the governor was appointed by the de facto president. At several points the governor of Buenos Aires – almost by definition one of the most powerful elected officials in the country – had presidential ambitions that resulted in tensions with the sitting president. These quarrels were always won by the latter, who often removed the troublesome governor via federal intervention. Moreover, presidents often attempted (and frequently succeeded) to impose their own candidates in the race for the governorship of Buenos Aires. For these reasons, provincial politics became increasingly intertwined with national politics after 1917 (Ollier 2010). A contributing factor has surely been the geographical proximity of the province to the Federal Capital: most *bonaerenses* live in the Greater Buenos Aires metropolitan area that surrounds the capital city of Buenos Aires, and the provincial capital of La Plata is merely sixty kilometres away from the Casa Rosada and the National Congress. Among other things this means that the media market for most *bonaerenses* is the same as the national media market based in the federal capital (while in all the other provinces the main media are newspapers, radios and TV stations with a strong local focus).

The gradual political integration of Buenos Aires politics and national politics (and the subordination of the former to the latter) was accompanied by the equally

---

8. Federal intervention is a power assigned by the Argentine constitution to the federal government to temporarily remove provincial authorities and replace them with an *interventor federal* appointed by the president.

9. For example the Partido Autonomista and Partido Liberal (Corrientes), the Movimiento Popular Neuquino (Neuquén), the Partido Bloquista (San Juan) and the Partido Social Patagónico (Tierra del Fuego).

gradual change in the nature of political conflict: the territorial cleavage (Buenos Aires vs. interior) that had dominated the new republic in the second half of the nineteenth century gave way to a party cleavage (Conservatives vs. UCR, originally revolving around the universal suffrage issue) that, critically, cut across provinces. Since then, Argentine elites and voters have been divided in terms of their partisanship (UCR vs. Peronists after 1945), their ideologies, their support or opposition to military governments, but never again in territorial terms. Ollier (2010: 61) stresses a paradox that is very much in line with the thesis of this chapter: the province with the most political and economic weight ends up being the least autonomous one. In fact, this pattern has continued to this day: the national government has subordinated Buenos Aires either by successfully promoting a reliable and close co-partisan as governor (e.g. Perón and Domingo Mercante in 1946, Alfonsín and Alejandro Armendáriz in 1983, Kirchner and Daniel Scioli in 2007, Macri and María Eugenia Vidal in 2015), by federally intervening the province (Ortiz and Manuel Fresco in 1940), or by forcing the resignation of the governor (Perón and Oscar Bidegain in 1974). A telling fact evidences the key influence of national politics in the province: three of the last six provincial governors were elected while serving as vice-presidents (Duhalde in 1991, Carlos Ruckauf in 1999 and Scioli in 2007; Vidal was Macri's vice-chief of government in the city of Buenos Aires when both were elected to their current posts).

The proportion of national legislators from Buenos Aires has been reduced in several ways since the nineteenth century. The first one was the federalisation of the city of Buenos Aires, which had the mechanical effects of absorbing some of the province's representatives and of creating one more district that elected national senators. Immediately before 1880, Buenos Aires accounted for 29.1 per cent of the lower chamber (twenty-five out of eighty-six national deputies), that is, a 'malapportionment bonus' of 2.7 per cent above its 1869 census population share of 26.4 per cent; however, by 1898 (after the reapportionment triggered by the 1895 census) Buenos Aires controlled only 23.3 per cent of the national deputies (twenty-eight out of 120), not far from its population share of 22.8 per cent (the 'malapportionment bonus' fell to 0.5 per cent; all figures taken or calculated from Reynoso 2012). Likewise, Buenos Aires' two senators represented 7.1 per cent of the upper chamber before 1880, but 6.7 per cent afterwards. From 1880 to 1951 the number of autonomous subnational units remained at fifteen (the federal capital and the fourteen provinces), but between 1951 and 1956 practically all the 'national territories' were legislated into provinces: Chaco (originally called 'Presidente Perón') and La Pampa (originally called 'Eva Perón') in 1951, Misiones in 1953, Chubut, Formosa, Neuquén and Río Negro in 1955, and Santa Cruz in 1956. This outburst of new provinces deepened senatorial malapportionment to extreme levels. By 1958, with twenty-two districts, the senators of Buenos Aires represented just 4.5 per cent of the upper chamber.[10] In terms of deputies the province recovered to 25.9 per cent (or fifty out of 193 deputies) due to its increasing demographic weight

---

10. One last province, Tierra del Fuego, was created in 1990, reducing still further the weight of Buenos Aires in the Senate.

(26.9 per cent of the country's population according to the 1947 census), but the 'malapportionment bonus' turned into a deficit: -1 per cent. Even this high share of representatives that the constitution granted Buenos Aires (by mandating that their distribution should be proportional to the population share of each province), eventually came under attack. Both the military governments of 1967–1973 and of 1976–1983 issued decrees with provisions that over-represented the smaller provinces (for details, see Reynoso 2012). Thus, in 1973 Buenos Aires elected only 28 per cent of all the deputies (68 out of 243) in spite of containing 37.6 per cent of the national population (the 'malapportionment deficit' deepened to a remarkable -9.6 per cent). The even more malapportioning decree of 1983 made the legislative share of Buenos Aires decline to 27.6 per cent even though its 1980 census population share grew to 38.9 per cent. The underrepresentation of the province reached a record of -11.3 per cent, a figure that has remained approximately constant up to the present. It may not be so surprising that, in spite of the implementation of three censuses in 1991, 2001 and 2011, Congress has not recalculated the number of deputies per province (article 45 of the national constitution orders such recalculation after each census). That national legislators originating in overrepresented (or fairly-represented) provinces fail to comply with the constitution in this respect may be understandable. That the governor and the national legislators of Buenos Aires do not do or say anything about it is more puzzling.

## Tentative Conclusions: Political Virtues and Normative Pitfalls of Incongruent Federalism

Seen from the point of view of the historical process of nation building among pre-existing dissymmetrical polities, the contemporary incongruent equilibrium is a happy outcome. Big and small, powerful and weak subnational units coexist peacefully within stable federations. The demographically and economically dominant units accept a federal bargain in which they are given less institutional power than democratic principles would imply. Over time they lose additional political and fiscal resources in favour of the smaller units. One possible interpretation is that the leaders of dominant units such as Buenos Aires or São Paulo rationally give up something in order to secure something else (that is, membership into a larger, safer polity). However, if this is the case, they do so at the expense of the rights and welfare of the citizens they represent.

When this stable and peaceful state of affairs is thought of in terms of citizens instead of units, several normative pitfalls come to light. Not only are the voters of large provinces and states extremely underrepresented in the upper houses (a very undemocratic situation, but one that is mandated by the constitution and that can be defended on nation-building grounds), but also they tend to face other types of discrimination that are less visible and defensible. Malapportionment in the lower chamber – with no normative or constitutional justification – exists in Argentina, Brazil and many other federal countries. Moreover, fiscal rules can also be extremely unfavourable to the citizens of the largest units, who only receive a small fraction of the fiscal resources allocated to the luckier inhabitants of small districts.

In sum, the incongruent equilibrium appears to be convenient from a conflict management perspective but undesirable from the point of view of the principles of fairness, equality and democracy: citizens that are equal in theory are given widely different political rights and fiscal resources according to their place of residence. Few of us would accept rules that weighted the votes of the poor, women or gays ten times less than those of non-poor, male and heterosexual citizens. Likewise, outrage would be widespread if a government decided to direct its public spending away from the former groups and in favour of the latter. However, this is basically what happens in Argentina. The grounds for discrimination is not socioeconomic status, gender or sexual orientation, but place of residence. By living in (or moving to) the province of Buenos Aires, an Argentine is very strongly discriminated against politically and fiscally.

I finish by highlighting a potential additional problem of the current equilibrium: the objective discrimination of *bonaerenses* or *paulistas* might someday be politicised. Both Argentina and Brazil have had conflicts between their largest state and the rest of the country in the past. In the same way that after years of democracy racial differences gave rise to indigenous parties in Bolivia or Ecuador (that is, a dormant cleavage was politicised), one cannot discard that strategic political entrepreneurs will decide to activate this obvious inequality among Argentines or Brazilians in order to gain votes. A different path-dependent process might then be set off: once political entrepreneurs make *bonaerenses* aware of their unfavourable situation, all the provincial political class will have incentives to take up the issue, for 'position taking' and for actually doing something about it. As the matter is talked about by provincial and national politicians and by the media, citizens will become more and more aware of it, will care more about it, and will expect their leaders to address it. A new territorial cleavage may emerge. I do not yet see any signs of such a process, but in the current context of party denationalisation and fragmentation in Argentina,[11] it is not hard to imagine a situation in which the politicians of Buenos Aires gradually become more *autonomistas*, as they were in the nineteenth century. The current equilibrium may be punctuated, and conflict may not be avoided after all.

## References

Baumgartner, F. and Jones, B. (1993) *Agendas and Instability in American Politics*, Chicago: University of Chicago Press.

Calvo, E. and Escolar, M. (2005) *La Nueva Política de Partidos en la Argentina: Crisis Política, Realineamientos Partidarios y Reforma Electoral*, Buenos Aires: Prometeo/ Pent Fundación para la Integración de la Argentina en el Mundo.

Cetrángolo, O. and Jiménez, J. (2004) 'Las Relaciones entre Niveles de Gobierno en Argentina', *Revista de la CEPAL* 84: 117–134.

---

11. See Calvo and Escolar 2005; Mustapic 2013; Gervasoni forthcoming.

Eaton, K. (2001) 'Decentralization, democratization, and liberalization: the history of revenue sharing in Argentina', *Journal of Latin American Studies* 33(1): 1–28.

Gervasoni, C. (2010) 'A rentier theory of subnational regimes: fiscal federalism, democracy, and authoritarianism in the Argentine provinces', *World Politics* 62(2): 302–40.

—— (forthcoming) 'Argentina's Declining Party System: Fragmentation, denationalization, factionalization, personalization and increasing fluidity in the new century', in S. Mainwaring (ed.) *Party Systems in Latin America: Institutionalization, decay, and collapse*, Cambridge University Press.

Gibson, E. and Calvo, E. (2000) 'Federalism and low-maintenance constituencies: territorial dimensions of economic reform in Argentina', *Studies in Comparative International Development* 35(3): 32–55.

Gibson, E., Calvo, E. and Falleti, T. (2004) 'Reallocative Federalism: Legislative overrepresentation and public spending in the Western Hemisphere', in E. Gibson (ed.) *Federalism and Democracy in Latin America*, Baltimore: The Johns Hopkins University Press, pp. 173–96.

Gimpelson, V. and Treisman, D. (2002) 'Fiscal games and public employment: a theory with evidence from Russia', *World Politics* 54(2): 145–183.

Gordin, J. (2006) 'Intergovernmental fiscal relations, "Argentine style"', *Journal of Public Policy* 26(3): 255–277.

Hunter, W. and Power, T. (2007) 'Rewarding Lula: executive power, social policy and the Brazilian elections of 2006', *Latin American Politics and Society* 49(1): 1–30.

Huntington, S. (1999) 'The lonely superpower (US military and cultural hegemony resented by other powers', *Foreign Affairs* 78(2): 35–49.

Jones, B. and Baumgartner, F. (2005) *The Politics of Attention: How government prioritizes problems*, Chicago: The University of Chicago Press.

Mainwaring, S. (1999) *Rethinking Party Systems in the Third Wave of Democratization: The case of Brazil*, Stanford: Stanford University Press.

McAdam, D., Tarrow, S. and Tilly, C. (2001) *Dynamics of Contention*, Cambridge: Cambridge University Press.

Mustapic, A. (2013) 'Los Partidos Políticos en la Argentina. Condiciones y Oportunidades para su Fragmentación', in C. Acuña (ed.) *¿Cuánto Importan las Instituciones? Gobierno, Estado y Actores en la Política Argentina*, Buenos Aires: Siglo Veintiuno-Fundación OSDE, pp. 249–90.

Ollier, M. (2010) *Atrapada sin Salida: Buenos Aires en la Política Nacional (1916–2007)*, San Martín: UNSAM Edita.

Oszlak, O. (2012 [1997]) *La Formación del Estado Argentino: Orden, Progreso y Organización Nacional*, Buenos Aires: Ariel.

Porto, A. (2004) 'Etapas de la Coparticipación Federal de Impuestos: Un Análisis Crítico', in A. Porto (ed.) *Disparidades Regionales y Federalismo Fiscal*, La Plata: Editorial de la Universidad de La Plata, pp. 155–99.

130 | Institutional Innovation and the Steering of Conflicts in Latin America

Porto, A. and Sanguinetti, P. (2001) 'Political determinants of intergovernmental grants: evidence from Argentina', *Economics and Politics* 13(3): 237–256.

Reynoso, D. (2012) 'El Reparto de la Representación: Antecedentes y Distorsiones de la Asignación de Diputados a las Provincias', *POSTData* 17(1): 153–192.

—— (2004) 'Bicameralismo y Sobre-representación en Argentina en Perspectiva Comparada', *Revista SAAP* 2(1): 69–94.

Ross, M. (2014) 'Conflict and Natural Resources: Is the Latin American and Caribbean region different from the rest of the world?' in J. C. Vieyra and M. Masson (eds) *Transparent Governance in an Age of Abundance: Experiences from the extractive industries in Latin America and the Caribbean*, Washington, D.C.: Inter-American Development Bank, pp. 109–42.

Samuels, D. and Snyder, R. (2001) 'The value of a vote: malapportionment in comparative perspective', *British Journal of Political Science* 31(4): 651–671.

Sartori, G. (1969) 'From the Sociology of Politics to Political Sociology', in S. M. Lipset (ed.) *Politics and the Social Sciences*, Oxford: Oxford University Press, pp. 195–214.

Schattschneider, E. (1960) *The Semisovereign People: A realist's view of democracy in America*, New York: Holt, Rinehart and Winston.

Snyder, R. and Samuels, D. (2004) 'Legislative Malapportionment in Latin America', in E. Gibson (ed.) *Federalism and Democracy in Latin America*, Baltimore: The Johns Hopkins University Press, pp. 131–72.

Stepan, A. (2004) 'Toward a New Comparative Politics of Federalism, Multinationalism, and Democracy: Beyond Rikerian Federalism', in E. Gibson (ed.) *Federalism and Democracy in Latin America*, Baltimore: The Johns Hopkins University Press, pp. 29–84.

Tarrow S. (1998) *Power in Movement*, 2nd edn, New York: Cambridge University Press.

Turgeon, M. and Calvacante, P. (2014) 'Desproporcionalidade da Representação dos Estados no Congresso Nacional e Seus Efeitos na Alocação dos Recursos Federais', Texto para Discussão, Brasilia: Instituto de Pesquisa Econômica Aplicada.

Wohlforth, W. (1999) 'The stability of a unipolar world', *International Security* 24(1): 5–41.

Zucco, C. (2008) 'The President's "New Constituency": Lula and the pragmatic vote in Brazil's 2006 elections', *Journal of Latin American Studies* 40(1): 29–49.

*Chapter Six*

# The Forgotten Principle of One Person, One Vote in the Chilean Electoral Map, 1988–2013

*Olivia Montecino Zúñiga and Patricio Navia*

Not all votes count the same in Chile. In fact, depending on the place of residency, the relative weight of each vote can substantially vary. In 2013, the four municipalities that comprise District 29 (D-29, San José de Maipo, Pirque, Puente Alto, La Pintana), in the Santiago Metropolitan Region, had a population of 803,976, while D-19, comprised by the municipalities of Independencia and Recoleta and also located in the Metropolitan Region, had a population of 224,029 persons. Though both districts are located a few miles apart in Santiago, D-29 has 3.6 times the population of D-19. There might historical reasons why districts located in different regions would have drastically different populations, but the high level of malapportionment within the same region, as observed in Chile, is unusual and calls into question the principle of one person, one vote.

In studies on the quality of democracy and strength of institutions, malapportionment can be analysed as an independent or as a dependent variable. If we want to understand the reasons why a country has an electoral map that favours certain regions or population groups, malapportionment will be the dependent variable explained by historical phenomena, geopolitical considerations or uneven changes in population patterns that have taken place after the initial design of the electoral map. However, when we want to understand the effects of malapportionment, the biased design of the electoral map can explain why public resources or subsidies are distributed in a given form.

In what follows, we review the literature on malapportionment both as a dependent and independent variable. After establishing the theoretical framework, we briefly explain how the electoral map in Chile was designed, under military rule, to favour political parties that supported the regime and hinder the electoral chances of opposition parties, grouped in the centre-left Concertación coalition. We then describe the evolution of malapportionment in Chile and associate it to the changes in population trends that have taken place since democracy was restored in 1990. As the electoral map did not change between 1989 and 2013, and as others have already shown in detail how the initial map was designed to favour right-wing parties (Navia and Rojas 2005; Navia 2003; Polga-Hecimovich and Siavelis 2015), we focus on how changes in population trends have altered the initial distortions in the population size of the different electoral districts in Chile. We argue that though the initial map was designed to favour right-wing parties and to lump together larger urban low income areas where the opposition to the military dictatorship was strongest, twenty-four years – and six legislative elections – after the first democratic election, malapportionment tends to favour the centre-left Concertación (renamed Nueva Mayoría in 2013) coalition and low income and low urbanisation municipalities.

### Origins and Effects of Malapportionment

Malapportionment is the discrepancy between the percentage of voters and representatives in the different electoral units of a country (Samuels and Snyder 2001a). An electoral map is malapportioned when the electoral units have a number of seats that is not proportionate to the population of that unit (Monroe 1994). As a result, the vote of some individuals ends up weighting more nationally than the vote of others. Malapportionment gives a higher seat share than their national vote share to parties that win seats in overrepresented districts. Malapportionment is seen as a pathology of electoral systems since it makes some people's vote weigh more than others' (Taagepera and Shugart 1989: 114).

Dahl asserts that one of the necessary requisites of democracy is that the preferences of different people weight the same on the decisions that governments make (Dahl 1971: 2). This condition, popularly known as the principle of 'one person, one vote', has been repeatedly mentioned as an important, and even a sine qua non, condition for the existence of democracy (Rousseau 1976; Nohlen 1998: 21). In Reynolds vs. Sims (377 U.S. 533, 1964), the U.S. Supreme Court unequivocally legitimised the principle by stating that 'an individual's right to vote for state legislators is unconstitutionally impaired when its weight is in a substantial fashion diluted when compared with votes of citizens living in other parts of the State'.

In several bicameral systems, like in the United States, malapportionment is common in one chamber. In many of those cases—but not in the United States—the malapportioned chamber is far less politically and institutionally relevant than the other, better apportioned, chamber (Samuels and Snyder 2001b). In fact, if one chamber is malapportioned, the expectation is that the other chamber will respect the 'one person, one vote' principle (Samuels and Snyder 2001a). As discussed, in many Latin American countries, malapportionment was designed to protect certain politically strategic and less populated regions (Samuels and Snyder 2001a; Navia and Rojas 2005). Yet, there does not seem to be a clear justification for why malapportionment ended up being present in both chambers and systematically would favour the same regions.

According to Samuels and Snyder (2001b), the origins of malapportionment can be found in the historical processes that resulted in the construction of national states. In Latin America, the overrepresentation of rural districts was a useful tool that facilitated the incorporation of landowning elites in nation and state formation in the nineteenth and early twentieth centuries. Malapportionment can be understood as a concession made by urban elites interested in consolidating the state to the landed rural elites. In order to get the landed elites to comply with the new rules, urban elites were willing to overrepresent rural areas in the composition of national congresses. Since most countries in Latin America did not include in their constitutions provisions for the periodic reallocation of seats to reflect population changes, the initial underrepresentation of urban areas further deteriorated as population changes brought more people to urban areas and the share of the national population in urban centres increased. Since the mid-1960s, drastic shifts in population trends that occurred with rapid urbanisation since the 1950s normally worsened the underrepresentation of urban areas. As most countries in Latin America lack automatic mechanisms for reallocation of seats based on changes in population trends, malapportionment has worsened since the third wave of democracy returned electoral politics as the only game in town in the region.

Malapportionment has consequences. It might lead to the rise of clientelism and might block the emergence of programmatically-oriented campaigns especially in overrepresented districts where fewer voters elect as many representatives as large urban centres (Hiroi and Neiva 2013). Malapportionment can also diminish competitiveness in elections and feed geographically-based electoral support, weakening ideologically-based support (Hiroi and Neiva 2013; Samuels and Snyder 2001b). This is particularly damaging to democracy in Latin America, where the malapportioned regions tend to be mainly rural and people in those regions have lower levels of education. In fact, in their study of malapportionment in the Brazilian Senate, Hiroi and Neiva (2013) show that in overrepresented states, senators tend to exercise more control over resources and allocation of services than in underrepresented states, where Senators have more scattered bases of support.

Malapportionment is also associated with income inequality in the long term. Some people who reside in lower income areas migrate to higher income areas in search of employment and opportunities. In Latin America, this has historically been associated with migration from rural to urban areas. As a result, population decreases in lower income areas and increases in higher income areas. When there are no automatic mechanisms to correct malapportionment, lower income areas end up being overrepresented and can exercise pressure to receive favourable treatment from the central government. Thus, income distribution patterns vary, as urban areas end up in a disadvantaged position as they lose weight in the distribution of seats in the legislature (Horiuchi 2004). The case of agricultural subsidies to rural states in the United States would fit this explanation. Yet, in Latin America, there does not seem to be evidence to support the argument that malapportionment favours the underrepresented regions.

Claiming that malapportionment has a negative effect on the quality of democracy in Latin America, Samuels and Snyder (2001a) identify four practical consequences of malapportionment in the region. First, there is an overrepresentation of rural districts – the effect of the old conservative parties effort to limit the electoral strength of the urban working class. Second, there is an estrangement between the executive and legislative, as the former responds to majority rule but the majority in the legislature might represent a national minority. Third, rural and peripheral overrepresented areas have the capacity to hold the underrepresented centre – usually urban – hostage. Fourth, there is the proliferation of subnational authoritarian enclaves, resulting from the excessive power and influence of malapportioned areas. Each of the four consequences undermines the quality of democracy in the region.

Public opinion does not easily realise the existence of malapportionment and its pernicious effects. In elections, people are not easily inclined to notice that the vote of one person in some regions weights more than the vote of another citizen elsewhere. People often focus on other features of electoral systems, but the importance of malapportionment cannot be overstated. Still, because it is not a priority for public opinion, correcting malapportionment is often not at the top of electoral reform demands.

In summary, malapportionment responds to historical variables, it has distributive effects in the present and it remains a problem as it is often overlooked by voters. Because of its distributive consequences, it is essential to understand the effects of malapportionment in the way in which votes are transformed into seats. It is also essential to assess whether the distributive effects that exist today are the same as those that were originally intended by malapportionment. After all, if the initial distributive effects no longer exist and the groups that the original designers sought to benefit with malapportionment are no longer benefitted, the intended effect of malapportionment no longer is effectively materialised. Thus, malapportionment might continue to have distributive consequences, but those consequences are different than those initially intended by those who introduced malapportionment in the design of the electoral map.

In Chile, as we discuss below, the electoral system was malapportioned before the breakdown of democracy in 1973 as it has since the restoration of democracy in 1990. The electoral map put in place in the 1989 election and effective until the 2013 election established malapportionment in both chambers. In fact, when first designed, the electoral map sought to overrepresent right-wing parties (Navia and Rojas 2005). The proportional representation system with an across-the-board two seat district magnitude, known as the binominal system, was also characterised by malapportionment.

We show the way in which malapportionment evolved in the Chamber of Deputies and in the Senate since the first democratic election in 1989 until 2013, the last election under which the original electoral map and electoral system was used. We assess the effect of malapportionment on regional and partisan representation. After showing that it was originally designed to over-represent right-wing parties, we analyse if the changes in population patterns have changed the political distortions caused by the malapportioned electoral districts.

We formally test three hypotheses. Our first hypothesis is that the initial malapportionment in 1988 has not changed across electoral units in the country. We justify the hypothesis on grounds that the initial map was specifically designed to favour right-wing parties using the electoral results of the 1988 plebiscite that brought the Pinochet dictatorship to an end. Though the plan had a short-term objective and the designers of the electoral map could not anticipate future population change patterns and the electoral preferences of different regions, we test the hypothesis of the long term effects of politically-motivated malapportionment design.

Our second hypothesis is that, regardless of how population patterns evolve, malapportionment continues to favour right-wing parties. Since the original designers could not anticipate population change patterns or electoral preferences, there are good reasons to question their ability to design an electoral map that would continue favouring right-wing parties. We analyse whether these parties continue to benefit from malapportioned districts.

Our third hypothesis is that malapportionment has hindered urban areas and areas that have developed more rapidly in recent years (and, thus, have attracted more population). Following Horiuchi (2004), we test to see if malapportionment in Chile has resulted from people leaving rural areas and moving to urban areas where they can have access to a better quality of life. As a result, rural districts will be even more overrepresented than they initially were when the electoral map was drawn in 1988.

In what follows, we first show how the initial map in 1988 was drawn to favour right-wing parties and then we assess, with population data and electoral results, the evolution of malapportionment and the parties that have benefited from the distorted map.

## The history of malapportionment in Chile

Malapportionment existed in Chile before the authoritarian regime (1973–1990). After an effort to correct malapportionment in the 1925 constitution, changes in population patterns and the inflexibility of authorities to modify the electoral map to incorporate those changes, ended up generating a deeply malapportioned map in Chile in the years prior to the 1973 democratic breakdown (Navia 2005).

In the pre-1973 period, the 1938 Electoral Law had established that the Chamber of Deputies would have 147 seats, following constitutional Article 37 that stated that each district would have one seat for every thirty thousand inhabitants and an additional seat for every fraction over fifteeen thousand inhabitants. However, though Article 37 tacitly required that the overall number of seats in the Chamber of Deputies increase together with a population increase, there was no change to the electoral map or the number of districts after the national census conducted in 1940, 1950, 1960 and 1970. In fact, the Chilean legislature systematically ignored the census results and kept the distribution of seats that reflected the population distribution in 1930 (Navia 2005).

In 1968, an electoral reform increased the number of seats in the Chamber of Deputies to 150, by adding one seat and creating an additional two-seat Chamber of Deputies district in the far south of the country. In addition, a new Senate district was created in the same region and assigned five seats (the same number of seats that each of the existing nine districts already had). That reform did not correct malapportionment. In fact, it worsened it, as the new districts were created in the under populated southern region of the country (Navia 2005).

Unlike what Samuels and Snyder (2001a) identify as the pattern for Latin America, malapportionment in Chile is not directly associated with the presence of authoritarian enclaves – at least not those related to the military dictatorship (1973–1990). There was plenty of malapportionment before the breakdown of democracy in 1973. Though, as Navia and Rojas (2005) have shown, the initial design of the electoral map, in place between 1989 and 2017, under military rule sought to overrepresent areas of the country where support for General Pinochet in the 1988 plebiscite had been highest. To be sure, there might have also been a geopolitical justification for overrepresenting the extreme northern and southern regions, but the massive distortions in representation elsewhere in Chile – especially the underrepresentation of Santiago and Concepción – can be explained by the fact that the democratic opposition to the military dictatorship was strongest in those two major urban centres (Navia and Rojas 2005).

In the late 1980s, as the end of authoritarian rule neared, and responding to the changes in the administrative division of the country undertaken under military rule, the Pinochet dictatorship decided to draw a new electoral map for the legislative elections that, according to the 1980 constitution, would take place in 1989. As the military dictatorship also adopted an electoral law that sought to reduce the number of parties in the country – the so-called binominal system, an across-the-board two-seat per district proportional representation system for the Chamber of Deputies and the Senate (Garretón 1990; Navia 2005), the drawing of the new electoral map became a priority. Though the electoral system was adopted before the 1988 plebiscite, the final design of the map was made after the plebiscite. As a result, the dictatorship had perfect knowledge of its support in the different regions of the country (Valenzuela and Siavelis 1991). Thus, since its origin, Chile's electoral map was distorted in favour of rural and more conservative sectors (Navia and Rojas 2005).

Before 1973, as a centralised country, Chile was comprised of twenty-five provinces. Each province was comprised of Departments and these Departments were subdivided into 287 municipalities. Provincial governors were appointed by the president. The military dictatorship rearranged the country into thirteen regions – with each regional *Intendente* also being appointed by the president. Regions were subdivided into fifty-one provinces and provinces were comprised of 335 municipalities. The drastic reorganisation of the territory undertaken by the military rendered the old electoral map based on provincial electoral districts useless. Thus, the military dictatorship decided to draw a brand new electoral map to assign the constitutionally mandated 120 seats in the Chamber of Deputies and the twenty-six elected seats in the Senate (Navia 2005).

Consequently, according to the common legislative procedure under military rule, the president sent a legislative bill to the Military Junta in August of 1988 to define the boundaries of the new electoral map. This bill sought to modify the existing Electoral Law (#18,700, promulgated on 19 April 1988) that established sixty two-seat proportional representation districts for the Chamber of Deputies and confirmed thirteen two-seat proportional representation Senatorial districts (one for each Region). The Electoral Law did not stipulate the boundaries of the sixty districts (Navia and Rojas 2005: 98). Thus, a new law had to be promulgated that established the boundaries for the sixty districts for the Chamber of Deputies.

The President's legislative bill justified the adoption of the two-seat proportional representation system as follows:

> The initiative seeks to establish a majoritarian electoral system that allows the representation, fundamentally, of public opinion dominant views, that has a certain reductive effect on the number of parties, that prevents the repetition of the disastrous electoral and partisan experiences of the past, that offers clarity to voters about the significance and consequences of their votes and that introduces pragmatism in the decisions for the good of the country, fostering moderation in all political actors. For all those reasons, the project establishes a uniform electoral system that is applied simultaneously – in the same elections, since that is what the constitution requires – and that allows for the election of a few deputies in each district, *namely two deputies per district*.

> (Congreso Nacional 1990: 39) (translation and italics are ours)

> Is it indifferent for the country to fall back on the same electoral and partisan situations of the decade before 1973, characterised by an absurd competition that seems to be more extremist? Is it not necessary to overcome ideological excesses and to give way to pragmatism and a better coexistence between different perspectives and viewpoints? Is it not indispensable that the system creates, or at least favours, moderation in political views and promotes, once for all, that the protagonists of Chilean politics be the more moderate positions?

> (Congreso Nacional 1990: 48) (translation and italics are ours)

As Navia and Rojas (2005) indicate, the Technical Report of the legislative bill submitted by the executive to the Military Junta on 11 August 1988 proposed the creation of sixty two-seat districts for the Chamber of Deputies. That way, the constitutional requirement of a 120-seat Chamber of Deputies would be met. The Technical Report also included a proposed electoral map with the boundaries for the sixty districts. One of the criteria for the map was that each of the thirteen regions would have a minimum of two districts (four seats) in the Chamber. The proposed map assigned two districts to the three least populated regions in the far north and the two least populated regions in the far south. The Santiago Metropolitan Region would receive fourteen districts. The other thirty-six districts would be assigned to the remaining regions in central and southern Chile. The underrepresentation of Santiago and, to a lesser extent, the rest of Central Chile was justified on grounds that 'it does not give those regions fewer districts than what they had in the pre-1973 map' (Congreso Nacional 1990: 54). The report did not refer to the fact that the pre-1973 map significantly underrepresented the central region and Santiago. Thus, even if the proposed map was an improvement over the old map, it was still very malapportioned (Navia and Rojas 2005: 98).

The legislative bill with the initial map was sent before the 1988 plebiscite was held and was subsequently modified after the plebiscite. In fact, when the corresponding bill was promulgated – Law 18,799 – the final map only gave each of the southern most regions one district and marginally increased the number of districts for the Metropolitan Region from fourteen to sixteen. The other ten regions kept the original number of seats. Within regions, however, the boundaries of the district changed significantly after the results of the 1988 plebiscite.

The democratic opposition criticised the electoral map as antidemocratic, arbitrary and illegitimate. Gutenberg Martínez, the Secretary General of the Christian Democratic Party (PDC), the largest opposition party, warned that 'we will not tolerate such a blatant imposition of an electoral manipulation aimed at preserving power in the hands of a regime condemned to losing' (El Mercurio, 4 April 1989, p. C9). The opposition's resistance to the electoral map being drafted by the Military Junta was worded on grounds that it violated the principle of one person, one vote. Martínez warned that 'these changes are the result of a coherent or methodological analysis that seeks to assign seats according to the number of voters in the country. On the contrary, they only seek to manipulate the map to give the government a better electoral representation' (in Navia and Rojas 2005: 100).

Ricardo Lagos, the president of the Party for Democracy – a leading member of the centre-left Concertación coalition, together with the PDC – criticised the map because 'it was made in function of the vote distribution of the plebiscite [...] it would be unthinkable in a democratic regime' (Navia and Rojas 2005: 100). Anibal Palma, president of the United Left (a member of the Concertación coalition) argued that the electoral map was a trick by the regime to favour allied parties artificially increasing their chances in areas where they are strongest and reducing the chances of the opposition in areas where the opposition is strongest (Navia and Rojas 2005: 100). The spokesperson for the Communist Party – not a member of the Concertación coalition – José Sanfuentes, criticised it as an antidemocratic electoral system that failed to respect the principle of one person, one vote: 'the map has been distorted by the Pinochet government to favour the far right, particularly the UDI [Independent Democratic Union] and other parties friendly to the government' (Navia and Rojas 2005: 100).

Military government sympathisers argued that any map would be arbitrary and would produce some kind of distortion. Junta Member and Commander of the Air Force Fernando Matthei reckoned that 'God did not draw the districts and thus the map is inevitably arbitrary' (Navia and Rojas 2005: 101). UDI leader Andrés Chadwick, defended the map arguing that legitimate discrepancies could exist about the most appropriate district boundaries but that the map 'sought to balance representation with regards to the number of voters and regional representation, which has been one of the priorities of the government' (El Mercurio, 13 April 1989, p. C4). Renovacion Nacional (RN) leader Fernando Maturana, defended the map claiming that criticisms were coming from candidates who did not like the shape of the districts they would have to run in (Navia and Rojas 2005: 101).

Yet, even supporters of the new electoral map acknowledged the existence of distortions. General Matthei acknowledged problems by stating that 'there are justified criticisms. But regardless of the shape of the map, there will be justified criticisms. We tried to do our best. It is difficult to achieve perfect proportionality. In other cases, the distortions are intentional. There are unquestionable electoral interests involved. We have also tried to underrepresent Santiago and to overrepresent the provinces to prevent that Santiago dominates the rest of the country. Many considerations were at play' (*El Mercurio*, 5 April 1989, p. A10).

A 16 April 1989 article in *El Mercurio* – the most influential newspaper in the country and a staunch conservative supporter of military rule – defended the electoral system and the map claiming that:

> the binominal system is a majoritarian system used, with some variations, in Great Britain, in the most developed members of the British Commonwealth, in the United States and [West] Germany, countries that have achieved stability based on large political currents. But in Chile, the opposition claims that we have a different reality: multipartism.

*El Mercurio* went on to warn that 'the doubt that remains out there is that whether a piece of legislation that fosters bipartisanship can modify the reality'. *El Mercurio* anticipated a distortion in favour of parties friendly to the regime:

> by simulating results based on the 1988 plebiscite, it is clear that the binominal system produces a seat allocation similar to the national vote. That is, globally, the No vote, which failed to get more than 66% of the vote, does not get more than 50% of the seats, while the Yes vote, which received more than 34% of the vote, gets the other 50% of the seats.

To justify the distortion, *El Mercurio* reckoned that,

> the way districts were drawn allows this reality to be reflected in each of them […] if the 5 October plebiscite results are reproduced, the Chamber of Deputies would be equally divided between the two political camps, each getting one seat in every district.

The anticipated distortion in the map led the Concertación to oppose the system and the map, but as *El Mercurio* reported,

> the Concertación, despite its criticism, announced that it would accept the law but that it would replace it with a proportional system when it wins office. Yet, that will depend on the composition of Congress, which will be partially determined by this new law.

(*El Mercurio*, 16 April 1989)

Since the results of the 1988 plebiscite triggered the transition to democracy – as the popular rejection of a new eight-term for Pinochet as president opened the way for democratic elections in late 1989 – the need to establish a new electoral map for the sixty districts for the Chamber of Deputies became urgent. The demand from democratic opposition parties to modify the authoritarian constitution also put pressure on the outgoing military government's legislative work. In mid-1989, the Pinochet government proposed a series of constitutional reforms and convened a referendum in late July for the popular ratification of the reforms. Though the opposition demanded more and deeper reforms, the Concertación coalition acquiesced to the reforms and called on voters to vote 'yes' on the referendum (Heiss and Navia 2007). Among the several reforms adopted, the number of seats in the Senate was increased from twenty-six elected senators to thirty-eight. That would require the creation of six new two-seat senatorial districts in the country. Since the original map for the Senate districts was based on the regional division of the country, the constitutional reform forced the government to divide existing regions into more than one senatorial district. New districts were created in the six most populous regions. The new composition of the Senate and the need to establish a new map for the composition of the Chamber of Deputies districts forced the military government to rush legislation to have the new system in place by mid-1989, before the deadline for candidate registration for the presidential and legislative elections scheduled for December of 1989.

## Malapportionment after 1990

How have the initial distortions evolved since the electoral map came into existence in the 1989 elections? After twenty-four years of democratic elections, is the map still favourable for right-wing parties that were the main supporters of the Pinochet dictatorship?

As Figure 6.1 shows, the districts from the far northern and southern regions of the country were severely overrepresented while the districts in the largest metropolitan areas were underrepresented. Districts in the Santiago Metropolitan Region were much bigger than districts elsewhere in the country, especially those in the far north and far south. For example, District 27 (El Bosque, La Cisterna and San Ramón), an urban lower class district in Santiago, had 5.3 times the population of District 59 (that comprised the entire Region of Aysén). Out of the sixty districts, thirty-five were over represented. In Santiago, out of the sixteen districts, fifteen were underrepresented. The heavy distortion against Santiago resulted from a concerted effort to underrepresent the capital city. Either because the government was interested in overrepresenting the provinces – as the official argument indicated – or because the government wanted to reduce the electoral power of the most important stronghold of the opposition, the new map overrepresented the extreme regions to the detriment of the Santiago Metropolitan Region.

By 2012, malapportionment had worsened. The most populous district in the country was D-29 (Puente Alto, La Pintana, Pirque, San José de Maipo), a lower class district in Santiago. D-29 had 8.1 times the population of the least populated district in Aysén (D-59). Since the map guarantees one district to each region, the least populous regions will inevitably always be overrepresented. Overtime, malapportionment worsened as the urban centres grew more rapidly than the least populated far away regions. Inter-regional malapportionment will continue to worsen if the urban population continues to grow faster than the population in the far away regions.

Yet, malapportionment also exists within regions. Thus, the argument that some far away regions explain malapportionment is not correct. Within the Santiago Metropolitan Region, the most populated district in 1988 was D-18 (Cerro Navia, Lo Prado and Quinta Normal). D-18 had 2.2 times the population of the least populous district in Santiago (District 22, downtown Santiago). The underrepresentation of some districts within the same region could not be explained by the official argument in favour of overrepresenting faraway regions. Because D-22 was among the highest income districts in Santiago – while D-18 was among the poorest districts and it also represented an opposition stronghold – the more plausible explanation for malapportionment within Santiago seems related to the intention of underrepresenting those districts where the opposition was strongest.

In 2012, the most populated district in the Metropolitan Region was D-29, with 3.6 times the population of the least populated district (D-19). The two districts are located a few miles apart in the capital city. The drastically different population of both districts clearly violates the principle of one person, one vote, as both districts elect the same number of representatives to the Chamber of Deputies.

Figures 6.1 and 6.2 show the malapportionment level in the sixty districts in the country in 1988 and 2012, ordered geographically (from north to south). The two figures show very clearly how malapportionment has worsened overtime. The differences between the most populated and least populated districts have drastically increased, between regions and within regions. In 1988, the most underrepresented districts had about two times the ideal population if the country had been divided into sixty districts with the same population in each. In 2012, the most underrepresented districts had more than three times the population they ought to have if each district had the same population. All the most underrepresented districts are located in the Metropolitan Region of Santiago (D-29, D-20 and D-16) and they all correspond to low middle-class areas.

In 1988, there were thirty-five overrepresented districts. That number increased to forty-four in 2012. That means that the underrepresentation of districts is now more heavily concentrated in a few largely underrepresented territories. Thirteen of the sixteen underrepresented districts in 2012 are located in the Santiago region. The most overrepresented districts continue to be in the far northern and far southern areas of the country, but some of the most overrepresented districts are now also located in the agricultural regions south of Santiago (Maule and Araucanía).

Malapportionment also exists in the electoral map for the Senate, as shown in Figures 6.3 and 6.4. In fact, malapportionment in Senatorial districts is far worse than in the Chamber of Deputies. Because the population of the country is heavily concentrated in the capital city of Santiago (Santiago Metropolitan Region) and

*Figure 6.1: Malapportionment by Chamber of Deputies districts in Chile, 1988*

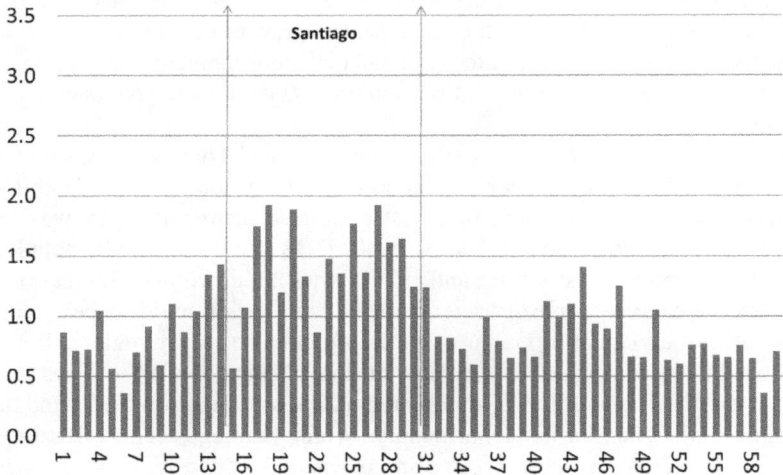

*Figure 6.2: Malapportionment by Chamber of Deputies districts in Chile, 2012*

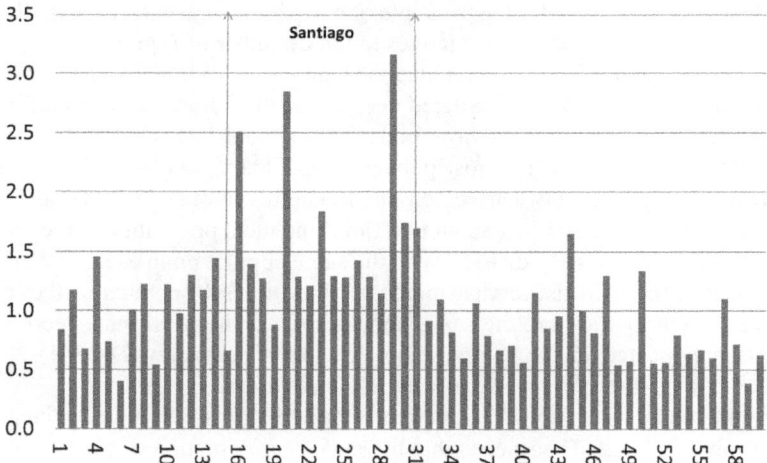

*Source:* Authors with data from www.elecciones.gov.cl (accessed 14 December 2014) and National Statistics Institute

that region only has two senatorial districts – as discussed, the 1989 constitutional reform increased the number of seats in the Senate and allowed for the division of the largest regions into two senatorial districts each – the population in the capital is severely underrepresented in the Senate. The two senatorial districts in Santiago (senatorial districts 7 and 8) were already the most radically affected by malapportionment in 1988. The senatorial districts in the far north and far south of the country were the most benefited by malapportionment. In 1988, only five of the nineteen senatorial districts had more population than they should have had if each district would have received the same number of people. Although there are historical and political reasons to justify the overrepresentation of faraway and underpopulated – and geopolitically strategic – regions, in the case of the Chilean Senate, the cost for the overrepresentation of the faraway regions is borne by the capital city.

*Figure 6.3: Malapportionment in senatorial districts in Chile, 1988*

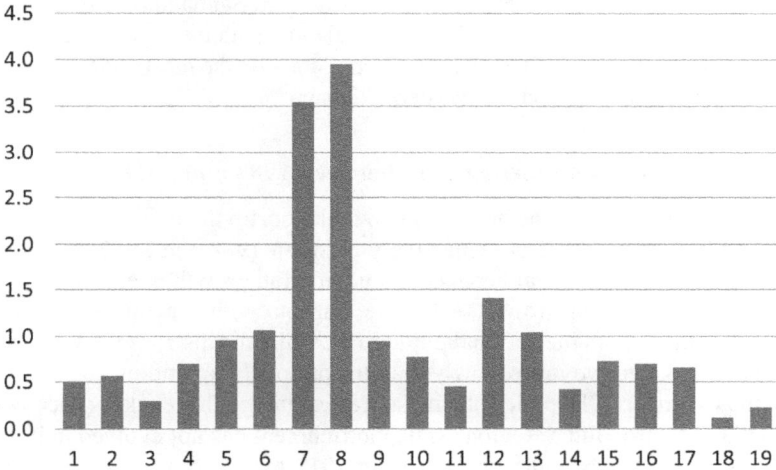

*Figure 6.4: Malapportionment in senatorial districts in Chile, 2012*

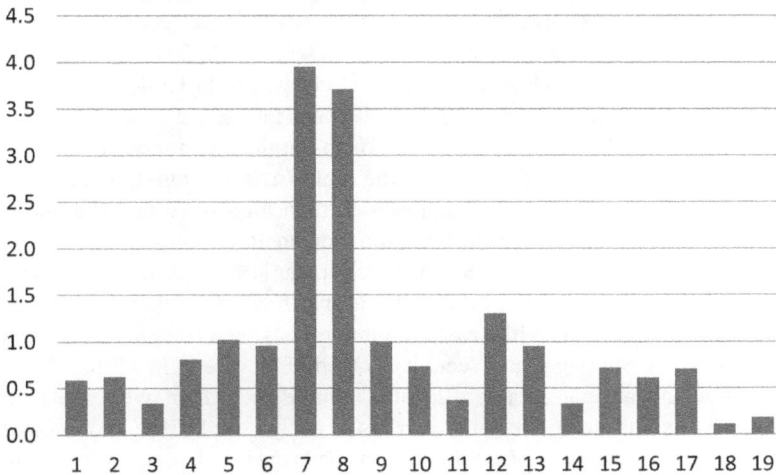

*Source:* Authors with data from www.elecciones.gov.cl (accessed 14 December 2014) and National Statistics Institute

As Figure 6.4 shows, malapportionment in the Senate did not worsen significantly between 1988 and 2012. Unlike what is observed for Chamber of Deputies districts – where malapportionment worsened – in senatorial districts, the level of malapportionment remained very stable between regions. As Santiago has grown marginally faster than the rest of the country, the number of underrepresented senatorial districts decreased from five in 1988 to only three in 2012. Yet, the two districts that are no longer underrepresented are now barely overrepresented.

Figure 6.4 does show a difference within Santiago in terms of overrepresentation. In 1988, the senatorial district that represents eastern Santiago was more underrepresented than the senatorial district in western Santiago (where the lowest income municipalities are located). As population patterns have shifted, since western Santiago has grown faster than eastern Santiago, the most underrepresented senatorial district in Chile today is western Santiago.

## The evolution of malapportionment between 1988 and 2012

Figures 6.5 and 6.6 show the net change in malapportionment in the Chamber of Deputies and Senate districts respectively between 1988 and 2012. Figures 6.5 and 6.6 show the differential between the population growth in each district and the national population growth. All those districts with a positive differential have grown faster than the national population, while the districts with a negative differential have grown more slowly than the national population.

In the Chamber of Deputies, the most drastic changes have taken place within the Santiago Metropolitan Region. Malapportionment has not evolved uniformly. Some districts are less underrepresented in 2012 than they were in 1988 while the underrepresentation has worsened in other districts. In D-16, D-20 and D-29, malapportionment has worsened significantly, as the population in those districts has grown far more rapidly than the population elsewhere in Santiago and elsewhere in the country. In other districts (D-17, D-18, D-19, D-25, D-27 and D-28), population growth has lagged behind elsewhere in Chile and thus those districts were less underrepresented in 2012 than they were when the map was initially drawn in 1988. As a result, even though Santiago continues to be the most underrepresented region in the country, the reality within Santiago has varied as some districts are now less underrepresented than they were in 1988 and other districts have seen their underrepresentation worsened.

In the Senate, malapportionment has varied far less than in the Chamber of Deputies. Again, the two senatorial districts that have been mostly affected are those located in Santiago. While eastern Santiago has seen its underrepresentation decline, western Santiago has seen it worsen. Elsewhere in Chile, Northern districts – where mining areas are located – have seen their overrepresentation decline, while southern agricultural districts in centre-south Chile have seen their overrepresentation increase. Since the population in those regions grew more slowly than the population elsewhere in Chile, they are becoming more overrepresented. In the far south regions of the country, the level of overrepresentation has not varied.

*Figure 6.5: Change in district-based malapportionment in the Chamber of Deputies between 1988 and 2012*

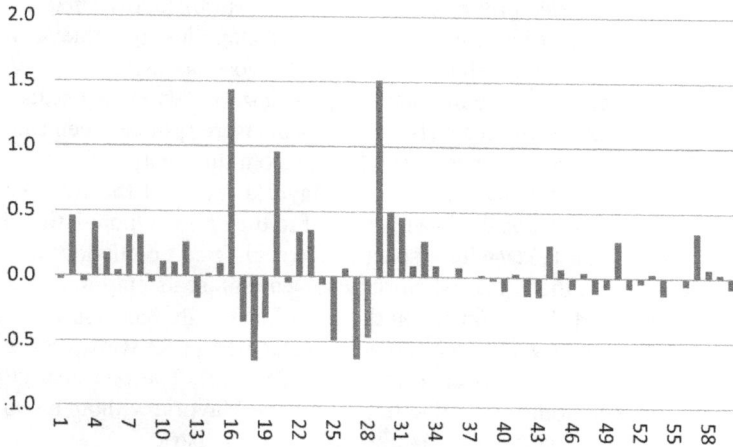

*Figure 6.6: Change in district-based malapportionment in the Senate between 1988 and 2012*

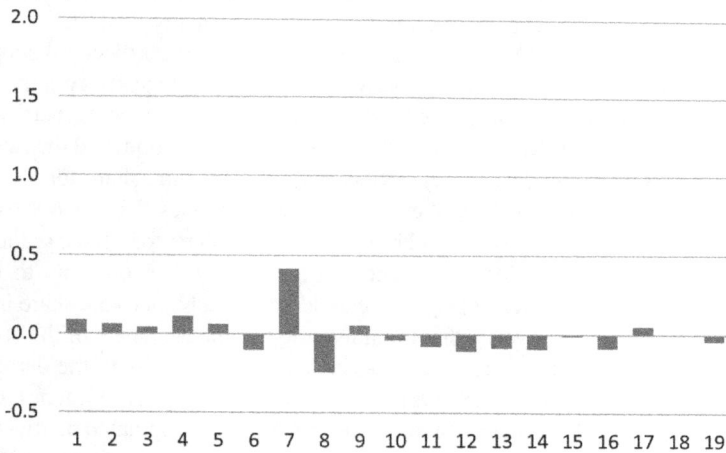

*Source:* Authors with data from www.elecciones.gov.cl (accessed 15 December 2014) and National Statistics Institute

## The effect of malapportionment in the Chamber of Deputies

When initially drawn, the map for the Chamber of Deputies districts sought to favour right-wing parties that were sympathetic to the outgoing Pinochet dictatorship. As time went by, population patterns changed and the electoral preferences of different regions and sectors evolved, the initial distortion in favour of right-wing parties declined. In fact, in the 2013 legislative election – the last election when the initial map will have been used – the centre-left coalition Nueva Mayoría – formerly known as Concertación – seemed to have benefitted from the distortions of the electoral map more than the centre-right Alianza coalition. In nine of the sixty districts for the Chamber of Deputies, the Nueva Mayoría received a high enough vote share to secure the two seats assigned (leaving the Alianza with no seats in those districts). The Alianza received two seats in only one district. In the other fifty districts, the two seats were split between candidates from the Nueva Mayoría, Alianza or candidates from third parties.

In the nine districts where the Nueva Mayoría received the two seats, the malapportionment level was 0.94 (with respect to the national population divided by sixty districts) and 0.71 (with respect to the registered population divided by sixty districts). Thus, the Nueva Mayoría received both seats only in districts that were overrepresented. The Alianza, on the other hand, only received two seats in one district (D-23) that was severely underrepresented (1.83 with respect to the population and 1.35 with respect to the eligible voters). The one district where the Alianza obtained both seats – and left the Nueva Mayoría without a seat – had twice the average population for Chamber of Deputies districts.

In the Senate in 2013, Nueva Mayoría gained both seats in two of the ten senatorial districts up for the election. The average malapportionment in those districts was 0.98 (with regards to the national population) and 0.68 (with respect to eligible voters). The Alianza did not gain both seats in any district.

To verify if the Nueva Mayoría (Concertación) has stronger electoral support in less populated districts, Figure 6.7 shows a scatterplot with the district population on the horizontal axis and the vote share for the centre-left coalition on the vertical axis. It is clear that the Nueva Mayoría vote share is higher in less populated districts. The slope of the curve shows that as population increases, the vote share for the Nueva Mayoría candidates for the Chamber of Deputies decreases. Figure 6.8 shows a scatterplot with the district level population and the vote share for Alianza candidates for the Chamber of Deputies. The slope in Figure 6.8 is the opposite to that in Figure 6.7. Alianza Chamber of Deputies candidates got a higher vote share in more populous districts. Thus, even if the initial intention of the designers of the electoral map was to group together larger populations that were friendly to the democratic centre-left opposition into fewer districts, the effect of malapportionment has been reversed. The centre-left Nueva Mayoría does better in less populated districts today while the Alianza tends to do better in more populous districts. Malapportionment in 2013 was more favourable to the Nueva Mayoría than to the centre-right Alianza.

## The effects of malapportionment in the Senate

As Figures 6.9 and 6.10 show, the effect of malapportionment on Senatorial districts is not as pronounced as in districts for the Chamber of Deputies. For the Concertación-Nueva Mayoría, the population of a senatorial district does not seem to have an effect on its vote share, as shown in Figure 6.9. The vote for Concertación senatorial candidates does vary depending on the population in each senatorial district. However, when we exclude the two largest senatorial districts

*Figure 6.7: District population and Concertación vote share, 2013*

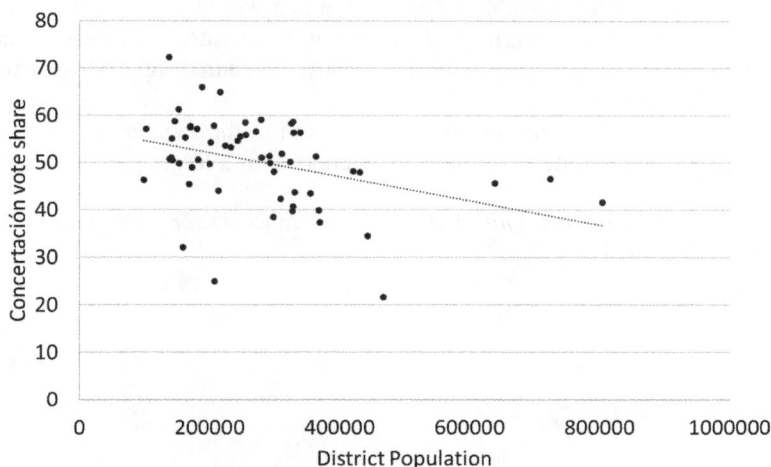

*Figure 6.8: District population and Alianza vote share, 2013*

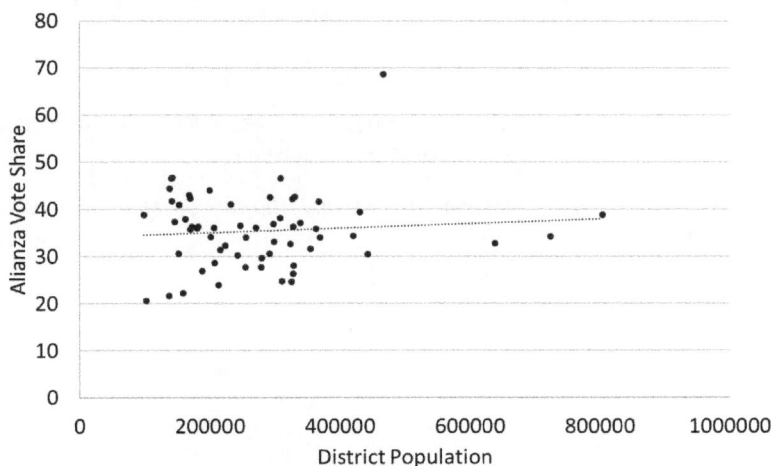

*Source:* Authors with data from www.elecciones.gov.cl (accessed 14 December 2014) and National Statistics Institute

in the country – located in the Santiago Metropolitan Region – there does seem to be a slight positive correlation between the population in each district and the vote share for the centre-left coalition. In regions other than Santiago, the Nueva Mayoría does better in more populous districts.

For the Alianza, as shown in Figure 6.10, there is a positive correlation between the population in senatorial districts and the vote share for that coalition. The more populous the senatorial district, the higher the vote share for the Alianza. Since the expectation is that the Alianza should do better in less populated districts – as the military dictatorship sought to draw a map that would be beneficial to right-wing parties, the evidence from Figure 6.10 shows that, after twenty-four years of democratic elections, malapportionment no longer favoured right-wing parties in senatorial elections in Chile.

Both in the Chamber of Deputies districts and in the senatorial districts, the Alianza had a higher vote share in 2013 in areas with a larger population. If the

*Figure 6.9: Population in senatorial districts and Concertación vote share in Senate elections, 2009–2013*

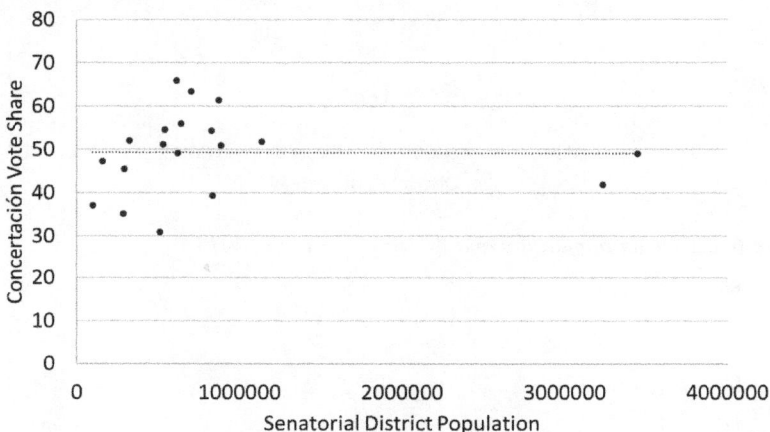

*Figure 6.10: Population in senatorial districts and Alianza vote share in Senate elections, 2009–2013*

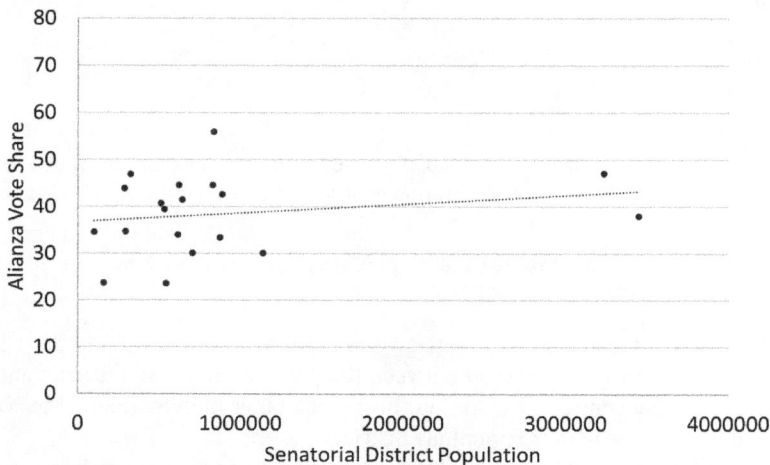

*Source:* Authors with data from www.elecciones.gov.cl (accessed 14 December 2014) and National Statistics Institute

initial intention of the military regime was to introduce malapportionment to favour right-wing parties, the longterm effects of a malapportioned map were no longer favourable to parties that were friendly to the government that first drew the electoral map.

## Socio-demographic conditions and malapportionment

Since the military dictatorship sought to group lower income areas into larger districts, the effect of malapportionment on the way votes are transformed into seats for the Nueva Mayoría and Alianza might be indirect. That is, if the way in which districts were drawn responded to the socio-economic composition of districts, then the effect on the Nueva Mayoría and Alianza will depend on the materialisation of the assumption that the centre-left coalition generates more support in urban low income areas while the centre-right coalition draws support from rural areas and higher income urban areas. If those electoral patterns were to change and the Alianza were to start drawing stronger support from low income urban areas, then the initial malapportionment would no longer be beneficial to the Alianza.

Figures 6.11 and 6.12 plot the relationship between district-level poverty and vote share for the Concertación and Alianza. As Figure 6.11 shows, the vote share for the Concertación/Nueva Mayoría increases as poverty increases. However, the vote share for the Alianza does not vary by poverty levels. The Alianza gets a similar vote share regardless of the poverty levels in each district.

We now move on to assess if there is a positive relationship between poverty levels and malapportionment. If the initial intent was to underrepresent areas where the Concertación was strongest and the Concertación drew more support in higher poverty areas, we must assess if higher poverty areas are still underrepresented in the electoral map today, twenty-four years after the map was introduced. Figures 6.13 and 6.14 show two scatterplots with poverty levels on the horizontal axis and malapportionment levels on the vertical axis – Figure 6.13 uses census data population numbers while Figure 6.14 uses the number of registered voters in every district. Both scatterplots show similar slopes. As poverty increases, malapportionment decreases. Districts with lower poverty levels tend to be underrepresented in 2013. That would mean that even if the initial objective was to underrepresent high poverty level areas where the centre-left coalition was strongest, after more than two decades since the map was first drawn, changes in population patterns and the asymmetrical growth experienced by the different regions of the country have altered the underrepresentation of impoverished areas. As urban areas have developed more and poverty levels are higher in rural areas, the most underrepresented districts now have lower levels of poverty than the more overrepresented districts.

Finally, we present evidence on the relationship between malapportionment and electoral support for the two leading coalitions, the centre-left Concertación/Nueva Mayoría and the conservative Alianza. Figure 6.15 shows a scatterplot with the level of malapportionment in every district and the vote share for the Concertación

*Figure 6.11: Poverty and Concertación vote share in Chamber of Deputies districts, 2013*

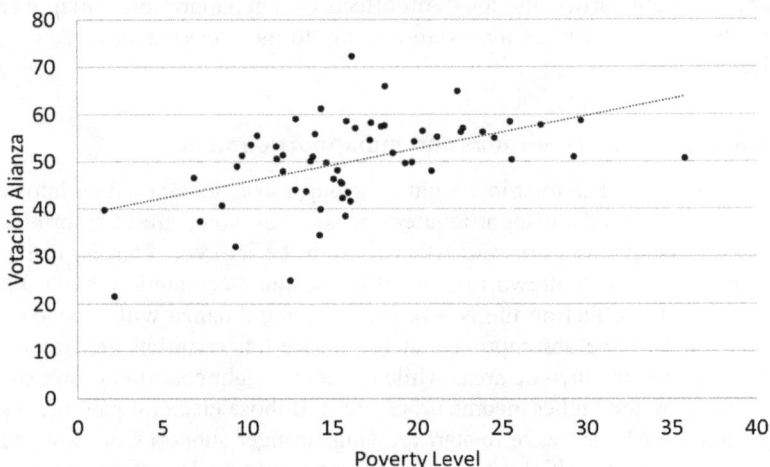

*Figure 6.12: Poverty and Alianza vote share in Chamber of Deputies districts, 2013*

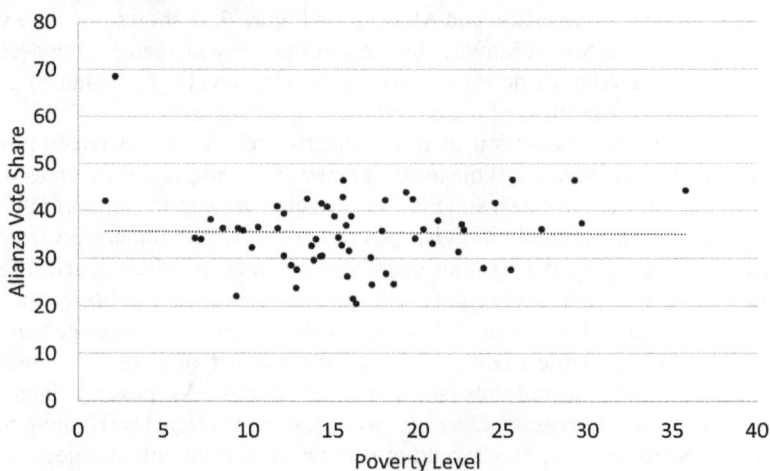

*Source:* Authors with data from www.elecciones.gov.cl (accessed 14 December 2014) and National Statistics Institute

in 1989. There was a weak positive correlation between malapportionment and electoral support for the Concertación. The centre-left coalition did slightly better in districts that were more underrepresented. Figure 6.16 shows the relationship between malapportionment and electoral support for the Concertación/Nueva Mayoría in 2013. Twenty-four years later, the slope has reversed. The centre-left coalition does better in districts that are overrepresented. If the initial intent of the designers of the electoral map was to hinder the Concertación by grouping

*Figure 6.13: Poverty level and malapportionment, Chamber of Deputies districts, 2013*

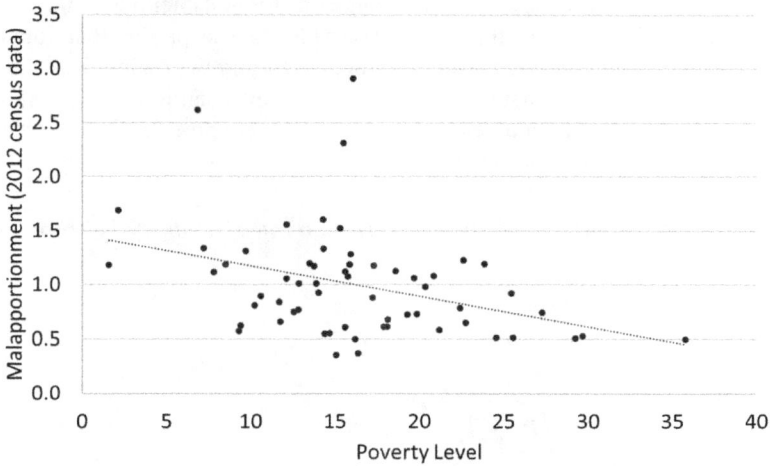

*Figure 6.14: Poverty level and malapportionment (based on number of voters in each district), 2013*

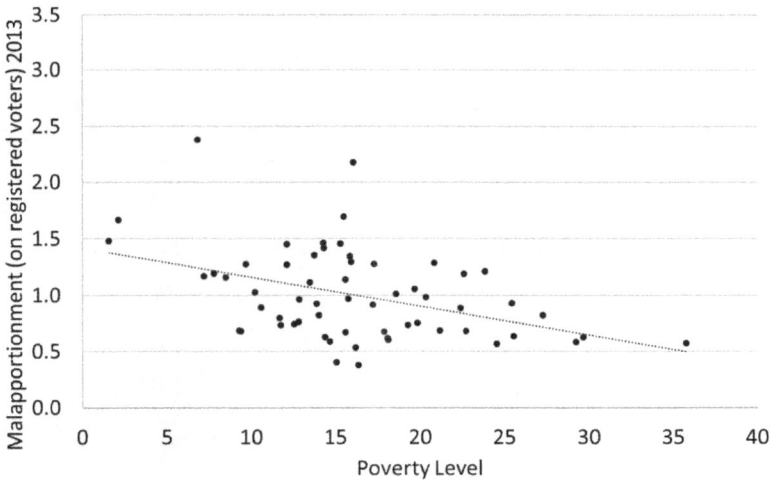

*Source:* Authors with data from www.elecciones.gov.cl (accessed 14 December 2014) and National Statistics Institute

centre-left electoral strongholds into bigger districts, the long term effect of that biased design has been reversed as the centre-left coalition now does better in districts that are overrepresented.

Figures 6.17 and 6.18 show the relationship between malapportionment and the Alianza vote share in Chamber of Deputies districts in 1989 and 2013 respectively.

In 1989, there was no noticeable relationship between malapportionment and the vote share for the right-wing coalition. Though the original intention of the military regime was to draw a map that was favourable for the parties that supported the dictatorship, the contrast between Figures 6.15 and 6.17 show that the map hindered the way in which support for the centre-left coalition was transformed into more votes rather than aided the way in which support for the conservative coalition was transformed into votes.

*Figure 6.15: Malapportionment and Concertación vote share in Chamber of Deputies election, 1989*

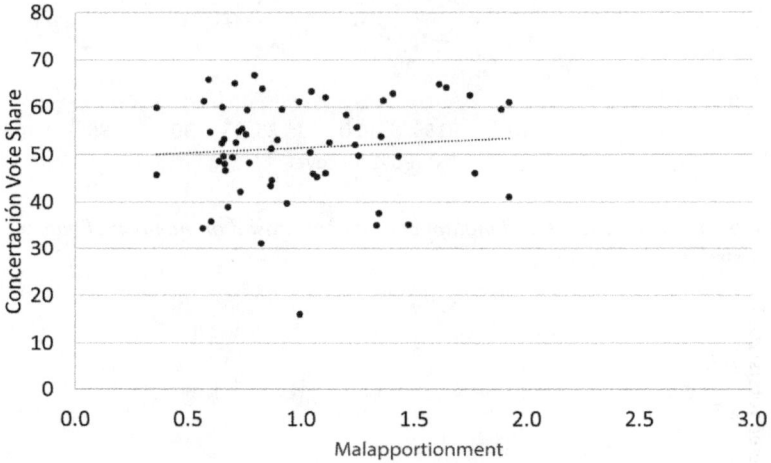

*Figure 6.16: Malapportionment and Concertación vote share in Chamber of Deputies election, 2013*

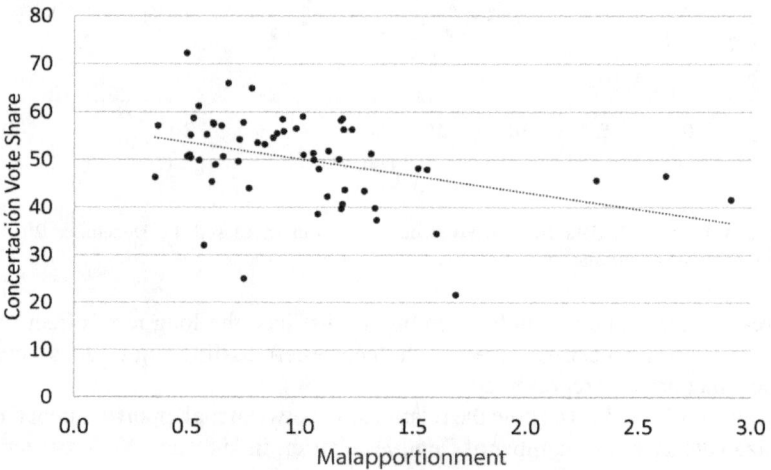

*Figure 6.17: Malapportionment and Alianza vote share in Chamber of Deputies election, 1989*

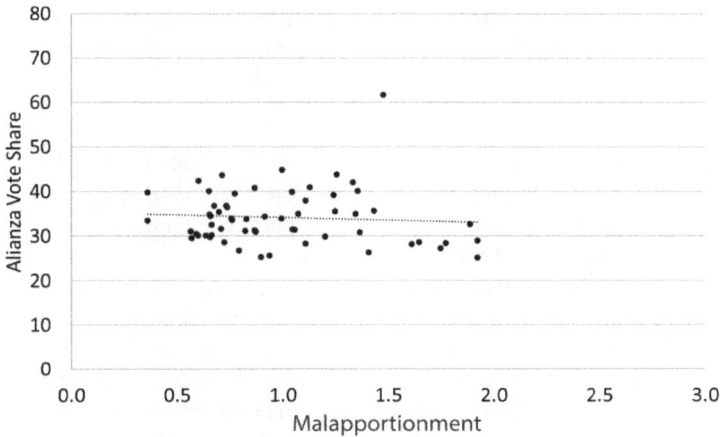

*Figure 6.18: Malapportionment and Alianza vote share in Chamber of Deputies election, 2013*

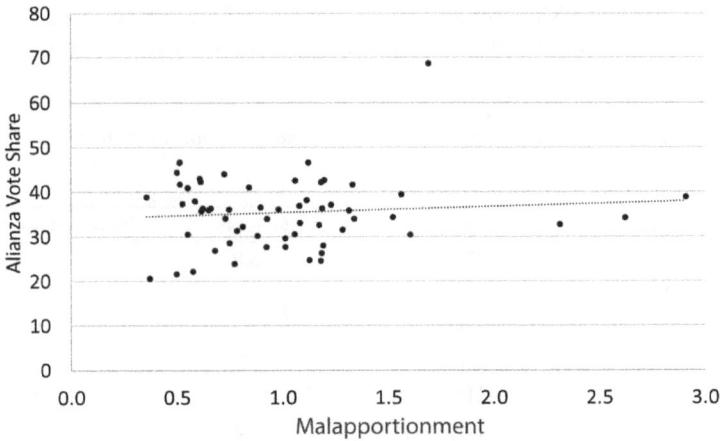

*Source:* Authors with data from www.elecciones.gov.cl (accessed 14 December 2014) and National Statistics Institute

Figure 6.18 shows the relationship between malapportionment and the vote share for the Alianza coalition in the 2013 legislative election. Here the relationship between malapportionment and support for conservative candidates is positive. The Alianza coalition does electorally better in districts that are underrepresented. Thus, the long term consequences of the biased design of the electoral map ended up being negative for the parties that were the initial intended beneficiaries of malapportionment.

## Malapportionment and support for political parties in 2013

The most common way of assessing malapportionment is a formula (MAL) that subtracts the vote share from the seat share received by each party (Samuels and Snyder 2001b). The sum of that subtraction is then divided by two. Formally, the formula is:

$$MAL= \tfrac{1}{2} \Sigma \, (s_i - v_i)$$

Where the value s stands for the share of seats and v stands for the share of votes for party i. Thus, when a party gets a higher vote share than its seat share, MAL will have a negative value. In cases where the parties get a higher seat share than its vote share, MAL will have a positive value.

Table 6.1 shows the national level malapportionment in the Chamber of Deputies election in 2013 for the most important parties that comprise the Alianza and Nueva Mayoría coalitions. Both coalitions had a positive MAL – that is, they both got a higher seat share than their vote share. The electoral system in place – with sixty districts that elect two deputies each – heavily punishes smaller coalitions and independent candidates. Since the threshold to win the first seat is fairly high, the system ends up rewarding the largest coalitions. Coalitions and candidates outside the Alianza and Nueva Mayoría received a combined vote share of 16.1%, but they only obtained 3.4 per cent of the seats in the Chamber of Deputies.

Within the Nueva Mayoría, all parties had a slightly higher seat share than their vote share, but no party benefited significantly more than others. In the Alianza,

*Table 6.1: Political party malapportionment at the national level in the Chamber of Deputies, 2013*

| Party/coalition | % votes | % seats | National level MAL |
|---|---|---|---|
| **Nueva Mayoría (Concertación)** | **47.7** | **55.8** | **4.1** |
| PDC | 15.6 | 17.5 | 1.0 |
| PRSD | 3.6 | 5.0 | 1.7 |
| PPD | 11.0 | 12.5 | 0.8 |
| PS | 11.1 | 12.5 | 0.7 |
| PC | 4.1 | 5.0 | 0.5 |
| Others | 2.3 | 3.3 | 0.5 |
| **Alianza** | **36.2** | **40.8** | **2.3** |
| RN | 14.9 | 15.8 | 0.9 |
| UDI | 19.0 | 24.2 | 2.6 |
| Others | 2.4 | 0.8 | –0.8 |
| **Others** | **16.1** | **3.4** | **–6.4** |
| **Total** | **100** | **100** | **0** |

Source: authors with data from the Electoral Service.

both RN and UDI benefited as well, but UDI benefited more as its 19 per cent vote share turned into a 24.2 per cent seat share in the Chamber of Deputies. In that respect, if the initial intention of the designers of the electoral system in place in Chile was to benefit right-wing parties, the long term effect of the design continues to be beneficial to the most conservative party in the country. To be sure, the distortion in favour of UDI results both from the electoral map and from the district magnitude that makes it easier for a coalition to secure half of the seats with only one-third of the votes. But the combined effect of district magnitude and the electoral map continue to benefit the party that was most closely associated with the Pinochet military regime.

Finally, Table 6.2 shows party-level malapportionment at the district level for the Chamber of Deputies in 2013. Unlike Table 6.1 that shows the distortion between vote shares and seat shares at the national level, Table 6.2 shows the district level distortion by averaging the distortions in the sixty districts for the Chamber of Deputies. The parties that comprise the Alianza and Nueva Mayoría coalitions are benefited by the effect of the low district magnitude of two seats per district that punishes independent candidates and candidates from smaller parties.

In addition, the effect of malapportionment is also noticeable. When comparing the average vote share and the average seat share for each party in all the districts where the party had a candidate, UDI is again the party that benefits the most from malapportionment. The fifty-six UDI candidates averaged 18.5 per cent of the votes in the districts where they competed, but UDI received 24.2 per cent of the

Table 6.2: Political party malapportionment at the district level in the Chamber of Deputies, 2013

| Party | # candidates | % Votes (average for all districts) | % seats in the Chamber | MAL district level average |
|---|---|---|---|---|
| **Nueva Mayoría** | | | | |
| PDC | 38 | 16.1 | 17.5 | 0.7 |
| PRSD | 12 | 4.2 | 5.0 | 0.4 |
| PPD | 25 | 11.0 | 12.5 | 0.8 |
| PS | 24 | 11.2 | 12.5 | 0.7 |
| PC | 8 | 4.1 | 5.0 | 0.5 |
| Others (NM) | 11 | 2.8 | 3.3 | 0.2 |
| **Alianza** | | | | |
| RN | 51 | 14.5 | 15.8 | 0.7 |
| UDI | 56 | 18.6 | 24.2 | 2.8 |
| Others Alianza | 13 | 2.3 | 0.8 | −0.7 |
| **Other candidates** | 232 | 15.4 | 3.3 | −6.0 |
| Total | 470 | 100 | 100 | 0.0 |

Source: authors with data from the Electoral Service.

seats in the Chamber of Deputies. With a MAL of 2.8, UDI was the party that most benefited from malapportionment in 2013 in Chile.

All other Concertación/Nueva Mayoría and Alianza parties also had positive values for the MAL index, meaning that they all had a higher seat share than their vote share. Since the MAL index includes the distortions caused by the electoral system and the electoral map, it does not solely reflect how the over and underrepresentation of different districts affects the way in which votes are transformed into seats.

## Conclusion

Since its adoption, the electoral system in Chile has been identified as a successful case of electoral engineering. The electoral designers in the authoritarian government sought to adopt a system that would favour right-wing parties by preventing the left-wing Concertación coalition from transforming its electoral majority into a commanding majority of seats in Congress. Although there is plenty of evidence that shows that the choice of creating sixty Chamber of Deputies districts and nineteen senatorial districts with two seats each and the use of proportional representation to assign the seats proved beneficial to help the Alianza coalition secure a larger seat share than its vote share (though the Concertación coalition also benefited by getting a higher seat share than its vote share), the drawing of the electoral map as a tool to distort electoral preferences in favour of right-wing parties has been mostly overlooked.

The sixty Chamber of Deputies districts and the nineteen senatorial districts bluntly violate the principle of one person, one vote. The electoral map was designed by the outgoing dictatorship to make it difficult for the centre-left coalition to transform its electoral majority into a seat majority in the Chilean Congress by grouping large strongholds of the Concertación into fewer, more populous districts and by creating less populated districts in regions where support for Pinochet and for right-wing parties was strongest.

The electoral map proved useful to help the right-wing Alianza coalition get a higher seat share than its vote share in the 1989 election. However, twenty-four years and six legislative elections later, given the changes in population patterns in the country and given the changes in the electoral preferences in under and overrepresented districts, the distortions produced by the malapportioned electoral map are no longer favourable to right-wing parties. Even though right-wing parties continue to benefit from the distortions caused by the two-seat binominal electoral system that makes it difficult for the coalition with the most votes to transform its electoral support into a commanding majority of seats, the electoral map is no longer beneficial to right-wing parties. In fact, the centre-left Nueva Mayoria (formerly Concertación) coalition gets its highest vote share in overrepresented districts while the Alianza coalition gets its highest vote share in underrepresented districts.

## References

Congreso Nacional (1990) *Historia de la Ley 18799: Folio 1–367*, Santiago: Biblioteca del Congreso.

Dahl, R. (1971) *Polyarchy: Participation and opposition*, New Haven: Yale University Press.

Garretón, M. (1990) 'Las condiciones sociopolíticas de la inauguración democrática en Chile', *Documento de Trabajo FLACSO* 444.

Heiss, C. and Navia, P. (2007) 'You win some, you lose some: constitutional reforms in Chile's transition to democracy', *Latin American Politics and Society* 49(3): 163–190.

Hiroi, T. and Neiva, P. (2013) 'Malapportionment and geographical bases of electoral support in the Brazilian Senate', *Journal of Politics in Latin America* 5(1): 127–150.

Horiuchi, Y. (2004) 'Malapportionment and income inequality: a cross-national analysis', *British Journal of Political Science* 34(1):179–183.

Monroe, B. (1994) 'Disproportionality and malapportionment: measuring electoral inequity', *Electoral Studies* 13(2):132–149.

Navia, P. (2003) 'You select the rules of the game and lose? Advantages and constraints when choosing electoral rules: the case of Chile', Ph.D. Dissertation, New York University.

—— (2005) 'Transformando votos en escaños: leyes electorales en Chile, 1833–2003', *Política y Gobierno* 12(2): 233–276.

Navia, P. and Rojas, P. (2005) 'Representación y tamaño de los distritos electorales en Chile, 1988–2002', *Revista de Ciencia Política* 25(2): 91–116.

Nohlen, D. (1998) 'Sistemas electorales y partidos políticos', Mexico DF: Fondo de Cultura Económica.

Polga-Hecimovich, J. and Siavelis, P. (2015) 'Here's the bias! A (re-) reassessment of the Chilean electoral system', *Electoral Studies* 40: 268–279.

Rousseau, J.-J. (1976) *Of the Social Contract or Principles of Political Right*, New York, Harper and Row.

Samuels, D. and Snyder, R. (2001a) 'Devaluing the vote in Latin America', *Journal of Democracy* 12(1):146–159.

—— (2001b) 'The value of a vote: malapportionment in comparative perspective', *British Journal of Political Science* 31(4): 651–671.

Taagepera, R. and Shugart, M. (1989) *Seats and Votes: The effects and determinants of electoral systems*, New Haven: Yale University Press.

Valenzuela, A. and Siavelis, P. (1991) 'Ley electoral y estabilidad democrática: Un ejercicio de simulación para el caso de Chile', *Estudios Públicos* 43: 27–87.

PART THREE

INSTITUTIONAL INNOVATION AND
REMODELLING IN LATIN AMERICA:
IDENTITY AND DISTRIBUTIVE CONCERNS

*Chapter Seven*

# Constitutional Courts as Third-Party Mediators in Conflict Resolution: The Case of the Right to Prior Consultation in Latin American Countries[1]

*Andrea Pozas-Loyo and Julio Rios-Figueroa*

## Introduction[2]

Ordinary courts help to solve conflicts. The basic social logic of courts is rooted in the triad for conflict resolution: whenever two actors come into a conflict that they cannot themselves solve they call upon a third for assistance (Shapiro 1981: 1). According to this simple but universal view of courts, the effectiveness and efficiency of the third-party is related to the extent that she is impartial to the issue in dispute and neutral to the parties in conflict, as well as to the extent to which it applies pre-existing legal norms after adversary proceedings (Shapiro 1981). Constitutional courts do more than help to solve specific conflicts: their authoritative interpretation of the constitution is a means for adapting existing institutions and rules of the political game to changing conditions. Constitutional jurisprudence also helps political actors and regular citizens adapt their views and preferences to make them compatible with the constitutional framework and principles. Constitutional courts are able to weigh in and mix different points of view, asking for opinions and discussion about the possibilities of constitutional interpretation to integrate popular, governmental, and other actors' views into constitutional interpretation (Friedman 1993). In a nutshell, constitutional courts can contribute to institutional stability allowing for the punctual adaptation of existing institutions and actors to changing conditions and challenges.

Constitutional courts are a relatively recent institutional innovation across Latin American countries. Although judicial review of legislation and certain government actions has been present in some countries in the region since the second half of the nineteenth century, it was not until the third-wave of democracy that we see a clear regional shift towards delegating this authority to judges who were also made independent (Rios-Figueroa 2011). In the last

---

1.  We are grateful to Tulia Falletti, Jorge Gordin, and Lucio Renno and the participants of the Diego Portales workshop for comments and suggestions.

2.  Parts of this chapter, in particular parts I and II, are based on Ríos-Figueroa (2016), where details of the theory are further developed.

three decades several institutional innovations took place in the systems of constitutional justice of the region: autonomous constitutional courts have been created in some countries, such as Brazil or Peru. Supreme Courts, or one of its chambers, have been invested with greater constitutional review powers, as in Mexico or Costa Rica. Access to constitutional justice has been broadened considerably in countries like Colombia or Costa Rica. At the same time, the list of justiciable rights has been expanded in virtually all constitutions of the region. In general, the gist of this institutional change is the incorporation of a new actor, the constitutional judges, with power to breathe new life into new or reformed constitutions across the region.

However, interesting variation not only in the timing but also in the content of judicial reforms across Latin American countries is expressed in diverse levels of independence, access, and judicial review powers of constitutional judges. These institutional elements are crucial for making constitutional courts effective forums to produce jurisprudence that allows for institutional stability through the gradual accommodation of the interests of the relevant actors. In this chapter, we take advantage of the variations in constitutional courts' levels of independence, access, and judicial review powers across Latin American countries to assess the role of these relatively new institutions in conflict resolution, emphasising how they help other institutions and actors to adapt to changing and challenging circumstances while keeping themselves within the constitutional framework.

To illustrate this role of constitutional courts we focus on an old conflict that has been reframed given the recently gained visibility of marginalised indigenous groups in Latin America. The conflict is between governments (and businesses), on the one hand, and indigenous communities, on the other, due to the attempts by the former to promote development via the extraction of natural resources or the construction of mega infrastructure projects in lands inhabited by the latter. Indigenous communities used to have few or no means to either stop or at least benefit from those development efforts. However, in 1989 the International Labor Organization (ILO) adopted the *Convention 169 on Indigenous and Tribal Peoples* that includes a right to prior consultation, which essentially requires that indigenous and tribal peoples be consulted on issues that affect them. In the Latin American countries that have ratified the *Convention 169*, the old conflict has been reframed as one pitting governments, seeking to encourage private investment with a view to promoting development, against indigenous peoples asserting their rights to use and enjoy their lands and to protect and manage them according to their own worldview. In this conflict, governments and indigenous communities claim to act according to their constitutional prerogatives and obligations.

This chapter is about the role that constitutional courts play in solving conflicts surrounding the right to prior consultation. In essence, it argues that constitutional courts' jurisprudence can serve as a road map guiding the behaviour of relevant actors and institutions under conditions of uncertainty, helping them to adapt to changing conditions (cfr. Goldstein and Keohane 1993: 16). Specifically, constitutional courts can reduce three types of uncertainties that lie at the heart of the seemingly incompatible goal of promoting simultaneously the rights of indigenous communities and economic development: uncertainty over the legal consequences of certain actions, uncertainty over the bounds of the exceptions and special circumstances allowed by the constitution, and uncertainty about how to balance clashing constitutional principles or rules in particular cases. Constitutional courts can provide a road map to drive through uncharted territory, helping actors determine their own goals and alternative political strategies by which to reach these goals within the bounds of the constitution.

In what follows, we first present the *Theory of Constitutional Courts as Mediators* (Ríos-Figueroa 2016), which argues that constitutional courts that enjoy high levels of independence, access, and judicial review powers can produce constitutional jurisprudence on the right to prior consultation that reduces uncertainty and promotes institutional stability and cooperation among conflictive actors. Then we illustrate our theoretical claim with instances from Colombia, Peru, and Mexico. In the final section of the chapter, we conclude by pointing to some general lessons on the role of constitutional courts in promoting (or not) institutional stability and cooperation through conflict resolution.

## A Theory of Constitutional Courts as Mediators

The political science scholarship on courts and judges stresses that courts not only check the government, disabling arbitrary actions, they can also enable the government to reach other goals. Specifically, recent scholarship theorises on the role that courts play in bringing about normatively appealing outcomes such as regime stability, human rights protection, or investment and economic growth by enhancing the *credibility* of government *commitments*, by providing focal points that help solve *coordination* problems, or by transmitting information that reduces the uncertainty that hinders *cooperation* between actors (e.g. Barro 1997; Blomquist and Ostrom 2008; Frye 2004; Gibler and Randazzo 2011; Milgrom, North, and Weingast 1990; North and Weingast 1989; Reenock, Staton, and Radean 2012; Sutter 1997; Weingast 1997). Through different mechanisms, therefore, constitutional courts can thus promote institutional stability and cooperation among actors.

To be clear, constitutional courts can help obtaining those goals but they do so through the solution of specific disputes. What makes the difference between courts simply solving specific disputes and courts that, in addition, contribute to obtain larger goals is *how* the court proceeds about solving them. The literature on conflict resolution offers two contrasting decision-making styles, that of the arbitrator and of the mediator. In essence, an *arbitrator* simply adjudicates responsibility based on the record and the disputing parties 'are confined by traditional legal remedies that do not encompass creative, innovative, and forward-looking solutions to disputes' (Sgubini, Prieditis, and Marighetto 2013: 2). In contrast, mediators help the parties reach a mutually satisfactory agreement 'facilitating dialogue in a structured multi-stage process assisting the parties in identifying and articulating their own interests, priorities, needs and wishes to each other' (Sgubini, Prieditis, and Marighetto 2013: 3).

Constitutional jurisprudence can approach the style of the mediator in resolving disputes. Mediator-like jurisprudence should aim at solutions that transcend the present conflict and instead look forward to forge a creative solution that integrates the views of the actual actors in the dispute with the more permanent roles of the institutions, groups, or principles that they represent (see Uprimny 2004: 73–75; see also Bush, Baruch and Folger 2004). Mediator-like jurisprudence does that by reducing the types of uncertainty established at the beginning of this chapter, and it is creative, forward-looking, and transparent in its argumentation that should be robustly grounded on constitutional principles and norms. This idea is not foreign to constitutional scholarship, especially the strand that consider constitutional courts as deliberative institutions according to which judges weigh reasons for and against an action, they deliberate, and then offer reasons for their decisions to the public (Ferejohn and Pasquino 2003, 2010).

The *Theory of Courts as Mediators* essentially posits that to the extent that constitutional courts are independent, accessible, and have ample judicial review powers they are more likely to produce mediator-like jurisprudence: they can obtain and credibly transmit relevant information to the actors in a conflict in a way that helps them address the underlying uncertainty that causes their conflict. Constitutional courts that are more accessible gather more information on how the actors in a conflict are actually operating under existing rules, and on whether the application (or lack thereof) of such rules is producing the expected results. Courts that review different types of cases, that have higher levels of docket control, and also higher levels of discretion over how to decide cases, are more able to transform such information into creative and forward-looking jurisprudence. Finally, courts that are more independent are more credible when transmitting such information. When courts lack independence they will tend to act as delegates of the actor to which they are subordinated. When courts have independence but they have meagre judicial review powers, or access to them is very limited, they would tend to act as arbitrators not as mediators.

In sum, independence is linked to the court's capacity to be credible. Access is related to the court's capacity to get information. And judicial review powers are related to the court's capacity to transform and transmit such information in an effective manner. In this theory, independent, accessible, and powerful constitutional courts transmit information via their jurisprudence, which has to have certain characteristics to be informative and cooperation enhancing. Let us look closer at the concepts of judicial independence, judicial access, and judicial review powers and explain how they combine to produce informative, mediator-like jurisprudence.

## Judicial Independence: Credibility in Transmitting Information

In the most basic scheme of courts as third-party dispute settlers (Shapiro 1981) 'independence' is the bedrock for judges' legitimacy before the parties in the dispute, the political actors, and the public at large (see, e.g. Bybee 2010). It is thus a key element for courts, and under the courts-as-mediators framework it is a necessary condition for judges to be credible. Without independence, judges would be mere delegates of those who control them undermining the credibility of the information they could transmit because it will always be biased towards the views of the controllers. In order to gauge independence it is useful to look at so-called *de jure* judicial independence, i.e. the formal rules that we think provide incentives to judges to decide based on her preferences. These incentives are contained in the appointment, tenure, and removal mechanisms and impact on whether the preferences of a judge diverge from those of the parties in the case, as well as on the extent to which judges can evaluate the cases before them, free from undue pressures. It is possible to state three conditions that appointment, tenure, and removal mechanisms should meet in order for judges to enjoy *de jure* independence:[3]

(i)   At least two different organs of government (e.g. president and congress; the Supreme Court and the president; a judicial council and congress, etc.) appoint constitutional judges, or it is not the case that a single organ appoints a majority of judges in quota systems.

Whereas the above appointment condition is key to make the preferences of the judge differ from those of the government, conditions on tenure and removal mechanisms are important for judges to be the 'authors of their own opinions' (Kornhauser 2002: 42–45). If tenure is too short constitutional judges face incentives to curry favour with both the current and the incoming government with an eye in their next employment. Their views on issues, therefore, will likely be unduly influenced by what these parties prefer. Tenure need not be for life, but it should give judges a sufficiently long time horizon so that autonomous behaviour is incentivised. Similarly, if removal procedures are too easy, judges face a credible threat of removal if they vote according to their mind, given that their preferences diverge from those of the executive and the legislative. In a general way, the tenure and removal mechanisms should meet the following conditions:

(ii)  The length of tenure of judges is at least longer than the appointer's tenure; and,
(iii) The process to remove judges is initiated by at least two-thirds of the legislature, and never by the executive.

### Access to Constitutional Courts: Acquiring Information

Access to constitutional courts is directly related to how courts get information, how much information, and how often they have the chance to intervene in a conflict. This is a critical element of the *Theory of Courts as Mediators*. Constitutional courts are in a privileged position to learn how existing rules are

---

3.   *See* Ríos-Figueroa (2011; 2016) and Ríos-Figueroa and Staton (2012) for more details on institutional incentives on judicial independence. On appointment mechanisms *see* (Malleson and Russell 2003).

actually working through reviewing specific complaints and controversies (Clark and Staton 2013). More access also implies that more actors can more easily sound the 'fire alarm' (McCubbins and Schwartz 1984) so that the court learns where exactly things are getting out of the proper constitutional bounds. In a nutshell, access is crucial because the more cases reach the court, the more the court learns, and the more information it can transmit. Notice that the constitutional court receives information from the plaintiff and from the defendant, which allows the court to learn both sides of the same issue. Moreover, the constitutional court also directly gets information on a particular topic or actor's behaviour from amicus briefs, other government actors (e.g., the solicitor general or the *procurador*), international court rulings, or experts that can be summoned by the court itself.

Constitutional judges with a continuous flow of cases not only will get more and more varied information, they will also be more able to express their jurisprudential preferences under favourable circumstances. If judges receive only a few scattered cases the scarcity of information is compounded by the fact that the chances that these cases arrive under non-favourable political circumstances are relatively higher. Moreover, wide and easy access to instruments of constitutional review implies that more and more diverse cases reach the judges allowing them to make subtler distinctions. On the contrary, when legal standing is restricted to state actors, the court gets fewer cases and political actors are parties to the case, which implies fewer external sources of information. Notice also that while other institutional elements augment the flow of cases, such as the automatic constitutional review of certain governmental decisions, still others reduce it, such as time restrictions to challenge certain government actions.

It is possible to assess the degree of access to constitutional courts by focusing on the scope of legal standing before the courts. In other words, one can look at how many instruments of constitutional review there are in a country and who are the actors that can use them. For instance, in some countries such as Mexico only political authorities can file constitutional challenges against laws in the abstract, but in other countries, such as Colombia, any citizen can file this type of suit. Because the instruments of constitutional review and their characteristics are stated in national constitutions, this is also a *de jure* proxy for access.[4]

*Constitutional Review Powers: Processing and Transforming Information*

The constitutional review powers of a court determine how the court processes and transmits the information that it gets. In other words, they are directly related to whether the court can produce informative and creative, i.e. mediator-like,

---

4. Therefore, the limitations of this proxy have to be taken into account. For example, this does not consider the capacities of actors to actually bring cases to the constitutional court. Specifically, for cases to reach the court it is necessary to have a legal opportunity structure, a support structure for legal mobilisation, and also an institutional framework that facilitates litigation (see, e.g., Epp 1998; Smulovitz 2010; Wilson 2006). Moreover, actual judicial decisions can give hope or promote despair on potential litigants with similar cases (Gauri and Brinks 2008; Helmke and Staton 2011).

jurisprudence. Constitutional review powers are related to how many different types of cases the court gets (e.g. abstract or concrete, *a priori* and *a posteriori*), to how much control over its docket a court has,[5] and to how much discretion a court has over the particular way in which a decision is processed and framed. A court that has discretion over its docket and sentencing guidelines can avoid cornering one actor asking it to comply with a resolution that is highly unlikely to be complied with, strategically managing conflict between the actors and avoiding setbacks for its own decisions. Discretion to pick cases also matters for efficiency, especially when the flow of cases to the court is very high (Clark and Strauss 2010).

Docket control and discretion on how to decide cases allow judges to better transmit information to the actors involved in a dispute and to better manage confrontation levels with and among them. Constitutional judges who can pick their legal battles can reduce the costs associated with their decisions. Flexibility on how to decide cases is greater when, for instance, there are no limits on time-to-disposition of cases, no limits on the topics that can be challenged with a given instrument, no super-majority requirements to reach a decision of unconstitutionality, or no instrument-dependent effects of judicial decisions. This last type of flexibility also helps judges to tailor their sentencing guidelines to reduce the likelihood of non-compliance, promote deliberation and cooperation, and minimise the chances of setbacks for its decisions.

To assess constitutional review powers and access to constitutional courts, an alternative is to look at the incentives set in formal mechanisms of judicial review. These incentives are of two types. The first impact the number of opportunities judges have to make decisions on a given topic (which is related to access, as mentioned before). The second impact the flexibility judges have to pick and choose which cases to hear and how to decide them. In conjunction, both types determine what and how many cases judges hear, how they craft their decisions, and the extent to which they can manipulate the degree of confrontation with the actors adversely affected by them. Therefore, these incentives are crucial for how for much information they get, and from whom, and for how effectively the constitutional courts can transmit the information they get. These incentives are contained in the characteristics of the instruments for judicial review available in a country (e.g. the *amparo* suit, the action of constitutionality, or the constitutional controversy), including who is entitled to use each of these instruments, how hard is to file them, or who is affected by decisions on them.

In sum, we suggest assessing levels of judicial independence, access, and judicial review powers through *de jure* incentives that are to be found in a country's

---

5.    The writ of *certiorari* in the case of the United States is the obvious and most famous example. Most countries do not give to constitutional judges something like the *certiorari* power but some recognise the possibility of choosing which cases to hear from one type of instrument but not others (e.g. the *tutela* in Colombia). Other countries give to judges the possibility to attract some cases that are heard in lower courts when they consider them important enough (e.g. Mexico, Argentina).

constitution. To be sure, how these rules operate in practice may diverge from what they are intended to produce. Incentives found in formal rules constitute approximations to the concepts of interest, and would need to be contrasted to actual judicial decisions in a diversity of cases and situations, in order to fully gauge the impact of the incentives on behaviour. We use the *de jure* incentives as a standard against which we can then assess whether or not the expectations set in them are fulfilled (see Pozas-Loyo and Ríos-Figueroa 2007). We also take into account that institutional incentives are likely to be more effective under certain political conditions than under others. Specifically, we expect these incentives to be more effective under divided government and also with higher levels of public support for the courts, conditions that are also positive for compliance with judicial decisions (e.g. Ríos-Figueroa 2007; Staton 2010; Vanberg 2005).

Notice that under the Courts as Mediators framework, compliance with judicial decisions takes a distinctive character. Specifically, the informative jurisprudence implies that courts tailor decisions to produce agreements between conflictive actors, thus their decisions do not shame, do not create sharp winners and losers and underscore the iterated relation both among the parties and with the court. Moreover, in this framework compliance goes hand in hand with the transmission of information. For instance, courts-as-mediators can make use of forums where the parties in the conflict develop responses to the problems. These forums provide information to the parties about their preferences and view of the conflict, but they also increase public awareness and increment the costs on the parties for not complying (Botero 2014: 30). Transmitting information effectively does not assume compliance, but arguably simply issuing creative and forward-looking jurisprudence would incentivise the actors in the conflict to apply the solution suggested by the mediator.

## Constitutional Jurisprudence on Prior Consultation in Latin America

The last decade witnessed an impressive rate of economic growth in several Latin American countries coupled with the reduction of poverty levels but also with an increment in the number and intensity of social conflicts. The causes of these conflicts vary but a significant proportion of them, including some of the most prominent, are associated with natural resources management and with resource exploitation and infrastructure projects. These conflicts pit two divergent views of development against one another. On the one hand, states seek to encourage private investment with the objective of promoting development without being viewed as infringing the relevant constitutional norms. On the other hand, indigenous peoples assert their rights to use and enjoy their lands and to protect and manage them according to their own worldview, safeguarded by the constitution and the international law. Both actors are pursuing good ends and both claim to act as required by the constitution and the international legal norms. How can these conflicting views be properly accommodated? How to promote economic development without jeopardising the rights and the identity of indigenous peoples?

The *right of prior consultation* presumably can help to reconcile these two aims. It was established in the Convention 169 on Indigenous and Tribal Peoples of the International Labor Organization (ILO). The spirit of consultation and participation constitutes the cornerstone of Convention No. 169 and all its provisions are based upon it. Essentially, the idea is to establish a requisite that indigenous and tribal peoples have a say on issues that affect them, and that they are able to engage in free, prior, and informed consultation in policy and development processes that affect them. Regarding the dilemma between development and indigenous people, prior consultation implies a collective right of indigenous communities, whose lands or environments could be potentially affected by resource extraction or mega-development projects, to be consulted before projects begin.

But what constitutes a 'free and 'prior' consultation? Who should organise the consultation and how? Does the prior consultation right imply veto power? What proceeds if agreement is not reached after the consultation? How should the different interests involved be balanced? Should they always be balanced or are there circumstances under which one of the interests always out-weights the other?

In this section we empirically evaluate the theory of courts as mediators using a most-similar cases research design on Colombia (since 1991), Peru (since 2002), and Mexico (since 2000) to investigate the constitutional courts' decision to regulate the right of prior consultation. These countries are similar regarding relevant variables that may lead to courts regulating this right. Specifically, in this period according to all existing indexes (e.g. Cheibub and Gandhi 2004), the three countries are democracies with healthy levels of political competition and no unified governments. This is relevant because political fragmentation has been shown to be a fertile context for judges to decide sincerely given that the political organs that could react to their decisions face coordination problems (e.g. Ríos-Figueroa 2007). Moreover, in the three countries democratically elected governments have attempted to develop infrastructure or mining projects that have been challenged by indigenous communities on the grounds that their right to prior consultation has been violated. Finally, in the three countries these communities have sued the government and the suit has reached the constitutional court.

These three countries, of course, also share other relevant characteristics that are related to constitutional judges' behaviour such as the civil-law tradition, a presidential system of government, the signing and ratification of the international treaties and Convention 169 of the ILO where the right to prior consultation is specified, and the jurisdiction of the Inter American Human Rights Court. But interestingly the countries differ in the variables that make it more likely that the constitutional court will behave as a mediator. In a nutshell, only Colombia shows high levels (*de jure* and *de facto*) of independence, access, and judicial review powers. Peru, in contrast, has low levels of independence, and medium levels of access and judicial review powers. Mexico, finally, has high levels of independence but low levels of judicial review powers and very low levels of access. The argument according to the theory is that only Colombia exhibits the necessary conditions that make it more likely that the constitutional court acts as a mediator. Table 7.1 summarises this discussion.

*Table 7.1: Most-similar research design: right to prior consultation*

|  | Y | X₁ | X₂ | X₃ | X₄ |
|---|---|---|---|---|---|
|  | Judicial mediation on the right to prior consultation | Governmental development projects in indigenous lands | Signing of Convention 169, and law suits based on it | Competitive democratic elections | High independence, access, and powers of const. court |
| Colombia | YES | YES | YES | YES | YES |
| Peru | NO | YES | YES | YES | NO |
| Mexico | NO | YES | YES | YES | NO |

## Colombia: The Constitutional Court, 1991–2013

The Colombian Constitution of 1991 radically transformed the justice system and, in particular, the constitutional jurisdiction. First, an autonomous constitutional court with nine members enjoying an eight-year tenure was created. Each one of three different organs (the Council of the State, the Supreme Court, and the Executive) appoints three constitutional judges, with the approval of the Senate. In addition, to the public action of constitutionality and the automatic review of declaration of states of emergency and emergency decrees, the powers of constitutional review of the newly created court were expanded considerably with the creation of the *tutela*. This is an instrument for the review of rights protection that is widely and easily accessible to the citizens who, almost immediately, began using the courts to defend their rights.[6] The *tutela* can be filed with any judge in Colombia who is then obliged to submit her decision to the Constitutional Court, which in turn has the discretionary power to select for revision only those *tutela* decisions it considers relevant.[7]

Colombian constitutional judges enjoy institutional incentives to have many opportunities to assert their preferences, and to receive lots of information on how actors operate under actual rules. In a nutshell, since 1991 the Colombian Constitutional Court is independent and powerful enough to become a cooperation-enhancing mediator. Since 1991 the governing party does not have a majority in the legislative branch of government, the country has enjoyed relatively high levels of stability in economic terms, and the Colombian Constitutional Court enjoys relatively high public support (Rodríguez-Raga 2011; Wilson 2009). In other

6. Access to the Constitutional Court in Colombia is much easier than in Peru and Mexico and other countries and this has consequences on a broader set of court's outcomes that involve rights protection (Ansolabehere 2010).

7. The Constitutional Court receives all the *tutelas* decided by Colombian judges from all over the country after two judicial decisions had been made. *Tutelas* can also be filed against judicial decisions when procedural matters are violated, or when the substance contradicts the constitution according to the petitioner. The Constitutional Court, after receiving literally hundreds of thousands of *tutelas*, only reviews the ones it considers relevant and transcendent.

words, Colombia since 1991 operates under favorable socio-political conditions making the institutional incentives that affect the independence and the powers of constitutional judges more likely to be more effective.

The Colombian Constitutional Court (CCC) has a rich jurisprudence regarding the right of Prior Consultation.[8] In what follows we give an account of a subset of these decisions, in which we underscore how specific decisions have reduced the three types of uncertainty we discussed earlier in the theory of constitutional courts as mediators.

## T-428 1992 MP CIRO ANGARITA[9]

This case involved the construction of a highway that affected the indigenous community of Cristianía in Antioquia. The construction had been contracted by the Ministry of Public Works (*Ministerio de Obras Públicas*) without consulting the indigenous authority. The CCC decided to grant the Amparo to the community and to order

> to suspend the construction of the Andes-Jardín highway's extension in the affected area (km 5+150 to 6+200), until an evaluation of the ecological impact has been completed, and all necessary precautions have been taken to avoid any additional damages to the community [...] (T-428 1992).

In this early decision the CCC made clear, against the decision of a lower court judge, that these conflicts were not about 'particular interests versus the general interest', but involve a clash between two collective interests'. Moreover it stated that given that 'the interest of the indigenous community [...] was grounded on fundamental rights extensively protected by the Constitution' (T-428 1992), it should be given full consideration, and could not be dispatched merely by the utilitarian argument that the project had a positive impact on a larger amount of people. This was the first step to approach the cases that involved prior consultation using, what we have called, mediation jurisprudence since it clearly opposed an arbitrational approach of the lower court judge. This decision reduced the uncertainty regarding the consequences of omitting prior consultation making clear that it would imply costs, and distanced itself from a resolution with a winner-takes-all structure.

---

8.  The Colombian Court has more than forty decisions that makes reference to the *Convention 169 on Indigenous and Tribal Peoples* of the International Labor Organization (ILO) See: (OIT 2009: 9 available at http://www.ilo.org/public/spanish/bureau/inst/download/wow_2009_es.pdf (last accessed 27 January 2017).

9.  MP stands for *Magistrado Ponente*, the author of the opinion. The decision can be reached at http://www.corteconstitucional.gov.co/relatoria/ (last accessed 27 January 2017).

## SU-39 1997 MP ANTONIO BARRERA

This case involved the environmental license for seismic prospecting activities in Samoré, with the end of finding oil fields. The U'wa community claimed that the license was not legal since a prior consultation process had not taken place. The CCC determined that the government had thirty days to initiate a consultation with the U'wa community, and that this process ought to comply with the criteria established in the decision. This is a very clear case of judicial mediation. With it the CCC considerably reduced the uncertainty over the legal consequences of certain actions, in particular it gave decisive steps forward in defining what constitutes prior consultation. With it the Court established forward-looking criteria that took in consideration the iterated interactions between the Government and the indigenous communities. Moreover, with this decision the CCC also continued with the task of reducing the uncertainty regarding how to balance the constitutional principles involved in the dispute.

To appreciate the previous points let us quote the CCC at large:

> [T]he institution of the consultation to the indigenous communities that can be affected by the exploitation of natural resources, implies the adoption of communication and understanding relations, characterised by mutual respect and good faith [...] aiming to achieve that a) the community has full knowledge on the projects destined to explore and exploit natural resources in the territories that they occupy or that belong to them, and of the procedures and activities required to execute them. b) That the community is informed and illustrated on the ways that the execution of those projects can imply to negative impacts, or undermine the elements that constitute the grounding of their social, cultural, economic and political cohesion, and therefore the foundation for its survival as a distinct human group [...] c) That the community is given the opportunity to freely, and without external interferences, convene its members or representatives to evaluate the advantages and disadvantages of the project on the community, [that] their concerns and wishes regarding the defense of their interests are heard and that they express their opinion on the viability of the project. The aim is that the community has an active and effective participation in the authority's decision making procedure such that the final decision is to the extent possible an acceptable agreement to all parties.

> (SU-39 1997 MP Antonio Barrera Carbonell, our translation[10])

As a consequence of these criteria, the court concluded that 'informative workshops' did not constitute prior consultation, and established the rule that the agent responsible for organising the consultation was not the private company involved with the project, but the government. This decision was also conducive to

---

10. The decision can be reached at http://www.corteconstitucional.gov.co/relatoria/ (last accessed 27 January 2017).

the reduction of the uncertainty of how to balance clashing constitutional interests. In it the CCC put forward the following principle:

> The exploitation of natural resources in the indigenous territories makes it necessary to harmonise two conflicting interests: the necessity of planning the natural resources management and harnessing [Article 80 of the Colombian Constitution] and of securing the protection of the ethnic, cultural, social, and economic integrity of indigenous communities [...] an equilibrium or balance must be sought [Article 330 of the Colombian Constitution].
>
> (SU-39 1997 MP Antonio Barrera Carbonell, our translation)[11]

The CCC applied this general principle to the decision-making process in cases that involved prior consultation. In particular it clarified what proceeds when agreement is not reached after the community has been properly consulted.

> When no agreement is possible, the authority's decision must be devoid of arbitrariness and authoritarianism, it must therefore be objective, reasonable and proportional to the constitutional aim that requires that the State protects the [...] identity of the indigenous community [...] mechanisms must be devised to reduce, correct or restore the effects that the authority's measures produce or can generate to the detriment of the community or its members.
>
> (SU-39 1997, our translation)

The reduction of the uncertainty over what proceeds when no agreement is reached has been incremental, as the theory of constitutional courts as mediators claims. For instance, another important decision in this respect is the C-891/02 in which the CCC dealt with an unconstitutionality suit against the Mining Law. In it the CCC clarified the consequences of lack of agreement after a proper prior consultation vis-à-vis a legislative project. It stated that agreement was not necessary for the legislative process to proceed and gave further clarification to what constitutes 'prior consultation'.

## C-208 2007 MP RODRIGO ESCOBAR

This is an unconstitutional suit against the Statute of the Teachers Professionalisation. The plaintiff, a member of the Indigenous Community Nasa 'KWET WALA', asked the CCC to declare the partial unconstitutionally

---

11. Other important decisions regarding how to balance these interests is SU-383 2003 MP ÁLVARO TAFUR in which the Organization of the Indigenous Peoples of the Colombian Amazonia (OPIAC) claim that the Program of Eradication of Illicit Crops had not incorporated prior consultation and resulted in considerable environmental damage. In addition this case is interesting because it shows that the right to prior consultation might need to be balanced with other constitutional principles such as 'the inherent right of the Colombian State to define and apply [...] the criminal policies, among them the eradication of illicit crops plans and programs [...]'(SU-383 2003).

of the Decree 1278 claiming that it did not consider the right of the indigenous communities to an education that respects and develops its cultural identity. He further argued that to make this right effective the requirements of a University degree and of winning an open competition for the post should not apply to teachers working in indigenous areas.

The CCC argued that this law was constitutional to the extent that it does not apply to schools in the indigenous territories, and that the legislature should make a statute of professionalisation that takes into consideration the rights of the communities. It also established that while this new statute was in place a prior norm that did not include these requirements applied to the indigenous territories. In this decision the CCC reduced the uncertainty regarding the bounds of exceptions allowed to the cultural identity right. It stated that these limits are related with 'what is truly intolerable because it damages the most valued good of human kind' such as the right to life, the prohibition against torture and slavery, individual responsibility for one own behaviour, and legal procedure of crimes and punishments (C-208 2007).

Another important decision that involved the reduction of uncertainty over the bounds of exception is the C-030 2008 MP RODRIGO ESCOBAR, an unconstitutionality suit against the general forestry law that established what should be understood as 'a law having a direct effect' on an indigenous community, and therefore clarified which laws do not require prior consultation.[12] Finally, T-129 2001 MP ALEJANDRO MARTÍNEZ is another good example of reduction of uncertainty over the limits of prior consultation. It involved three important projects that affected the Embera-Katio and Embera-Dobida peoples. In it, among other norms, the CCC established that in the cases where all the alternative projects of development would imply the disappearance of the community as such, the right of the community would take precedence and no balance should be sought.

### Peru: The Constitutional Tribunal (PCT), 2001–2013

The Constitution of 1993 includes in its Article 201 the Constitutional Tribunal as the 'organ in charge of protecting the constitution'. The Peruvian Constitutional Tribunal (PCT) is composed of seven members elected by a two-thirds majority of the members of Congress for a period of five years without the possibility of immediate re-election (Art. 201). The PCT decides, in its original jurisdiction docket, conflicts of competence and actions of constitutionality, and in its appellate jurisdiction, *habeas corpus, amparo, habeas data*, and action of compliance (Art. 202). Access to the PCT is, in comparison to the Colombian Constitutional Court, more difficult. Legal standing in actions of constitutionality is restricted to political or collective actors such as the president, the attorney general, the *defensor del pueblo*, 25 per cent of members of Congress, regional presidents and

---

12. This is also an important decision vis-à-vis the reduction of uncertainty over the legal consequences of certain actions since it established the judicial implication of the omission of a prior consultation, and further clarified the necessary conditions for this requirement to be satisfied.

local mayors (in matters of their competence), 5000 citizens whose signatures have to be validated by the electoral court, 1 per cent of the inhabitants of a certain municipality against ordinances by their municipal government, and professional associations (in matters of their competence) (Art. 203) (see Dargent 2009: 254). Article 4 of the organic law of the PCT again requires a supermajority of six votes, out of seven, for the tribunal to declare a norm unconstitutional.[13]

The PCT was not properly installed until June 1996, because there was a protracted negotiation process to appoint the first set of judges. As soon as it started working, the PCT got the politically difficult case regarding whether Fujimori's attempt at re-election in 2000 was constitutional. In January 1997, the PCT circulated an opinion arguing that it was not (see details in Conaghan 2005: 126–132). The three judges who stood for the unconstitutionality of Fujimori's re-election were removed via impeachment on 29 May 1997, which meant that the PCT continued to function with only four members whose preferences were close to the president's. Interestingly, four judges was the minimum required by law for the PCT to continue working and decide all types of cases except actions of constitutionality. Fujimori's regime collapsed at the end of the year 2000 and on November of that same year the three impeached judges were reinstalled in the PCT. The four judges who were close to Fujimori ended their terms in 2001, and in May 2002 four new judges were elected. According to César Landa (2007: 280) this event marks two periods of the PCT, 'the tribunal in captivity' (1997–2002), and the 'tribunal in liberty' (2002-).

The actual composition of the 'tribunal in liberty' included some high calibre and neutral magistrates. To attain the required two-thirds vote, the four majoritarian groups in Congress arrived at an agreement that allowed each of them to name a magistrate. As Dargent (2009: 271) explains, 'in order to reach the two-thirds requirement for the candidates' appointment, parties were careful to nominate candidates that were acceptable to all of the political groups'. This mechanism produce judges that, even though they could be linked to a particular political group, were individuals with personal prestige as politicians or lawyers (Dargent 2009: 271). In addition, these four judges joined the three independent magistrates still in the court, which permitted a plural mixture of past and new magistrates. The PCT from 2003 to 2008 was indeed quite remarkable in the type and breadth of jurisprudence it produced.

However, the length of tenure of Peruvian judges is quite short (five years), which means that even high-calibre and professional judges face uncomfortable choices regarding the pace and the depth of the jurisprudence they want to produce. Moreover, the short length of judges' tenure coincides with the tenure of their appointers (congressmen) making this a highly unstable institution and an easy prey for political manipulation. Essentially, during each president's administration the full membership of the constitutional tribunal is renewed (see Ponce and Tiede 2014). The performance of the Tribunal from 2003 to 2008, which demonstrated

---

13.  On 20 October 2002 this article was modified making the requirement of five votes, out of seven, to declare a norm unconstitutional.

how consequential a Tribunal can be, paradoxically also partly caused its demise because political actors wanted to influence the composition of such organ. As John Ferejohn put it, the judicalisation of politics leads to the politicisation of the judiciary, which is successful if the right incentives, conditions, and protections for the judicial institutions are not in place (Ferejohn 2002). A case in point is the appointment process of four new constitutional judges in 2007–2008, which was not transparent and was far from the way in which the election took place in 2002. This time, the process involved resignations, internal fights, and the loss of collegiality that characterised the Tribunal from 2002 to 2007 (Justicia Viva 2008).[14] The changes in composition were felt also in the quality and depth of jurisprudence produced by the Constitutional Tribunal.

As was the case with our account of the Colombian constitutional court jurisprudence on prior consultation, the aim of this section is to exemplify the type of decisions that the Peruvian Constitutional Tribunal has had in prior consultation cases to illustrate the theoretical argument we defend. Therefore, the aim is not to present an exhaustive account of the decisions, but provide an analysis that illuminates why we argue this Tribunal has not produced mediation jurisprudence in this important area.

We argue that the PCT has failed to systematically reduce uncertainty because its decisions have lacked an important requisite: consistency. Jurisprudential consistency is a necessary condition to reduce all types of uncertainty, for instance clarifying what are the legal consequences of certain actions reduces uncertainty, and hence enables the lessening of conflict to the extent that it is known that such criteria will stand in the future interactions among the parts. Hence, jurisprudential inconsistency taints the reduction of uncertainty that can be obtained through the decisions of a Constitutional Court. Furthermore, this type of inconsistency breaks the rule-making character of constitutional decisions since a rule that is later negated is no longer a rule. Finally, we will present instances of backward-looking and winner-take-all decisions. In sum, we want to show that the jurisprudence of the PCT in prior consultation cases lacks the characteristics of mediation jurisprudence.

### *06316-2008-PA/TC and Resolution N06316-2008-AA*

06316-2008 PA/TC is an *amparo* suit against the Ministry of Energy and Mining. The plaintiff, the Interethnic Association for the Development of the Peruvian Rain Forest (AIDESEP) argued that contracts that such Ministry had made with Perupetro S.A., Barrett Resource Peru Corporation and Repsol YPF for the exploitation and

---

14. In fact, a first set of judges already selected by Congress was removed after Congress faced strong opposition from NGOs and public opinion regarding the characteristics of some of the judges and the lack of transparency in the election process. A new set of four judges had to be appointed and even then some judges whose closeness with a political party had been denounced were elected. In 2013, again, Congress had to cancel the appointment of four new judges due to heavy criticisms of some of the judges and of the process of election, and the appointment process had to be done again.

extraction of oil, violated several rights of the *waorani, pananujuri,* and *aushiris* indigenous communities of the 'proposed territorial reservoir Napo Tigre' (their right to life, ethnic identity, property, etc.) and that those contracts had been done without prior consultation with the communities. Therefore, the plaintiff asked for the nullification of the contracts and the suspension of all extractive activities. The PCT decided that the suit was unfounded since the plaintiff had not accredited the communities' status as communities in voluntary isolation.

Additionally, in Peru the parts of a suit can ask the Tribunal to clarify specific points of its decision. In this case the AIDESEP ask the Court to clarify part of the decision we have just presented. Resolution N06316-2008-AA is the decision that responds to that request for clarification. The PTC has taken inconsistent decisions regarding the right to prior consultation, which arguably have tainted its capacity to reduce uncertainty. In 06316-2008-PA/TC the PTC implies that the prior consultation is enforceable only after this decision:

> [we] consider that the right to prior consultation must, in this case, be enforced in a gradual way by the companies involved and with the supervision of the competent entities. With this the Tribunal will put in place a plan of shared commitments between the private companies involved, that will not see their actions paralysed and the communities [...] who cannot renounce their rights.

> (06316-2008-PA/TC, p. 30. Our translation)[15]

This pronouncement implies that the enforcement of this right will be gradual once the cited plan is put in place, but that it is not enforceable before that. This particular point, which is more clearly restated in its recourse to clarification, is in clear opposition with previous and posterior decisions in which the Tribunal clearly and explicitly established that the right of prior consultation was enforceable since 1995.

In the resolution to the request for clarification (N06316-2008-AA) the PTC 'establish[ed] that [prior] consultation was enforceable from the publication of the STC 0022-2009-PI/TC'. That meant that the right of prior consultation was enforceable, only from the 9 of June 2010, and not from 2 February 1995, which is the date of entry into force of the *Convention 169 on Indigenous and Tribal Peoples*. The argument was that the legislative branch had not produced law to regulate this treaty, thus enforcing it would affect the legal security of the parts involved.

> In terms of efficacy, the normative character of the treaty has been difficult precisely because of the omission of an appropriate normative development that [...] has generated legal insecurity [...] that affects not only the indigenous

---

15. The decision can be found in http://www.tc.gob.pe/tc/jurisprudencia/constitucional (last accessed 27 January 2017).

people but also those people who have developed action without the State having required previously carrying out a consultation.

(f.j. exp N0616-2008-AA)

This claim is in clear contradiction with previous and posteriors decisions from the PCT. For instance, in the 00022-2009-PI/TC it clearly establishes that:

[it] is not a constitutionally valid argument to excuse the enforcement of fundamental rights due to the absence of legal regulation [...] that would be to leave in the hands of the state discretionarily the observance of fundamental rights [...].

(00022-2009-PI/TC, p. 12)

Or

all activity of public authorities must consider the direct application of the norms consecrated in international treaties of human rights (Exp. N02798-2004-HC/TC, p. 8).

Now the resolution 06316-2008-PA/TC is also a good instance to exemplify the lack of other characteristics we associate with jurisprudential mediation. It is arguably backward-looking and exhibits a winner-take-all structure. The PCT argues that after the Ministry of Energy and Mining granted the contracts to the companies, the latter acted in good faith grounded on the legal security and trust that those contracts transmitted (p. 27) The tribunal claims that the nullification of those contracts would affect the legal security of the companies. Needless to say: the legal security of the communities is not balanced.

First, this argument emphasises the past actions and expectations of one of the parties in conflict, it is not centred on the iterated relation between the government and the companies on the one side, and the communities on the others. Its reasoning does not focus on establishing rules that can reduce the conflict of future interactions, but on adjudicating the concrete conflict at hand. Moreover, the decision has a winner takes all structure, where the Waorani, Pananujuri, and Aushiris indigenous communities are left without any possibility to ask for their right of prior consultation to be enforced.

In sum, in this section we have exemplified the type of decisions that the Peruvian Constitutional Tribunal has had in prior consultation cases to illustrate how it has not systematically behaved as a mediator in the conflicts involving the right to prior consultation.

## Mexico: The Supreme Court (SC), 2000–2013

A key constitutional reform in 1994 empowered the Mexican Supreme Court and also reduced and renewed its membership in order to increase its legitimacy and independence vis-à-vis the other branches of government (see Fix-Fierro 2003). The 1994 reform increased the judicial review powers of the Mexican Supreme Court judges by creating instruments of both concrete and abstract control with the possibility of generating *erga omnes* effects and it granted the judges an effective fifteen-year tenure. While in independence levels this puts the Mexican Court somewhat above Colombia (and definitely more than Peru), regarding judicial review powers Mexico is below both of them. This is clearest regarding access to the Mexican Supreme Court that after the 1994 reform was still very limited: legal standing in the two new instruments of constitutional review created or strengthened in the reform (the action of unconstitutionality and the constitutional controversy, respectively) is allowed only to political authorities such as political parties, the representatives of the three branches of government, or a legislative minority. Ordinary citizens do not have the standing to use these instruments, and this is also true for most autonomous organs such as the Federal Electoral Institute (IFE) or the Federal Institute of Transparency and Information (IFAI) (see Ansolabehere 2010).[16] Moreover, the other instrument for constitutional review, the *amparo* suit, remained weak mainly because of its limited, *inter partes*, effects, and also for its de facto inaccessibility for ordinary citizens due to its technical complexity and high cost (see Pou Giménez 2012).[17]

The incentives on independence, access, and powers established by the reform of 1994 found a fertile political context to implant and grow. This context is essentially the increasing electoral competition and the gradual melting down of the PRI-regime. As part of the reform of 1994, the whole membership of the Supreme Court was renewed. But this time most of the judges proposed in 1995 by the president and confirmed by the Senate were the product of consensus between at least two political parties, more often the PRI and the right-leaning PAN (*Partido Acción Nacional*) (Magaloni, Sánchez, and Magar 2011). In contrast to the past, to be able to be part of the Supreme Court candidates should not be perceived as unconditional to the PRI, and they need to be respected lawyers.[18] Moreover, since 1997 there is divided government in Mexico and in 2000 the PRI lost the presidency for the first time in 71 years.

As in the case of Colombia and Peru, the following step is to instantiate the theoretical claim we make, that is to provide some evidence consistent with the claim that the low levels of judicial review powers have had a negative impact on the development of mediation jurisprudence.

---

16. The exception is the National Commission of Human Rights, CNDH, but only since 2006.

17. Since 1987 (but strengthened in 1994) the court enjoys the so-called *facultad de atracción*, the possibility to take cases that it deems important from lower courts in order to decide on them. This does not amount to *certiorari* power, but it does give the court the possibility to go after some cases in order to make a jurisprudential contribution. However, the Court only started using this for politically relevant cases in 2007–8 (Abad 2014).

18. Moreover, since 1997 Mexico has lived in a fragmented political context where the party of the president does not control legislative majorities. This increasing political diversity in the legislative and the executive branch, as well as in the local governments, decreased the threat of retaliation to rulings disliked by political actors (Rios-Figueroa 2007).

As we noted above, the low level of access is arguably the most significant characteristic of the judicial review powers in Mexico, and its direct consequence is that there is not a profuse jurisprudence on prior consultation. *Prima facie*, one would expect that a country of the size of Mexico – with a large number of indigenous communities, and numerous developmental projects – would have an impressive jurisprudence on prior consultation, especially after more than two decades from the 1994 judicial reform and the ratification the *Convention 169 on Indigenous and Tribal Peoples*. However, this expectation is not grounded: there are few and pretty recent cases that deal in depth with this right, so paradoxically the strongest evidence for our claim is the lack of a long and rich jurisprudence on this area.

Among the recent cases that deal with prior consultation one that has attracted more attention is the *amparo* suit 631/2012. In 2010 the government of the state of Sonora promoted the construction of an aqueduct to transport a large amount of water from the Yaqui River. In 2011 the Ministry of Environment and Natural Resources (SEMARNAT) gave the required permission without prior consultation to the Yaqui community that depends on the river for their economic and cultural survival. The Yaqui community presented an *amparo* against those governmental acts.

The Supreme Court recognised that the prior consultation right of the Yaqui community had been violated; that 'it was not enough that the responsible authority made the project public [...] through diverse media'. The Supreme Court made clear that the community should have been consulted (631/2012 Resolution, p. 88), and negated the validity of the permission that the SEMARNAT gave to the project and required a new assessment that incorporated the consultation with the community. However, in a statement issued as a clarification of its decision, the Supreme Court permitted that the aqueduct continued functioning without the required permissions and before the consultation had concluded. This clarification was in tension with its own decision that emphasised the need to respect the right of consultation (it also opposes the international standards). The tensions inherent to this decision undercuts its capacity to reduce the uncertainty, and to establish clear norms that ease the future conflicts between the government and the indigenous communities vis-à-vis the extraction of natural resources or the construction of infrastructure.

## Conclusion

In this chapter we argued that constitutional courts can contribute to institutional stability allowing for the punctual adaptation of existing institutions and actors to changing conditions and challenges. We claimed that courts can do that through jurisprudence that approaches the mediator style of conflict resolution, and that only courts that are independent, accessible, and that have ample judicial review powers can do so. We analysed conflicts that involved the right to prior consultation and evaluate the theory using a most similar research design on Colombia, Peru, and Mexico. We argue that the conditions for mediator-like jurisprudence are only present in the Colombian Constitutional Court (1991–2013).

In a series of other decisions, the Colombian Constitutional Court has produced a line of informative jurisprudence on the right to prior consultation. In a case where the U'wa community claimed it had not been consulted before an environmental license for seismic prospecting activities with the goal of finding oil fields was granted, the court determined that the government had 30 days to initiate a consultation with the U'wa community and that this process ought to comply with the criteria established in the decision (SU-039 1997 MP Antonio Barrera Carbonell). In this clear case of judicial mediation, the Court took decisive steps forward in defining what constitutes prior consultation, for instance arguing that 'informative workshops' did not constitute prior consultation. In other decisions (e.g. C-208 2007 MP Rodrigo Escobar Gil; C-030 2008 MP Rodrigo Escobar Gil) the court continued to build a doctrine that attempted to balance the differing rights of the communities and the developmental state, reducing the uncertainties that surround this issue-area.

In contrast, the Peruvian Constitutional Tribunal and the Mexican Supreme Court have produced jurisprudence that is closer to arbitration, not mediation, style of conflict resolution. In Peru, lack of consistency (produced by low independence) has produced erratic jurisprudence on the right to prior consultation. For instance, the Peruvian Tribunal first accepts that some contracts for a development project violate indigenous community rights but when the community requests their nullification, the Tribunal does not nullify them based on convoluted arguments (see *06316-2008-PA/TC and Resolution N06316-2008-AA*). In the case of Mexico, a country with a large number of indigenous communities and numerous developmental projects, the jurisprudence on prior consultation is rare, which we argue can be explained by the lack of access to the Supreme Court. And when a case reaches the court, the Court has managed to discourage further litigation. For instance, in a recent *amparo* suit 631/2012 in which the Yaqui community challenges the construction of an aqueduct promoted by the government of the state of Sonora, the Supreme Court first recognised that the right to prior consultation of the Yaqui community had been violated, but then in a statement issued as a clarification of its decision, the Supreme Court permitted the aqueduct to continue functioning without the required permissions and before the mandated consultation had concluded.

The theory of courts as mediators is more applicable to the extent that the source of conflict is informational, i.e. when underlying the conflict between two or more parties there is one of the types of uncertainty discussed in this chapter. Of course, there are other sources of conflict between parties such as distributional sources. In a post-electoral conflict when two parties are claiming to have won the election, any resolution involves clear winners and losers. In these cases, according to the literature on conflict resolution, an arbitrator style (disposing authoritatively who wins and loses the particular dispute) would perhaps be a better approach. An interesting avenue for future research is to evaluate whether courts, such as the Colombian Constitutional Court or the Costa Rican *Sala Cuarta* that are independent, highly accessible, and have substantial powers of judicial review, vary their kinds of decisions depending on whether the source of the underlying conflict is mainly distributional or informational.

## References

Abad, A. (2014) *La Protección de Los Derechos Fundamentales En La Novena Época de La Suprema Corte de Justicia de La Nación*, Mexico: IIJ-UNAM / Porrúa.

Ansolabehere, K. (2010) 'More Power, More Rights? The Supreme Court and society in Mexico', in J. Couso, A. Hunneus and R. Sieder (eds) *Cultures of Legality: Judicialization and political activism in Latin America*, New York, NY: Cambridge University Press, pp. 78–111.

Barro, R. (1997) *Determinants of Economic Growth: A cross-country empirical study*, Cambridge: MIT Press.

Blomquist, W. and Ostrom, E. (2008) 'Deliberation, learning, and institutional change: the evolution of institutions in judicial settings', *Constitutional Political Economy* 19(3): 180–202.

Botero, S. (2014) *Judicial Impact and Court-Promoted Monitoring in Argentina.* Paper presented at the Latin American Studies Association Annual Meeting, Chicago, IL, May 21–24.

Bush, R., Baruch, A. and Folger, J. (2004) *The Promise of Mediation: The transformative approach to conflict*, New York, NY: Jossey-Bass.

Bybee, K. (2010) *All Judges Are Political – Except When They Are Not: Acceptable hypocrisies and the rule of law*, Stanford, CA: Stanford University Press.

Cheibub, J. and Gandhi, J. (2004) 'Classifying political regimes: a sixfold classification of democracies and dictatorships', *Annual Meeting of the American Political Science Association*, Chicago, IL.: APSA.

Clark, T. and Staton J. (2013) 'Optimal Dockets', Working paper on file with author.

Clark, T. and Strauss, B. (2010) 'The implications of high court docket control for resource allocation and legal efficiency', *Journal of Theoretical Politics* 22(2): 247–268.

Conaghan, C. M. (2005) *Fujimori's Peru: Deception in the public sphere*, Pittsburgh, PA: University of Pittsburgh Press.

Dargent, E. (2009) 'Determinants of judicial independence: lessons from three "cases" on Constitutional Courts in Peru (1979–2007)', *Journal of Latin American Studies* 41(2): 251–278.

Epp, C. (1998) *The Rights Revolution: Lawyers, activists, and Supreme Courts in comparative perspective*, Chicago: University of Chicago Press.

Ferejohn, J. (2002) 'Judicializing politics, politicizing law', *Law and Contemporary Problems* 65(3): 41–68.

Ferejohn, J. and Pasquino, P. (2010) 'The countermajoritarian opportunity', *University of Pennsylvania Journal of Constitutional Law* 13(2): 353–360.

——— (2003) 'Constitutional Courts as deliberative institutions: towards an institutional theory of constitutional justice', in S. Wojciech (ed.) *Constitutional Justice, East and West*, London: Kluwer International, pp. 21–36.

Fix-Fierro, H. (2003) 'Judicial Reform in Mexico: What next?', in E. Jensen and T. Heller (eds) *Beyond Common Knowledge: Empirical approaches to the rule of law*, Stanford, CA: Stanford University Press, pp. 240–289.

Friedman, B. (1993) 'Dialogue and judicial review', *Michigan Law Review* 91(4): 577–682.

Frye, T. (2004) 'Credible commitment and property rights: evidence from Russia', *American Political Science Review* 98(3): 453–266.

Gauri, V. and Brinks, D. (2008) 'Introduction: The elements of legalization and the triangular shape of social and economic rights', in V. Gauri and D. Brinks (eds) *Courting Social Justice: Judicial enforcement of social and economic rights in the developing world*, New York: Cambridge University Press, pp. 1–37.

Gibler, D. and Randazzo, K. (2011) 'Testing the effects of independent judiciaries on the likelihood of democratic backsliding', *American Journal of Political Science* 55(3): 696–709.

Goldstein, J. and Keohane, R. (1993) 'Ideas and Foreign Policy: An analytic framework', in J. Goldstein and R. Keohane (eds) *Ideas and Foreign Policy: Beliefs, institutions, and political change*, Ithaca, NY: Cornell University Press, pp. 3–30.

Helmke, G. and Staton, J. (2011) 'The Puzzle of Judicial Politics in Latin America', in G. Helmke and J. Ríos-Figueroa (eds) *Courts in Latin America*, New York, NY: Cambridge University Press, pp 306–331.

Justicia Viva (2008) *Balance Al 2008 Del Tribunal Constitucional Peruano: El TC Que Se Nos Fue Y El TC Que Se Nos Viene*, Lima: Instituto de Defensa Legal.

Kornhauser, L. (2002) 'Is Judicial Independence a Useful Concept?', in S. Burbank and B. Friedman (eds) *Judicial Independence at the Crossroads: An interdisciplinary approach*, New York: Sage Publications Inc., pp. 45–55.

Landa Arroyo, C. (2007) *Tribunal Constitucional y Estado Democrático*, Lima: Palestra.

Magaloni, B., Sánchez, A. and Magar, E. (2011) 'Legalists vs Interpretativists: The Supreme Court and the Democratic Transition in Mexico', in G. Helmke and J. Ríos-Figueroa (eds) *Courts in Latin America*, New York, NY: Cambridge University Press, pp. 187–218.

Malleson, K. and Russell, R. (2003) *Appointing Judges in an Age of Judicial Power*, Toronto: University of Toronto Press.

McCubbins, M. and Schwartz, T. (1984) 'Congressional oversight overlooked: police patrols versus fire alarms', *American Journal of Political Science* 28(1): 165–179.

Milgrom, P., North, D. and Weingast, B. (1990) 'The role of institutions in the revival of trade: the medieval law merchant, private judges, and the champagne fairs', *Economics and Politics* 2(1): 1–23.

North, D. and Weingast, B. (1989) 'Constitutions and commitment: the evolution of institutions governing public choice in 17th century England', *Journal of Economic History* 49(4): 803–832.

Ponce, A. and Tiede, L. (2014) 'Evaluating theories of decision-making on the Peruvian constitutional tribunal', *Journal of Politics in Latin America* 6(2): 139–164.

Pou Giménez, F. (2012) 'Judicial Review and Rights Protection in Mexico: Assessing the recent Amparo constitutional reforms', Working paper on file with author.

Pozas-Loyo, A. and Rios-Figueroa, J. (2007) 'When and Why 'Law' and 'Reality' Coincide? De jure and de facto judicial independence in Chile and Mexico' in A. Rios-Cazares and D. Shirk (eds) *Evaluating Transparency and Accountability in Mexico: National, local and comparative perspectives*, San Diego, CA: University of San Diego Press.

Reenock, C., Staton, J. and Radean, M. (2012) 'Legal institutions and democratic survival', *The Journal of Politics* 75(02): 491–505.

Ríos-Figueroa, J. (2016) *Constitutional Courts as Mediators. Armed conflict, civil-military relations, and the rule of law in Latin America*, New York, NY: Cambridge University Press.

—— (2007) 'Fragmentation of power and the emergence of an effective judiciary in Mexico, 1994–2002', *Latin American Politics Society* 49(1): 31–57.

—— (2011) 'Institutions for Constitutional Justice in Latin America', in G. Helmke and J. Ríos-Figueroa (eds) *Courts in Latin America*, New York, NY: Cambridge University Press, pp. 27–54.

Ríos-Figueroa, J. and Staton, J. (2012) 'An evaluation of cross-national measures of judicial independence', *Journal of Law, Economics and Organization* 30(1): 104–137.

Rodríguez-Raga, J. (2011) 'Strategic prudence in the Colombian Constitutional Court, 1992–2006', University of Pittsburgh.

Sgubini, A., Prieditis, M. and Marighetto, A. (2013) *Arbitration, Mediation and Conciliation: Differences and similarities from an international and Italian business perspective*. Available at http://www.mediate.com/articles/sgubinia2.cfm (accessed 27 January 2017).

Shapiro, M. (1981) *Courts: A comparative and political analysis*, Chicago: University of Chicago Press.

Smulovitz, C. (2010) 'Judicialization in Argentina: Legal culture or opportunities and support structures?', in J. Couso, A. Huneeus, and R. Sieder (eds) *Cultures of Legality: Judicialization and political activism in Latin America*, New York, NY: Cambridge University Press, pp. 234–253.

Staton, J. (2010) *Judicial Power and Strategic Communication in Mexico*, New York: Cambridge University Press.

Sutter, D. (1997) 'Enforcing constitutional constraints', *Constitutional Political Economy* 8(1): 139–150.

Uprimny, R. (2004) *Orden Democrático Y Manejo de Conflictos*, Bogotá: Universidad Pedagógica Nacional.

Vanberg, G. (2005) *The Politics of Constitutional Review in Germany*, New York: Cambridge University Press.

Weingast, B. (1997) 'The political foundations of democracy and the rule of law', *American Political Science Review* 91(2): 245–263.

Wilson, B. (2006) 'Legal opportunity structures and social movements: the effects of institutional change on Costa Rican politics', *Comparative Political Studies* 39(3): 325–351.

—— (2009) 'Institutional Reform and Rights Revolutions in Latin America: The Cases of Costa Rica and Colombia', *Journal of Politics in Latin America* 1(2): 59–85.

*Chapter Eight*

# (How) Do National Authoritarian Regimes Manage Conflictive Ethnically Diverse Populations? Evidence from the Case of Mexico

*Allyson Lucinda Benton*

## Introduction

How do national authoritarian regimes manage ethnically diverse conflictive populations? Scholars that examine whether and how national politicians use political institutional arrangements to manage ethnically diverse societies have tended to focus on national democratic systems. At the national level, scholars debate the relative merits of parliamentary (Lijphart 1977) and presidential (Horowitz 2000) systems for managing ethnically divided societies and preventing conflict. They also debate the expected effects of electoral laws used to select national legislatures on ethnic relations, with some arguing that systems that facilitate the formation of ethnic parties best reduce the chances of ethnic conflict (Lijphart 1977; Sartori 1994) and others arguing that such systems only serve to aggravate existing inter-group tensions (Horowitz 1985; Wilkinson 2004). At the regional level, scholars examine how national district lines and subnational government affects ethnic group saliency. They argue that national district lines and the presence of subnational governments that crosscut ethnic groups reduce the political salience of ethnic groups in national politics (Horowitz 2000, 2007; Posner 2005; Wilkinson 2004).

Yet, national democrats are not the only ones that might seek political institutional solutions for managing ethnically diverse populations. National autocrats often find themselves ruling ethnically diverse populations as well, posing a potential risk to the stability of national authoritarian regimes. Ethnic group membership binds community members together (Horowitz 2000), raising the chances that ethnic group members can be called upon and mobilised to undertake sustained social and political activities. When harnessed by and thus firmly embedded in national authoritarian political structures, ethnic group members can be co-opted and counted on to provide sustained support for authoritarian rule. However, because shared ethnic identity can be used to resolve what amounts to as a serious collective action problem, when ethnic group members are alienated from authoritarian systems, they can be easily organised to engage in sustained opposition to national authoritarian regimes.

Despite the potential risks to national authoritarian regimes, little research has been conducted on the ways through which national autocrats manage ethnically divided societies. Of course, it could be argued that repression (or the threat of it) is always a useful tool used by autocrats to manage potentially disruptive ethnic groups into passive compliance or active support of the regime. However, many regimes well known for relying on force or the threat of it to maintain control range widely in their levels of stability and rates of survival, with repression appearing to play no systematic role in guaranteeing regime support (Gandhi 2008). Indeed, repression or the threat of it often has no effect on citizens in these systems: most either remain passive or actively support even brutally repressive regimes (Blaydes 2011).

For this reason, scholars have begun to examine the range of ostensibly democratic political tools that national autocrats often deploy – instead of or alongside the use of force – for ensuring citizen cooperation and compliance with their regimes. They note that national autocrats often deploy parties, elections, legislatures, and constitutions (e.g., Blaydes 2011; Boix and Svolik 2013; Brownlee 2007; Gandhi and Przeworski 2007; Gandhi 2008; Levitsky and Way 2010; Lust-Okar 2006; Svolik 2012; Wright 2008; Negretto 2013), as well as political structures, like decentralized and subnational levels of government (e.g., Jin, Qian and Weingast 2005; Montinola, Qian, and Weingast 1996; Qian and Weingast 1996; O'Brien and Li 2000; Landry 2008; Oi and Rozelle 2000; Manion 1996; Eaton 2006; Falleti 2011), as do national democrats to ensure regime support. Such ostensibly democratic institutions are said to help manage inter-elite rivalries and co-opt citizens into national authoritarian projects, with autocrats most likely to deploy such institutions when citizens' capacity to organise against and thus threaten the regime is high (Gandhi 2008). Given the enhanced capacity of groups with shared ethnic identities to coordinate and mobilise to defend their shared interests, I argue that national autocrats should be particularly keen to use political institutional innovations – instead of, or in addition to (the threat of) force – to ensure that ethnic groups do not organise against the regime. In other words, national autocrats should turn to many of the same political institutional arrangements to manage ethnically diverse societies as national democrats.

In this study, I focus on one political institutional tool that should be particularly useful for national autocrats facing large ethnic populations: political decentralisation. Most ethnic identities are shaped at the local level, organised from the ground up, and thus count on an inherently local logic (Horowitz 2000). Political decentralisation should thus be a useful tool for managing ethnically diverse societies in two ways. First, the presence of subnational governments reorients ethnic group attention to lower-level constituencies and thus reduces the political salience of shared ethnic identities that extend beyond these local borders (Horowitz 2000; Posner 2005; Wilkinson 2004; Horowitz 2007). Second, national autocrats' subnational regime officials benefit from valuable local political and social expertise useful for managing local ethnic group dynamics. The incentive for national autocrats to rely on political decentralisation thus rises with indigenous group membership and their tendency to organise along shared ethnic identity and to challenge the regime.

I examine the incentive for national autocrats facing large ethnic populations to engage in political decentralisation using the case of Mexico. Mexico is a good case for study for substantive and methodological reasons. From a substantive perspective, it fits three important requirements. First, Mexico counts on a large indigenous population. The share of indigenous language speakers totals about 10 per cent of the nation's population but with these groups heavily concentrated in the southern states of Chiapas, Oaxaca, and those in the Yucatán Peninsula. Second, scholars examining indigenous groups in Mexico often note that Mexico's long time national electoral authoritarian regime, run by the *Partido Institucional Revolucionario* (PRI) during most of the twentieth century, faced frequent indigenous protests, mobilisation, and regime opposition (Yashar 2005; Anaya Muñoz 2006; Mejia Piñeros and Sarmiento Silva 1987; Trejo and Aguilar 1999; Trejo 2001a, b, 2012). Third, scholars note how the national PRI sometimes devolved political decision making to subnational regime officials, namely, its state governors who were charged with managing social conflict and delivering regime support (Bernstein 1993; Hernández Rodríguez 2008; Díaz-Cayeros 2006; Langston unpublished book manuscript). This suggests that the national PRI leaders could have decentralised decisions about the best way to manage ethnic diversity and conflict to subnational officials as well, even though this proposition has not yet been tested empirically.

From a methodological perspective, two unusual features of the Mexican case raise the internal validity of any empirical analysis or estimates of the tendency of national autocrats to undertake political decentralisation in response to indigenous communities. First, Mexico's national electoral authoritarian government was organised around a constitutionally federal structure with its territory divided into states, in turn subdivided into municipalities, with regular national and subnational elections held according to a stable electoral calendar. This allows me to identify and observe the regime's variety of subnational (state and municipal) regime officials that could have been charged with managing political control, should the national regime have chosen to undertake such political decentralisation. Second, and most important, an unusual political reform undertaken during the last decade of PRI rule in the state of Oaxaca allows me to directly measure an instance where the PRI undertook decentralised political control to some subnational officials and cases where it did not.

Specifically, Oaxaca's PRI-run state government formally codified new electoral rules in 1995 that decentralised the authority to design new methods for selecting local governments to municipal leaders in some municipalities but not to all. These *'Usos y Costumbres (UyC)'* or 'Uses and Customs' rules were adopted in 412 municipalities in 1995, rising to 418 in 1997, with the remainder retaining the state's centrally determined rules for universal candidate and voter suffrage rights and the individual secret ballot. Oaxaca's UyC systems thus give us a unique opportunity to examine how the nature of ethnic-based conflict affects strategies for national authoritarian political decentralisation.

## Research on Political Institutions and Ethnic Diversity in Democratic Systems

Scholars have long noted that shared ethnic identity binds people together more strongly than other common social, economic, or political characteristics or experiences, although the explanations for this range from shared primordial genetic or familial traits to constructed psychological or sociological ones (Horowitz 2000). Ethnic affinity thus allows ethnic leaders to influence group members to suppress individual needs for the benefit of the group in a sustained way (Horowitz 2000). Although ethnic elites and entrepreneurs might choose to moderate perceptions of intra-group ethnic affinities and member relations with other ethnic or non-ethnic associations in order to avoid unrest, they might also choose to exaggerate these same ethnic affinities and differences from other associations in order to incite inter-group conflict and rebellion (Horowitz 2000).

Even so, ethnic group membership also often coexists with other group affiliations, leading scholars to examine how the relative saliency of ethnic membership compared to other identities depends on national political institutional arrangements (Horowitz 2000; Posner 2005; Wilkinson 2004; Chandra 2004; Laitin 1998). Scholars studying ethnic diversity in national democratic systems in Africa and Asia, for example, examine how different political institutional configurations can be used to shape ethnic identity and its political salience (Horowitz 2000; Posner 2005; Wilkinson 2004; Chandra 2004; Laitin 1998). Narrow national districts that crosscut ethnic group lines reduce the salience of ethnic group divisions, leading members to focus on other identities instead (Horowitz 2000; Posner 2005), thereby reducing the chances that ethnically divided societies will experience conflict. This is especially the case when such institutional structures are coupled with national or local electoral laws that reduce the number of political parties in the system or that force parties to appeal across ethnic groups rather than separately to them (Wilkinson 2004; Varshney 2002). Likewise, federal institutions that shift the point of political focus of ethnic voters to lower levels of government (Horowitz 2007) also reduce the salience of ethnic identities and thus the chances of ethnic conflict and rebellion as well.

Interestingly, scholars of Latin American politics argue that ethnic groups are always well placed to take advantage of the narrow districts and lower levels of government that emerge with decentralising reforms (Van Cott 2008). Latin America's indigenous groups 'have a tradition of regularly scheduled and occasional deliberative assemblies, at which leaders are chosen, important decisions are made, and cultural identities and community solidarity are built and maintained' (Van Cott 2008). The region's indigenous communities also often have a long history of obligatory community service (Van Cott 2008). Scholars of Latin American ethnic politics thus often argue that decentralising reforms that allow indigenous groups greater involvement in deciding local affairs, either through elections or participatory democracy, can be used to raise the legitimacy of governmental institutions in the eyes of their members, thereby addressing ethnic diversity and reducing the chances of intergroup conflict and rebellion against national governments (Van Cott 2008; Wampler 2008; McNulty 2011; Hiskey and Seligson 2003; Eaton 2004; Madrid 2012). Politically decentralised systems also raise ethnic group participation in local politics and policy making, reducing their incentive to engage in conflict and rebellion as well (Hiskey and Seligson 2003; Madrid 2012; McNulty 2011; Van Cott 2008; Wampler 2008).

Research to date has thus focused on how political institutions work to manage ethnic diversity in national democratic systems. However, national democrats are not the only ones that face ethnic diversity and the chance of ethnic conflict. National autocrats also often face ethnically diverse populations whose tendency toward conflict can destabilise their regimes. It may thus be the case that national autocrats rely on some of the same political institutional solutions as democrats to manage ethnically diverse populations as well. That this might be the case should not be that surprising. Scholars have often noted that national autocrats deploy many of the same national political institutional arrangements as national democrats to ensure political stability and the survival of their regimes. They often use national elections (Geddes 2005; Lust-Okar 2006; Blaydes 2011; Levitsky and Way 2010), national political parties (Brownlee 2007; Magaloni 2006; Blaydes 2011; Geddes 2005; Greene 2007; Svolik 2012), and national legislatures (Gandhi 2008; Boix and Svolik 2013; Gandhi and Przeworski 2007; Wright 2008) to channel intra-regime, regime-opposition, and regime-mass conflict, stabilising national authoritarian rule.[1] And, a growing number of scholars examine how decentralisation can facilitate regime governance as well (Jin, Qian and Weingast 2005; Montinola, Qian and Weingast 1996; Qian and Weingast 1996; Landry 2008).

Even so, national autocrats' political goals and strategies for using national political institutions are not the same as those of national democrats. Unlike national democrats, national autocrats use political institutional configurations to engineer political outcomes favourable to their regimes, leading them to engage in frequent manipulation of the political institutions they deploy in this regard. This is nowhere better seen than in the ways that national autocrats manipulate electoral rules managing the selection of national authoritarian legislatures, with electoral rules that legally bias results in favour of the national regime as a top choice (Malesky and Schuler 2011; Schedler 2006; Birch 2011). Unlike national democrats, national autocrats also need not implement their institutional strategies universally or evenly. National autocrats can formally and legally tailor political institutions to regional regime needs (Birch 2011), engineer district magnitudes and boundary lines (Malesky 2009), manage candidate selection and list placement (Malesky and Schuler 2011; Díaz-Cayeros and Langston 2003; Langston 2001), and allocated campaign resources (Langston and Morgenstern 2009). They can

---

1. Some scholars note that creation of national political institutions can facilitate democratic transitions in some contexts (e.g. Lindberg 2009; Wright 2008; Wright and Escribà-Folch 2012; Bunce and Wolchik 2010; Howard and Roessler 2006), or indicate that transitions are underway (Brownlee 2007; Gandhi and Lust-Okar 2009).

also engage in selective informal and illegal political practices as well, including the selective enforcement of formal electoral rules, selective candidate intimidation and voter coercion, and selective vote-buying and fraud (Schedler 2002; Kitschelt and Wilkinson 2007; Birch 2011). It thus may be the case that national autocrats use political decentralisation not merely to reduce the salience of ethnic group affiliation or to raise ethnic group participation but also to co-opt or manage ethnic group members more firmly into supporting the national authoritarian regime. I explain below.

**National Authoritarian Political Decentralisation for Managing Ethnic Diversity**

I argue that national autocrats decentralise political control to subnational regime officials to manage ethnic diversity and to better manage ethnic group leaders and members into supporting the national authoritarian regime. I build on research on the benefits of decentralisation in national authoritarian regimes. Scholars have long argued that subnational governments in nationally authoritarian systems are better able to determine local constituent needs than national governments (Jin, Qian, and Weingast 2005; Montinola, Qian, and Weingast 1996; Qian and Weingast 1996). The decentralisation of administrative and fiscal decisions to subnational regime officials can thus raise the level of policy innovation and efficiency because subnational officials enjoy better information about local conditions and constituent needs than national officials (Jin, Qian, and Weingast 2005; Montinola, Qian, and Weingast 1996; Qian and Weingast 1996). Likewise, scholars have also begun to argue that national autocrats likely perceive similar potential benefits from the decentralisation of political authority as well (Benton 2016a, b). Because of their regional positions, subnational regime officials should be better at determining local political and social dynamics than national autocrats, and thus better at deciding the most effective methods for managing and building national authoritarian regime support (Benton 2016a, b).

Of course, the extent of the benefits of decentralisation to national authoritarian regimes depends on other economic, social, and political factors (see, for example, research by O'Brien and Li 2000; Blanchard and Shleifer 2001; Oi and Rozelle 2000; Grindle 2007; Zhuravskaya 2000; Uchimura and Jütting 2007; Ko and Zhi 2013). Any decentralisation, whether administrative, fiscal, or political, is a risky endeavour for national authoritarian regimes. Subnational officials do not always manage decentralised administrative and fiscal authorities in ways that balance local constituent needs with national political goals (see, for example, O'Brien and Li 2000; Blanchard and Shleifer 2001; Oi and Rozelle 2000; Grindle 2007; Zhuravskaya 2000; Uchimura and Jütting 2007; Ko and Zhi 2013), undermining the benefits of decentralisation to the national authoritarian regime and its chances for survival. Even so, that national autocrats, even military regimes (Eaton 2006; Falleti 2011), regularly undertake administrative and fiscal decentralisation reveals that they expect these measures to deliver benefits to the regime. Likewise, scholars have begun to show that national autocrats also decentralise political control to subnational regime officials in core districts and recently marginal ones as well, in order to raise the chances that in so doing they can retain aggregate support and territorial control (e.g., Benton 2016a, b).

I argue that national autocrats have an incentive to decentralise decisions about political control to subnational regime officials when facing ethnically diverse communities. Shared ethnic identity binds community members together and can raise the chances that they will mobilise to undertake sustained social or political activities, either for or against the regime. National autocrats must thus constantly evaluate the most reliable and efficient means for keeping ethnic communities aligned with the national authoritarian regime. I argue that this leads national autocrats to delegate decisions about the management of ethnically diverse communities to subnational regime officials whose superior knowledge about local social and political dynamics raise the chances that they will find innovative ways for engineering regime support among these groups, especially compared to national authoritarian leaders who are further removed. In contrast, the absence of large ethnic communities reduces the need for national autocrats to relinquish political authority to subnational regime officials based on ethnic considerations. They will, instead, prioritise other political and social dynamics when considering whether to decentralise political control (as explained by Benton 2016a, b).

The incentive to undertake political decentralisation to subnational regime officials among ethnically diverse communities rises with their tendency to engage in conflictive behaviour. Generally speaking, national authoritarian leaders should prefer to decentralise political management to only those subnational officials in charge of non-conflictive communities (Benton 2016a, b). It is risky to grant subnational regime officials political authority amidst social volatility, even if national leaders trust that local officials will work on behalf of the regime. The potential costs of any mismanagement of, or failure to mitigate, local political and social tensions are too high for national autocrats to risk, with this chance greatest among subnational regime officials only just recently empowered to develop their own strategies for managing local affairs (Benton 2016a, b). National authoritarian leaders should thus generally prefer to retain central control over regions or localities experiencing conflict or unrest, in order to prevent them from spinning further out of regime control (Benton 2016a, b).

However, when local unrest is based in ethnic group grievances, the political risks to and thus calculations of national autocrats change. The dynamics of ethnic-based conflict mean that it is more dangerous to national authoritarian regimes than non-ethnic based conflict. The natural affinities tying ethnic group members together mean that any shared grievances and conflictive activities they engage in to make them known can be sustained in the long term. This raises the chances that localities experiencing ethnic-based conflict can move into outright rebellion against the regime, with this anti-regime conflict spilling over into neighbouring communities as well. Any concerns that national officials may have about the capacity of subnational regime officials to manage conflictive communities are outweighed by the risk of allowing ethnic group grievances to go unaddressed. As such, national autocrats find it in their best interest to assume the risks of decentralisation to subnational regime officials in highly conflictive ethnically diverse places in exchange for the benefits of subnational officials' superior local political and social knowledge about the best way to manage ethnic communities. This means that the incentive for national autocrats to decentralise political decisions to subnational regime officials grows with the size of the ethnic group population in the community, and especially with their tendency toward conflictive behaviour.

That national autocrats would accept the risk of political decentralisation to subnational regime officials facing conflictive ethnic populations should not be that surprising. Scholars of national democratic systems have noted that decentralising reforms that directly involve subnational officials and local communities in their design and implementation deliver better results than those that are directed and designed exclusively by national governments (Eaton 2004; Van Cott 2008; Wampler 2008; McNulty 2011; Hiskey and Seligson 2003). In the case of national democratic systems, this means the bottom-up decentralising reforms produce better political participation, representation, and governance, thereby strengthening national democratic system stability. In the case of national authoritarian regimes, however, this implies that bottom-up decentralising reforms will contribute to national authoritarian regime governance and thus regime stability as well, although through its effects on political control. Scholars have often noted that many activities associated with ethnic groups are not particularly democratic. Indigenous community identities in Latin America, for example, have been long thought antithetical to the individualism embedded in liberal democracy. Building community identities requires preventing dissent, which is often accomplished through community participation but also through community exclusion, intimidation, and violence (Van Cott 2008; Fox 1996; Andersson and Van Laerhoven 2007; Blair 2000). Certain indigenous group characteristics are also known to trigger anti-democratic tendencies within systems of participatory democracy (Van Cott 2008). As such, when national autocrats allow subnational regime officials to involve ethnic populations in the design of local institutions, they not only reduce the chances of ethnic conflict and rebellion, they also reinforce local and thus national authoritarian rule.

## A Good Case for Study: Electoral Authoritarian Mexico

I test the argument using the case of electoral authoritarian Mexico. Mexico is a good case for study for several reasons. Mexico's *Partido Institucional Revolucionario* (PRI) managed the typical electoral authoritarian regime during the twentieth century, ensuring control over elections for national, state, and municipal offices until the 1980s when it began to allow opposition victories in a few municipal and state elections. In 1997, the PRI yielded control over the lower chamber of congress and the party lost the presidency in 2000, signalling the end of its electoral authoritarian regime.

Scholars regularly note that national PRI leaders sought to maximize regime member loyalty and citizen support while minimising political and social backlash against the regime (Hernández Rodríguez 2008; Bernstein 1993; Magaloni 2006), and that it used a variety of economic resources and political tools to this end. Scholars show how the PRI-ruled national government used state-led economic development (Greene 2007), tax policy (Díaz-Cayeros 2006), discretional fiscal transfers (Magaloni 2006; Cornelius, Craig, and Fox 1994; Díaz-Cayeros 2006), the delivery of other clientelist benefits (Bruhn 1997; Fox 1994), and the rotation of bureaucratic appointments and elected positions (Smith 1979; Díaz-Cayeros 2006) to manage regime member loyalty and guarantee citizen support.

Scholars also note that national PRI autocrats relied on political institutional arrangements to reinforce PRI rule. Formal universal electoral laws like party registration rules, ballot structures, and electoral formulas (Díaz-Cayeros and Magaloni 2001; Molinar 1991; Méndez de Hoyos 2006) and access to campaign media (Lawson 2002; Langston unpublished book manuscript) were used to bias elections in favour of the PRI. National PRI officials also selectively strategised the selection of candidates (Díaz-Cayeros and Langston 2003; Díaz-Cayeros 2006; Langston 2001, unpublished book manuscript) and the distribution of campaign resources (Langston and Morgenstern 2009; Langston unpublished book manuscript). And, PRI officials informally and illegally managed the selective application of electoral laws (Fox 2007), like access to the ballot (Díaz-Cayeros and Langston 2003; Díaz-Cayeros 2006) and voting secrecy (Molinar 1991; Fox 2007). The party monitored, coerced, and intimidated candidates and voters, as well as regularly bought votes and stuffed ballot boxes (Cornelius 2004; Fox 1994; Magaloni 2006; Molinar 1991; Simpser 2013).

Most research to date has been conducted on national level regime strategies for managing political control. However, several scholars have noted that national PRI autocrats appear to have devolved many decisions about regime political affairs to state governors (Bernstein 1993; Hernández Rodríguez 2008; Díaz-Cayeros 2006; Langston unpublished book manuscript). Governors who did not deliver social stability and elite cohesion, and party member loyalty and citizen support, at election time are often said to have been removed from office or stymied in their careers (Hernández Rodríguez 2008; Bernstein 1993). National and state PRI leaders are known to have allowed a variety of informal local political practices – ranging from exclusionary autocratic rule by local strongmen to surprisingly inclusionary forms of local governance – to operate in local government as well, as long as social order was maintained and PRI support preserved (Recondo 2007; Anaya Muñoz 2006; Hernández Rodríguez 2008; Anderson 1971; Bernstein 1993; Padgett 1966; Baily 1988; Rodríguez 1987). Some scholars have noted the types of political intervention undertaken by state PRI leaders in municipal political affairs (Hernández Rodríguez 2008; Anderson 1971; Bernstein 1993; Padgett 1966; Baily 1988; Rodríguez 1987), while others have highlighted the all-powerful role of governors over political matters in their states (Martínez Cabañas 1985; Rodríguez 1987; Bernstein 1993; Hernández Rodríguez 2008).

Importantly for the purposes of the argument made here, anecdotal evidence also suggests that Mexico's PRI-ruled national electoral authoritarian regime decentralised decisions about the management of regime support but that they did not do so evenly across their domain. Not all state governors enjoyed the same political capacity or will to manage state politics in ways that were always aligned with national PRI goals, with even strongly loyal state PRI leaders sometimes flouting national PRI demands (Hernández Rodríguez 2008; Bernstein 1993). Because any mismanagement of state political affairs, economic resources, and social dynamics could undermine national PRI rule, national PRI rulers thus likely discriminated among state governors when decentralising decisions about regime support (Benton 2016a, b), although this proposition has only begun to be tested systematically (for example, by Benton 2016a, b).

This means that national autocrats should have discriminated among states and localities for political decentralisation by variation in the size and nature of regional and local indigenous populations as well. The Mexican government estimates the number of indigenous language speakers at about 10% of the nation's total population, but with these groups heavily concentrated in the southern regions, especially in the states of Chiapas, Oaxaca, and those in the Yucatán Peninsula. Interestingly, scholars examining indigenous groups in Mexico often note that the PRI-ruled national authoritarian government frequently faced indigenous protests, mobilisation, and regime opposition during the twentieth century (Yashar 2005; Anaya Muñoz 2006; Mejia Piñeros and Sarmiento Silva 1987; Trejo and Aguilar 1999; Trejo 2001a, b, 2012). Although scholars sometimes examine the ways that opposition parties harnessed ethnic grievances against the PRI-led national electoral authoritarian regime (Trejo 2004, 2012; Yashar 2005), few have examined whether and how national PRI autocrats may have also sought to manage ethnic populations and conflict as well in order to bring these communities and their activities in line with national regime goals. And, no one has examined how political institutions, and especially political decentralisation, may have been used in this regard.

Yet, the PRI's use of political institutional arrangements alongside its frequent reliance on state and local officials to deliver social stability and political control suggests that national autocrats may have sought to use politically decentralised forms of decision-making to manage indigenous populations as well. That the electoral authoritarian PRI-ruled regime ratified the International Labour Organization's Convention 169 in 1990 to acknowledge the rights of indigenous peoples and reformed the national Constitution in 1992 to recognise its multicultural indigenous heritage, serves to highlight the regime's political concerns about its volatile indigenous population.[2] Sixteen PRI-run state governments joined the national government and undertook constitutional reforms to recognise their indigenous heritages, mostly in the early to mid-1990s, although one state (Guerrero) undertook reforms as early

---

2.   The PRI-run national government also produced the 1996 San Andrés Accords on indigenous rights and cultures in response to the 1994 rebellion in Chiapas, but secondary legislation was dramatically watered down by the time of its 2001 approval (López Bárcenas 2010).

as 1987 (López Bárcenas 2010).[3] A few states even moved beyond symbolic state constitutional recognition to codify such rights into secondary laws (Anaya Muñoz 2003, 2005; López Bárcenas 2010). Many states, however, also allowed indigenous groups to incorporate customary laws and practices informally into local (municipal and sub-municipal town-level) political processes, rather than relying on formal legislation (Anaya Muñoz 2003, 2005, 2006; de León Pasquel 2001). Even so, the logic guiding whether PRI-run state governments allowed or disallowed indigenous customs to affect local political decision-making and election processes, and especially how this may have fitted into national leaders' strategies for engineering PRI support, is as yet largely unstudied. In the next section, I show how Mexico's state of Oaxaca can be used to examine the logic driving the distribution of political authority to subnational regime officials to manage conflictive ethnic populations.

### Testable Expectations of the Argument for Indigenous Oaxaca, Mexico

Systematic analysis of the structure of decision making within national electoral authoritarian regimes presents a challenge to researchers. Credible data that measures the level of decentralisation in political decision making, especially as regards political manipulation, is difficult, if not impossible to collect. This is certainly the case for Mexico, which explains the general lack of analysis beyond qualitative accounts of the way that state governors were incorporated into the PRI's national electoral authoritarian system. Conveniently, however, the state of Oaxaca approved a unique electoral reform during the last decade of national PRI rule that can help test arguments about the decentralisation of political decision making in response to ethnic diversity and conflict. Oaxaca's PRI-ruled state government proposed, and its state legislature approved, new electoral rules on 30 August 1995 that divided municipalities into those allowed to create new rules for selecting local governments according to local '*Usos y Costumbres*' (UyC) or 'Uses and Customs' and those required to use centrally determined state election rules, called '*Partidos Politicos*' (PP) or 'Political Parties' systems. UyC systems were adopted in 412 municipalities in 1995, rising to 418 in 1997. The remainder of Oaxaca's 570 PP municipalities maintained state level PP systems. These systems are still in use today, and total 417 since 2012.

Oaxaca's UyC systems revolve around a central decision-making body, the *Asamblea General Comunal* or General Community Assembly (AGC), where the formal selection of municipal authorities takes place. The AGC is run by a *Mesa de Debates* or Supervisory Board comprised of incumbent municipal officials, and sometimes of elders' councils as well. The *Mesa de Debates* is charged with determining which rules will be used that election cycle to select new municipal leaders in the AGC. The AGC is the public town hall meeting whose participants, either as leaders in the *Mesa de Debates*, voters, or candidates, can be restricted

---

3.    Three other states adopted constitutional reforms after 2000 (López Bárcenas 2010).

by sex, age, marital status, birth and/or residency requirements, and participation in local unpaid community service (*tequio*) and fulfilment of a series of unpaid community administrative positions (*cargos*). The *Mesa de Debates*, and thus AGC meetings, can choose to select municipal authorities using a variety of voting mechanisms, ranging from secret individual ballots to publicly cast (single and multiple) votes, according to simultaneous or sequential procedures. The original 1995 UyC reform made the participation of political parties in UyC elections optional, but reforms to the UyC law in 1997 prohibited political parties from presenting candidates in these systems.

The variety of rules that can be used within UyC systems means that these systems can vary quite dramatically from one another, as well as from year to year, since rules and procedures can be changed. From a political decentralisation perspective, UyC rules give municipal leaders the capacity to manage elections in ways normally considered politically manipulative by scholars of electoral malpractice (e.g., Birch 2011; Schedler 2002) because they allow municipal leaders the flexibility to restrict candidate and voter political rights, sometimes quite heavily, as well as to deny any participants the individual secret ballot. That municipal leaders, through the *Mesa de Debates* charged with running the AGC, have the power to determine the combination of UyC practices that will be used each election year means that they can design their own subnational rules of the game, implying that state autocrats formally devolved considerable political power to municipal UyC leaders with the 1995 UyC electoral reform. Oaxaca's PP municipalities, in contrast, must adhere to centrally determined state level electoral rules, restricting the capacity of PP municipal authorities to design strategies for managing local political control apart from state leaders. This is not to say that PP municipal leaders do not also seek to engineer election outcomes, but that state leaders did not formally confer this authority to them. State leaders thus retained a greater capacity to determine the nature of electoral manipulation in PP municipalities.

Scholars of Oaxaca's political history and UyC systems note that the decision to adopt UyC rules came on the tail of decades of political conflict that in the 1990s threatened to destabilise state politics and state PRI rule. Beginning in the 1960s, student organisations, labour associations, and peasant groups began to organise to defend their interests against the state government and state PRI officials, becoming active in each other's struggles and forming alliances to facilitate cooperation in pressuring the state government on a variety of themes, including respect for increased local political autonomy and democratisation (Anaya Muñoz 2006; Bustamante *et al.* 1978; Foweraker and Craig 1990). These groups fought for, among other things, control over natural resources, better agricultural working conditions, land rights, better local public services, indigenous rights, respect for indigenous culture, recognition for traditional forms of local governance, an end to state PRI intrusion into local affairs, and local democratisation (Mejía Piñeros and Sarmiento 1987; Anaya Muñoz 2006; Barbas and Bartolomé 1999; Reina 1988). Interestingly, state officials had long used informal UyC-type political practices prior to the 1995 UyC reform to select party lists for municipal offices

(Guerra Pulido 2000; Elizarrarás Álvarez 2002; Recondo 2001, 2002, 2007). Local strongmen able to create municipal party lists and avoid the presentation of competing lists from members of their communities would then register their lists as having received 100 per cent PRI support. However, if municipal leaders selected candidates that state level authorities did not approve of, even if registering them as PRI 'winners', state leaders would intervene and have the state legislature replace them with interim leaders and often call for new elections (Anaya Muñoz 2006; Eisenstadt 2007). This added to pre-existing local-state tensions.[4]

Oaxaca's state officials frequently clamped down on mobilisations, especially in the 1970s and 1980s, when it needed to ensure social control and PRI support (Anaya Muñoz 2006; Bailón Corres 1999; López Monjardín 1986; Martínez Vázquez 1990). However, local protests against PRI rule led Governor Heladio Ramírez López (1986–1992) to seek to placate local demands by granting additional informal autonomy to some local leaders (Anaya Muñoz 2006). The rise of the armed Ejército Zapatista de Liberación Nacional (EZLN) insurgency in the nearby state of Chiapas in 1994 led subsequent state officials to move to take more formal political action. Oaxaca's state officials worried that the EZLN would trigger stronger mobilisation against the state PRI-led government because many indigenous organisations in the state expressed sympathy for the Zapatistas (Anaya Muñoz 2005, 2006).[5] In early 1995, Governor Diódoro Carrasco Altamirano (1992–1998) moved to implement formal political measures that would become the UyC municipal electoral reform of September 1995 (Anaya Muñoz 2006).

The ultimate assignment of municipalities into UyC and PP system categories was decided by a small group of state officials from the newly created state electoral institute in consultation with leaders of the PRI and opposition parties in the state (Anaya Muñoz 2006; Recondo 2007). Academic experts on local social and political dynamics also took part (Anaya Muñoz 2006; Recondo 2007). Most scholars examining the logic behind UyC assignment have thus tended to focus on the political factors motivating UyC assignment, sometimes controlling for indigenous population and conflict and sometimes not. In places under PRI control, some scholars argue that state leaders ultimately favoured the placement of UyC systems among municipalities with a history of strong PRI support and weak opposition presence (Anaya Muñoz 2006). Others take a more nuanced view and argue that national autocrats decentralised political control to subnational officials ruling over both core PRI and some marginal PRI districts whose populations had only recently shifted against the regime, with an eye toward preserving aggregate PRI support and territorial PRI control (Benton 2016a, b).

4. Such activities led candidates from indigenous associations and other opposition groups to protest state decisions, even in the 1970s, with many municipalities during this period and since then experiencing post-election conflicts that often resulted in citizen deaths (Eisenstadt 2007). In early 1990s, well over 10 per cent of Oaxacan municipalities experienced violent post-election conflicts (Eisenstadt 2007).

5. Although the armed insurgency was short-lived, Zapatista leaders evaded capture and continued to demand local indigenous autonomy and political liberalisation.

In places under opposition control, scholars argue that PRI-run state leaders negotiated UyC and PP assignment with state level opposition party leaders, with opposition party leaders strongly opposing UyC systems in their municipalities because they believed that these rules would facilitate the return to PRI rule (Anaya Muñoz 2006). Others show that opposition leaders were allowed to determine their own political fates and often chose to adopt UyC rules in localities under their control (Benton 2016a, b). Interestingly, few scholars have examined whether variation in municipal indigenous population and conflict also affected UyC assignment among Oaxaca's 570 municipalities, despite the fact that most agree that the 1994 Zapatista rebellion in neighbouring Chiapas prompted Oaxaca's state officials to undertake municipal UyC reform in 1995 in the first place.[6] And, those that have considered whether indigenous considerations mattered for UyC assignment have dismissed them, noting that many highly indigenous municipalities received PP systems while many nonindigenous localities were assigned UyC rules (e.g., Cleary 2005; Eisenstadt and Ríos 2014). This research has had the unfortunate effect of dissuading scholars from taking a closer theoretical and empirical look. However, if the argument made here about the role of political decentralisation for managing conflictive ethnically diverse populations is correct, then these factors should have contributed to determining the assignment of UyC systems across Oaxaca's 570 municipalities, even if the political factors were the primary motivating factor at work. That is, state PRI leaders should have prioritised UyC systems among its most indigenous municipalities, focusing particular attention among those with highly conflictive tendencies, all else being equal. And, state PRI leaders should have prioritised PP systems among its least indigenous municipalities, with the incentive to assign PP systems highest among those municipalities experiencing prior conflict. However, UyC regimes were only useful in managing ethnic conflict for PRI-run state officials insofar as they were conferred to subnational PRI members who could be trusted to use them to engineer pro-PRI results. In opposition hands, UyC rules could have been used to engineer ethnic communities against the PRI. State autocrats thus should have chosen to impose UyC rules in PRI-run places according to indigenous population and the presence of conflict, leading to the following testable expectations of the argument:

*H1: In places under PRI control, UyC regime assignment will be more likely where indigenous populations are largest, all else being equal.*
*H2: In places under PRI control, UyC regime assignment will be more likely where indigenous groups have been associated with prior conflict, all else being equal.*

In contrast, Oaxaca's PRI-run state autocrats should have left opposition parties to decide the UyC fates of municipalities under their control, with the rationale motivating them different from that of the PRI. Just as with PRI state leaders, leaders in opposition-run municipalities should have found it in their political interests to adopt UyC rules in places with high indigenous populations.

---

6.    Scholars have found that the size of the indigenous population played no role (Cleary 2005).

However, unlike PRI state leaders, opposition leaders should have been wary of placing UyC systems in highly conflictive indigenous communities, for fear that placing decision making in local leaders' hands would further undermine local social stability already at risk. This leads to the following:

*H3: In places under opposition control, UyC regime assignment will be more likely where indigenous populations are largest, all else being equal.*
*H4: In places under opposition control, UyC regime assignment will be less likely where indigenous groups have been associated with prior conflict, all else being equal.*

It is important to note that testing the argument requires finding evidence for all four hypotheses. It is important to show that the logic behind UyC adoption in PRI-run places responds to the size of ethnic communities and to their tendency toward conflict, as well as that the logic of UyC adoption is different in opposition-led localities. If the logic driving UyC assignment were the same across PRI-run and opposition-led places, I could not conclude that top-down political considerations drove PRI state autocratic decisions, nor that top-down political considerations drove opposition UyC choices either, something that would be contrary to the argument that autocrats use political decentralisation to facilitate the management of ethnic communities and conflict.

## Statistical Analysis

I evaluate the testable hypotheses using logistic regression analysis. The dichotomous dependent variable (*UyC Adoption 1995*) captures whether the municipality was formally codified as a UyC system (1 = yes, 0 = no) in September 1995. The principal explanatory variables include the share of indigenous population (*Indigenous Pop.*)[7] and the presence of post-electoral conflicts in 1992 and 1995 after state elections (1 = yes, 0 = no) (*Conflicts 1992; Conflicts 1995*).[8] To account for whether the PRI or an opposition party controlled the municipality, I code whether the opposition came in first place (1 = yes, 0 = no) or not, calling this variable *Opposition Wins 1995*. I construct this variable as such to ease interpretation of the results, as explained further below.

The principal control variables include two factors also said to matter for UyC adoption (e.g., Benton 2016a, b): the amount of support won by the PRI in the municipality in the 1995 state elections and the change in PRI support from the previous 1992 state elections, called *PRI Support 1995* and *Chg. PRI 1992–95*.[9] I also include controls for the share of population living on ejido or communal lands (*Ejido Pop.*) (e.g. Recondo 2007; Anaya Muñoz 2006)[10] and for the total

---

7.  Data from INEGI. *Indigenous Pop. 1995* is the share of indigenous language speakers over age five.
8.  I am grateful to Todd Eisenstadt for providing this data.
9.  Data from IEEO.
10. Data from CONAPO. *Ejido Pop. 1990* is municipal population share on ejido or communal lands.

size of the municipal population (logged) (*Total Pop.*).[11] UyC systems should be easier to implement in places with communal land organisations and more difficult to implement in large urban areas. For the sake of model parsimony, I exclude the percent share of Catholic population as it produced no effect (I do not consider more complex measures of religious division, unlike Trejo 2004, 2012). I exclude other factors shown to matter for later PRI support in UyC systems – migration, poverty, fiscal resources (e.g. Benton 2012; Goodman and Hiskey 2008; Hiskey and Goodman 2011) – but that should have played no role in original UyC adoption.

I use fully dummy-interactive models on the pooled sample of all 570 municipalities to evaluate evidence for the four testable hypotheses. Because the testable hypotheses explain how the strategies for UyC assignment among municipalities under PRI control were different from under opposition control, I must demonstrate the causal effect of ingenuous populations and conflict on UyC adoption among Oaxaca's PRI-run municipalities, as well as show where it was statistically different from that observed in opposition-led places. The fully dummy-interactive models account for the possibility that different logics were at work among these UyC and PP systems. I thus interact the dummy *Opposition Wins 1995* variable with all independent variables, so that the constituent terms measure their effect in PRI-run municipalities and the dummy-interactive terms capturing (the difference in) their effect in opposition-led places. The following two subsections consider the results for PRI-run and opposition-led places separately.

*Table 8.1: Indigenous population, conflict, and UyC adoption in Oaxaca, Mexico*

|  | Model 1 | Model 2 |
|---|---|---|
| Conflicts 1992 | -2.812*** | -1.118 |
|  | (0.765) | (2.931) |
| Conflicts 1995 | -0.254 | 1.304 |
|  | (0.461) | (1.929) |
| Indigenous Pop. | 1.531*** | 0.564 |
|  | (0.441) | (1.637) |
| Conflicts 1992 * Indig. Pop. | 1.781* | 2.896 |
|  | (1.113) | (4.609) |
| Conflicts 1995 * Indig. Pop. | 0.517 | -6.142 |
|  | (0.909) | (4.035) |
| PRI Support 1995 | 3.026** | 2.349 |
|  | (1.423) | (1.851) |
| Conflicts 1992 * PRI Support 1995 |  | -2.421 |
|  |  | (4.688) |

(Continued)

---

11. Data from INEGI.

*Table 8.1: Continued*

|  | Model 1 | Model 2 |
| --- | --- | --- |
| Conflicts 1995 * PRI Support 1995 |  | -2.796 |
|  |  | (3.481) |
| Indig. Pop. * PRI Support 1995 |  | 1.685 |
|  |  | (2.551) |
| Conflicts 1992 *Indig. Pop * PRI Support 1995 |  | -2.352 |
| Support 1995 |  | (7.201) |
| Change PRI 1992–95 | -10.25*** | -10.34*** |
|  | (3.630) | (3.709) |
| PRI Support 1995 * Chg. PRI 1992–95 | 13.80** | 13.99** |
|  | (5.631) | (5.867) |
| Ejido Pop. 1991 | 2.000** | 2.351** |
|  | (0.917) | (1.009) |
| Total Pop. (log) | -1.292*** | -1.348*** |
|  | (0.174) | (0.182) |
| *Opp. Wins 1995* | *13.59* | *24.32\*\*\** |
|  | *(9.437)* | *(7.157)* |
| *Opp. * Conflicts 1992* | *2.648\** | *58.80\*\*\** |
|  | *(1.365)* | *(22.49)* |
| *Opp. * Conflicts 1995* | *1.533* | *194.6\*\*\** |
|  | *(1.398)* | *(49.68)* |
| *Opp. * Indig. Pop.* | *1.384* | *38.48\** |
|  | *(1.571)* | *(20.84)* |
| *Opp. * Conflicts 1992 * Indig. Pop.* | *-9.299\*\** | *-343.9\*\*\** |
|  | *(3.790)* | *(104.6)* |
| *Opp. * Conflicts 1995 * Indig. Pop.* | *1.849* | *33.56* |
|  | *(3.322)* | *(77.81)* |
| *Opp. * PRI Support 1995* | *-2.622* | *-26.85* |
|  | *(10.19)* | *(20.43)* |
| *Opp.* Conflicts 1992 * PRI Support 1995* |  | *-156.4\*\*\** |
|  |  | *(59.26)* |
| *Opp.* Conflicts 1995 * PRI Support 1995* |  | *-593.3\*\*\** |
|  |  | *(150.7)* |
| *Opp. * Indig. Pop. * PRI Support 1995* |  | *-106.8\** |
|  |  | *(59.99)* |

(Continued)

*Table 8.1: Continued*

| | Model 1 | Model 2 |
|---|---|---|
| *Opp. * Conflicts 1992 *Indig. Pop * PRI Support 1995* | | 817.6*** |
| | | (246.6) |
| Conflicts 1995 *Indig. Pop * PRI Support 1995 | | 11.38* |
| | | (6.560) |
| *Opp. * Conflicts 1995 *Indig. Pop * PRI Support 1995* | | 99.95 |
| | | (195.2) |
| *Opp. * Change PRI 1992–95* | −18.24 | 23.55 |
| | (17.83) | (19.48) |
| *Opp. * PRI Support 1995 * Change PRI 1992–95* | 56.27 | −101.2 |
| | (52.55) | (66.15) |
| *Opp. * Ejido Pop.* | 13.19** | 37.98*** |
| | (6.727) | (11.13) |
| *Opp. * Total Pop.* | −2.044 | −3.354*** |
| | (1.389) | (0.970) |
| Constant | 8.444*** | 9.230*** |
| | (1.848) | (2.124) |
| Pseudo-R-Squ. | 0.4069 | 0.4364 |
| BIC | −2919.123 | −2754.969 |
| Log-Likelihood | −199.363 | −189.454 |
| Chi-Squared | 144.29*** | 218.21*** |
| Number Obs. | 569 | 569 |

*Note:* Logistic Regression. Dependent Variable: UyC Adoption 1995 (1 = yes, 0 = no). Robust standard errors in parentheses. Observations do not total 570 due missing data. * $p < 0.10$, ** $p < 0.05$, *** $p < 0.01$.

## UyC Assignment in PRI-Run Municipalities

I first consider the logic of UyC adoption in PRI-run municipalities. Model 1, Table 8.1 examines the effect of conflictive indigenous populations on UyC adoption in PRI-run and opposition-led places. Hypothesis 1 predicted that PRI-run municipalities with larger indigenous populations would be more likely to adopt UyC systems. Hypothesis 2 predicted that this tendency would be strengthened by the presence of social conflict. I expect that the constituent term measuring the share of indigenous population (*Indigenous Pop.*) in a municipality and the interaction between its indigenous population and the presence of post-election conflicts (*Conflicts 1992 * Indig. Pop.* and *Conflicts 1995 * Indig. Pop.*) will be positive and significant in Model 1. As expected, the 1.531 coefficient for *Indigenous Pop.* and the 1.781 coefficient for *Conflicts 1992 * Indig. Pop.* were both significant at the

*Figure 8.1: Predicted probability UyC adoption according to indigenous population and conflict across Oaxaca's municipalities*

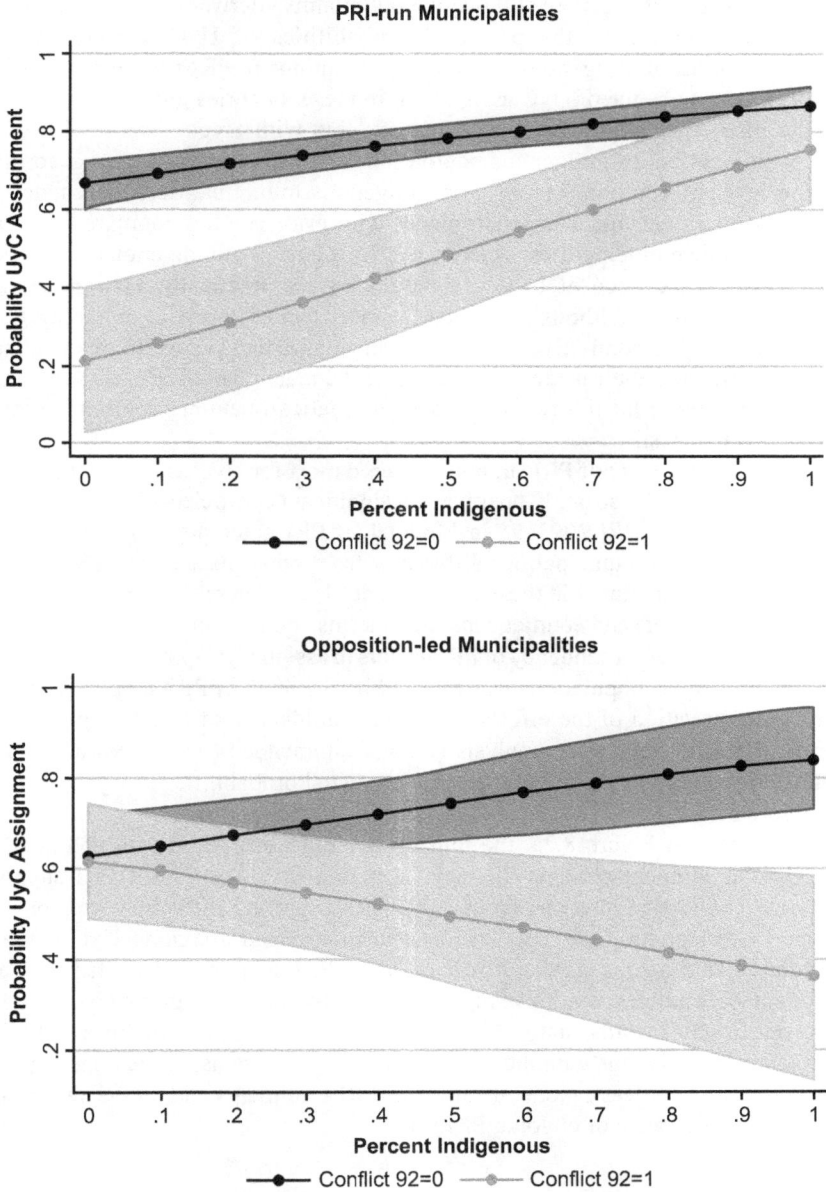

**PRI-run Municipalities**

**Opposition-led Municipalities**

*Note:* Figures based on Model 3, Table 8.1, and Table 8.2.

p < 0.1 level. Interestingly, post election conflicts after the 1995 elections (*Conflicts 1995*) did not have a significant effect on UyC adoption. This is likely due to the fact that these conflicts were still playing out months afterwards.

Figure 8.1a graphs the predicted probabilities of UyC adoption across different shares of indigenous municipal populations in PRI-run municipalities. As shown, the chance of UyC assignment in these localities grew with the share of the municipal indigenous population, in line with Hypothesis 1. However, the positive effect of indigenous population for UyC adoption varied according to the level of conflict. Among non-indigenous municipalities, the chance of UyC adoption was much lower in places with prior conflict compared to more socially stable municipalities, as expected. As the level of indigenous population share rose, the chance of UyC assignment rose dramatically as well, in line with Hypothesis 2. Although PRI state leaders tended to avoid assigning UyC systems in highly conflictive places, lest they aggravate pre-existing social and political tensions, their incentive to delegate the management of local social and political affairs to local leaders increased dramatically among conflicted highly indigenous places.

Although the level of PRI support mattered most for UyC assignment (Benton 2016b), as shown by strongly positive and significant coefficients for *PRI Support 1995* and *Change PRI 1992–95* in Model 1, if PRI autocrats treated conflictive highly indigenous municipalities differently from other places, then PRI support should not have mattered in these cases. Model 2 thus interacts *PRI Support 1995* with the indigenous and conflict constituent terms and their interaction, in order to determine whether the tendency of PRI leaders to assign UyC systems to conflictive highly indigenous populations was affected by the level of PRI support. Because direct interpretation of the effects, sign, and significance of complex interaction terms in logistic regression analysis is not recommended (Ai and Norton 2003), I move directly to an examination of the predicted probabilities of UyC adoption in Figure 8.2a.

As shown in Figure 8.2a, the impact of indigenous population and conflict on UyC assignment remains the same across different levels of PRI support, with the confidence intervals around the lines capturing different levels of PRI support overlapping. State PRI leaders tended to avoid assigning UyC systems to conflictive places, regardless of patterns of PRI support, but tended to use a different logic among conflictive highly indigenous places, assigning UyC systems to them. In other words, state PRI autocrats sought to appease highly conflictive indigenous populations with the assignment of UyC systems, in the hope that this would, in the very least, moderate any anti-PRI sentiments and, at the very most, raise their acceptance of ongoing PRI rule.

## UyC Assignment in Opposition-Led Municipalities

I now consider the logic of UyC adoption in opposition-led municipalities. Testing the argument and the hypotheses requires demonstrating that the decision criteria for the distribution of UyC systems among opposition-led municipalities tend

*Figure 8.2: Predicted probability UyC adoption according to PRI support, indigenous population, and conflict across Oaxaca's municipalities*

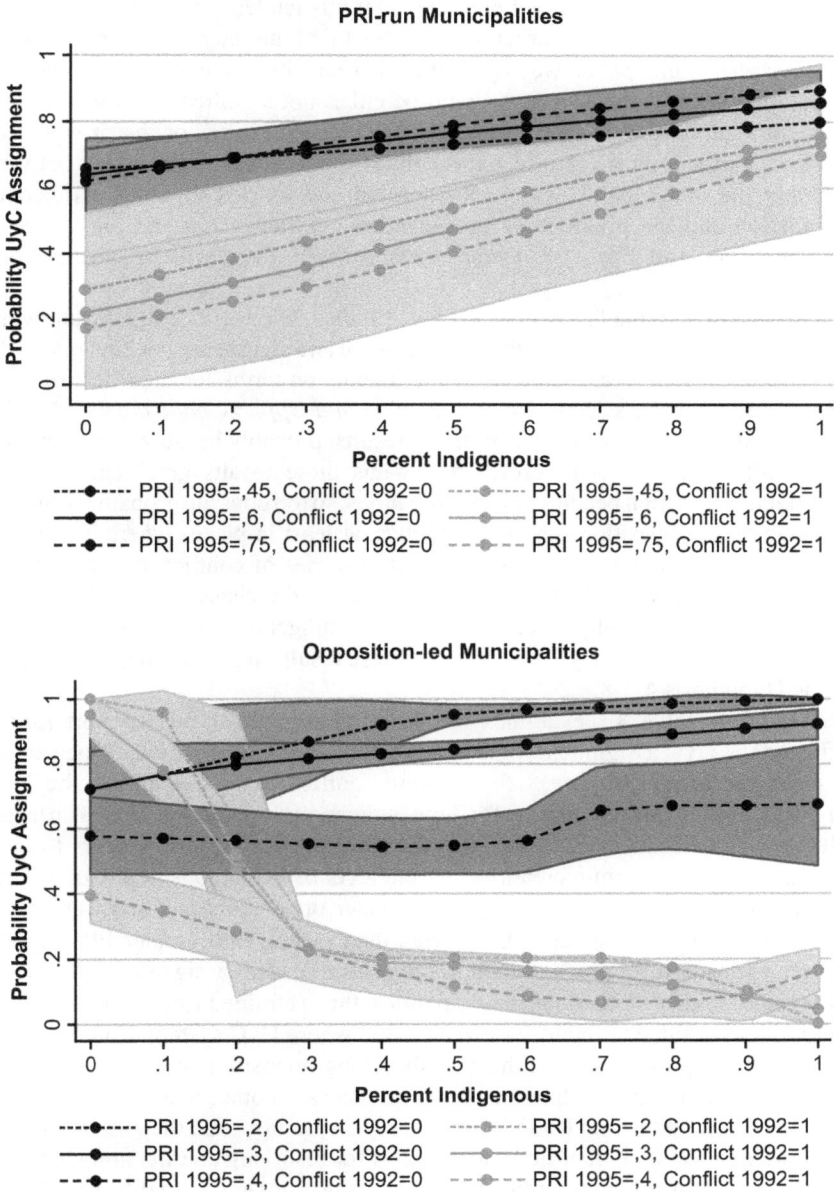

**PRI-run Municipalities**

**Opposition-led Municipalities**

*Note:* Figures based on Model 4, Table 8.1, and Table 8.2.

to be different from PRI-run places. Hypothesis 3 predicted that opposition-led municipalities with larger indigenous populations would be more likely to adopt UyC systems, but Hypothesis 4 predicted that this tendency would be dampened by the presence of social conflict. I thus expect that the interaction term between whether the municipality was opposition-led and its percent share indigenous population (*Opp.* * *Indig. Pop.*) would be either not significant, showing that it was not significantly different from that for PRI-led places, or that it would be positive and significant. I also expect that the three-way interactions between whether the municipality was opposition-led and its percent share indigenous population and the presence of post-election conflicts (*Opp.* * *Conflicts 1992* * *Indig. Pop.* and *Opp.* * *Conflicts 1995* * *Indig. Pop*) will be negative and significant.

As shown in Table 8.1, Model 3, *Opp.* * *Indig. Pop.* was not significant, while *Opp.* * *Conflicts 1992* * *Indig. Pop* was negative and significant (-9.299, $p < 0.01$), as expected. [As above, the effect of the interaction terms for the effect of 1995 post-election conflicts (*Opp.* * *Conflicts 1995 and Opp.* * *Conflicts 1995* * *Indig. Pop.*) produced no statistically significant results, probably because these conflicts were still playing out.] Figure 8.1b presents these results graphically. As the municipal population becomes more indigenous, so too does the probability of UyC assignment in opposition-run municipalities, at least in places where indigenous groups were not conflictive. In places with histories of conflict, however, larger indigenous populations had the opposite effect on the chances of UyC adoption compared to PRI-run places: conflictive highly indigenous municipal populations lowered the chances of UyC assignment. These results are in line with Hypothesis 3 and Hypothesis 4.

Model 4, Table 8.1 examines whether the strength of PRI support further affected the UyC assignment logic in opposition-run municipalities. Once again, I graph the results (Figure 8.2b). Among conflictive municipalities, the level of PRI support did not matter for how indigenous population shares affected UyC assignment decisions. However, the level of PRI support appears to have mattered in peaceful municipalities. As the level of indigenous population grew, municipalities with lower PRI support (greater opposition support) were much more likely to be assigned UyC systems than places with greater PRI support (lower opposition support). Although opposition leaders assigned UyC systems in peaceful highly indigenous municipalities, they refrained from assigning them in places where their support was weaker and where UyC systems could be used to manipulate politics against them. Only strong opposition leaders dared adopt UyC systems in highly indigenous peaceful places. In other words, in contrast to PRI autocrats, opposition leaders did view UyC systems – and their assignment in high indigenous municipalities – as a means for resolving conflict among highly ethnic populations. Any conflict in highly indigenous municipalities tended to be organised against the state PRI. Instead, opposition leaders assigned UyC systems where they could be used to prevent a return of the PRI, with these leaders having little incentive to use them to dampen anti-PRI sentiments among their populations.

## Conclusions and Implications for Future Research

The original goal of this chapter was to examine how national authoritarian governments manage ethnically diverse populations and respond to conflict among these communities. Most research on the usefulness of political institutional arrangements for managing ethnic groups and conflict has been conducted in nationally democratic settings. However, national authoritarian regimes often must rule over ethnically diverse populations that can threaten regime survival. Ethnic group affiliation ties members together in ways that allow them to suppress individual needs in favour of group ones, allowing ethnic group leaders to mobilise and direct their activities to achieve important ends. As such, mobilised ethnic group activities can present a clear benefit but also a clear threat to national authoritarian regimes whose survival depends on maintaining aggregate regime support and territorial control. Because national authoritarian regimes are also widely known to use political institutional arrangements to manage regime support, it thus stands to reason that they may also use institutions to manage ethnic populations and conflict as well.

With this possibility in mind, I examined how national autocrats might use political decentralisation to manage ethnically diverse and conflictive populations. The reliance on subnational regime officials to manage ethnic communities might deliver benefits to the national authoritarian regime, given that subnational regime officials often count on better local social and political knowledge than national autocrats, thereby allowing them to develop highly tailored strategies for managing ethnic communities that can at once appease their leaders and members and bring their activities in line with the national authoritarian regime. I thus argue that autocrats will consider decentralising political decision making about how to manage regime support and control to subnational officials in charge of large ethnic communities, and that this tendency will increase with the conflictiveness of these populations.

I test this argument on the case of Mexico's state of Oaxaca. In the final decade of electoral authoritarian rule by the *Partido Revolucionario Institucional* (PRI), subnational regime officials in the state of Oaxaca approved new rules for municipal governance that transferred the authority to decide municipal rules and decision-making processes to local governments in some municipalities but not in all. Statistical analysis of the application of these '*Usos y Costumbres*' (UyC) rules across municipalities shows that state autocrats assigned them among high indigenous populations. Specifically, among PRI-run municipalities, state autocrats assigned them in municipalities with large and conflictive indigenous populations. Interestingly, among opposition-led places, opposition parties tended to assign UyC rules in places with large but non-conflictive indigenous populations. This different assignment logic attests to the different logics guiding autocratic and opposition political dynamics.

Although focusing on electoral authoritarian Mexico, this study seeks to add to the literature on national authoritarian regimes by examining the role of subnational officials in them, something that has not yet been widely or systematically studied.

Of course, the focus on a single state in Mexico could raise criticism about the generalisability of the findings. However, it is important to note two things. First, the concentration on Oaxaca raises the internal validity of the results tracing the effect of ethnicity and conflict on political decentralisation, even among regime-led and opposition-held regions. Second, it is precisely the nature of the issue and the argument under examination that requires a scaled-down empirical approach. The difficulty in finding systematic data measuring variation in the decentralisation of political authority to subnational regime officials makes top-down empirical tests of arguments about it difficult, if not impossible. A bottom-up analysis using unique or proxy measures to capture variation in the level of decentralisation of decision making in individual or small numbers of subnational units is a more reasonable empirical approach. And, this is precisely the road taken by the numerous scholars studying national authoritarian administrative and fiscal decentralisation cited here who focus on specific subnational regions to test their arguments.

Although I only test the argument on one Mexican state, two things suggest a similar logic may have been at work guiding similar political decentralisation and the informal adoption of UyC systems in other states with indigenous communities. First, there is considerable variation in the level of recognition of indigenous rights and cultures across Mexico's states during the last decade of national electoral authoritarian rule (Anaya Muñoz 2003, 2005; López Bárcenas 2010). Second, many states allowed indigenous groups to incorporate customary laws and practices informally into local (municipal and sub-municipal town-level) political processes, rather than relying on formal legislation (Anaya Muñoz 2003, 2005, 2006; de León Pasquel 2001; Fox 2007; Cornelius 2004). Indeed, that many of Oaxaca's municipalities were allowed to use UyC practices informally prior to formal UyC reform suggests that these informal UyC rules were widely accepted in this state and thus probably in others as well.

That national autocrats in Mexico or other national electoral authoritarian systems would be inclined to involve subnational officials in their strategies for managing regime support, and especially, ethnically diverse and conflictive populations, does not mean that their efforts always worked. Other endogenous and exogenous factors – like economic crises brought on by domestic economic policy decisions and/or sudden changes in the global economy – can undermine their efforts and their regimes' chances of survival. Even within the limited borders of Oaxaca, Mexico, UyC electoral rules did not play out in the way that state autocrats had hoped (Anaya Muñoz 2006; Recondo 2007; Benton 2012), with the assignment of UyC rules often associated with greater, rather than lower, levels of political conflict in subsequent years (Eisenstadt 2007; Eisenstadt and Ríos 2014). Even so, the logic outlined here was still the best (and perhaps only) political response for managing ethnically diverse and conflictive populations. That Oaxaca's PRI-run state electoral authoritarian regime lasted another ten years beyond Mexico's national democratic transition, resulting in its survival as a subnational authoritarian enclave (Gibson 2005; Giraudy 2009; Benton 2012), supports this point.

## References

Ai, C. and Norton, E. (2003) 'Interaction terms in logit and probit models', *Economic Letters* 80:123–129.

Anaya Muñoz, A. (2003) 'La Política del Reconocimiento en Oaxaca: La Preservación de una Governabilidad Priísta y el Desarrollo del Proyecto de Autonomía Indígena en el Estado', *Relaciones* XXIV(97): 267–305.

—— (2005) 'The emergence and development of the politics of recognition of cultural diversity and indigenous people's rights in Mexico: Chiapas and Oaxaca in comparative perspective', *Journal of Latin American Studies* 37(3): 585–610.

—— (2006) *Autonomía Indígena, Gobernabilidad y Legitimidad en México*, Distrito Federal: Universidad Iberoamericana and Plaza y Valdés.

Anderson, R. (1971) 'The Functional Role of the Governors and their States in the Political Development of Mexico, 1940–64', PhD, Department of Political Science, University of Wisconsin.

Andersson, K. and Van Laerhoven, F. (2007) 'From local strongman to facilitator: institutional incentives for participatory municipal governance in Latin America', *Comparative Political Studies* 40(9): 1085–1111.

Bailey, J. (1988) *Governing Mexico: The statecraft of crisis management*, New York: St. Martin's Press.

Bailón Corres, J. (1999) *Pueblos indios, elites y territorio*, Distrito Federal, México: El Colegio de México.

Barbas, A. and Bartolomé, M. (eds) (1999) *Configuraciones étnicas para las autonomías*, Distrito Federal, Mexico: INI and Conaculta.

Benton, A. (2012) 'Bottom-up challenges to national democracy: Mexico's (legal) subnational authoritarian enclaves', *Comparative Politics* 44(3): 253–271.

—— (2016a) 'How "participatory governance" strengthens authoritarian regimes: evidence from electoral authoritarian Oaxaca, Mexico', *Journal of Politics in Latin America* 8 (2): 37–70.

—— (2016b) 'Configuring authority over electoral manipulation in electoral authoritarian regimes: Evidence from Mexico', *Democratization* 1–23. doi: 10.1080/13510347.2016.1236789.

Bernstein, T. (1993) 'Fifty Years of State Governors in Mexico: Middle Elites and Political Stability', PhD Diss., Department of Government and Foreign Affairs, University of Virginia.

Birch, S. (2011) *Electoral Malpractice*, Oxford: Oxford University Press.

Blair, H. (2000) 'Participation and accountability at the periphery: democratic local governments in six countries', *World Development* 28(1): 21–39.

Blanchard, O. and Shleifer, A. (2001) 'Federalism With and Without Political Centralization: China versus Russia', *IMF Staff Paper*, Washington, DC: IMF.

Blaydes, L. (2011) *Elections and Distributive Politics in Mubarak's Egypt*, Cambridge: Cambridge University Press.

Boix, C. and Svolik, M. (2013) 'The foundations of limited authoritarian government: institutions and power-sharing in dictatorships', *Journal of Politics* 75(2): 300–316.

Brownlee, J. (2007) *Authoritarianism in an Age of Democratization*, Cambridge: Cambridge University Press.

Bruhn, K. (1997) *Taking on Goliath: The emergence of a new left party and the struggle for democracy in Mexico*, University Park: Pennsylvania State University Press.

Bunce, V. and Wolchik, S. (2010) 'Defeating dictators: electoral change and stability in competitive authoritarian regimes', *World Politics* 62(1): 43–86.

Bustamante, R. (ed.) (1978) *Oaxaca, una lucha reciente: 1960–1978*, Distrito Federal, Mexico: Ediciones Nueva Sociología.

Chandra, K. (2004) *Why Ethnic Parties Succeed*, Cambridge: Cambridge University Press.

Cleary, M. (2005) 'Indigenous Autonomy in Southern Mexico', Midwestern Political Science Association, Chicago, Illinois, April 7 - 9.

Consejo Nacional de Población (CONAPO) http://www.conapo.org.mx (accessed 15 January 2014).

Cornelius, W. (2004) 'Mobilized Voting in the 2000 Elections: The changing efficacy of vote buying and coercion in Mexican electoral politics', in J. I. Domínguez and C. Lawson (eds) *Mexico's Pivotal Democratic Election: Campaign effects and the presidential race of 2000*, Stanford: Stanford University Press.

Cornelius, W. A., Craig, A. and Fox, J. (1994) *Transforming State-Society Relations in Mexico: The national solidarity strategy, U.S.-Mexico contemporary perspectives series 6*, La Jolla, Calif.: Center for U.S.-Mexican Studies University of California, San Diego.

de León Pasquel, L. (ed.) (2001) *Costumbres, leyes y movimiento indio en Oaxaca y Chiapas*, Mexico: Centro de Investigaciones y Estudios Superiores en Antropologia Social and Miguel Ángel Porrúa.

Díaz-Cayeros, A. (2006) *Federalism, Fiscal Authority, and Centralization in Latin America*, Cambridge: Cambridge University Press.

Díaz-Cayeros, A. and Langston, J. (2003) 'The Consequences of Competition: Gubernatorial Nominations and Candidate Quality in Mexico: 1994–2004', in *Documento de Trabajo, División de Estudios Políticos*, No. 160, Distrito Federal: Centro de Investigación y Docencia Económicas.

Díaz-Cayeros, A. and Magaloni, B. (2001) 'Party dominance and the logic of electoral design in Mexico's transition to democracy', *Journal of Theoretical Politics* 13(3): 271–293.

Eaton, K. (2004) *Politics Beyond the Capital: The design of subnational institutions in South America*, Stanford, Ca.: Stanford University Press.

—— (2006) 'Decentralization's nondemocratic roots: authoritarianism and subnational reform in Latin America', *Latin American Politics & Society* 48(1): 1–26.

Eisenstadt, T. (2007) 'Usos y costumbres and postelectoral conflicts in Oaxaca, Mexico, 1995–2004: an empirical and normative assessment', *Latin American Research Review* 42(1): 50–75.

Eisenstadt, T. and Ríos, V. (2014) 'Multicultural institutions, distributional politics, and postelectoral mobilization in indigenous Mexico', *Latin American Politics and Society* 56(2): 70–92.

Elizarrarás Álvarez, R. (2002) 'Gobernabilidad y Autonomía Indigena: Mótivos y Efectos en el Reconocimiento de los Usos y Costumbres en Oaxaca', Licenciatura B.A Thesis, Ciencia Política, Instituto Tecnológico Autónomo de México (ITAM).

Falleti, T. (2011) 'Varieties of authoritarianism: the organization of the military state and its effects on federalism in Argentina and Brazil', *Studies in Comparative International Development* 46(2): 137–162.

Foweraker, J. and Craig, A. (eds) (1990) *Popular Movements and Political Change in Mexico*, Boulder: Lynne Rienner Publishers.

Fox, J. (1994) 'The difficult transition from clientelism to citizenship: lessons from Mexico', *World Politics* 46: 151–184.

Fox, J. (1996) 'How does civil society thicken? The political construction of social capital in rural Mexico', *World Development* 24(6): 1089–1103.

—— (2007) *Accountability Politics: Power and voice in rural Mexico*, Oxford: Oxford University Press.

Gandhi, J. (2008) *Political Institutions Under Dictatorship*, Cambridge: Cambridge University Press.

Gandhi, J. and Lust-Okar, E. (2009) 'Elections under authoritarianism', *Annual Review of Political Science* 12: 403–422.

Gandhi, J. and Przeworski, A. (2007) 'Authoritarian institutions and the survival of autocrats', *Comparative Political Studies* 40(11): 1279–1301.

Geddes, B. (2005) 'Why Parties and Elections in Authoritarian Regimes?', paper presented to American Political Science Association, California: UCLA.

Gibson, E. (2005) 'Boundary control: subnational authoritarianism in democratic countries', *World Politics* 58(1):101–132.

Giraudy, A. (2009) 'Subnational Undemocratic Regime Continuity after Democratization: Argentina and Mexico in Comparative Perspective', PhD, Department of Political Science, University of North Carolina at Chapel Hill.

Goodman, G. and Hiskey, J. (2008) 'Exit without leaving: political disengagement in high migration municipalities in Mexico', *Comparative Politics* 40(2): 169–188.

Greene, K. (2007) *Why Dominant Parties Lose: Mexico's democratization in comparative perspective*, Cambridge: Cambridge University Press.

Grindle, M. (2007) *Going Local: Decentralization, democratization, and the promise of good governance*, Princetion: Princeton University Press.

Guerra Pulido, M. (2000) 'Usos y Costumbres o Partidos Polítocos: Una Decisión de los Municipios Oaxaqueños', Licenciatura B.A Thesis, Ciencia Política y Relaciones Internacionales, Centro de Investigación y Docencia Económicas, A.C.

Hernández Rodríguez, R. (2008) *El centro dividido: La nueva autonomiá de los gobernadores*, Mexico, DF: El Colegio de México.

Hiskey, J. and Goodman, G. (2011) 'The participation paradox of indigenous autonomy in Mexico', *Latin American Politics and Society* 53(2): 61–86.

Hiskey, J. and Seligson, M. (2003) 'Pitfalls of power to the people: decentralization, local government performance, and system support in Bolivia', *Studies in Comparative International Development* 37(4): 64–88.

Horowitz, D. (1985) *Ethnic Groups in Conflict*, Berkeley: University of California Press.

——— (2000) *Ethnic Groups in Conflict*, 2nd edn, Berkeley: University of California Press.

——— (2007) 'The many uses of federalism', *Drake Law Review* 55: 953–966.

Howard, M. and Roessler, P. (2006) 'Liberalizing electoral outcomes in competitive authoritarian regimes', *American Journal of Political Science* 50(2): 365–381.

Instituto Estatal Electoral y de Participación Ciudadana de Oaxaca (IEEPCO) http://www.ieepco.org.mx (accessed 14 January 2014).

Jin, H., Qian, Y. and Weingast, B. (2005) 'Regional decentralization and fiscal incentives: federalism, Chinese style', *Journal of Public Economics* 89(9–10): 1719–1742.

Kitschelt, H. and Wilkinson, S. I. (eds) (2007) *Patrons, Clients, and Policies*, Cambridge: Cambridge University Press.

Ko, K. and Zhi, J. (2013) 'Fiscal decentralization: guilty of aggravating corruption in China?', *Journal of Contemporary China* 22(79): 35–55.

Laitin, D. (1998) *Identity in Formation*, Ithica, NY: Cornell University Press.

Landry, P. F. (2008) *Decentralized Authoritarianism in China: The Communist Party's control of local elites in post-Mao era*, Cambridge: Cambridge University Press.

Langston, J. (2001) 'Why rules matter: changes in candidate selection in Mexico's PRI, 1988–2000', *Journal of Latin American Studies* 33(3): 485–511.

——— (unpublished book manuscript) *Democratization and Party Change: Mexico's evolving PRI, 1980–2012*.

Langston, J. and Morgenstern, S. (2009) 'Campaigning in an electoral authoritarian regime: the case of Mexico', *Comparative Politics* 41(2): 165–81.

Lawson, C. (2002) *Building the Fourth Estate: Democratization and media opening in Mexico*, Berkeley: University of California Press.

Levitsky, S. and Way, L. (2010) *Competitive Authoritarianism: Hybrid regimes after the Cold War*, Cambridge: Cambridge University Press.

Lijphart, A. (1977) *Democracy in Plural Societies*, New Haven: Yale University Press.

Lindberg, S. (2009) *Democratization by Elections: A new mode of transition*, Baltimore, Maryland: The Johns Hopkins University Press.

López Bárcenas, F. (2010) *Legislación y derechos indígenas en México*, México, DF: Centro de Estudios para el Desarrollo Rural Sustentable y la Soberanía Alimentaria, Càmara de Diputados, lXi legislatura.

López Monjardín, A. (1986) *La lucha por los ayuntamientos: una utopía viable*, Distrito Federal, Mexico: Siglo XXI.

Lust-Okar, E. (2006) 'Elections under authoritarianism: preliminary lessons from Jordan', *Democratization* 13(3): 456–471.

McNulty, S. (2011) *Voice and Vote: Decentralization and participation in post-Fujimori Peru*, Stanford, CA: Stanford University Press.

Madrid, R. (2012) *The Rise of Ethnic Politics in Latin America*, Cambridge: Cambridge University Press.

Magaloni, B. (2006) *Voting for Autocracy: Hegemonic party survival and its demise in Mexico*, Cambridge: Cambridge University Press.

Malesky, E. (2009) 'Gerrymandering–Vietnamese style: escaping the partial reform quilibrium in a nondemocratic regime', *The Journal of Politics* 71(01): 132–159.

Malesky, E. and Schuler, P. (2011) 'The single-party dictator's dilemma: information in elections without opposition', *Legislative Studies Quarterly* 36(4): 491–530.

Manion, M. (1996) 'The electoral connection in the Chinese countryside', *American Political Science Review* 90(4): 736–748.

Martínez Cabañas, G. (1985) *La Administración Estatal y Municipal de Mexico*, Mexico, DF: Instituto Nacional de Administración Pública.

Martínez Vázquez, V. (1990) *Movimiento Popular y política en Oaxaca: 1968–86*, Distrito Federal, Mexico: Conaculta.

Mejía Piñeros, M. and Sarmiento Silva, S. (1987) *La lucha indígena: un reto a la ortodoxia*, Distrito Federal, Mexico: Siglo XXI and CEHAM.

Méndez de Hoyos, I. (2006) *Transición a la Democracia en México: Competencia Partidista y Reformas Electroales, 1977–2003*, Distrito Federal: Faculdad Latinoamericana de Ciencias Sociales, Sede Académica de México (FLACSO) and Distribuciones Fontamara, SA.

Molinar, J. (1991) *El Tiempo de la Legitimidad. Elecciones, Autoritariasmo y Democracia en México*, México, DF: Cal y Arena.

Montinola, G., Qian, Y. and Weingast, B. (1996) 'Federalism, Chinese style: the political basis for economic success', *World Politics* 48(1): 50–81.

Negretto, G. (2013) 'Authorian Constitution Making: The role of the military in Latin America', in T. Ginsburg and A. Simpser (eds) *Constitutions in Authoritarian Regimes*, New York: Cambridge University Press, pp. 83–110.

O'Brien, K. and Li, L. (2000) 'Accommodating "democracy" in a one-party state: introducing village elections in China', *The China Quarterly* Special Issue: *Elections and Democracy in Greater China* 162: 465–489.

Oi, J. and Rozelle, S. (2000) 'Elections and power: the locus of decision-making in Chinese villages', *The China Quarterly* 162: 513–539.

Padgett, L. (1966) *The Mexican Political System*, Boston, Ma.: Houghton Mifflin Company.

Posner, D. (2005) *Institutions and Ethnic Politics in Africa*, New York: Cambridge University Press.

Qian, Y. and Weingast, B. (1996) 'China's transition to markets: market-preserving federalism, Chinese style', *Journal of Policy Reform* 1(2): 149–185.

Recondo, D. (2001) 'Usos y Costumbres, Procesos Electorales, y Autonomía Indígena en Oaxaca', in L. de León Pasquel (ed.) *Costumbrres, Leyes y Movimiento Indio en Oaxaca y Chiapas*, Distrito Federal, México: Centro de Investigaciones y Estudios Superiores en Antropología Social (CIESAS), pp. 91–113.

―――― (2002) 'État et Coutumes Électorales dans L'Oaxaca (Mexique): Réflexions Sur Les Enjeux Politiques Du Multiculturalisme', PhD Dissertation, Droit, Sciences Sociales et Politiques, Sciences Économiques et de Gestion, Université Montesquieu-Bordeaux IV.

―――― (2007) *La política del gatopardo: Multiculturalismo y democracia en Oaxaca*, Distrito Federal Mexico: CIESAS and DEMC.

Reina, L. (ed.) (1988) *Historia de la cuestión agraria mexicana. Estado de Oaxaca. 1925–1986*, Mexico: Juan Pablos Editor, Gobierno del Estado de Oaxaca, UABJO, and Centro de Estudios Históricos del Agrarismo en México.

Rodríguez, V. (1987) 'The Politics of Decentralization in Mexico: Divergent Outcomes of Policy Implementation', PhD, Department of Political Science, University of California, Berkeley.

Sartori, G. (1994) *Comparative Constitutional Engineering: An inquiry into structures, incentives and outcomes*, London: Macmillan.

Schedler, A. (2002) 'The Menu of Manipulation', *Journal of Democracy* 13(2): 36–50.

―――― (2006) *Electoral Authoritarianism: The dynamics of unfree competition*, Boulder, Colorado: Lynne Rienner Publishers.

Simpser, A. (2013) *Why Governments and Parties Manipulate Elections: Theory, practice, and implications*, New York: Cambridge University Press.

Smith, P. (1979) *Labyrinths of Power: Political recruitment in Twentieth-century Mexico*, Princeton, New Jersey: Princeton University Press.

Svolik, M. (2012) *The Politics of Authoritarian Rule*, New York: Cambridge University Press.

Trejo, G. (2001a) 'The Political Foundations of Ethic Mobilization and Territorial Conflict in Mexico', *CIDE* Working Paper, Number 135.

―――― (2001b) 'Religious Competition, State Action and the Renaissance of Indigenous Identities in Chiapas', *CIDE* Working Paper, Number 136.

―――― (2004) 'Indigenous Insurgency: Protest, Rebellion and the Politicization of Ethnicity in 20th Century Mexico', PhD, Department of Political Science, University of Chicago.

—— (2012) *Popular Movements in Autocracies: Religion, repression and indigenous collective action in Mexico*, New York: Cambridge University Press.

Trejo, G. and Aguilar, J. (1999) 'Ethnicity and Electoral Conflict in a Weakly Divided Society', *CIDE* Working Paper, Number 108.

Uchimura, H. and Jütting, J. (2007) 'Fiscal Decentralisation, Chinese Style: Good for health outcomes?', *OECD Development Centre*: OECD.

Van Cott, D. (2008) *Radical Democracy in the Andes*, Cambridge: Cambridge University Press.

Varshney, A. (2002) *Ethnic Conflict and Civic Life*, New Haven: Yale University Press.

Wampler, B. (2008) 'When does participatory democracy deepen the quality of democracy? Lessons from Brazil', *Comparative Politics* 41(1): 61–81.

Wilkinson, S. (2004) *Votes and Violence: Electoral competition and ethnic riots in India*, Cambridge: Cambridge University Press.

Wright, J. (2008) 'Do authoritarian institutions constrain? How legislatures affect economic growth and investment', *American Journal of Political Science* 52(2): 322–343.

Wright, J. and Escribà-Folch, A. (2012) 'Authoritarian institutions and regime survival: transitions to democracy and subsequent autocracy', *British Journal of Political Science* 42(2): 283–309.

Yashar, D. (2005) *Contesting Citizenship in Latin America: Indigenous movements and the postliberal challenge*, Cambridge: Cambridge University Press.

Zhuravskaya, E. (2000) 'Incentives to provide local public goods: fiscal federalism, Russian style', *Journal of Public Economics* 76: 337–368.

## Chapter Nine

# Political Ambition and Subnational Redistributive Spending

*Lucas González and Germán Lodola*

## Introduction

Government spending is a powerful tool subnational incumbents can utilise to favour different social groups in a federation. As such, it spreads out redistributive conflicts over who gets what (and how) in multi-level democracies. Schematically, subnational governments can either benefit specific groups by allocating public resources to particularistic goods or they can favour a large majority of citizens by delivering collective goods. In this chapter, we analyse the institutional, contextual, and individual-level factors that affect subnational governments' redistributive spending choices. In contrast to prior research that has concentrated on both institutional and contextual determinants of government spending, we emphasise that individual factors largely explain why subnational incumbents decide to reward certain groups of citizens over others thus shaping redistributive conflicts within their territorial jurisdictions.

Our central claim is that subnational executives' (i.e., state governors) office ambitions – whether they are national-centred or state-centred – affect their decisions to strategically allocate social infrastructure (collective) and civil administration (particularistic) expenditures by delineating different electoral linkages between politicians and citizens. More concretely, governors who seek to remain in their districts will favour their core supporters and invest in patronage-based networks of political support by distributing targeted particularistic goods. On the contrary, governors who aspire to gain popularity beyond their districts in order to build a national career will target larger constituencies by providing collective goods, which are broader in scope and more visible.

There is a vibrant tradition of theoretical research on redistributive politics that has examined the conditions that provide incentives for incumbent politicians or parties to spend government funds on public goods that benefit the vast majority of citizens, rather than on private goods narrowly targeted to specific groups (e.g., Persson and Tabellini 1999, 2000; Bueno de Mesquita *et al*. 2003; Robinson and Torvik 2005). More empirically oriented studies have identified three broad categories of factors that affect government spending: structural, institutional and contextual. The structural explanations point to the negative impact of pre-existing social cleavages such as religion, caste, and ethnic divisions (Alesina, Baqir and Easterly 1999; Betancourt and Gleason 2002; Miguel and Gugerty 2005;

Chandra 2007), economic deprivation and income inequality (Londregan and Poole 1993; Perotti 1996; Huber, Mustillo and Stephens 2008) on the provision of public goods. The institutional accounts refer to a wide range of key political features that are thought to shape incumbents' redistributive incentives including political regimes, electoral systems, political parties and party systems, bicameralism and malapportionment, divided government, executive powers, and federalism (Hibbs 1977; Alesina 1987; Boix 1988; Alt and Lowry 1994; McCarty 2000; Lizzeri and Persico 2001; Ansolabehere, Snyder and Ting 2003; Chhibber and Nooruddin 2004, Rodden 2005; Berry 2008). Finally, the contextual analyses highlight that the timing of elections (the political business cycle),[1] and the macroeconomic environment (Pierson 2001) affects both the level and shares of government spending.

We draw on some of these insights, particularly on political-institutional explanations, but argue that prior research has neglected examining the impact of individual-level factors on government expenditure choices. Perhaps the most decisive individual factor that lies at the heart of a politician's behaviour is her office goals (Schlesinger 1966: 6). Thus, in studying and empirically testing the effect of governors' ambitions on subnational expenditure patterns, particularly on their motivations to allocate public or private goods, we aim to increase our knowledge on the micro-foundations of spending redistribution and territorial power-building in federalised (multi-level) countries.

Our analysis focuses on Argentina, which is an ideal case for examining this issue due to its particular political institutions. The highly decentralised nature of the country's federalism makes provincial governors dominant players in their fiefdoms, influential national actors, and competitive aspirants to the presidency. Moreover, federal fiscal institutions and provincial budgetary rules commonly grant governors a substantial level of discretion over the use of public moneys (Jones, Sanguinetti and Tommasi 2000; Bonvecchi and Lodola 2011). Finally, governors in the period we study vary considerably in terms of their career goals. This variation allows us to explore whether different modalities of individual ambitions eventually lead to different spending patterns by affecting the nature of the electoral connection between candidates and voters, and the construction of networks of political support.

There has been a recent growth of literature on the institutional power and political influence of provincial governors in Argentina. A first strand of research has focused on their ability to control politicians' career advancement (Jones 2001, 2008; De Luca, Jones and Tula 2002; Lodola 2009), and so to influence the voting behaviour of their copartisan legislators in both the Chamber of Deputies (Jones and Huang 2005; Jones, Hwang and Micozzi 2009) and the Senate (Kikuchi and Lodola 2014). A second group of scholars has pointed to changes in the distribution of fiscal resources and policy responsibilities between governors and presidents, and how this phenomenon affected the

---

1. For extensive reviews of this literature see Drazen (2000) and Franzese (2002).

intergovernmental balance of power (Benton 2009; Falleti 2010; Bonvecchi and Lodola 2011; González 2016). A third body of works has examined the causes of subnational variation in the level of democracy, and the conditions for territorial democratisation (Gervasoni 2010; Behrend 2011; Gibson 2012). Finally, a fourth stream of analyses has explored whether provincial governments strategically rely on pork-barrel or patronage activities to amass political support, and who is rewarded from these investments at the ballot box (Remmer 2007; Stokes 2005; Calvo and Murillo 2004; Lodola 2010). Our study speaks to this last area of research by examining how governors manipulate public resources in order to survive politically and fulfil their office aspirations, arguably their primary concerns. This chapter also has theoretical implications beyond Argentina. Students of redistributive politics have devoted a great deal of attention to examining the link between government spending and office retention across national institutions and actors. Yet little scholarly effort has been made to study, as we do here, this connection using subnational political actors as units of analysis.[2] This lacuna is important because without an understanding of how individual motivations shape expenditure patterns at the subnational level, we lack the whole structure of incentives that operates on redistributive conflicts in federalised polities.

Our empirical results indicate a strong effect of governors' political ambitions on public spending across Argentine provinces. Concretely, we substantiate that gubernatorial incentives for increasing expenditures in social infrastructure are stronger in provinces where the governor manifests a national-centred ambition. By contrast, incentives for increasing jobs, wages and salaries in the provincial civil administration are stronger where the governor has a state-centred (typically re-election) goal. We explain these different results by stressing the varied nature of electoral linkages between office-seeking politicians and their constituencies (Kitschelt 2000; Kitschelt and Williamson 2007). Our central argument is that different office ambitions promote different modes of citizen-politician linkages. Governors who nationalise their office ambition need to gain popularity abroad their provinces so that they will favour the provision of collective (non-excludable) goods that are visible and target broader constituencies. In contrast, governors who seek to remain in their home provinces will favour the allocation of particularistic (excludable) goods because this form of spending is much safer in their expected returns and allows the incumbent to build a patronage-based network of political support that reinforce provincial dominance.

We also find empirical evidence that some political-institutional variables affect subnational expenditure allocations in Argentina. As reported by prior research, political fragmentation (both electoral and legislative) reduces gubernatorial incentives to allocate collective goods while fosters particularism. Contrary to previous works, however, we find that electoral uncertainty as measured by the margin of victory have no statistical association with spending patterns. With

---

2. Some notable exceptions are Calvo and Murillo (2004), Chhibber and Nooruddin (2004), Besley, Persson and Sturm (2005), Remmer (2007).

regards to the role of contextual variables, the statistical results show that election cycles have minimal to no effect depending on model specifications. Finally, in contrast to past studies on fiscal federalism, we demonstrate that governors from provinces that found a greater portion of public expenditures through their own revenues (as opposed to fiscal dependency from intergovernmental transfers) are positively associated with civil administration outlays, even after controlling for relevant macroeconomic and demographic variables.

The rest of the chapter is organised as follows. The second section discusses the defining features of gubernatorial politics in Argentina, and provides descriptive evidence on the structure of provincial governors' political ambitions. The third section expands upon the theoretical arguments that underlie our hypotheses on how incumbents' office goals, as well as other institutional and contextual factors, affect the way in which governors use public spending as an electoral strategy for fulfilling their personal aspirations. The fourth section describes our data and operationalises the relevant variables. The fifth section tests our hypotheses and discusses the statistical results. The last section considers the potential generalisability of our findings, and how they contribute to the current debates on political careerism and subnational redistributive politics.

## Gubernatorial Politics and Career Ambitions in Argentina

In this section we outline the fundamental aspects of gubernatorial politics in Argentina, and describe the modalities of political ambitions held by provincial governors in the 1993–2004 period.

Argentina is a highly decentralised federal republic composed of twenty-three provinces and an autonomous city. The country is commonly regarded as a textbook example of robust federalism, that is, a multi-level polity where subnational territorial units (provinces) comprise the most salient arena of political competition for national power (Mainwaring 1991; Stepan 2004). Politically, each province has the authority to determine its own constitution and electoral system thus generating one of the most complex institutional architectures in the world. All subnational jurisdictions have popularly elected governors for four-year terms. However, the rules of gubernatorial election have exhibited considerable variation both across provinces and through time. During the period covered in this chapter, twenty-one provinces eventually allowed for the immediate re-election of governors, with seventeen of them limiting gubernatorial incumbency to two consecutive terms, one province to three terms, and the remaining permitting indefinite re-election.[3]

---

3. Four provinces reformed their gubernatorial electoral rules in this period: one of them introduced the possibility of reelection for two consecutive terms, while the other three indeed limited governors' static aspirations by moving from allowing unlimited mandates to permit only one re-election. With regards to the electoral formula, Argentine governors have been typically elected according to the plurality rule, with a few provinces using the majority runoff system. Some jurisdictions introduced adapted versions of the *apparentment* rules (*Ley de Lemas*) to allow different candidates from the same party to compete against each other at the time of the general election.

The institution of gubernatorial re-election – along with provincial electoral rules that allow governors to improve their control over local legislatures by introducing a majoritarian bias or premium seat (Calvo and Micozzi 2005) – contributed to the political consolidation of regional elites, typically structured around a dominant family clan, a personalistic leader, or a small group of local politicians.[4]

There are other institutional factors that make provincial governors almost unbeatable contenders in their districts. First, career opportunities are essentially decided by subnational – not national – party bosses given Argentina's party-centred electoral system (the closed list proportional representation), and provincial party delegations' control of candidate nomination procedures (Jones 1997, 2001, 2008; De Luca, Jones and Tula 2002; Jones, Saiegh, Spiller and Tommasi 2002; Jones and Hwang 2005; Lodola 2009). As almost every elective position and an overwhelming majority of appointed posts are determined within the provinces, and there is a lack of stable civil service rules typical of merit-based systems, governors – who are *de jure* and/or *de facto* presidents of the incumbent parties – can distribute electoral candidacies and public jobs with ample discretion. Second, governors also retain tight control over campaign financing, and enjoy virtually full authority over a vast amount of resources transferred from the central government that can help politicians get elected. This is mainly due to the country's peculiar federal fiscal system, which prioritises gubernatorial – rather than presidential – discretion over the use of sizeable intergovernmental transfers and royalties for the extraction of natural resources in the provincial territories (Bonvecchi and Lodola 2011).[5] Third, although the division of budgetary powers between the governor and the local legislature varies greatly across provinces (Jones, Sanguinetti and Tommasi 2000), there is a tendency towards governors' institutional dominance over the budgetary process. This tendency, as we mentioned above, is reinforced by the fact that local legislatures are usually politically controlled by governors: in our sample, the governor's party enjoyed majority in the legislature as high as 70 per cent of the time, while it captured an average of 54.3 per cent of the seats.[6]

Because governors have a greater say over the way in which provinces are financed and local politics is arranged, the gubernatorial post has become a critical vehicle for achieving national stature. Since the return of democracy, provincial

---

4.  Personalistic leadership does not necessarily imply absence of political parties because personalism is not often exercised in the same way. Some personalistic leaders – in Argentina and elsewhere – favour the construction of enduring party organisations, while others are indifferent or even antithetical to parties.

5.  A significant number of Argentine provinces raise extremely low proportions of their budgets and depend heavily on revenues from the federal government. The bulk of this money comes directly from a revenue-sharing mechanism and is transferred by statute with no strings attached. Other smaller transfers have specific purposes, but in practice the central government finds it difficult to monitor or sanction the misuse of these funds.

6.  Data on provincial legislatures always refer to the lower chamber. Depending on their constitutions, provinces have either unicameral or bicameral legislatures which are renewed either partially or totally every two or four years. In the time-frame we study here sixteen provinces had a unicameral system.

chief-executives have been the most competitive contenders for the presidency as six out of eight presidents were previously governors.

We assume that governors strategically harness public expenditure to marshal vote support that may increase their chances of political survival. Particularly, we are concerned about whether or not – and how – governors' priorities towards the allocation of collective (social infrastructure) and private (civil administration) goods are affected by their career aspirations.

Research on political careerism and ambition in Latin America has mostly focused on exploring political recruitment, career pathways to power, and office retention of presidents and congressional legislators.[7] In contrast, there has been only limited scholarly attention devoted to the study of subnational political actors, in particular state governors. The few extant studies on gubernatorial careerism in the region have examined how individual candidates to the statehouse are ultimately recruited and nominated by established parties or elites (Siavelis and Morgenstern 2008).

For example, Power and Mochel (2008: 229–38) analyse candidate selection for the governorship in Brazil between 1990 and 2002. Based on descriptive and anecdotal evidence, the authors contend that both partisan and regional factors help explain variation in the types of gubernatorial candidates selected. Thus candidates from leftist (ideological) political parties and pluralistic states (i.e., where politics is not controlled by a personal clique or a traditional political clan) are more likely to build their careers in a party organisation than candidates from rightist (catchall) parties and oligarchic states, who are more independent from partisan ties. In a similar vein, De Luca (2008: 204–15) shows that party-centred electoral and candidate selection rules in Argentina generate aspirants to the governorship with personal electoral appeal (such as senators, federal deputies, and mayors of large cities), and substantial economic resources so as to maintain their own machines or get the support of the party machine, and thus have stable prior political careers underwritten by their parties. Finally, in what constitutes the most elaborated research on gubernatorial recruitment in Latin America, Camp (2008, 2010) studies some changing patterns in the social background and career paths of Mexican governors throughout the twentieth century. The evidence substantiates that the generation of governors from the recent democratic period is more localistic than previous generations. Indeed, most of these new governors were born in small provincial cities, remained in their home state or nearby for their secondary and tertiary education, and began their professional careers linked to their parties in a local political position.

This literature has contributed substantially to our understanding of state-executive recruitment processes in federal countries with different electoral systems and nomination procedures. Nonetheless, the emphasis on gubernatorial recruitment has often neglected to explore the defining attributes of governors'

---

7. This literature is legion. For references, see Siavelis and Morgenstern (2008) and the literature quoted therein.

political ambitions, and how these personal aspirations affect their behaviour – in this chapter, their redistributive strategies – in office.

The rest of this section discusses the structure of Argentine governors' office ambitions based upon an original dataset that contains biographic information on each *acting* governor (i.e., any individual who occupied the governorship for at least six months) between 1993 and 2004.[8] Data collection drew upon multiple sources – such as governors' biographies, non-academic studies that gathered personal information on politicians (CIPPEC 2002, 2009), official data on candidate nominations, and pictures of party ballots taken at the Archives of the National Electoral Court. The sample includes 103 individual cases: ninety-two popularly elected governors, seven elected vice-governors, and four interim governors.[9]

The systematic examination of political ambition is problematic because ambition is a psychological predisposition rather than an observable behaviour (Hibbing 1986). Ideally, we would like to have measures of such predispositions for each governor over their entire time in office. This information, however, is almost impossible to collect as it would demand interviewing governors to know their 'true' office goals. To address this limitation, we use a governor's observed decision to pursue a given office (or to quit politics for whatever reason) as a surrogate for her psychological predisposition, which is assumed to exist prior to her spending decisions in office and constant during the entire gubernatorial mandate (Herrick and Moore 1993: 772). This strategy allow us to infer governors' ambitions from the posts (both nominated and elected) they actually occupied or vied for. Certainly, this is an impure measure because we infer pure preferences from observable choices. For example, it has been shown that incumbents usually choose to retire when their electoral prospects look dim and to run for office when they are assured of winning (Coates and Munger 1995). Hence, our approach is likely to introduce bias in the statistical estimates, specifically to underestimate

---

8. This criterion excludes five cases of interim governors from the provinces of Corrientes and Santiago del Estero who only served as provincial executives for a few weeks or days. We also exclude federal interventions to these jurisdictions.

9. On average, vice-governors and interims occupied the governorship for almost fifteen consecutive months. They did so either because the elected governor stepped down to assume the presidency (three cases), a presidential cabinet position (1), or a seat in Congress (1), resigned from office (5) – typically to avoid an impeachment from the provincial legislature – or died (1). We have strong reasons to include both vice-governors and interims in the analysis. Argentina's electoral rules mandate elected governors to resign from office in order to get a job in the public administration or to occupy (but not to run for) any other elected position. In these cases, as well as when the governor resigns, is impeached or dies, the vice-governor (occasionally, an interim) completes the gubernatorial term. Most provincial constitutions allow vice-governors and interims to vie for office, including gubernatorial reelection. Indeed, almost 73 per cent of the vice-governors and interims in our dataset ran for an elected post (55 per cent did it for re-election) when their mandates expired, and three-quarters of them succeeded in their attempts. These numbers suggest that governors' substitutes have access to the perks and resources of office and use them strategically for career advancement. Therefore, excluding these cases from the sample would arbitrarily reduce observations and lead to selection bias.

the effect of political ambition because we do not observe the performance that vulnerable incumbents would have had if they had run for office.

Furthermore, we accept that an 'ambition' – whether in politics or anything else – commonly entails long term trends, and not necessarily remains constant for any one person over a lifetime. We do not analyse, however, sequences of positions (attempted to be) occupied by a salient governor. Rather, we only consider the first, single position (failed to be) captured by a governor immediately after the end of her executive term. In this way, we simplify the political ambition process because it rarely involves a one-shot, unidirectional movement.

Figure 9.1 displays data on the career choices and electoral performance of the four salient gubernatorial cohorts (from 1995 to 2007) included in our sample.[10] The information shows gubernatorial running and winning rates, and turnover from both electoral defeats and retirements. The first notable observation is that Argentine governors usually sought to get an elected office (including re-election) at the end of their executive terms. Indeed, the average running rate is 81 per cent and it is highly stable over time. The second pattern to observe is that governors who vied for an elected position were unquestionably successful in reaching their office goals. Note that the gubernatorial winning rate (as percentage of incumbents competing for office) averaged nearly 84 per cent in the period with relatively minor fluctuations among cohorts. Third, gubernatorial turnover was persistently low, especially after 1995 once most provinces had incorporated re-election clauses, thus averaging 32 per cent in the period. Of this percentage, as we will see in greater detail below, the smallest group (around 40 per cent) corresponds to electorally defeated governors, while the largest group is composed of governors who quit electoral politics either voluntarily or forced by local political crises and governmental scandals.

Table 9.1 provides more detailed information on the political ambitions held by the 103 Argentine governors included in our analysis. We contend that governors can be motivated by two fundamental modalities of careerism, each involving a unique electoral connection: national-centred and state-centred. The former refers to the observed desire of continuing a professional career in the home province. The latter denotes the goal of moving to the national level. We prefer this distinction to the seminal conceptualisation of static (to retain current office) and progressive (to gain higher office) ambitions (Schlesinger 1966), because adopting this classical distinction would inevitably entail defining a hierarchy of careers. Yet there is a lively debate among scholars as to how offices are arranged, and to whether they are ordered into a stable hierarchical ladder or they shift fluidly (Schlesinger 1991; Francis and Kenny 2000). Moreover, in the

---

10. With a few minor exceptions gubernatorial contests in the period under analysis were held in 1991, 1995, 1999, and 2003. To preserve consistency, those governors who assumed office in a different year from the ones mentioned above are considered as members of the most proximate prior cohort. For example, Corrientes held gubernatorial elections in 1993 so we coded the elected governor as member of the 1991 cohort.

*Figure 9.1: Career choices and electoral performance of governors in Argentina (salient cohorts, 1995–2007)*

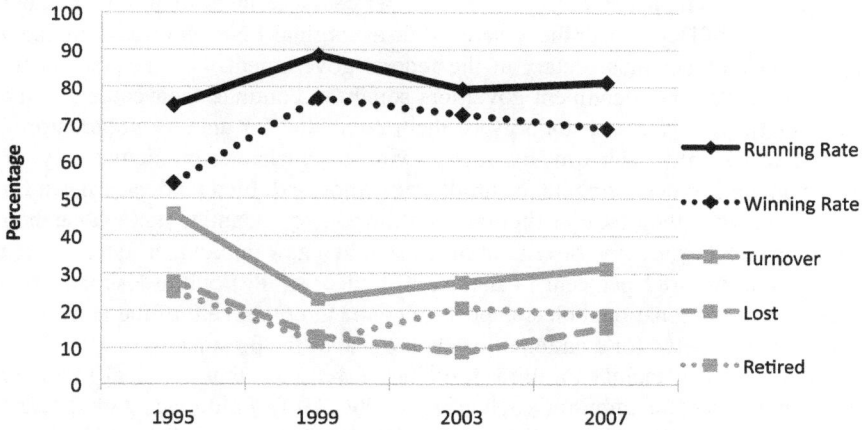

*Source:* Authors' compilation.

context of Argentina's robust federalism it is not obvious whether a national office (but the presidency) is hierarchically superior or inferior to a provincial position.[11]

Especially in the small and poorer provinces, moving to the nation can be a political punishment rather than a reward. As a former legislator of Formosa expressed it:

> There is an old adage here: who goes to the [national] capital loses his power in the province [...] becomes a political dead. We called the Chamber of Deputies [and the Senate] the *elephants' cemetery*. If you go there, someone else occupies your space here, where the real business is done.[12]

In the same token, a former senator, rival of presidents Néstor Kirchner (2003–2007) and Cristina Fernández de Kirchner (2007–present), explained:

> That happened twice in my province. When the vice-governor Eduardo Arnold began to annoy politically, the governor Néstor Kirchner sent him to the Chamber of Deputies. Bye, that's it, he killed Arnold. Later, when the vice-governor Sergio Acevedo began to increase a bit his political influence in the province, Kirchner also nominated him to head the list of national deputies.[13]

---

11. See also Samuels (2003), who notes that despite the possibility of consecutive re-election many federal deputies in Brazil decide not to stay in the chamber but to revert back to the state and municipal governments.

12. Interview with Aníbal Hardy, Formosa, April 6, 2006.

13. Interview with Alfredo Martínez. Ciudad de Buenos Aires, November 22, 2005.

The frequencies presented in Table 9.1 show that around a third of the governors attempted to obtain a national level position at the expiration of their terms: almost 6 per cent the (vice) presidency, close to 28 per cent a congressional seat at either the Chamber of Deputies or the Senate, while a marginal 1 per cent was nominated as cabinet member or secretary at the federal government. On the other hand, 47.6 per cent of the incumbent governors sought to continue their careers at the provincial level. The vast majority of them competed for another gubernatorial period, while only 7 per cent became provincial legislators, municipal mayors, or provincial cabinet members. Naturally, governors exhibit a tendency to run for re-election when they are constitutionally allowed to do it, and to nationalise their careers when they are not. Seven out of ten sought a new gubernatorial term when it was permitted (82 per cent of them did it successfully), while less than two attempted to get a national elected post. In contrast, 66 per cent of the lame duck governors competed for a national legislative seat or the presidency.

Table 9.1 also includes a third direction of ambition that classical literature refers to as 'discrete ambition' (Schlesinger 1966: 10ff). Politicians with discrete ambition voluntarily withdraw from public life after serving only for a limited time in a single office, commonly to pursue some narrow objective. Strictly speaking, Argentine governors in our sample do not fully fit into this definition since virtually all of them were professional politicians who had held an elective or appointed post before conquering the statehouse: on average, governors had served in three different positions (only 15 per cent of them had served in only one post) for a

*Table 9.1: The structure of gubernatorial political ambitions in Argentina (salient cohorts, 1995–2011)*

| Structure of Political Ambitions | Percentage |
| --- | --- |
| *National Ambition* | **34.9** |
| President | 4.8 |
| Vice-President | 1.0 |
| Senator | 11.6 |
| National Deputy | 16.5 |
| Federal Bureaucracy | 1.0 |
| *Provincial Ambition* | **47.6** |
| Governor | 40.8 |
| Mayor | 1.0 |
| State Deputy | 3.9 |
| State Bureaucracy | 1.9 |
| *Discrete (Retirement)* | **17.5** |
| Voluntary | 7.8 |
| Non-voluntary | 9.7 |

Source: Authors' compilation. N = 103.

tenure of 12.3 years.[14] Hence, given our purposes in this chapter, we include in the discrete category only those governors who did not run for any elected office or were not appointed to any political position at the end of their executive mandates. The information provided distinguishes between voluntary and involuntary (i.e., legal impeachments and resignations) retirements, with values of almost 8 and 10 per cent of the total governors respectively.[15] As it can be appreciated, only rarely did Argentine governors decide to quit politics voluntarily while a non-marginal number were either impeached by their provincial legislatures or forced to resign due to severe government crises.

## Subnational Redistributive Spending

In this section we discuss a set of theoretical expectations on the determinants of subnational government spending, and offer testable hypotheses on how provincial governors' office ambitions as well as other institutional and contextual factors could potentially affect gubernatorial incentives to strategically divvy up public resources to collective and particularistic goods. Table 9.2 offers a summary of the initial hypotheses based on past empirical research and our argument about the potential impact of political ambition on government spending.

It is important to underscore that we conceive difference in subnational governments' redistributive orientations in relative terms only. That is, incumbent governors must decide how to allocate a basket of goods, which differ in their relative budgetary cost, expected electoral return and level of electoral risk, to voters. We expect that governors in all provinces use both collective and particularistic goods to appeal to their constituents. But these two modalities of spending are offered in different combinations depending, at least in part, on the nature of incumbents' political ambitions. Our central argument is that governors' ambitions affect their spending incentives because different types of offices entail different electoral connections (or linkages) between candidates and voters.

Different electoral constituencies coexist in a federalised (multi-level) polity. We assume a two-level polity in which subnational incumbents' behaviour – in particular their decisions concerning public expenditures – constitutes a signal towards voters. We also assume that voters in both (the national and subnational) constituencies are sensible to such a signal so that they evaluate governors by observing the level and type of spending (and taxes) they execute in their provinces. Governors who aspire to national office need to gain popularity on board their districts and maximise the number of votes obtainable from both constituencies. In redistributive terms, these governors will privilege the expenditures with the highest positive territorial spill-overs. We thus hypothesise that as a governor's

---

14. There are only two amateur governors in our sample. These are F-1 car racer Carlos Reutemann, and popular singer Ramón 'Palito' Ortega.

15. Relying on qualitative data (mainly national and local newspapers) and some personal interviews, we built an inventory of the 'motives' that could have led Argentine governors to retire from politics. A complete list of these cases is shown in the Appendix.

*Table 9.2: Summary of hypotheses*

| Hypothesis | Independent Variable | Social Spending | Civil administration Spending |
|---|---|---|---|
| Individual | | | |
| H1 | Office ambitious | + | – |
| Political-institutional | | | |
| H2 | Party system fragmentation | – | + |
| H3 | Electoral uncertainty | + | – |
| H4 | Vertical copartisanship | empirical | empirical |
| H5 | Provincial revenues | + | – |
| Contextual | | | |
| H6 | Electoral cycles | + | + |
| H7 | Macroeconomic conditions | empirical | empirical |

career becomes nationalised she will attempt to assemble the increasingly more heterogeneous electorate through the provision of collective rather than particularistic goods. The logic behind this expectation is that collective goods constitute non-excludable benefits that target broader constituencies. This peculiarity reduces the transaction costs between potential beneficiaries thus resulting in beneficiaries being more cost-effective.

In sharp contrast, governors who possess a state-centred political ambition, especially those seeking re-election, have strong incentives to deliver particularistic goods. Because this form of spending is excludable as it targets specific individuals, it does not yield spill-overs beyond the province thus reducing overall electoral payoffs. However, it is much safer in their expected returns than collective goods. Assuming some capacity of vote monitoring as that exhibited by relevant parties in Argentina (Stokes 2005), particularistic goods provide a better oversight to assure that citizens receiving a material benefit will vote for the incumbent and not defer to the opposition. In many Argentine provinces, one of the most commonly offered particularistic good is a government job. These jobs are a key weapon to build stable provincial networks of political support. In return for getting a job in the civil administration, individuals are expected to participate in observable services such as the party daily-life and electioneering activities. Essentially, patronage-based networks contribute to the enduring territorial dominance of governors by shaping expectations about the future distribution of public jobs over an elaborate network of party operatives able to monitor voters and dissuade them from migrating to the opposition (Robinson and Verdier 2003; Calvo and Murillo 2004). This discussion led us to hypothesise that as a governor's career remains localised she will attempt to mobilise provincial voters through the provision of particularistic rather than collective goods.

Along with this individual-level factor, two political-institutional features are considered to affect incumbents' motivations to manage public outlays with political survival and career advancement goals: the party system and electoral competiveness. The former factor refers to both the extent of party competition (i.e., the number of participants that incumbents confront when competing for votes) and legislative fragmentation (i.e., the number of parties in the provincial legislature). The latter factor denotes a crucial aspect of electoral competition: the uncertainty of winning that the incumbents face (i.e., the margin of victory). These two characteristics are interrelated but should also have a distinct impact on public goods provision.

Researchers have recurrently argued that two-party systems provide a greater share of collective goods and longer periods of fiscal solvency than multiparty systems (Cox 1997; Hallerberg and von Hagen 1999; Persson and Tabellini 1999; Bueno de Mesquita *et al.* 2003; Mukherjee 2003; Chhibber and Nooruddin 2004; Hallerberg 2004). The general argument is that when only two parties compete for office (especially in winner-takes-all systems like that used in most Argentine provinces) each of them needs to assemble a majority in order to win the election. Each party has therefore to build electoral alliances across different social groups through, as we have seen, the provision of collective goods that are highly visible and widely valued. As political parties face other viable competitors and the party system becomes more fragmented, it is riskier (and too costly) to spend resources in building broad electoral coalitions because other parties can make more direct offers to narrower segments of the electorate. Hence, under party system fragmentation – a large number of effective competing parties – it is safer for incumbents to mobilise specific groups of the voting population through the allocation of particularistic goods rather than all citizens through collective goods.

An analytically distinct, but related, mechanism might be at work simultaneously. Political fragmentation can be considered an indicator of social heterogeneity or the degree to which policy preferences in a society diverge.[16] Extant research has documented a strong negative relationship between social heterogeneity – both in isolation and in interaction with the mechanical effects of the electoral system – and the provision of public goods. The usual account for this relation lies in the increased costs of collective action that groups face when their preferences are not homogeneous. In line with this reasoning, we anticipate that an increase in the effective number of parties represented in a provincial legislature would be detrimental to the provision of collective goods and would instead result in more particularism.

The second political-institutional factor that might affect subnational spending decisions is electoral competition or the uncertainty the incumbent faces about winning the election. In general, extant research highlights the benefits of electoral

---

16. Social heterogeneity can manifest itself through various channels, but recurrent topics in the literature refer to some relevant social dimension such as ethnicity, religion, landowner-peasant relations, and income inequality. Compared to these dimensions, we acknowledge that political fragmentation is a 'soft' indicator of social heterogeneity.

competition and alternation in encouraging the provision of public goods. The theoretical expectation is that those incumbents who confront a competitive (uncertain) election will derive expenditure towards 'lumpy' goods and more universalistic forms of spending in an attempt to catch more votes. For example, Hecock (2006) shows that subnational governments in Mexico with more competitive elections spend more on education. Conversely, incumbents who anticipate winning with a large margin of victory face low pressure to be responsive to their constituents. Thus, under political monopoly – or at least reduced political contestation – where politicians have no fear of being removed from office, voters are tied to the incumbents who are likely to bribe voters through particularistic goods. Despite these theoretical considerations, it is important to note that Argentina has experienced a notable pro-incumbency vote at the subnational level. The effect of such an incumbency bias in the voting trend would be to diminish the potential impact of electoral uncertainty on public expenditures as Argentine governors, on average, tend not to face many risky elections.

An additional political-institutional factor that might shape the spending choices of subnational governments, especially in countries like Argentina with relative disciplined parties, is vertical co-partisanship. Some researchers claim that partisan harmony between presidents and governors is conducive to spending reductions, a finding observed in Argentina during the mid-1980s and 1990s (Jones, Sanguinetti and Tommasi 2000). The central argument is that the president, who has better incentives for fiscal conservatism than state governors because the former is held responsible for macroeconomic outcomes, has additional coercive tools to compel governors from the same party to behave in line with national fiscal objectives. Furthermore, inasmuch as the electoral success of co-partisan governors depends in part on voters' assessment of the national government (the coattails effect) subnational leaders have incentives to minimise macroeconomic profligacy that might result from overspending (Rodden 2005; Wibbels 2006). Nonetheless, if the connection between overspending and macroeconomic performance is not acknowledged by voters, co-partisan governors might be tempted to be more – not less – fiscally profligate because they might expect easier access to bailouts from the central government. Empirical work on Germany (Rodden 2005), India (Khemani 2007) and Italy (Bordignon and Turati 2005) shows that regional governments have higher spending and fiscal deficits precisely when they belong to the same party as that occupying the presidency. It is therefore an empirical question whether vertical co-partisanship is associated with subnational overspending or fiscal conservatism.

The last political-institutional factor we address and test refers to the sources of provincial income. According to public finance literature, the incentives to expand government expenditures vary with the sources of income. Larger levels of nontax revenues – mainly coming from federal fiscal transfers – generates incentives for state expansion, particularly for expanding public employment and other forms of patronage distribution (Remmer 2007; Rodden 2002; Rodden and Wibbels 2002). The argument is that citizens and politicians view intergovernmental grants and locally-generated revenues through different lenses. Federal transfers create the fiscal illusion that subnational expenditures are funded by non-residents. In doing so, these transfers break the link between taxes and benefits, thus making voters less likely to sanction overspending. Subsidised by a sustained inflow of revenues coming from the centre, and protected from being electorally punished for their fiscal behaviour, governors sooner or later manipulate public spending to construct territorial power based on a large state apparatus.[17] For incumbents that are uncertain about how voters will respond to targeted benefits, supplying particularistic goods to their core friends is preferable to delivering collective goods to their swing neighbours. Conversely, to the extent that governors rely on broad-based domestic taxation to finance the provision of services, there is a close link between the benefits provided by these services and the costs to the local taxpayers. Under such conditions, voters have incentives to monitor authorities' fiscal behaviour making governors less likely to invest domestically-generated revenues in financing a large civil administration and more likely to spend these resources on delivering collective goods.

In addition to the individual and institutional factors described above, we also want to examine the effect of contextual variables on subnational government expenditure. These variables include the timing of elections and the macroeconomic conditions.

Because budgetary resources are limited, politicians should allocate spending when it is more needed. The concern of incumbents for their political survival is arguably greatest in periods proximate to elections, when they will seek to improve the lots of their voters. The conventional view is that incumbents pursue expansionary policies prior to elections in anticipation of a potential alternation of power in the electoral cycle (Levitt and Snyder 1995), and voters' reliance upon retrospective judgments on the functioning of the economy. Empirical evidence of electoral business cycles, however, is mixed. On the one hand, some studies of both well-established and less developed democracies find evidence consistent with the opportunistic manipulation of the economy (Ames 1987; Kiefer 2000; Clark 2005). Within this tradition a number of scholars argue that pre-electoral spending tends to be biased towards patronage or civil administration expenditures (Rogoff 1990; Gimpelson and Treisman 2002) because incumbents presumably seek to expand patronage appointments among their adherents. Others instead suggest that spending before elections is biased towards observable public investment projects (Khemani 2003) and social security policies (Wibbels 2006). On the other hand, however, there is some relevant research that has found no systematic evidence of pre-election spending booms. For example, Alesina *et al.* (1999) substantiate that there are no patterns of this in OECD countries. Based on a time-series analysis of six Latin American countries, Remmer (1993) demonstrates that some nations exhibit the predicted pattern of manipulation while others do not. Finally, a group of comparative analysts indicate that politicians might differ in whether public spending is to be

---

17. Furthermore, as provincial bureaucrats anticipate flows of revenues from the centre they have incentives to increase the resources allocated to them.

used after – rather than before – the elections (Ames 1987: 13; Remmer 2007). This might be especially the case of a newly elected government that needs to reinforce its territorial presence on the ground, or incumbents that negotiate to honour pre-electoral support conditional upon the observed electoral results and voters' behaviour.

Finally, our analysis incorporates some macroeconomic contextual variables that are expected to influence the amount and share of different types of spending. According to Wagner's law of increasing state activity, economic development should foster both social infrastructure and civil administration spending as it creates demands for new government services to satisfy the needs of the population. Yet expenditures can also be expanded in hard economic times in order to safeguard the population against private sector unemployment (Gimpelson and Treisman 2002). Empirical evidence on this issue is also mixed. On the one hand, relying upon time series and cross-sectional data Wu, Tang, and Lin (2010) find strong support for Wagner's law, a finding confirmed by several country-specific studies (Lin 1995; Yousefi and Abizadeh 1992). On the other hand, however, numerous comparative and single case analyses report weak or no association between economic development and government spending (Afxentiou and Serletis 1996; Akitoby *et al.* 2006; Afzal and Abbas 2010).

We also consider the potential effect of income inequality on public expenditure. The usual account for this relationship is that income inequality yields to a lower (suboptimal) supply of public goods because, first, it elicits cooperation dilemmas between the rich and the poor as these groups have heterogeneous preferences over which goods should be provided and, second, it privileges the position of established elites who have asymmetric access to public services (Dayton-Johnson 2000; Khwaja 2009). Finally, we consider the province population size because it might affect the leeway a province has over its spending. The argument goes in both directions. The biggest provinces have incentives to overspend because they might expect to be bailed out by the central government if they 'fail'. But the smallest provinces might also be tempted to overspend because their size limits the negative macroeconomic effects of their behaviour (Rodden 2005).

In sum, our theoretical approach builds on existing political-institutional and contextual explanations that emphasise the role of party systems, electoral competition, and election cycles. We also introduce the effect of individual level factors (incumbents' office ambitions) on subnational government spending. Although other important work has looked at related questions in Argentina and elsewhere, we are the first to empirically examine this set of determinants together. In doing so, we better capture the complexity and causal heterogeneity of provincial governors' decisions to allocate collective and particularistic goods.

## Data and Methods

To assess whether individual, institutional or contextual factors better explain variation in subnational government spending across Argentina's provinces, we

*Figure 9.2: Social infrastructure spending, by province (1993–2004)*

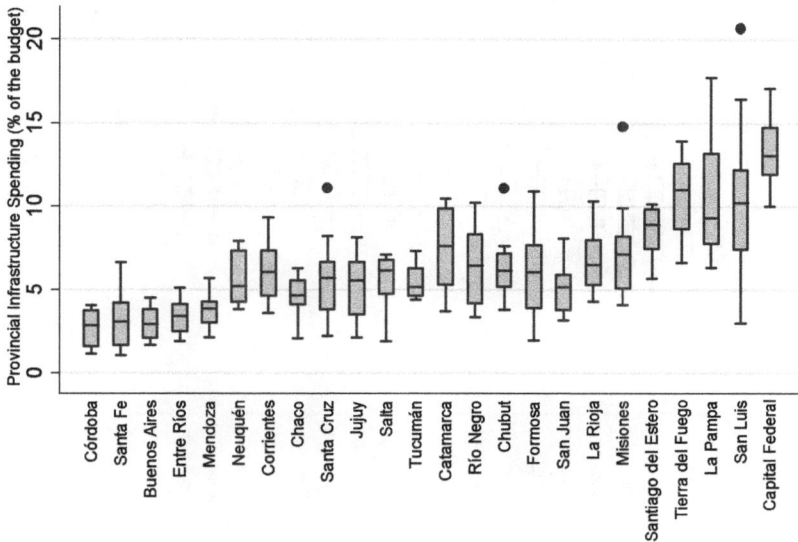

*Source:* Dirección de Análisis de Gasto Público y Programas Sociales, Secretaría de Política Económica, Ministerio de Economía.

collected official data on provincial expenditures for the 1993–2004 period.[18] Our dependent variables are government spending on social infrastructure and on civil administration, both measured as shares of the total provincial budget (expressed in constant *pesos*) and naturally logged to reduce skewness. The former type of spending includes expenditure on housing, urban development, sanitary engineering, water supply, sewerage, and sewage. Because capital investment on social infrastructure is geographically targeted – and, as such, non-excludable – it is considered a semi-public or collective good.[19] The latter type of spending includes personal allocation (jobs, wages and salaries) to finance the provincial civil administration. Because this expenditure only targets specific individuals (i.e., public workers) it is excludable and then a classic example of particularistic good.[20]

Figure 9.2 displays the annual percentage of the total provincial budget that each province devoted to social infrastructure and civil administration during the

---

18. Data were provided by the Dirección de Análisis de Gasto Público y Programas Sociales, Secretaría de Política Económica, Ministerio de Economía.

19. In measuring infrastructure expenditures, we deliberately excluded spending on capital projects such as credits to specific economic sectors and firms, which are sectorally targeted club goods.

20. This measurement naturally excludes administrative expenditures associated with the delivery of goods and services, including social security services.

*Figure 9.3: Civil administration spending, by province (1993–2004)*

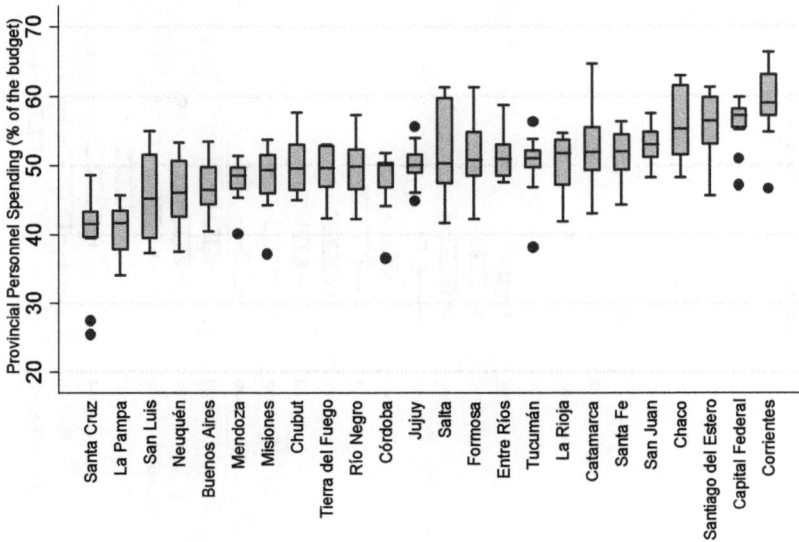

*Source:* Dirección de Análisis de Gasto Público y Programas Sociales, Secretaría de Política Económica, Ministerio de Economía.

period under study. As it can be seen, percentages vary widely across jurisdictions. On average, these values range from a minimum of 1.05 per cent (Santa Fe, 2003) to a maximum of 20.7 (San Luis, 1998), with a median of 6.4 and a standard deviation of 3.4 per cent. The provinces with the highest averaged percentages are Ciudad de Buenos Aires (the richest district), San Luis and La Pampa, while those with the lowest percentages are the metropolitan provinces of Córdoba, Santa Fe, and Buenos Aires.

As for public spending on civil administration, Figure 9.3 shows that variation across provinces is less remarkable but still considerable. Indeed, it ranges from a maximum of 66.3 per cent (Corrientes, 1993) to a minimum of 25.5 (Santa Cruz, 2003), with a mean of 50.1 and a standard deviation of 6.3. The jurisdictions that comparatively devoted more resources to personnel expenditure are Corrientes, Ciudad de Buenos Aires, and Santiago del Estero, while those with the lowest percentages are Santa Cruz, La Pampa, and San Luis.

The crucial independent variables included in our estimations are designed to measure provincial governors' office ambitions at the end of their mandates, political fragmentation (both electoral and legislative), political competitiveness, vertical co-partisanship, provincial vertical fiscal balance, gubernatorial and presidential electoral cycles, and provincial socio-economic conditions.

First, the effect of our individual-level factor (i.e., governors' office ambitious) is captured through an ordinal variable measuring the level of gubernatorial career nationalisation. Values of this variable are 0 (governors who quit politics), 1 (governors with provincial-centred ambition), and 2 (governors with national-centred ambition). We also estimated, with almost identical statistical results, our models with a 0–3 ordinal variable distinguishing between governors with municipal and provincial ambitions. Second, we operationalise the set of political-institutional variables discussed in the previous section. Regarding the impact of provincial political fragmentation, we are concerned with both the number of political parties competing in elections for gubernatorial office and the relative seat share that each party possesses in the provincial legislature. Although there is, of course, a direct connection between the number of votes and seats, different electoral rules in the Argentine provinces lead to substantially different mechanisms of translating votes into legislative seats (Calvo and Micozzi 2005). Therefore, we measure political fragmentation through the effective number of competitive/legislative parties, a concept that weights the number of parties by their vote share and size in the local legislature, respectively (Laasko and Taagepera 1979).[21] The former variable ranges from a minimum of 1.6 competitive parties to a maximum of 9.7, with a mean of 3.2 and a standard deviation of 1.1. The latter variable ranges from 1.0 legislative party to 5.1, with a mean of 2.1 and a standard deviation of 0.7. To empirically assess the role of electoral competition we compute the margin of victory (i.e., percentage point difference) between the winning party and the second largest recipient of votes in each gubernatorial election. Provincial variation ranges from a vote difference of 84.5 per cent to 2.9, with a mean and standard deviation of 17.1 and 15.3 per cent respectively. We also include a dummy variable for vertical co-partisanship coded 1 if the incumbent governor shares the president's party (55 per cent of the cases in our dataset), 0 otherwise. The last political-institutional variable incorporated to our models measures the tax structure of each province as the rate of nontax revenues to own-source revenues. This variable ranges from 86.8 to 3.1 per cent with a mean of 20.5 and a standard deviation of 17.1 per cent. Recall that we expect social infrastructure to increase and civil administration to decrease with higher levels of provincially-generated revenues.[22]

With regards to the contextual factors that are paramount in affecting government expenditures, we separately include in our models dummy variables indicating the presence of a gubernatorial and a presidential election year. We finally incorporate a number of variables typically used by comparative research on redistributive politics to explore whether the socio-economic conditions of each province are causally related to different patterns of subnational government spending. Thus, the models include the provincial GDP per capita in each year, the annual rate of

---

21. Data to build these variables come from Calvo and Escolar (2005), and our own calculations based on the Atlas Electoral Andy Tow, http://www.andytow.com (accessed 10 December 2016).

22. Data to construct this variable was obtained from the Dirección Nacional de Coordinación Fiscal con las provincias, Secretaría de Hacienda, Ministerio de Economía.

national economic growth, the annual share of the provincial population under the poverty line (or unsatisfied basic needs), and the population size.

To test our theoretical expectations, we employ a pooled cross-sectional time-series dataset that consists of Argentina's twenty-four provinces between 1993 and 2004. As it becomes standard in similar studies, we rely on ordinary least square (OLS) estimators with panel corrected standard errors (PCSE) to remedy for panel heteroskedasticity and spatial correlation (Beck and Katz 1995). Most cross-national studies on spending have employed fixed-effects models to control for omitted variable bias. There is considerable debate, however, over the merits of including fixed effects. Besides the fact that such controls are atheoretical, their inclusion mitigate the effect of exogenous time-invariant variables, and severely skews the estimated effects of partially invariant variables over time (Beck 2001). For these reasons, the reported results do not include fixed effect estimators. A potential problem with our models, as it has been noted in past works, is the incremental and sticky nature of budgetary spending. Correlations for the two spending variables of interest across the four years of each gubernatorial term reveal the presence of certain continuity in the level of expenditure. Yet we decided not to include a lagged dependent variable for two main reasons. First, in practical terms, including a lagged variable would seriously diminish the number of observations given the limited time span in our dataset. Second, as Achen (2000) has demonstrated, because the inclusion of a lagged dependent variable in cases with short time series may lead to autocorrelation and then to an underestimate of the effect of other explanatory (and theoretically more interesting) variables.

**Discussion**

The estimates of four different specifications of our basic model examining the effect of individual, political-institutional, and contextual variables on subnational government spending in Argentina are reported in Table 9.3 and Table 9.4. The models are identical with the only exception of the variable measuring provincial political fragmentation: the effective number of competitive parties (Table 9.3), and the effective number of legislative parties (Table 9.4). In both tables, Model 1 tests for gubernatorial electoral cycles while Model 2 does it for presidential cycles.

The first result to notice is that the empirical tests provide strong support for our claim that the direction of governors' office ambitions affects gubernatorial incentives to strategically deliver collective and particularistic goods. Indeed, as the statistically significant positive sign of the ambitious variable indicates, governors spend proportionally more budgetary resources on social infrastructure projects when they possess a national-oriented aspiration. Conversely, as shown by the significant negative sign of the same variable, governors with provincial-oriented office ambitions tend to devote more resources to finance the civil administration. In substantive terms, on average, a governor with nationalised political ambition spends 5 per cent (Model 1, column 1) more of the budgetary resources in social infrastructure than a governor with provincialised office goals, whereas the latter dedicates 1.3 per cent (Model 1, column 2) more of these monies

*Table 9.3: Determinants of provincial government spending, 1993–2004 (1)*

| Variables | Model 1 | | Model 2 | |
|---|---|---|---|---|
| | Social Infrastructure | Civil Administration | Social Infrastructure | Civil Administration |
| Office Ambitious | .050** | −.013** | .050** | −.013** |
| | (.023) | (.006) | (.023) | (.006) |
| Political Fragmentation, ENCP (ln) | −.244*** | .064*** | −.242*** | .067*** |
| | (.085) | (.021) | (.085) | (.021) |
| Margin of Victory (ln) | .031 | −.007 | .032 | −.007 |
| | (.021) | (.006) | (.021) | (.006) |
| Vertical Copartisanship | .005 | −.037** | .005 | −.037** |
| | (.048) | (.016) | (.048) | (.017) |
| Gubernatorial Election Year | −.019 | −.026 | | |
| | (.087) | (.026) | | |
| Presidential Election Year | | | −.018 | −.022 |
| | | | (.082) | (.025) |
| Provincial Revenues (ln) | −.011 | .043*** | −.011 | .043*** |
| | (.045) | (.011) | (.045) | (.011) |
| Provincial GDP, per capita | .000*** | −.000*** | .000*** | −.000*** |
| | (.000) | (.000) | (.000) | (.000) |
| National Economic Growth | .010* | −.005*** | .010* | −.005*** |
| | (.006) | (.002) | (.006) | (.002) |
| Provincial Poverty | .015*** | .008*** | .015*** | .008*** |
| | (.003) | (.001) | (.003) | (.001) |
| Provincial Population | −2.11*** | −.051 | −2.11*** | −.051 |
| | (.313) | (.082) | (.314) | (.082) |
| Constant | 1.31*** | 3.59*** | 1.31*** | 3.58*** |
| | (.161) | (.063) | (.159) | (.063) |
| N | 278 | 278 | 278 | 278 |
| Groups | 24 | 24 | 24 | 24 |
| R2 | 0.302 | 0.361 | 0.302 | 0.361 |
| Prob > chi2 | 0.0000 | 0.0000 | 0.0000 | 0.0000 |

Note: PCSE Regression. Standard errors in parentheses. Dependent variable: share of the provincial budget allocated to social infrastructure and civil administration (natural log). ENCP: effective number of competitive parties.* p < .10; ** p < .05; *** p < .01

*Table 9.4: Determinants of provincial government spending, 1993–2004 (2)*

| Variables | Model 1 | | Model 2 | |
|---|---|---|---|---|
| | Social Infrastructure | Civil Administration | Social Infrastructure | Civil Administration |
| Office Ambitious | .056** | −.014** | .056** | −.014** |
| | (.023) | (.006) | (.023) | (.006) |
| Political Fragmentation, ENLP (ln) | −.039* | .072** | −.039* | .074** |
| | (.022) | (.030) | (.022) | (.030) |
| Margin of Victory (ln) | .099 | −.008 | .099 | −.009 |
| | (.101) | (.006) | (.101) | (.006) |
| Vertical Copartisanship | .018 | −.041** | .018 | −.042** |
| | (.053) | (.017) | (.052) | (.017) |
| Gubernatorial Election Year | −.007 | −.027 | | |
| | (.094) | (.025) | | |
| Presidential Election Year | | | −.012 | −.023 |
| | | | (.090) | (.025) |
| Provincial Revenues (ln) | −.009 | .036** | −.008 | .036** |
| | (.041) | (.014) | (.041) | (.014) |
| Provincial GDP, per capita | .000*** | −.000*** | .000*** | −.000*** |
| | (.000) | (.000) | (.000) | (.000) |
| National Economic Growth | .013** | −.005*** | .013** | −.005*** |
| | (.006) | (.002) | (.006) | (.002) |
| Provincial Poverty | .015*** | .007*** | .015*** | .007*** |
| | (.003) | (.000) | (.003) | (.001) |
| Provincial Population | −2.11*** | −.055 | −2.11*** | −.056 |
| | (.338) | (.085) | (.339) | (.085) |
| Constant | 1.15*** | 3.64*** | 1.15*** | 3.64*** |
| | (.145) | (.058) | (.145) | (.058) |
| N | 278 | 278 | 278 | 278 |
| Groups | 24 | 24 | 24 | 24 |
| R2 | 0.291 | 0.367 | 0.291 | 0.365 |
| Prob > chi2 | 0.0000 | 0.0000 | 0.0000 | 0.0000 |

Note: PCSE Regression. Standard errors in parentheses. Dependent variable: share of the provincial budget allocated to social infrastructure and civil administration (natural log). ENCP: effective number of competitive parties. *p < .10; **p < .05; ***p < .01

to finance the provincial bureaucracy.[23] Not only are coefficients of the political ambition variable statistically robust (at the .05 level) in all model specifications, but they also contain some substantive impact, especially in the case of social infrastructure considering that the media for this type of spending is 6.4 per cent of the provincial budget. Thus, we would expect a governor with national ambition to spend nearly 78 per cent more to back these projects than a governor who aspires to continue her professional career within the province.

Second, our results also lend credence to the hypotheses that link political fragmentation with subnational expenditure patterns. As it can be appreciated, there is a statistically significant negative relationship between the effective number of parties (irrespective of whether we use votes or seats as indicators) and social infrastructure spending. Therefore, increased fragmentation in either the electoral market or the local legislature decreases gubernatorial incentives to provide collective goods. In line with our theoretical expectations, moreover, there is a positive significant relationship between party system fragmentation and personnel spending. Substantive results demonstrate that for every percentage increase in the effective number of competitive parties, the budgetary share of spending on social infrastructure diminishes 0.24 per cent (Model 1, column 1), while spending on civil administration increases .06 per cent (Model 1, column 2).[24] Taken together, these results suggest that the greater the fragmentation of the party system (the more the number of parties), the more provincial governors are forced to focus on the narrow objectives of specific groups and individuals rather than on the shared benefits of broader constituencies.

Third, contrary to our theoretical expectations and much past research, we find no empirical evidence that electoral uncertainty – as measured by the margin of victory – has a real impact on redistributive spending in the Argentine provinces. Although the coefficients for this variable have always the expected sign, they do not reach the standard levels of statistical significance.

Fourth, with regards to the effect of vertical (federal-provincial) copartisanship, the results are somewhat mixed. On the one hand, no matter how we estimate the models, belonging to the president's party has no causal effect on the level of social infrastructure spending. On the other hand, however, this variable has a strong and significant inverse effect on civil administration spending. On average, provinces where the governor is a member of the president's party spend significantly less (between 3.7 and 4.2 per cent depending on the model) in personnel expenditure than provinces ruled by governors from the opposition. This result seems to confirm the argument than presidents are capable of compelling their copartisan

---

23. Recall that the dependent variable is expressed in its log-transformed state and the political ambition variable is in its original metric. In such models, the format for interpretation is that the dependent variable changes by 100*(coefficient) per cent for a one unit increase in the independent variable holding all other variables in the model constant.

24. Because variables of the effective number of parties are log-transformed, their impact is measured as the per cent change in the share of spending while the effective number of parties increases by 1 per cent.

governors to behave more conservatively, at least regarding the financing of the state apparatus.

The one counterintuitive finding from the regression results is that provinces with higher shares of income coming from domestic taxation spend proportionally more public outlays on civil administration (between 3.6 and 4.3 per cent). This finding contradicts a common expectation of prior work on fiscal federalism and public finance that subnational dependence on federal fiscal transfers generates incentives to allocate particularistic goods and thus increase the size of the public administration. Yet it should be noticed that this result is the artifact of an outlier: the Ciudad de Buenos Aires, which collects an average of 82 per cent of its total income from local taxes, whereas the other provinces only collect an average of 16 per cent from domestic tax sources. Once this outlier is dropped from the analysis the positive relationship is no longer statistically significant.

Fifth, the estimated coefficients for both gubernatorial and presidential election years do not reach statistical significance. Thus, we do not find empirical support for the conventional wisdom that governing parties at the provincial level in Argentina tend to increase spending during electoral times through either public works or salary bonuses for provincial public sector employees.

Finally, the macroeconomic variables included in the models are highly robust and tend to perform as expected. Good economic performance, both at the national and provincial levels, is positively related to the allocation of social infrastructure and negatively to the provision of public jobs and salaries. Economic growth then fosters provincial governments to invest in public work – mainly urban – services, and indirectly reduces the size of civil administration as private employment increases. The poverty and population variables partially conform to expectations as provinces with a larger share of poor households spend proportionally more on both types of expenditures, while more populated provinces spend less.

## Conclusion

Redistribution conflicts in a federation usually take place within the territorial boundaries of subnational jurisdictions. Hence, in order to understand the nature of several distributional conflicts in multi-level systems it is critical to examine how subnational incumbents strategically divvy up the public money to benefit certain groups of citizens over others.

This chapter assesses the role played by individual, political-institutional and contextual factors in shaping subnational government spending – particularly, the ability of provincial governors to strategically deliver collective and particularistic goods – across Argentina's provinces. In doing so, this analysis contributes to an understanding of public goods provision and redistributive conflicts in an important federal country where governors are regarded as textbook examples of powerful subnational political actors and federal institutions provide subnational executives with ample spending discretion.

We draw on the existing literature on public finance and fiscal federalism for building our key arguments, but we introduce an important innovation to the institutional and contextual approaches commonly used to study government spending in comparative politics. We focus on the influence that governors' office ambitions have on their strategic decisions to allocate the public money. That is, we examine the micro-foundations of subnational government spending.

Our analysis provides systematic evidence of the effect that gubernatorial ambitions have over different types of government expenditure. On average, governors with national-oriented ambitions systematically spend more resources to finance social infrastructure projects and less to public employment. Moreover, provincial party-system fragmentation – but not political competition – generates incentives to deliver particularistic rather than collective goods. We found partial evidence regarding the impact of federal-provincial copartisanship as it reduces particularism but does not affect the provision of collective goods, and no evidence of the presence of election (neither gubernatorial nor presidential) cycles.

This chapter leaves a number of significant questions open for further research. First, with regard to the nature of incumbents' ambitions, it would be important to obtain data on whether or not they change their future political ambitions while in office. Second, future research should consider other factors that might influence incentives to allocate collective and particularistic goods such as subnational public debts as well as the interactions between institutional and individual variables. Third, researchers should consider the importance of other types of universalistic forms of spending to examine whether the structure of incumbents' incentives differ when they distribute private, collective, and public goods.

## APPENDIX

*Table 9.1A: Motives of gubernatorial retirement in Argentina (salient cohorts, 1995–2011)*

| Name of Governor | Voluntary Retirement | Motive |
|---|---|---|
| Arnoldo Castillo | Yes | Advanced Age |
| Juan Manuel de la Sota | Yes | Party Politics* |
| Néstor Braillard Poccard | No (impeached) | Scandal |
| Sergio Montiel | Yes | Party Politics* |
| Mario Moine | Yes | Quit Politics** |
| Roberto Domínguez | No (resigned) | Political Crisis |
| Carlos Ficosecco | No (resigned) | Political Crisis |
| Carlos Ferraro | No (resigned) | Avoid Impeachment |
| Angel Mazza | No (impeached) | Scandal |
| Felipe Sapag | Yes | Party Politics* |
| Juan Carlos Rojas | Yes | Party Politics* |
| Alfredo Avelín | No (impeached) | Scandal |
| Sergio Acevedo | No (resigned) | Political Crisis |
| Jorge Obeid | Yes | Quit Politics** |
| Carlos Mujica | No (resigned) | Avoid Impeachment |
| Mercedes A. de Juarez | No (resigned) | Political Crisis |
| José Estabillo | Yes | Party Politics* |
| Mario Collazo | No (impeached) | Scandal |

*Source*: Authors' compilation. Notes: (*)The person was engaged in a noteworthy partisan activity. (**)The person did not hold any elective or appointed position, and was not engaged in a partisan activity.

# References

Achen, C. (2000) 'Why Lagged Dependent Variables Can Supress the Explanatory Power of Other Independent Variables', Presented at the Annual Meeting of the Political Methodology, Los Angeles.

Afxentiou, P. and Serletis, A. (1996) 'Government Expenditures in the European Union: Do They Converge or Follow Wagner's Law?', *International Economic Journal* 10(3): 33–47.

Afzal, M. and Abbas, Q. (2010) 'Wagner's law in Pakistan: another look', *Journal of Economics and International Finance* 2(1): 12–19.

Akitoby, B., Clements, B., Gupta, S. and Inchauste, G. (2006) 'Public spending, voracity and Wagner's Law in developing countries', *European Journal of Political Economy* 22(4): 908–924.

Alesina, A. (1987) 'Macroeconomic policy in a two-party system as a repeated game', *The Quarterly Journal of Economics* 102(3): 651–678.

Alesina, A., Baqir, R. and Easterly, W. (1999) 'Public goods and ethnic divisions', *The Quarterly Journal of Economics* 114(4): 1243–1284.

Alt, J. and Lowry, R. (1994) 'Divided government, fiscal institutions and budget deficits: evidence from the States', *American Political Science Review* 88(4): 811–828.

Ames, B. (1987) *Political Survival: Politicians and public policy in Latin America*, Berkeley: University of California Press.

Ansolabehere, S., Snyder Jr., J. and Ting, M. (2003) 'Bargaining in bicameral legislatures: when and why does malapportionment matter?', *American Political Science Review* 97(3): 471–481.

Beck, N. (2001) 'Time-series-cross-section data: what have we learned in the past few years?', *Annual Review of Political Science* 4(1): 271–293.

Beck, N. and Katz, J. N. (1995) 'What to do (and not to do) with time series cross-section data', *American Political Science Review* 89(3): 634–647.

Behrend, J. (2011) 'The unevenness of democracy at the subnational level: provincial closed games in Argentina', *Latin American Research Review* 46(1): 150–176.

Benton, A. (2009) 'What makes strong federalism seem weak? Fiscal resources and presidential-provincial relations in Argentina', *Publius: The Journal of Federalism* 39(4): 651–676.

Berry, C. (2008) 'Piling on: multilevel government and the fiscal common pool', *American Journal of Political Science* 52(4): 802–820.

Besley, T., Persson, T. and Sturm, D. (2005) 'Political Competition and Economic Performance: Theory and Evidence from the United States', NBER Working Paper No. 11484.

Betancourt, R. and Gleason, S. (2000) 'The allocation of publicly-provided goods to rural households in India: on some consequences of caste, religion and democracy', *World Development* 28(12): 23–34.

Boix, C. (1988) *Political Parties, Growth and Equality: Conservative and social democratic economic strategies in the world economy*, Cambridge, UK: Cambridge University Press.

Bonvecchi, A. and Lodola, G. (2011) 'The dual logic of intergovernmental transfers: Presidents, Governors, and the politics of coalition-building in Argentina', *Publius: The Journal of Federalism* 41(2): 179–206.

Bordignon, M. and Turati, G. (2005) 'Bailing Out Expectations and Health Expenditure in Italy: An empirical approach', Unpublished Manuscript, Universita Cattolica di Milano.

Bueno de Mesquita, B., Smith, A., Silverson, R. and Morrow, J. (2003) *The Logic of Political Survival*, Cambridge, MASS: MIT Press.

Calvo, E. and Escolar, M. (2005) *La nueva política de partidos en la Argentina: Crisis política, realineamientos partidarios y reforma electoral*, Buenos Aires: Prometeo-PENT.

Calvo, E. and Micozzi, J. (2005) 'The Governor's backyard: a seat-vote model of electoral reform for subnational multiparty races', *The Journal of Politics* 67(4): 1323–1335.

Calvo, E. and Murillo, M. (2004) 'Who delivers? Partisan clients in the Argentine electoral market', *American Journal of Political Science* 48(4): 742–57.

Camp, R. (2008) *Mexico's Mandarins, Crafting a Power Elite for the 21st Century*, California: University of California Press.

—— (2010) *The Metamorphosis of Leadership in a Democratic Mexico*, Oxford: Oxford University Press.

Centro de Implementación de Políticas Públicas para la Equidad y el Crecimiento, 2002 and 2009, *Directorio Legislativo: Quiénes son nuestros legisladores y cómo nos representan*, Buenos Aires: CIPPEC.

Chandra, K. (2007) *Why Ethnic Parties Succeed: Patronage and ethnic headcounts in India*, Cambridge, UK: Cambridge University Press.

Chhibber, P. and Nooruddin, I. (2004) 'Do party systems count? The number of parties and government performance in the Indian States', *Comparative Political Studies* 37(2): 152–187.

Clark, W. (2005) *Capitalism, Not Globalism: Capital mobility, Central Bank independence, and the political control of the economy*, Michigan: University of Michigan Press.

Coates, D. and Munger, M. (1995) 'Win, lose, or withdraw: a categorical analysis of career patterns in the House of Representatives, 1948–1978', *Public Choice* 83(1–2), 95–111.

Cox, G. (1997) *Making Votes Count: Strategic coordination in the world's electoral systems*, Cambridge: Cambridge University Press.

Dayton-Johnson, J. (2000) 'Determinants of collective action on the local commons: a model with evidence from Mexico', *Journal of Development Economics* 62(1): 181–208.

De Luca, M. (2008) 'Political Recruitment of Presidents and Governors in the Argentine Party-Centered System', in P. Siavelis and S. Morgenstern (eds), *Pathways to Power: Political recruitment and candidate selection in Latin America*, University Park: Pennsylvania State University Press, pp. 189–217.

De Luca, M., Jones, M. and Tula, M. (2002) 'Back rooms or ballot boxes? Candidate nomination in Argentina', *Comparative Political Studies* 35(4): 413–436.

Drazen, A. (2000) *Political Economy in Macroeconomics*, Princeton: Princeton University Press.

Falleti, T. (2010) *Decentralization and Subnational Politics in Latin America*, New York, NY: Cambridge University Press.

Francis, W. and Kenny, L. (1996) 'Position shifting in pursuit of higher office', *American Journal of Political Science* 40(3): 768–786.

Franzese, R. (2002) 'Electoral and partisan cycles in economic policies and outcomes', *Annual Review of Political Science* 5: 369–421.

Gervasoni, C. (2010) 'A rentier theory of subnational regimes: fiscal federalism, democracy and authoritarianism in the Argentine Provinces', *World Politics* 62(2): 302–40.

Gibson, E. (2012) *Boundary Control: Subnational authoritarianism in federal democracies*, Cambridge: Cambridge University Press.

Gimpelson, V. and Treisman, D. (2002) 'Fiscal games and public employment: a theory with evidence from Russia', *World Politics* 54: 145–183.

González, L. (2016) *Presidents, Governors, and the Politics of Distribution in Federal Democracies: Primus contra pares in Argentina and Brazil*, London: Routledge.

Hallerberg, M. (2004) *Domestic Budgets in a United Europe*, Ithaca: Cornell University Press.

Hallerberg, M. and von Hagen, J. (1999) 'Electoral Institutions, Cabinet Negotiations, and Budget Deficits within the European Union', in J. Poterba and J. von Hagen (eds) *Fiscal Institutions and Fiscal Performance*, Chicago: University of Chicago Press, pp. 209–32.

Hecock, D. (2006) 'Electoral competition, globalization, and subnational education spending in Mexico, 1999–2004', *American Journal of Political Science* 50(4): 950–961.

Herrick, R. and Moore, M. (1993) 'Political ambition's effect on legislative behaviour: Schlesinger's typology reconsidered and revisited', *The Journal of Politics* 55(3): 765–776.

Hibbing, J. (1986) 'Ambition in the House: behavioral consequences of higher office goals among U.S. Representatives', *American Journal of Political Science* 30(3): 651–665.

Hibbs, D. (1977) 'Political parties and macroeconomic policy', *American Political Science Review* 71(3): 1467–1487.

Huber, E., Mustillo, T. and Stephens, J. (2008) 'Politics and social spending in Latin America', *The Journal of Politics* 70(2): 420–436.

Jones, M. (1997) 'Federalism and the number of parties in Argentine congressional elections', *The Journal of Politics* 59(2): 538–549.

—— (2001) 'Political Institutions and Public Policy in Argentina: An overview of the formation and execution of the national budget', in S. Haggard and M. McCubbins (eds), *Presidents, Parliaments, and Policy*, Cambridge, MA: Cambridge University Press, pp. 149–182.

—— (2008) 'The Recruitment and Selection of Legislative Candidates in Argentina', in P. Siavelis and S. Morgenstern (eds), *Pathways to Power: Political recruitment and candidate selection in Latin America*, University Park: Pennsylvania State University Press, pp. 41–75.

Jones, M. and Hwang, W. (2005) 'Party government in presidential democracies: extending cartel theory beyond the U.S. Congress', *American Journal of Political Science* 49(2): 267–282.

Jones, M., Hwang, W. and Micozzi, J. (2009) 'Government and opposition in the Argentine Congress, 1989–2007: understanding inter-party dynamics through roll call vote analysis', *Journal of Politics in Latin America* 1(1): 67–96.

Jones, M., Saiegh, S., Spiller, P. and Tommasi, M. (2002) 'Amateur legislators-professional politicians: the consequences of party-centered electoral rules in a federal system', *American Journal of Political Science* 46(3): 356–369.

Jones, M., Sanguinetti, P. and Tommasi, M. (2000) 'Politics, institutions, and fiscal performance in a federal system: an analysis of the Argentine Provinces', *Journal of Development Economics* 61(2): 303–333.

Khemani, S. (2003) 'Political cycles in a developing economy: effect of elections in the Indian state', *Journal of Development Economics* 73(1): 125–154.

—— (2007) 'Party politics and fiscal discipline in a federation: evidence from the states of India', *Comparative Political Studies* 40 (6): 691–712.

Khwaja, A. (2009) 'Can good projects succeed in bad communities?', *Journal of Public Economics* 93(7–8): 899–916.

Kiefer, D. (2000) 'Activist macroeconomic policy, election effects, and the foundation of expectations: evidence from OECD countries', *Economics and Politics* 12: 137–154.

Kikuchi, H. and Lodola, G. (2014) 'Gubernatorial influence and political career effects in senatorial voting behavior: the Argentine case', *Journal of Politics in Latin America* 6(2): 73–105.

Kitschelt, H. (2000) 'Linkages between citizens and politicians in democratic polities', *Comparative Political Studies* 33(6–7): 845–879.

Kitschelt, H. and Wilkinson, S. (2007) *Patrons, Clients, and Policies: Patterns of democratic accountability and political competition*, Cambridge: Cambridge University Press.

Laakso, M. and Taagepera, R. (1979) 'Effective number of parties: a measure with application to Western Europe', *Comparative Political Studies* 12(1): 3–27.

Levitt, S. and Snyder Jr, J. (1995) 'Political parties and the distribution of federal outlays', *American Journal of Political Science* 39(4): 958–980.

Lizzeri, A. and Persico, N. (2001) 'The provision of public goods under alternative electoral incentives', *American Economic Review* 91(1): 225–239.

Lodola, G. (2009) 'La Estructura Subnacional de las Carreras Políticas en Argentina y Brasil', *Revista Desarrollo Económico* 194(49): 247–286.

—— (2010) 'The Politics of Subnational Coalition Building: Redistributive electoral strategies in Argentina and Brazil', Ph.D. Dissertation, Department of Political Science, University of Pittsburgh.

Londregan, J. and Poole, K. (1993) 'Poverty, the coup trap, and the seizure of executive power', *World Politics* 42(2): 151–183.

McCarty, N. (2000) 'Proposal rights, veto rights, and political bargaining', *American Journal of Political Science* 44(3): 506–522.

Mainwaring, S. (1991) 'Politicians, parties, and electoral systems: Brazil in comparative perspective', *Comparative Politics* 24(1): 21–43.

Miguel, E. and Gugerty, M. (2005) 'Ethnic diversity, social sanctions, and public goods in Kenya', *Journal of Public Economics* 89(4): 2325–2368.

Mukherjee, B. (2003) 'Political parties and the size of government in multiparty legislatures: examining cross-country and panel data evidence', *Comparative Political Studies* 36(6): 699–728.

Perotti, R. (1996) 'Growth, income distribution, and democracy: what the data say', *Journal of Economic Growth* 1(2): 149–187.

Persson, T. and Tabellini, G. (1999) 'The size and scope of government: comparative politics with rational politicians', *European Economic Review* 43(4–6): 699–735.

—— (2000) *Political Economics: Explaining economic policy*, Cambridge, MA: M.I.T. Press.

—— (2003) *The Economic Effects of Constitutions*, Cambridge, MA: MIT Press.

Pierson, P. (2001) *The New Politics of the Welfare State*, Oxford: Oxford University Press.

Power, T. and Mochel, M. (2008) 'Presidents, Ministers, and Governors in Brazil', in P. Siavelis and S. Morgenstern (eds) *Pathways to Power: Political recruitment and candidate selection in Latin America*, Pennsylvania: Pennsylvania State University, pp 229–38.

Remmer, K. (1993) 'Political economy of elections in Latin America', *American Political Science Review* 87(2): 393–407.

—— (2007) 'The political economy of patronage: expenditure patterns in the Argentine provinces, 1983–2003', *The Journal of Politics* 69(2): 363–77.

Robinson, J. and Torvik, R. (2005) 'White elephants', *Journal of Public Economics* 89(2–3): 197–210.

Robinson, J. and Verdier, T. (2003) 'The Political Economy of Clientelism', Unpublished Manuscript, University of California, Berkeley.

Rodden, J. (2002) 'The Dilemma of Fiscal Federalism: Grants and Fiscal Performance around the World', *American Journal of Political Science* 46(3): 670–687.

—— (2005) *Hamilton's Paradox: The promise and peril of fiscal federalism*, Cambridge: Cambridge University Press.

Rodden, J. and Wibbels, E. (2002) 'Beyond the fiction of federalism: macroeconomic management in multi-tiered systems', *World Politics* 54(4): 494–531.

Rogoff, K. (1999) 'Equilibrium political budget cycles', *American Economic Review* 80: 21–36.

Samuels, D. (2003) *Ambition, Federalism, and Legislative Politics in Brazil*, Cambridge: Cambridge University Press.

Schlesinger, J. (1966) *Ambition and Politics: Political careers in the United States*, Chicago: Rand McNally & Company.

—— (1991) *Political Parties and the Winning of Office*, Ann Arbor: University of Michigan Press.

Siavelis, P. and Morgenstern, S. (2008) *Pathways to Power: Political recruitment and candidate selection in Latin America*, University Park: Pennsylvania State University Press.

Stepan, A. (2004) 'Electorally generated veto players in unitary and federal systems', in E. Gibson (ed.) *Federalism and Democracy in Latin America*, Baltimore: The Johns Hopkins University Press, pp. 323–61.

Stokes, S. (2005) 'Perverse accountability: a formal model of machine politics with evidence from Argentina', *American Political Science Review* 99(3): 315–325.

Stratmann, T. and Baur, M. (2002) 'Plurality rule, proportional representation, and the German Bundestag: how incentives to pork-barrel differ across electoral systems', *American Journal of Political Science* 46(3): 506–514.

Wayne, F. L. and Kenny, L. W. (2000) *Up the Political Ladder: Career paths in U.S. politics*, Thousand Oaks, CA: Sage Publications, Inc.

Wibbels, E. (2006) 'Dependency revisited: international markets, business cycles, and social spending in the developing world', *International Organization* 60(2): 433–468.

Yousefi, M. and Abizadeh, S. (1992) 'Growth of state government expenditures: empirical evidence from the United States', *Public Finance* 47(2): 322–339.

*Chapter Ten*

# An Institutional Architecture for Social Inclusion: The Creation of the *Bolsa Família* Programme and the Social Development Ministry in Brazil[1]

*Lucio R. Renno*

## Introduction

Institutions and organisations are the fruit of human ingenuity to solve problems and mitigate conflicts. They are born from occasion and action. In other words, there are macro-level factors that create the opportunity for institution building, but these are only consummated if humans are willing to create rules, bureaucratic bodies, and agencies that materialise the drive to construct or reconstruct a legal framework that embodies the solutions for problems and conflicts. Hence, to understand the creation of problem-solving and conflict-mitigating bodies of rules and organisational structures it is important to explore both contextual factors that bolster the emergence of institutional innovations as well as agents' motivations.

All of this is known. An ever-growing body of literature, transversal to several disciplines, too extensive to cite in detail here, but discussed to some extent in the introductory chapter to this volume, has uncovered the many determinants of institutional craftsmanship. The specific contribution hereby proposed is to focus on two elements that facilitate institutional innovation: one at the macro-level and another at the micro-level. The first is in the essence of the central discussion proposed by this book: weak institutions can be an opportunity for institutional change, whereas strong institutions can lead to a lock-in situation, blocking the opportunities for change, even if conflicts and problems originally intended to be solved linger on or new ones emerge. The case studied here is clearly one in which the absence of strong welfare-state institutions in Brazil allowed for the creation of entirely new ones, in a short period of time.

Still, institutions do not spontaneously generate from particles of dust. There must be agents willing to invest time, energy, and resources to transform reality. Individual level motivations gain central stage and institution building can only be

---

1.  I would like to thank Jorge Gordin, Timothy Power, and Rebecca Abers for very helpful comments. I am also grateful to the many people directly involved in the process of constructing the institutional basis for inclusion in Brazil that gracefully consented interviews.

understood from a creationist perspective in which intelligent design and devotion motivates coordinated and intentional acts leading to specific, desired outcomes.[2]

Action is purposeful, even if outcomes are not entirely under the control of motivated actors. Even if we assume that the end result, which can be a specific policy, agency, organisation or set of rules, is a consequence of conflict and negotiation, it emerges from actors taking advantage of and acting upon specific circumstances, with a strong commitment and relentless effort to achieve a desired goal. Hence, we must also focus on the architects of institutional innovation and their motivations, not just on environmental conditions.

Motivations might be of varied types and natures, and difficult to theorise and measure. However, we propose here a concept that might be useful in describing the micro-foundations of institution building: voluntarism. Voluntarism is the unwavering dedication to the achievement of a specific goal based on a deep ingrained belief that, in so doing, a significant contribution to the solution of a problem or conflict will be accomplished. Hence, voluntarism is the unconditional commitment to the eradication of a specific social, economic, political problem with public implications. It is the expression of true-believers' devotion to addressing a significant collective issue and their personal and professional investment in achieving their established goals. As we will argue later, voluntarism is an attribute of policy entrepreneurs, as defined by John Kingdon (2003).[3]

The combination of a pre-existing weak institutional order and the emergence of agents committed to addressing a specific collective problem (voluntarists) increases the probability of the emergence of new institutions. We explore this combination of elements in understanding the construction of the *Bolsa Família* programme (BFP) in Brazil. We further argue that the creation of this specific public policy, a targeted social welfare programme, is fundamental to comprehend the emergence of the Social Development Ministry (Ministério do Desenvolvimento Social – MDS) in Brazil, during Lula da Silva's first mandate. Obviously, the MDS is larger than the BFP, but it was certainly because of the investment made in the latter that the former gained relevance and a reason for being (*raison d'être*). The BFP is the core of MDS' mission. We can, therefore, argue that the MDS only exists because of the centrality of the BFP in the Worker's Party (PT) and Lula da Silva's agenda of solving the problem of inequality and social injustice in Brazil. Hence, we see the emergence of an important institutional innovation, the MDS, probably the most significant legacy of the Workers' Party at the national level, as a consequence of the adoption and development of a specific public policy. Policies can motivate the creation of bureaucratic agencies, and not just the other way around. We explore the creation of both here, as in this case they are irreparably intertwined.

---

2.  Parallelism with religious rhetoric is mere coincidence.

3.  The use of the term voluntarism here is not to be confused with the political philosophy concept of voluntarism, associated with advocates of non-political strategies to achieve a free society summarised more recently by Watner, Smith, and McElroy in *Neither Bullets nor Ballots: Essays on Voluntaryism* (1983).

In addition to the theoretical arguments above, a few other necessary factors are important to explain the case at hand. First, the existence of the previous policy failure (Carpenter 2010) of the Fome Zero Program and a threat to BFP itself because of inept early implementation were paramount for important shifts in the leadership of the program, with definitive impact on its final outcome. Second, the insulation from political pressures of a specific network of highly qualified bureaucrats is also central. The concept of bureaucratic insulation (*insulamento burocrático*), important to understand efficiency in the public services in Brazil, was also important here (Nunes 1997; Abers and Keck 2013). Insulation from political pressures was important for the second generation of BFP policy entrepreneurs to correct the mistakes of the programmes' initial proposers. It was the combination of creativity and innovation, in the first generation of policy entrepreneurs and the professionalisation and organisational competence of the second generation that allowed for the BFP to become the success it currently is. Nonetheless, these different people, highly motivated and well trained, embodied the voluntarism necessary to create a new institution and to put it in motion, with significant implications for the levels of poverty and inequality in Brazil and the health and education of the poor. Finally, the creation of a reputation of effectiveness and professionalisation (Carpenter 2010), after facing hurdles in the early stages of the programme's implementation, was fundamental to consolidate it. This occurred mostly through a network of specialists conducting policy evaluation and through an effective communication strategy with the media. Hence, consolidation requires orchestrated efforts by a network of supporters. In this case, it is also interesting to notice how policy evaluation can be used as a tool to construct a positive reputation and to legitimise a policy program. Committed sympathetic analysts play a significant role in constructing institutional reputations: this may be an intentional strategy.

The next section further provides details of the BFP program and the structure of the MDS. Next, the theory behind the creation of the BFP and the MDS in Brazil is detailed and illustrated with empirical evidence based on interviews and existing studies. It must be kept in mind that theory and empirics overlap in explaining how these institutions came to be in Brazil. The model proposed is obviously generalisable, but its foremost goal is more modest, namely understanding a concrete and important case: the construction of the BFP and MDS in Brazil. The explanation provided emerges both from conceptual constructions based on other cases as well as from prior studies of the specific case at hand. The final section concludes.

But, before moving on, it must be said that the predominant methodological approach is based on the ideas of grounded theory (Charmaz 2006), where pre-existing explanatory categories are merged with new, data driven, insights in the iterative process of creating new theoretical explanations for a relevant, context-bound process. I conducted twelve (12) in-depth interviews between March and October of 2014 in Brasilia, Brazil with actors directly involved in the creation of the BFP and the MDS.[4] The purpose of the interviews was to invite agents to narrate the creation of the BFP and the MDS from their point of view. Interviews were based on a short script, very flexible in nature, which aimed at probing respondents about details in the processes they witnessed first-hand. There was scarce interviewer intervention to avoid response contamination. The identities of the interviewees are completely secondary to the narratives told: hence, they will not be disclosed. It suffices to say that the respondents were directly involved in the creation of the BFP and MDS in different stages of the process. Finally, data collection was completed when interviews no longer provided new relevant information and became redundant. In this case, redundancy was fundamental to validate and confirm prior narratives, increasing the reliability of the data. In addition, prior studies about the same case were fundamental to further detail and confirm the historical facts related to the institution-building processes reported by respondents. In sum, a modest attempt of triangulating information from different sources and informants was fundamental to increase the consistency of the story hereby told. The final narrative that emerges amalgamates the different information aiming at a cohesive history of a current event.

### The *Bolsa Família* and the MDS in Brazil

The *Bolsa Família* programme is the most successful social policy in Brazilian history. Based on November 2, 2015 data from the MDS website, there are 13,971,124 beneficiary families in Brazil and R$23,132,229,726.00 (roughly US$6,005,727,332.60 at the exchange rate for the same date above) was spent in 2015. In 2014, 14,003,441 families benefitted from the programme and R$27,187,295,233.00 (US$7,058,003,249.80 at the exchange rate for the corresponding date) was spent. This makes the BFP one of the largest Conditional Cash Transfer (CCTs) programmes in the world and unparalleled in Brazilian history (Cecchini and Madariaga 2011; Soares, Ribas, and Osório 2010). Its sheer magnitude also puts the BFP as one of the most studied cases, from various different angles, among all CCTs (Freitas 2007; Hunter and Power 2007; Marques and Mendes 2007, 2009; Moura 2007; Nicolau and Peixoto 2007; Soares and Terron 2008; Zucco 2008, 2013; Zucco and Power 2013; Licio *et al.* 2009; Bohn 2011, 2013; Peixoto and Rennó 2012; Sugiyama and Hunter 2013; Hunter and Sugiyama 2014; Layton and Smith 2015). Hence, explaining its origins and its relevance to the construction of welfare policies in Brazil provides a great opportunity to understand how institutions are built and contributes to highlight how a very impressive experiment of policy and institutional innovation came to be. Furthermore, we argue that the machinery involved in its maintenance and in providing information for its constant evaluation and monitoring explain the

---

4.   Participation was voluntary and anonymity guaranteed. Hence, interviews and direct extracts from interviewees' statements will not be used in the analysis presented. The interviews were significant to understand the overall characteristics of the process, the actors involved, and their commitment to the cause rather than to provide a specific test for a hypothesis.

relevance of the MDS in Brazil and how it became a powerhouse for social policy in the Brazilian government. In fact, we argue here that the greatest institutional innovation of the Workers' Party at the Federal level in Brazil is precisely the creation of the BFP and its institutional architecture embodied by the MDS.

The Ministry of Social Development (MDS), however, is more than the BFP. Created in 2004, it is today organised around four main programmes: conditional cash transfers to citizens, social aid/assistance, food and nutrition security, and policy evaluation and information management on social issues. The MDS is the backbone of Brazil's welfare state programmes. Each of the four areas are coordinated by a specific Sub-Secretary in the Ministries organisational chart, in addition to the Minister's cabinet and Executive Secretary (numbers one (1) and two (2) in the hierarchy). The Secretaria Nacional de Assistência Social (SNAS) (*Social Assistance National Secretary*) is responsible for the social assistance programmes of the Federal government and the National Social Assistance Fund. The Secretaria Nacional de Renda e Cidadania (SENARC) (*Citizen Income National Secretary*) is responsible for the management of the *Bolsa Família* programme. The Secretaria Nacional de Segurança Alimentar e Nutricional (SESAN) (*Food and Nutritional Security National Secretary*) focuses on food and nutrition safety. The Secretaria de Avaliação e Gestão da Informação (SAGI) (*Information Management and Evaluation National Secretary*) is responsible for the monitoring and evaluation of social policies in Brazil. It also produces reports and studies, makes data available to the public, and trains agents that collaborate with the Ministry's diverse programmes. More recently, the Secretaria Extraordinária para Superação da Extrema Pobreza (SESEP) (*Extreme Poverty Alleviation Extraordinary Secretary*) was created to conduct Dilma Rousseff's Brasil Sem Miséria Program, which articulates various policy programs aiming at combating extreme poverty.

It is clear, therefore, that the MDS is a combination of various facets of social and economic inclusion programmes, born from agendas espoused by diverse social movements and groups. The MDS incarnates a set of core principles of Lula da Silva's first term in office and was the result of the former president's personal commitment to the eradication of extreme poverty, starvation, and the reduction of social and economic inequality in Brazil. Its construction was neither immediate nor planned in advance. It was the result of conflict, perseverance, commitment, learning, and hard work by several different people during distinct moments and facing different challenges. However, it was the result of motivated action, with clear learning processes from its prior pitfalls, involving many individuals, and with clear leaders in different moments. As Abers and Keck point out, institution building is messy, with design and implementation phases being intertwined (2013: 5–6). It was a coordinated effort to construct an institutional architecture of welfare policies and social inclusion in Brazil. The details of this construction will emerge over the course of the narrative, with an emphasis on the moments and agents involved in the process.

The opportunity structure for the creation of the MDS came from the ascendance to power of the PT and from a lack of prior institutional constraints that could limit the scope for creativity. Its actual configuration, however, was moulded by the voluntarism of the many individuals involved in the process, mostly activists with distinct backgrounds. It is to the narration of the creation process of the *Bolsa Família* programme and the MDS that we now turn our attention to.

## Micro and Macro Foundations of Institution Building

Some elements are central to understanding the emergence of the BFP and the MDS in Brazil. The two main factors include a) the structural weakness of the then existing social welfare institutions in the country and b) the voluntarism of a group of agents within the PT government between 2002 and 2006. Secondary plots include policy failures and follows reputation-building strategies that assist in reorganising the programme and consolidating it as the leading initiative of the MDS.

## Weak Institutions as an Opportunity

To understand how the MDS and BFP came to be, it is important to understand what preceded both. The central argument here is that the story of social assistance and welfare policies in Brazil, prior to the Worker's Party's spell at the Federal Government, is one of institutional instability and failure in addressing issues of poverty and inequality substantively. It was not until 2001, the last year of Fernando Henrique Cardoso's second term in office that systematic policies started to emerge in order to directly attack poverty and inequality in the country. But, at that moment, initial attempts were fragmented across several agencies and there were many questions about the effectiveness of the policies adopted. The scenario of decentralisation on the implementation of such policies created a juxtaposition of jurisdictions and increased the odds of conflict. Prior to that, scarce attempts of social and economic inclusion marked Brazilian history, but none as institutionally solid and well organised as the MDS experience. We explore below three distinct moments in the history of welfare policies in Brazil so as to show how the recent moment is extremely different from what existed before and how it was designed free of institutional constraints that existed prior to their emergence. This new moment is marked by institutional innovation and by policy diffusion, as the new experience was influenced by similar programmes implemented outside of Brazil as well as scaled-up from subnational pilot programmes; but with improvements. Hence, strong prior institutions that condition the adoption of innovation did not limit the current moment. It allowed for policy advocates, based on unconditional dedication (voluntarism) to a cause, to advance an entirely new approach to the problem and to embed it in an institutional web that will be hard to unravel in the future.

Our parcelling of history, however, is based on an important threshold event in Brazil, the 1988 Constitution. Promulgated immediately after a twenty plus years interregnum of military governments based on extraordinary powers of the executive branch, the 1988 Constitution created the opportunity for more effective social policies in Brazil. As any constitution, it did not design the actual policy programmes, but it oriented the Brazilian state towards combating poverty and inequality, by decentralising power, empowering civil society and control institutions and opening the opportunities for change. Albeit some criticism of its excessive details, it is unquestionable that the 1988 Constitution was born from a desire of social inclusion and it is understandable that it become known as the 'Constituição Cidadã' (Citizenship Constitution or Constitution of the Citizen). But first, a warning: it is not the goal here to investigate in detail all of the different moments. The intention is only to argue that Brazilian history is marked by the inexistence of systematic, well organised, deep ingrained policy programmes regarding welfare policies. This does not mean the complete lack of attempts in the past, but we highlight their frugal nature.

## Brazil Prior to the 1988 Constitution: Social Assistance as Charity to the Poor

Wendy Hunter (2014) provides a very instructive overview of social policies in Brazil from the Getúlio Vargas' period to the present day. Her main point is that there was a transition from corporatist inclusion in the past to a more universalistic model that was constructed gradually over the course of the second half of the twentieth century in Brazil and quickly deepened after 2001.

The Vargas period is marked by contribution-based social policies, enacted for those who were in the formal sector and affiliated with labour unions. Hence, Vargas extended institutional social benefits to the portion of the population who had a 'carteira de trabalho', a labour identification document, indicating the citizen was working, or had worked in the past, and was, only then, entitled to social programmes. As Hunter points out, 'the formal-informal cleavage mapped out roughly onto an urban-rural divide' (2014: 20). Hence, most of the Brazilian populations, especially the neediest ones, were still kept out of the social security schemes. Therefore, Vargas' social protection framework is classically seen as a form of co-optation of workers' organised sectors, trading benefits for support, in the traditional form of corporatism associated with many similar regimes in that period across Latin America.

It is also during this era that the federal government starts to provide subsidies for basic goods, often transferred to and distributed at subnational levels. In addition, as Hunter argues: 'states and municipalities also operated their own programmes, many of which became grist for the machinations of patronage-oriented politicians' (2014: 22). This tradition operated in a way in which citizens and politicians perceived social assistance as favours granted to the poor citizens in society: regarded as a charity and not as a securely held right, an entitlement (Hunter 2014: 22). Hence, we notice here an expansion, in the final years of the Vargas' Estado Novo period, of social assistance beyond the formal sector, but never conducted in universalistic terms and without any form of social control or accountability. This was prevailed as an idea of social assistance associated with favours to the poor by philanthropists, first in the private sector and then in the public one. The creation of the Conselho Nacional de Serviço Social in 1938 was a step in this direction and it was used to filter demands for the allocation of resources to states and municipalities.

Even more exemplary of this movement is the creation of the Legião Brasileira de Assistência (LBA) in 1942, by First Lady Darcy Vargas. LBA began during World War II as an institution that provided assistance to the families of Brazilian soldiers fighting in Europe. With the end of the war, it gradually increased its scope by focusing on poor families in general. LBA was always coordinated by the First Ladies and provided no clear, universal and transparent mechanism for the distribution of public resources to the poor. So much so that, in 1991, under the direction of Rosane Collor, it was involved in several major scandals. It was finally extinguished on 1 January 1995, as one of Cardoso's first actions in government. The LBA is a paradigmatic case of this entire period, in which welfare policies are confused with 'assistencialismo', clientelism, and patronage. It was a selective form of inclusion, which did not alter the structural roots of poverty and inequality in Brazil.

It is during the subsequent period, with the 1946 Constitution and the restoration of democracy in Brazil that the 'assistencialista' model deepens. Nothing changes from the prior period and the State now serves mostly the purpose of certifying private institutions that through philanthropy and charity assist the poor in a fragmented, decentralised fashion. The perspective of rights and entitlement is weakened and women, wives of politicians in the federal, state and municipal levels usually conduct social assistance institutions.

The Military Dictatorship, beginning with the Coup D'Etat of 1964, changes this predicament. Even though political rights were extensively restricted during the years of the Military Dictatorship, much was accomplished in increasing the inclusion of the poor through social assistance. Several institutions still existing today were then created. A very important one that became operational during the Military Regime was the Funrural, the rural social security programme installed in 1972 (Delgado and Cardoso Jr. 1999). This program expanded the benefits created during the Vargas' period to workers in rural areas, dramatically increasing the coverage of the welfare state in Brazil. Even though all elderly people in rural areas qualified for the programme, and in spite of not having contributed in the past, they still had to provide evidence of previous work in rural areas (Hunter 2014: 26). Hence, it was still linked to the traditional format of social security in Brazil, based on contributions or prior work history. Even though the traditional charity oriented perspective of social assistance that prevailed in the democratic period of 1946 to 1964 was better organised and formalised during the Military period, the general thrust of the system was kept unchanged.

## Brazil from 1988 to 2001: Social Assistance as Rights

The 1988 Constitution marks a clear rupture with the past, even though it takes a few more years for its requisites to be fully implemented and executed. It is in the 1988 Constitution that social assistance becomes recognised as a right that must be assured by public institutions. This implies a clear rupture with the past, transforming into a right what was before a favour. Social assistance, based on a citizenship principle and provided to whoever needs it, is placed alongside with the concept of social insurance, grounded in a contributory principle (Hunter 2014: 25). Therefore, not just the ones who contributed financially in the past, or who had worked in the past and could prove it, became seen as holders of rights to social assistance. For instance, health coverage is universalised through the Sistema Unico de Saúde (SUS). But, the Constitution itself did not provide for the implementation or creation of specific programmes. It assured the right and forced the State to act, but actual changes and the implementation of programmes foreseen in the Constitution was the creation of the successive governments that came to power.

During this period, it is important to highlight a few specific social policies that altered the nature of the welfare state in Brazil. First, the Benefício de Prestação Continuada (BPC), fully implemented in 1996, comes to mind as it is based not on contribution, but on need. All families who could attest their level of poverty and their age (over sixty-five), qualified to become a beneficiary. The programme still benefits a specific group, based on age and income, but it does not require any prior contribution. This is a very important distinction from how social welfare was conducted in Brazil. As Hunter argues, the BPC, because it did not require any prior contribution, provides an important safety net for those who did not qualify for other existing programmes (2014: 26).

The Lei Orgânica de Assistência Social (LOAS) of December 1993, details the Constitutional provisions about social assistance. It creates the Conselho Nacional de Assistência Social and contributes to the extinction of the CNSS, created in the Vargas Period. The LOAS institutionalises social assistance in Brazil by creating participatory mechanisms and establishes mechanisms for the social control over social policy. It stipulates the need for local councils, plans and specific funds for social assistance in Brazil and establishes the framework for the National Conferences on Social Assistance, which become major national events to elaborate social policy in the country.

In 1995, as part of the LOAS effort, the Cardoso government created the Comunidade Solidária programme, which was headed by First Lady Ruth Cardoso, a renowned anthropologist, which proposed a new scheme for conducting social assistance. The general view of this period is that sectorial actions by ministries are the principal form of state action in combating poverty and inequality, but that in the long term it is through civil society activism that solutions to social injustice would be constructed (Monteiro 2011: 36). The Comunidade Solidária tried to activate and engage civil society, but ultimately it failed having achieved very little in the way of concretely reducing inequality and poverty in the country. Its long-term, diffuse perspective simply did not produce tangible results.

In addition to the Comunidade Solidária, which ended in 2002, with the demise from power of the Cardoso government, it is important to highlight that the LOAS also amplified the institutionalisation of social assistance in Brazil by creating the Fundo Nacional de Assistência Social (FNAS). FNAS transfers money to state and municipalities to support public and private sector initiatives related to poverty alleviation. Finally, also as a consequence of the LOAS, in 2003 the Sistema Único de Assistência Social (SUAS) is created, enhancing the partnership between federal, state and municipal levels in the coordination of social assistance in the country, creating the Centros de Referência de Assistencia Social (CRAS) and Centros de Referência Especializada de Assistência Social (CREAS), which provide at the local level, many different services for Brazilian citizens in situations of vulnerability.

Hence, directly from the 1988 Constitution, a full framework of social assistance emerged in the country, pushed mostly after 1994, creating a true architecture of inclusion in the country. However, most of the initiatives implemented were somewhat limited in their coverage and depth. The adoption of conditional cash transfer programmes in 2001 at the national level provided a completely new perspective on social assistance. In particular, it is not until 2004, when the MDS is fully operationalised that an entirely new, integrated, universalistic, and transparent institution of welfare policies is created in Brazil.

## Brazil after 2001: The Emergence of the Welfare State in Brazil

The final year of the Cardoso government saw an outpouring of social programmes, providing an extremely relevant safety net for individuals facing situations of poverty, inequality, and exclusion. The end of Cardoso's second term represented a shift in focus from policies and reforms aiming at economic stability and the creation of fiscal responsibility in Brazil, which constituted the essence of his first seven years in office, to the fight for social justice through cash transfer programmes. The failed experience of the Comunidade Solidária or the pressing need for economic stabilisation may have, somewhat, delayed the implementation of such programmes earlier in the PSDB government. Still, at the federal level, it is the Cardoso government who first adopts policy programmes based on cash transfers to individuals as a way of promoting social and economic inclusion: an achievement that should not be undervalued. But it should not be overstated as well. This last year can be understood as a transition period to the full-blown development of social policies in the PT government.

The key programme then was the Bolsa Escola, a programme based on educational achievement as a condition for money transfers to families. This programme was the scaling-up of similar policies adopted in early experiments at the state and municipal levels in Brazil. Hence, the Cardoso government nationalised programmes that were being developed at the subnational level. Policy diffusion played a role in the scaling-up of social policies in Brazil. But, in addition to the Bolsa Escola, there were many other programmes coordinated by different ministries: Bolsa Alimentação and Auxílio Gás are probably the most noted.

The numbers, shown below, are impressive, indicating that the Social Democrat's commitment to social policies was not trivial. The social agenda during Cardoso might have taken too long to be implemented and its full impact on society was never really assessed, but the movement we focus on in this paper, the creation of the BFP and the MDS, certainly owes much to the first steps at the national level taken then.

Nevertheless, I concur only slightly with Marcus Melo's (2008) claim that the success of social policy in Brazil is a result of cumulative experiences, of policy emulation, and 'stealing' of good ideas by each of the PT and PSDB coalitions. Instead of simple emulation by the PT, Cardoso's contribution to the construction of a welfare network in Brazil should not be overestimated either.

There are many more differences than similarities between the PT and PSDB approaches to social policies. The degree of continuity was smaller than that of change. Policies only resemble themselves. There are significant differences in institutional design, forms of implementation, and, more importantly, the bureaucratic infrastructure that supports them. There is nothing comparable to the BFP and the MDS in the PSDB period in government at the federal level. Unquestionably, the most significant institutional innovation brought on by the PT at federal level, its main institutional reform during its now sixteen years in power, was the construction of the MDS lead on by the crystallisation of the BFP.

So much so, that today, almost all states in the Union, including those governed by the PSDB such as São Paulo, emulated the MDS by creating Secretarias de Desenvolvimento Social. This is evidence that the idea behind the MDS has caught on, and that it has become an integral part of social policy governance in Brazil.

Still, choices made in the Cardoso period, especially the decentralised implementation of several different programmes in distinct ministries, are key to understanding the more recent developments that ensued in the Lula administration. But, to a certain extent, they are not much more than a preface to the real story that needs to be told.

This is not to say that there weren't many policy heroes in the Cardoso period, all engaged and fully committed to attacking the lifelong problems of inequality and poverty. Certainly, there was plenty of voluntarism then, by significant actors who pushed forward the social policy agenda. In fact, Rosani Cunha, who later played a decisive role in restructuring the BFP in Lula's first term, and will take a lead role in the story we tell here, was an important player in the organising of social policies in the Health Ministry during Jose Serra's tenure as minister in Cardoso's second term. In addition, the late Ruth Cardoso and Vilmar Faria definitely deserve to be seen as important institutional architects of a welfare safety net in Brazil. However, the timing of the process was off and a different perspective predated it: that of the Comunidade Solidária, which had a much more diffuse, ambiguous, and ambitious mission and vision. Unfortunately, the Comunidade Solidária did not amount to much in reducing social and economic inequalities and has been all but forgotten. Therefore, voluntarism must not be equated with success: it is a component of the successful building of institutions, but not the only one. There are plenty of cases in which voluntarism led to misfortunes: malfunctioning institutions and or even once-to-be institutions that never came to existence. Environmental factors and opportunities condition the success of institution building and these were not present at the end of the PSDB tenure in office.

In the final years of the Cardoso government there were six main programmes in existence, as documented by Ana Fonseca in the Relatório da Equipe de Transição da Área Social (2002):

- Agente Jovem, established by Portaria 879 on 3 December 2001, benefitting youngsters with ages between fifteen and seventeen years old in a situation of poverty or social risk, from families with per capita income up to a minimum wage. The responsible ministry was the Ministério da Previdência e Assistência Social (MPAS) and it benefitted 105,446 individuals with the payment of R$65,000 per month. The total expenditure for the programme until October 2002 was R$38,030,628.00, according to data provided by Monteiro (2011). Corrected for inflation at November 2015 prices, to increase comparability with data for the BFP, this amounts to R$89,737,210.54.[5]

- Programa de Erradicação do Trabalho Infantil (PETI), created in 1996 and reformulated by the Portaria 458 of 2001. It benefitted families with per capita income of one minimum wage and infants between seven (7) and fourteen (14) years old who were working in activities considered painful and degrading. It was also implemented by MPAS and beneficiaries received R$25.00 in rural areas and R$40.00 in urban areas. 810,348 families received the benefits totalling R$306,036,226.00 transferred by October 2002 (Monteiro 2011). The corrected, real value is R$722,124,211.20.

- Bolsa Escola instituted in 2001 by Law 10.219/01. The Bolsa Escola programme benefitted children in the ages between seven (7) and fourteen (14) years old enrolled in public schools, from families with a per capita income of R$90.00. Only families with children in school attendance over 85 per cent could receive the benefit of R$15.00 per child up to the limit of R$45.00 per family. 10.7 million families received the benefit in October 2002, totalling R$1,277,720,000.00 spent by then in 2002 alone and R$3,014,912,839.56 at November 2015 value. The Ministry of Education implemented Bolsa Escola.

- Bolsa Alimentação instituted in 2001, by Decreto 3934, benefitting pregnant women, nursing mothers, sons and daughters of HIV positive mothers, and children up to seven (7) years old in families with per capita income up to one minimum wage received a benefit of R$15.00 per beneficiary up to the limit of three. 1,403,010 beneficiaries add up to a total of R$115,000,000.00 (R$271,354,425.50 at 11/2015 values). It was implemented by the Ministry of Health.

---

5. I used the Brazilian Central Bank website to calculate the real values at prices for November of 2015, so as to increase comparability with the current values spend in the BFP. The correction was based on the INPC inflation index. See, https://www3.bcb.gov.br/CALCIDADAO/publico/ exibirFormCorrecaoValores.do?method=exibirFormCorrecaoValores (accessed in November 2015).

- Auxílio Gás, created in 2002 by Law 10.453, was executed by the Ministry of Mines and Energy, benefitting families with per capita income of one minimum wage, with a R$15.00 bimonthly subsidy for the payment of gas bills. The programme benefitted 8,556,785 recipients totalling R$502,139,720.00 (R$1,184,850,741.23 at 11/2015 prices) spent by October 2002.
- Bolsa Renda, created in 2002 by Law 10.458/2002, implemented by the Ministry of Interior, benefitting families resident of municipalities affected by droughts and registered in the Bolsa Escola programme. Beneficiaries received R$30.00 and 842,000 families received in total R$332,428,142.00 (R$784,398,673.85 for 11/2015 prices) in October 2002.

Hence, if we add the expenditures of all the programmes in the PSDB government for the duration of their existence (over one year), correcting for inflation at November 2015 prices, the lump sum spent is R$6,067,378,102. Comparing 2002 and 2015, the overall amount spent increased a whopping R$17,064,851,624.00 (US$4.422.206.127.67 for 11 February 2015 exchange rate) and that is comparing only the eleven months of 2015 with the more than one year of programmes' duration in the Cardoso period. If we add the entire amount spent by the PT governments since 2003, the comparison between both parties' administrations is absolutely ludicrous and unnecessary. The PT owns the social policy agenda in Brazil.

Whereas the PT (Workers' Party) starts its government with the social policy agenda at the heart of its governing platform, in the PSDB (Brazilian Social Democratic Party) it was practically the government's last breath. Hence, the opportunity for the PSDB to fully develop the programme was a stillbirth and it was up to the PT to deepen and reinvent how social policy and a welfare safety network should be implemented in Brazil.

Overall this initial moment was victim to several problems: inefficiency caused by multiple layers of actors; different agencies controlling different programmes with distinct registries and rules. Hence, its role in the story of how a welfare infrastructure was built in Brazil must not be exaggerated.

Hence, the *Bolsa Família* programme (BFP) of the Workers' Party represents the reorganisation and consolidation of the building of an institutional architecture of inclusion in Brazil. It institutionalised social policy and increased its coverage. Unification of all the social programmes was the key difference implemented by the Lula administration. It seems simple to achieve, but was only forged through conflict, negotiation and the extremely hard work of several institutional architects, whose voluntarism we will soon discuss. Furthermore, the significant institutional reform of the Worker's Party tenure in office is exactly the construction of the Social Development Ministry, the most efficient institution in combating poverty and inequality in Brazilian history.

The main innovations brought about by the PT were the centralisation of all of the above programmes in the *Bolsa Família* and the consolidation of a single, very effectively managed registry of the means tested families in Brazil. Strengthening the unified registry (*cadastro único*) for families living under economic vulnerability and unifying the several programmes into a single one, administered by a single institution, the MDS, has been the great innovation on welfare state policies promoted by the PT. Ana Fonseca, who coordinated the transition team on social issues in preparation for Lula's first term in office, is very clear that the main problem regarding social policies that the incoming PT administration should address was the overlapping of programmes in different ministries, and fragmented implementation (Fonseca 2002). The fragmentation of the programmes initiated in the Cardoso period generated inefficiency in monitoring beneficiary responsibilities (*condicionalidades*) and caused trouble in coordinating the distinct programmes.

This assessment was in the roots of the organisation of a study group, at the President's office, to advance the agenda of social policy making in the government. This group was to study ways to unify the registry and it became the seed for the future MDS. In addition to centralising the process, reducing its fragmentation and increasing the efficiency in organising the registry of social policy beneficiaries, the group also advanced the idea of using the Caixa Econômica Federal, a federal bank, to distribute the monies allocated by the social programmes. This bank has a great decentralised presence in Brazil, facilitating access to the resources through a bankcard that all beneficiaries of the programme received. The operational difficulties of getting the money to the citizen were reduced with the support of Caixa Econômica. These are significant advances in relation to what existed before in Brazil.

However, there was a different view within the PT camp, led by José Graziano and based on the Fome Zero programme, an encompassing set of propositions that also oriented the construction of the PT proposals for the 2002 elections. The Fome Zero was much broader than the assessments made by Fonseca and they were translated into the new government by Graziano's transition report on food and nutrition security. This programme proposed a very complex arrangement that would fight hunger in Brazil and assured production of food by stimulating cooperative mechanisms.

In spite of Fonseca's recommendations, this division prevailed during the first year of Lula da Silva's first term in office. Graziano became the minister of Ministério Extraordinário de Segurança Alimentar e Combate à Fome (MESA), which housed the Fome Zero group. In addition, the PT created the Ministério da Assistência e Promoção Social (MAPS), which was headed by Benedita da Silva. In addition, a special advisory body of the Presidency, headed by Miriam Belchior was also launched. Within the special advisory body, many debates took place about how to better structure social programmes in the PT government. The first year of the government, therefore, was marked by a continued discussion about the most effective way of administering social policies. Hence, divergence between different groups within the government, and even the Workers' Party, were addressed when the government had already started. This is to show how the actual governing agenda is constructed while in office, not prior or during the campaign, and through harsh and time-consuming involvement of many different stakeholders.

It is curious to note that Ana Fonseca's transition report, which already identified and presented solutions to the many problems of a fragmented coordination of social policies, was not very influential in the government at that moment. The debate about concentrating the programmes and strengthening the unified register lingered on, without conclusion, in the first six months of Lula's first term. In fact, only the second semester of 2003 saw some advances, mostly articulated by the special advisory group to the President and the downfall of the centrality of the Fome Zero programme in the country.

Fome Zero was Graziano's pet programme in MESA. It was an all-encompassing programme that aimed at putting issues of hunger and food security in the core of the government's agenda. It was an ambitious project, which included several actions, in different fronts, to improve Brazilian's living conditions and relied on a multipronged strategy that included principles of solidary economy, nutritional safety, and cash distribution. It was also a long-term project that raised doubts about its short-term effectiveness.

The government soon realised the risks of embarking on a programme with such characteristics. Early in the first year, Graziano's agenda suffered severe attacks from many fronts under the claims that obesity, not hunger, was a central problem of the country. Little by little, Graziano's agenda was delegitimised and lost momentum within the government. Benedita da Silva, who could have occupied a leadership position, then, was never able to formulate a consistent policy alternative. She also suffered from repeated criticism and failed to convince the government and the public of her ability to lead a key policy agenda of the government. Neither was ever able to bounce back and slowly but surely lost ground to a distinct, more pragmatic and less ambitious project, which aimed at achieving quick wins. Neither saw the end of Lula's first year in government as ministers. The same fate followed Cristovam Buarque in the Ministry of Education.

It was to attenuate the fiasco of the first semester, in which the government's social policy agenda appeared ineffective, and to find solutions that could be implemented swiftly, that a technical group was constituted in June of 2003 to integrate the income transfer programmes. Certainly the inability of ministers with jurisdiction over the government's social agenda (MESA, Health, Education, MAPS) to finally decide about its general framework and to establish an implementation strategy was a key motivation of the government in creating the group. It included actors that would later become pivotal in the PT administration and hold important positions in the government's structure.[6] It was a group of

---

6. The group was formed by Miriam Belchior and Tereza Campello, from the Assessoria Especial da Presidência da República (AESP/PR); Darci Bertholdo and Tereza Cotta from the Casa Civil; Ricardo Henriques, Rosane Mendonça, Cláudio Roquete and Agostinho Guerreiro from the Ministério da Assistência e Promoção Social (MAPS); Flávio Botelho and Maya Takagi from the Ministério Extraordinário de Segurança Alimentar e Combate à Fome (MESA); Gastão Wagner, Elisabetta Recine, Michele Oliveira and Marcelo Duarte from the Ministério da Saúde; Rubem Fonseca, Marcelo Aguiar and Maurício Carvalho from the Ministério da Educação and from the

technocrats, composed by middle range bureaucrats and scholars in the area of social policies and poverty. The result of the intense work that took place between June and August of 2003 was the unification of all social programmes under one banner, *Bolsa Família*. The Executive Secretary, headed by Ana Fonseca and directly linked to the Presidency, would coordinate the *Bolsa Família* programme. The official launch of the programme occurred on 20 October 2003. This special office in the Presidency was the seed of what was to become the MDS.

In January 2004 the MDS was finally created. The MESA and MPAS were extinguished and Ministers Graziano and Benedita da Silva fired. After a first year of many failures in both ministries in assuring their prominence in conducting social policies in Brazil, a new alternative prevailed. The first minister of the MDS was Patrus Ananias, a politician from Minas Gerais, who stayed in office until 2010 and had a central role in consolidating the ministries' leadership in the social programmes. Ana Fonseca was to be the Executive Secretary of the newly created ministry. The *Bolsa Família* programme, which was the central justification for the creation of the MDS was to be coordinated by the Secretaria Nacional de Renda de Cidadania – Senarc, and the ministry would also encompass issues of food and nutrition safety and social assistance. Hence, the MESA and MPAS were engulfed by the MDS, spurred from the centralisation of social policies around the BFP.

## Institutional Vacuum and the Opportunity for Creation

Based on the brief historical narrative provided above, it becomes clear that after 2001 there was an exponential increase in activity regarding the establishment of welfare policies in Brazil. What is more, there was a continuous and somewhat articulated construction of an institutional framework to accelerate social and economic inclusion. This was constructed based on institutional opportunity provided by the weakness of prior infrastructure to promote social inclusion. Up until the 1988 Constitution, welfare policy in Brazil was limited to the formal sectors, to those who could provide evidence of having worked on the past and contribution based. Excluded populations that did not qualify for the existing social security schemes were attended by irregular, particularistic programmes that lacked transparency, and were based on philanthropy and charity. The best example is the leading role that First Ladies had on such programmes and how poorly structured they were. Social assistance was confused with favour exchange, providing chances for opportunistic behaviour in the form of clientelism and patronage.

The 1988 Constitution opened the opportunities to a new understanding of social assistance: it turned favours into rights. Citizens became entitled to social assistance programmes, which opened the doors to the formal structuring of welfare policies in Brazil. But, the Constitution was not self-applying. It required

---

Ministério do Planejamento, Nelson Machado (SE), Elvio Gaspar and George Soares. IPEA was represented by Anna Maria Peliano and Nathalie Beghin and the Caixa Econômica Federal by Ana Fonseca and Isabel Costa.

further regulations that detailed the mechanism of access to federal funds. It created the opportunity for activists and stakeholders to engage the State in formulating innovations on how to treat inequality and poverty. Hence, the weakness of prior institutions, mostly their limitations in providing the inclusion of significant social groups and the window of opportunity created by the Constitution, spurred a new wave of policy innovation in Brazil that led to a new institutional architecture much more efficient in promoting inclusion. It stimulated activists to invest their time, energy, heart and souls in the creation of a new order of things. Weak institutions made it possible for those who were engaged in promoting innovations in the sector to construct a new alternative, based mostly on their view of how to solve these problems and on their voluntarism to fully dedicate to this task. Hence, we must now turn our attention to the architects of this new moment. We have, in part, started doing so already.

## Voluntarism and the Creation of the BFP and MDS

To talk about voluntarism is to focus on the actors: their motivations and abilities to implement change and to create innovation. We are not interested here in theorising the strategies such actors adopt, which is done, for instance, by Rebecca Abers and Margaret Keck (2013). The emphasis is on how people's commitment to a specific agenda and their personal determination allow for the construction of new institutions, which is related to two factors: innovation and novelty on one hand and organisation and consolidation on another. These are distinct moments in the construction of institutions. The first stage requires innovative thinking, creativity, and the ability to convince others, which entails negotiation. These factors are related to the practical authority Abers and Keck (2013) theorise about. The second phase of institution building requires organisational capacity to make the institution work.

Not necessarily, the same people will accomplish both missions. However, all must be entirely committed to their purposes and dedicate themselves entirely to achieve them. That is the essence of voluntarism – dedication to achieving a goal, *no matter what*. Voluntarism epitomises a type of commitment and dedication that demands effort, time, energy, and personal concessions. It is a personal attribute of few, independent of partisan and ideological motivations. Voluntarism is the personification of protagonism and relentless hard work dedicated to a specific goal. Hence, the focus is on the agents and what they do to achieve such goals. Voluntarism, it is true, is made visible mostly through success cases of a concrete outcome; the creation of institutional innovation. However, it must not be equated with success. In this case, it is the conjunction between contextual factors and individual motivation that must be considered as sufficient and necessary conditions for institution building or remodelling.

Voluntarism is a necessary condition for institution building: all successful institutional architects hold this trait. But, it is not a sufficient condition. Many actors with such frame of mind and disposition for work have failed in achieving their goals of recreating, remodelling or starting an institution anew. Hence, motivation must be married with contextual opportunity: the right moment, the right wave, must present itself so that committed riders can surf it all the way, as John Kingdon would say (2003).

In fact, I argue that voluntarism is the main quality held by policy entrepreneurs. It's their defining trait. Policy entrepreneurs are 'advocates who are willing to invest their resources – time, energy, reputation, money – to promote a position in return for anticipated future gain in the form of material, purposive, or solidary benefits' (Kingdon 2003: 179). Hence, in addition to the already known list of abilities and attributes an institutional architect must have: 1) a sense of the opportunities and of positioning oneself well to take advantage of them; 2) having a clearly defined agenda; 3) holding political connections; 4) negotiating skills; 5) persistence, policy entrepreneurs must be ready to commit fully and work hard to achieve their goals. Voluntarism is such dedication. It is a conviction about the correct thing to do.

Injustice will certainly be committed in identifying the actors involved in the process of constructing the MDS and the *Bolsa Família*. Many will be left out. But, the goal here is to point out the dedication and commitment of the leading stakeholders in the process, whose direction was fundamental to the process. In sum, we narrate below the role played by policy and institutional heroes.

## Voluntarism, Policy Failure, Institutional Innovation and Consolidation

It is clear from the historical overview that several actors had an active role in the creation of the MDS and that the definitions and resolutions of conflicts within the government in favour of the centralisation of social policies on the *Bolsa Família* programme created a trajectory that favoured some positions over others. In other words, some actors and their views prevailed.

Clearly, an important decision took place midway in 2003 to empower the Executive Secretariat of the *Bolsa Família* programme, Ana Fonseca. As we might recall, this process unfolded under the leadership of Miriam Belchior, then a special analyst of the Presidency in the working group responsible for proposing the unification of social programmes. On the other hand, two actors lost their leadership positions: Benedita da Silva and José Francisco Graziano. Graziano's group in particular had proposed an alternative view of how social programmes should be conducted in the PT government, much more oriented to food and nutrition safety. His view on how programmes should be managed did not prevail. Instead, a much more pragmatic approach, led by Belchior and Fonseca, was adopted.

The 2003 debates led by Belchior, were extremely intensive, surrounded by great expectations, and frequent, especially between April and September. The group met numerous times, for hours on end, to try to make compatible the different views within the government about how to conduct what was an essential aspect of its agenda, social inclusion. It is absolutely important to highlight here something that came up repeatedly in interviews: the dedication and effort put into the project by this group was astounding. They were fully committed to the opportunity offered to them by President Lula himself of finding a solution to what was to become the government's most important banner in its administration: combating inequality and alleviating poverty. The actors involved in the process, with a special emphasis on Belchior and Fonseca, took advantage of the opportunity and worked unceasingly and uninterruptedly, in a very concentrated way, to construct the new policy programme and the institutional framework to support it. It was not just their technical ability or negotiation capabilities, albeit important, that assured the formatting of the new institution, but their incessant drive to work: it was their voluntarism that pushed them through.

Remember, Lula da Silva was elected with the promise of reducing inequalities in Brazil and combating poverty. His initial agenda focused on alleviating hunger and the Fome Zero programme embodied this promise quite well. However, it proved to be overly ambitious and its impacts would have been noticeable only in the long run. More immediate relief was in order. Hence, Lula concentrated the debates about social inclusion and social policies close to him, in his personal office. He brought the issue to the centre of government. First, he empowered Belchior to lead the study group that would propose solutions. Second, once the diagnostic and proposal was defined and accepted by the involved players, Lula again placed the Executive Secretariat of the *Bolsa Família* programme, where Ana Fonseca played a key role, also in the Presidency.

Hence, Lula placed the social policy agenda in the centre of power of his first mandate. The centrality of the topic in Lula's agenda and his commitment to the issue were key for providing the incentives for the quick wins the programme achieved. Hence, the decision to centralise the many social programmes and the choice of one model to do so, represented by Ana Fonseca's proposals in her transition report, came swiftly after intense debate and disputes within the government. After noticing that the main programmes headed by the Ministries of Health, Education, MESA and MPAS were not working, Lula did not hesitate in substituting the personnel involved to orient the subsequent moment of the government. This would happen again in the phase of organising the MDS and the *Bolsa Família*. In its consolidation phase, Fonseca and Belchior are substituted by other actors. Therefore, the link between contextual factors, opportunities, and individual drive, voluntarism, is fundamental to explain pivoting moments in the history of institutional design.

Also as result of the process, Lula selected Patrus Ananias, an experienced politician, to conduct the process of constructing the MDS. Patrus, differently from Francisco Graziano and Benedita da Silva (less so in her case), was an extremely experienced politician known for his ability to minimise conflict, construct common ground, and negotiate support (Moura 2012). All of these traits were important to assure the initial cohabitation of groups who had intensively competed over which social policy model would be implemented: food and nutrition activists, social assistance activists, and income transfer activists. All of these three sectors, which espoused different views and defended relatively competitive alternatives for social policies, coexisted in the new ministry, which had the *Bolsa Família* as its main social programme. In other words, Patrus would have to coordinate the relationship between two losing groups and the winning view. Over the long haul, his longevity in office and the success of the *Bolsa Família* programme are testament to his political abilities. However, this was not constructed without difficulties.

A first one had to do with the nomination of Ana Fonseca as Junior Minister (*secretário executivo*) of the new ministry, indicated by Lula da Silva himself and not by Patrus Ananias, the minister. Fonseca was to be responsible for the *Bolsa Família* programme in the ministry and she appointed André Teixeira as the Secretary of the Secretaria de Renda do Cidadão – Senarc. Patrus Ananias was to be responsible for all the other areas of the ministry. This situation clearly poses a potential problem for the Minister, as he has limited influence over a specific area of the Ministry he heads. In principal, such situations create necessary tensions between actors and weaken the chief-officer's command. Hence, a natural competition emerged and blame shifting between the two actors became a problem.

Ana Fonseca was an intellectual who defended minimum income policies to all citizens in need. She played a significant role in the transition to the PT administration and actively engaged in the study group responsible for the creation of the *Bolsa Família* programme. Hence, she was very active in 2002 and 2003. However, as Moura (2012: 210–212) points out, her preferred institutional approach was to keep the *Bolsa Família* in the presidency, failing to see all the institutional complexity involved in implementing a nation-wide programme from within the President's office. Nonetheless, *Bolsa Família*'s first months of existence, within the Presidency, were successful. However, gradually, it became clear that the bureaucratic infrastructure within the Presidency was insufficient. A bigger and structurally stronger organisation was necessary to run a programme of the BFP's magnitude.

The MDS is born from such necessity. Fonseca's position of maintaining it in the Presidency did not prevail and Lula invited a skilled politician, to lead the newly created MDS. Fonseca was respected as an intellectual who understood the political and ideological confrontations surrounding the BFP. Her ability to implement and manage the programme, however, was a different story. In fact, the administrative and organisational challenges for managing the biggest social policy programme in Brazil were immense. The programme required the administration of the unified register (*cadastro único*) and the monitoring of the conditionalities. It also involved a close relationship with thousands of Brazilian municipalities to update, refine, and improve the register, and enter the data on beneficiaries' responsibilities. It also involved the complexities of dealing with the Caixa Econômica Federal, a nationwide bank responsible for issuing the cards for programme beneficiaries and making sure the money was allocated transparently.

It didn't take long for the tasks of organising the *Bolsa Família* programme, of coordinating the relationship between the different groups within the MDS, and dealing with a new boss, Minister Patrus instead of President Lula, to prove to be too much for Ana Fonseca.

The main difficulties in managing the *Bolsa Família* programme began to be reflected in its operations. What had been challenges turned into crises when many problems began to be targeted by the media and by auditing courts.

Problems with the focalisation of the programme (people who shouldn't receive were receiving the benefit) and inability to assure the conditionalities were being respected became central criticism to how the programme was being conducted. The problem was clearly one of managing the BFP. Fonseca's dedication to the creation of a unified registry and single social programme, backed by Belchior's leadership in moving the agenda in this direction, was not enough to assure the consolidation of the programme. A new set of skills was necessary. The issue was to find equality motivated personnel but better equipped to the tasks of organising and consolidating the programme. Voluntarism was the constant: the set of technical abilities needed adjustment.

The highpoint of this process occurred on 17 October 2004 in the *Fantastico* Show of *Rede Globo*, a leading TV broadcast presented on Sunday nights on prime time in the largest television station of the country. The episode showcased the failures of the BFP in its first year of implementation, clearly characterising it as a fraud due to the uncontrolled transfer of funds to individuals. The BFP was portrayed as a policy failure, in the sense attributed to this type of event by Carpenter (2010). A policy failure is a crisis made visible by the media or by stakeholders that changes the way a specific programme is conducted, moving it towards new formats and alternatives that address the existing limitations (Carpenter 2010). Hence, a critical event, the showcase of the BFP's organisational and administrative drawbacks in a widely seen television programme altered the priorities in MDS so as to assure the continuation of the programme.

The crisis clearly empowered Patrus Ananias as Ana Fonseca was blamed for the managerial problems of the BFP. Remember, the original division of labour landed the BFP program on her lap. As criticism from within and from outside the government amounted, Lula da Silva gave Patrus autonomy to reorganise the functioning of the BFP. Immediately, Ana Fonseca was history. He brought in a new group of public managers with abilities to solve the administrative problems of the BFP, but who were aware of the daunting task ahead of them. This group played a decisive role in increasing the likelihood of the programme's consolidation.

Rosani Cunha, a mid-level bureaucrat member of the bureaucratic career *Gestora de Políticas Públicas*, a group of highly skilled public servants with a specific career and entry processes in the government (*concursos*), replaced Fonseca. Rosani Cunhas was a civil servant with significant experience in the Ministry of Health in the last years of the Cardoso administration, where she was responsible for that ministry's social registry. She then worked in the Casa Civil in Lula's first term and was regarded as a very competent professional. However, as was mentioned in a few interviews and confirmed by Moura's work on the topic (2012), Patrus was not considering her for the position. In fact, the choice of who was to replace Ana Fonseca was a difficult one. People involved in the process before had either failed in the first two years of Lula's term or were employed elsewhere. Aware of this and that the opportunity represented a unique chance to contribute to a very important task in the government and for the country, Cunha offered herself for the position in an interview with Minister Patrus during an airplane flight, on which she made sure she was included (Moura 2012: 124). This was important even to convince Patrus of her commitment, her dedication to the cause. She was determined to contribute to the construction of the *Bolsa Família* programme, as many interviewees attested. In addition, as Moura points out, this was also an opportunity to advance her career. Hence, her determination paid off. Cunha finally obtained the nomination a few weeks after the conversation with the Minister and of having convinced him of her knowledge about the topic and the viability of the solutions she proposed.

Once in office as Secretary of Senarc, Cunha nominated Lucia Modesto, also a public manager with great experience, as her coordinator of the single registry (*cadastro único*). Their first task was to take control of the Cadastro Único and remove it from the Caixa Econômica Federal to effectively manage it from within Senarc. Obtaining control over the management of the unified registry was fundamental to strengthen the MDS and its monitoring capabilities. A second task was to construct solid bases of oversight and control, to be able to better monitor the conditionalities of the programme. Hence, in a quite effective way, Cunha and Modesto were able to mitigate the main criticism of the BFP that had plagued Fonseca's period, expanding the programme to its current levels and professionalising its management. As many interviews show, this was done through immense and unquestioned dedication to the cause and in very adverse conditions, with limited personnel and infrastructure. It was due to the voluntarism, expressed through the hard work of these two leaders that the BFP blossomed.

Furthermore, as Moura points out, the duo was also able to establish a good relationship with the media, making sure that the prior problems were being addressed and with leading intellectuals in the area of social policies backing the advances made (2012: 129). The following few years, 2005 to 2008, were extremely important for the consolidation of the BFP through a network of policy analysts who consistently provided evidence of the programme's positive social and economic impact on society (de Brauw 2014; Soares *et al.* 2010; Campello and Neri 2013; Castro and Modesto 2010). The Instituto de Pesquisa Economica Aplicada (IPEA) (*The Institute for Applied Economic Research*) and the World Bank played a key role conducting and publishing several studies explaining the nuts and bolts of the programme and praising its effectiveness (Lindert *et al.* 2007). SAGI in the MDS did its part by collecting and disseminating information about the programme. Hence, it is interesting to see how an apparently neutral, scientific procedure based on the analysis of a social programme's impact becomes an instrument in its favour and abundantly used as part of its consolidation arsenal. The MDS and the BFP in particular, constructed a solid reputation of managerial excellence and efficiency, which Carpenter argues is fundamental in institutional innovation and construction (Carpenter 2010). Policy evaluation backed this reputation, playing a decisive role in increasing the programme's legitimacy. Therefore, the MDS' network with IPEA and academia was fundamental to consolidate the programme's leading role in Brazilian politics. Policy evaluation, therefore, has political implications.[7]

---

7. For an interesting debate on this matter, see the papers available at http://www.icpublicpolicy.org/ How-Policy-Evaluation-Praxis (accessed in November 2015). Also, see Guenther *et al.* (2010).

This is not to say that results were manipulated and data fabricated, but that the identification of positive outcomes reinforces processes of institution building and this is the role of policy evaluation as well.

The BFP and the MDS built a reputation of professionalism, competence, apartisanship (as Cunha and Modesto were not PT members), and an emphasis on technical decision making. Hence, as Carpenter argues, reputation became an asset for the BFP and strengthened its centrality within the MDS (2010: 66). It developed a technical reputation that increasingly legitimised its institutional design and that was constructed through public policy evaluation.

In addition to the relevance of policy evaluation, media communication strategies also contributed to increasing popular support for the BFP. A closer relationship with the media was established, enabling a restoration of the program's credibility (Carpenter 2010). Lindert and Vincensini (2010) had shown that media coverage about the BFP was predominantly negative after the Lula government, much more so than it had been during the early years of similar programmes under Cardoso's administration. Notwithstanding the possible media bias, once the problems were attenuated, a positive presence in the media was fundamental for the programme to increase its popular appeal and transparency. The many reforms adopted by Cunha and Modesto in the leadership of the program increased its transparency and addressed most of the criticism previously received. Their technical competence became a trademark of the programme, and it acquired a brand name based on success in promoting social inclusion. But this was done through strengthening the contacts with the media and promoting the positive angles of the programme, especially by making its favourable policy evaluations acknowledged by a bigger audience.

In sum, Cunha and Modesto's professional experience, coupled with their undisputed dedication and hard work to the cause of social inclusion, were key to understanding the consolidation of the *Bolsa Família* programme. Their managerial skills and pragmatism in solving the programme's main limitations proved imperative for its resonant success. However, technical ability is only effective if coupled with the passion and dedication typical of voluntarism. On the other hand, the ideas and commitment early in the process by Belchior and Fonseca were much more important during the founding moments of the BFP. Hence, these four women played important roles in constructing one of the most successful social policies in Brazil and Latin America. Their dedication to the cause and sense of opportunity arousing from different circumstantial features of the early days of the PT government proved fundamental to the definition of the main traits of the programme.

In addition, the leadership of Lula da Silva and of Patrus Ananias proved fundamental to place the BFP and the MDS in the centre of power in the Workers' Party's first two terms in office, from 2003 to 2010. Their role is also fundamental for understanding the creation of the MDS. If the first four women made the BFP programme a reality, it was the capacity of negotiation and commitment of Patrus that strengthened the MDS and helped consolidate it, even among serious crises.

All these actors share a common belief that the BFP was an important innovation in combating social exclusion and poverty relief in Brazil. They all were truly dedicated to the cause and made significant personal and professional investments and concessions in turning it into reality. It was through the voluntarism of this group that the opportunity created by weak welfare institutions in Brazil made way to one of the most important innovations in combating social inclusion in the country. The creation of the MDS based on the centrality of the BFP program in Brazil has made a significant difference in how social exclusion is dealt with and mitigated.

## Final Considerations

This chapter discussed an important case of institution building to deal with problems of social and economic exclusion. The construction of welfare policies in Brazil gained momentum with the 1988 Constitution and, more clearly, in 2001, with the adoption at the national level of several policies oriented to the mitigation of inequality and poverty under the heading of Conditional Cash Transfer programmes. These policies went beyond contribution-based policies to means tested, targeted schemes, based on the observation of conditionalities. This movement significantly increased the number of beneficiaries and created a professional and efficient safety net for individuals living in conditions of social vulnerability. We argued here that the advances were dramatic in relation to the traditional forms of social assistance in Brazil, prior to these recent developments. In addition, the changes implemented by the Workers' Party differentiate its contribution even in relation to its immediate PSDB predecessor, who must be recognised as the first to adopt nationwide CCTs in Brazil. Indisputably, the creation of the MDS, a bureaucratic agency that centralises and coordinates all aspects of social policies in the country, is the most significant institutional reform promoted by the Workers' Party at the federal level in Brazil.

Two factors are important in understanding the emergence of institutional innovation. First, there must be environmental conditions prone to stimulating institutional creativity and engineering. There are many factors to take into account, but we focused on an original perspective that puts the inexistence or weakness of prior institutional arrangements in the forefront, as an opportunity for ways to improve on it or start completely from scratch. In such contexts, agents have more leeway to improve on what exists.

Another key factor, therefore, is individual level motivation and action of such agents in creating institutions. The focus must fall upon those involved in the process, their strategies (Abers and Keck 2013), their characteristics (Mahoney and Thelen 2010), and their abilities (Kingdon 2003). We contribute to this list with a focus on policy entrepreneurs' motivations, especially the idea of voluntarism. Motivations can only be inferred from actions, but still they reflect a specific state of mind that is disposed to achieving some goal. Not all actors have such predispositions. We called it here voluntarism: a deep ingrained commitment to achieving a specific goal with collective and public repercussions. It is not the sheer motivation to advance one's career, even though this is also part of the explanation, but the conviction that a specific policy or programme can make a difference in addressing a key collective problem or address some social/political/ethnic/distributive conflict. This deep ingrained belief is not particular to a specific partisan or ideological position, but prevalent among those who are indignant, resentful, infuriated about some unjust, unacceptable, offending social/political/economic situation. Voluntarism is an unwavering dedication to solving a problem of the above magnitude and the agents with such motivation will spare no efforts, personal or professional, to achieve its goals. Hence, voluntarism is a categorical attribute of individuals: either you have it or you don't. It is not a continuum. This does not mean that individuals who have these traits will always be successful, but those who don't have it, most definitely won't be.

We employed this analytical framework to explain the emergence of the *Bolsa Família* programme in Brazil and, consequently, of the Ministry of Social Development. The creation of new institutions, oriented towards social policies, even with similar designations, has been spurred in many Latin American countries in the late 1990's and throughout the 2000's (Midaglia, Castillo and Fuentes 2010). Understanding their emergence in comparative perspective, but with an in-depth perspective combining micro and macro level factors is a profitable path of analysis.

In Brazil, what first started during the last year of the Cardoso administration as a scaling up of social policies originally developed at the local level, later became, after much conflict and dissent, an entirely new programme never seen before in Brazilian history. This new programme, the *Bolsa Família*, was the fruit of institutional learning and of voluntarists who fully committed to achieving it, in an environment ripe for institutional innovation. This policy programme, in its turn, became the catalyst for the construction of an institutional framework that coordinates and centralises the formulation, evaluation and implementation of social policies in Brazil: the Ministry of Social Development. This institutional apparatus has become an integral part of social policy governance in all of Brazil, emulated by states and municipalities and finding similar institutions in other countries (Midaglia *et al.* 2010). Interestingly, it was the need to improve upon and better structure a policy programme that spurred the creation of institutional innovation and an entirely new bureaucratic agency. Usually, this process is seen as the other way around: agencies create policies and are not a consequence of them. The MDS and the BFP are different in this way.

Categories such as voluntarism, opportunities of a weak institutional environment, policy failure and reputation building are essential to understand the creation of innovation and later the organisation and structuring of it into a consolidated organisation. It was the work of people with a special drive and the institutional vacuum they encountered that allowed for the creation and consolidation of the architecture of inclusion in Brazil represented by the BFP and MDS.

## References

Abers, R. and Keck, M. (2013) *Practical Authority: Agency and institutional change in Brazilian water politics*, New York: Oxford University Press.

Bohn, S. (2013) 'The electoral behavior of the poor in Brazil: a research agenda', *Latin American Research Review*, 48(2): 25–31.

—— (2011) 'Social policy and vote in Brazil: Bolsa Família and the shifts in Lula's electoral Base', *Latin American Research Review*, 46(1): 54–79.

Campello, T. and Neri, M. (2013) *Programa Bolsa Família: Uma Década de Inclusão e Cidadania*, Brasília: Ipea.

Carpenter, D. (2010) *Reputation and Power: Organizational image and pharmaceutical regulation at the FDA*, Princeton: Princeton University Press.

Castro, J. and Modesto, L. (2010) *Bolsa Família 2003–2010: Avanços e Desafios*, Brasília: Ipea.

Cecchini, S. and Madariaga, A. (2011) *Conditional Cash Transfer Programmes: The recent experience in Latin America and the Caribbean*, Santiago, Chile: United Nations.

Charmaz, K. (2006) *Constructing Grounded Theory: A practical guide through qualitative analysis*, London: Sage.

de Brauw, A. (2014) 'The Impact of Bolsa Família on Schooling: Girls' Advantage Increases and Older Children Gain', IFPRI Discussion Paper 1319, Washington, DC: International Food Policy Research Institute.

Delgado, G. and Cardoso Jr., J. (1999) 'O Idoso E A Previdência Rural no Brasil: A Experiência Recente da Universalização', *Texto para Discussão* No. 688, Rio de Janeiro: Ipea.

Fenwick, T. (2009) 'Avoiding governors: the success of Bolsa Família', *Latin American Research Review* 44(1): 102–131.

Fonseca, A. (2002) Relatório Transição Governamental – Análise das Políticas Sociais, unpublished document.

Freitas, R. (2007) 'O governo Lula e a proteção social no Brasil: desafios e perspectivas', *Revista Katálysis* 10(1): 65–74.

Guenther, J., Williams, E. and Arnott, A. (2010) 'The politics of evaluation: evidence-based policy or policy-based evidence?', Paper presented to the NARU Public Seminar Series, Darwin, 30 November 2010.

Hunter, W. (2014) 'Making citizens: Brazilian social policy from Getúlio to Lula', *Journal of Politics in Latin America* 6(3): 15–37.

Hunter, W. and Power, T. (2007) 'Rewarding Lula: executive power, social policy, and the Brazilian elections of 2006', *Latin American Politics and Society* 49(1): 1–30.

Hunter, W. and Sugiyama, N. (2014) 'Transforming subjects into citizens: insights from Brazil's Bolsa Família', *Perspectives on Politics* 12(4): 829–845.

Kingdon, J. (2003) *Agendas, Alternatives, and Public Policies*, New York: Longman.

Layton, M. and Smith, A. (2015) 'Incorporating marginal citizens and voters: the conditional electoral effects of targeted social assistance in Latin America', *Comparative Political Studies* 48(7): 854–881.

Licio, E., Rennó, L. and Castro, H. (2009) 'Bolsa Família e voto na eleição presidencial de 2006: Em busca do elo perdido', *Opinião Pública* 15(1): 31–54.

Lindert, K. and Vincensini, V. (2010) *Social Policy, Perceptions and the Press: An analysis of the media's treatment of conditional cash transfers in Brazil*, Discussion Paper No. 1008, Washington D.C.: World Bank.

Lindert, K., Linder, A., Hobbs, J. and de la Brière, B. (2007) *The Nuts and Bolts of Brazil's Bolsa Família Program: Implementing conditional cash transfers in a decentralized context*, SP Discussion Paper No. 0709. Washington D.C.: World Bank World Bank.

Mahony, J. and Thelen, K. (2010) 'A Theory of Gradual Institutional Change', in J. Mahony and K. Thelen (eds), *Explaining Institutional Change: Ambiguity, agency and power*, Cambridge, Cambridge University Press, pp. 1–38.

Marques, R. M. and Mendes, Á. (2007) 'Servindo a dois senhores: as políticas sociais no governo Lula', *Revista Katálysis* 10(1): 15–23.

Marques, R. M., Leite, M. G., Mendes, Á. and Ferreira, M. R. J. (2009) 'Discutindo o papel do Programa Bolsa Família na decisão das eleições presidenciais brasileiras de 2006', *Revista de Economia Política* 29(1): 114–132.

Melo, M. (2008) 'Unexpected Successes, Unanticipated Failures: Social policy from Cardoso to Lula', in P. Kingstone and T. Power (eds) *Democratic Brazil Revisited*, Pittsburgh: University of Pittsburgh Press, pp. 161–84.

Midaglia, C., Castillo, M. and Fuentes, G. (2010) 'El Significado Político de los Ministerios Sociales en Argentina, Chile y Uruguay', *Revista Chilena de Administración Pública* 15–16: 123–154.

Monteiro, I. (2011) *Integração de Políticas Sociais: Um Estudo de Caso Sobre o Bolsa Família*, Getúlio Vargas Foundation, Dissertação de Mestrado Profissional apresentada ao Centro de Pesquisa e Documentação de História Contemporânea do Brasil – CPDOC.

Moura, C. (2012) *O Programa Bolsa Família no Campo das Políticas Públicas*, University of Brasilia, Dissertação apresentada ao Departamento de Sociologia.

Moura, P. (2007) 'Bolsa Família: Projeto social ou marketing político?', *Revista Katálysis*, 10(1): 115–122.

Nicolau, J. and Peixoto, V. (2007) 'As bases municipais da votação de Lula em 2006', published online in Forum Internet as Position Paper 2. Available through: http://www.forumnacional.org.br/forum/pforum62a.asp (accessed December 2015).

Nunes, E. (1997) *Gramática Política do Brasil: Clientelismo e Insulamento*, Rio de Janeiro: Zahar Editores.

Oliveira, A. *et al.* (2007) 'Primeiros Resultados da Análise da Linha de Base da Pesquisa de Avaliação de Impacto do Programa Bolsa Família', in *Avaliação de políticas e programas do MDS: resultados*, Brasília, DF: MDS; SAGI.

Peixoto, V. and Rennó, L. (2011) 'Mobilidade social ascendente e voto: as eleições presidenciais de 2010 no Brasil', *Opinião Pública* 17(2): 304–332.

Soares, F., Ribas, R. and Osório, R. (2010) 'Evaluating the impact of Brazil's Bolsa Família: cash transfer programs in comparative perspective', *Latin American Research Review* 45(2): 173–190.

Soares, G. and Terron, S. (2008) 'Dois Lulas: A geografia eleitoral da reeleição (explorando conceitos, métodos e técnicas de análise geoespacial)', *Opinião Pública* 14(2): 269–301.

Sugiyama, N. and Hunter, W. (2013) 'Whither clientelism? Good governance and Brazil's Bolsa Família Program', *Comparative Politics* 46(1): 43–62.

Watner, C., Smith, G. H. and McElroy, W. (1983) *Neither Bullets Nor Ballots: Essays on voluntaryism*, Penn Valley, Calif.: Pine Tree Press/The Voluntaryists.

Zucco, C. (2008) 'The President's 'new' constituency: Lula and the pragmatic vote in Brazil's 2006 elections', *Journal of Latin American Studies* 40(1): 29–49.

—— (2013) 'When payouts pay off: conditional cash transfers and voting behavior in Brazil 2002–10', *American Journal of Political Science* 57(4): 810–822.

Zucco, C. and Power, T. (2013) 'Bolsa Família and the shift in Lula's electoral base, 2002–2006: a reply to Bohn', *Latin American Research Review* 48(2): 3–24.

*Chapter Eleven*

# Social Inclusion Comes First, not Ideology: Legislators' Budgetary Preferences in Brazil[*]

*Carlos Pereira and Frederico Bertholini*

## Introduction

This chapter disputes that conflict is a troubling constant in the current Brazilian institutional setting. The institutional setting that emerged from the 1988 Brazilian Constitution generated an extremely open political system and a very inclusive society. After twenty-one years of authoritarian regime, the first civilian government was under great pressure to respond to demands for social and political inclusion. A belief in social inclusion emerged as a reaction to the overwhelming social-economic inequality in Brazil, marked by one of the largest concentrations of wealth in the world. This belief produced a feedback loop with the growing political awareness among political and social groups on the need for policies capable of promoting radical changes towards social inclusion. Democracy with policies of social inclusion then became the only game in town.

We emphasise how the beliefs of social inclusion not only framed post-1988 institutions in Brazil but, foremost, still guide the true preferences of politicians within Congress. That is, regardless of politicians' different ideological orientations or budgetary and public policy preferences, rather than clashing against each other they ended up cooperating in supporting a very inclusive social and political agenda. On the other hand, when we observe the actual roll call voting behaviour within Congress, the main cleavage is not ideology, measured both in partisan ideological distribution and in individual terms, but rather in the division between government and opposition. Therefore, beliefs determine what and how politicians truly think but not necessarily their actual behaviour.

Political economy explanations of budgetary policy build on the idea that fiscal decisions and budget outcomes are the result of political processes that involve political actors and policymakers with a variety of interests and preferences. Rather than being a consequence of a single benevolent welfare-maximising policymaker, budget decisions in democratic regimes are instead the result of a

---

[*] A preliminary version of this paper was presented at the IDRC Workshop 'The Architecture of Diversity: Institutional Design and Conflict Management in Latin America', Universidad Diego Portales, 28–29 July 2014. We are grateful for the comments and suggestions provided by the participants of the workshop, especially Lucio Renno and Jorge Gordin.

complex and tricky process that involves the interactions of a variety of players with their own beliefs and their own prescriptions of how public resources should be allocated and prioritised. When government officials, legislators, economic actors and civil society get involved in budget negotiations and decisions they do have their own views about the needs of a society, and may have their own expectations about the political benefits they can obtain from certain policies, once implemented.

Most of the literature, usually based on cross-country analysis, has emphasised political and institutional aspects on budgetary and fiscal outcomes keeping in mind that the budget process is part of a broader policy-making process (Stein and Tommasi 2008). Surprisingly, however, this literature has failed to take into account the political actors' preferences. Even when scholars acknowledge the importance of political players on budget outcomes, they do not bring their policy preferences to the centre stage of the analysis. At maximum, scholars analyse how political players interact in practice at each stage of the budget process and the particular institutional context in which the budgetary game is played out (Hallerberg, Scartascini and Stein 2009).

One of the reasons that may justify this gap is the difficulty to obtain systematic data and information on political players' preferences and beliefs. When politicians' preferences are taken into account it mostly takes place, for instance, in roll call votes as revealed preferences of the legislators on the floor of a Congress. Roll call votes may not be free from strategic bias, given that legislators' revealed preferences sometimes might be away from politicians' true preferences on public policies.

Legislators, for instance, may vote in favour of allocating a certain amount of resources in a particular policy area, or a specific local region, as a consequence of party discipline, as a result of a position-taking strategy fulfilling their local constituencies' preferences or because they belong to a governing coalition, rather than their own recipes or views of how the world should work. Thus, roll call may work only as a complementary dimension to the whole picture made up by the revealed and the true budgetary preferences of politicians and not the definitive one. This could be particularly true in institutional settings in which the executive and party leaders are strong players with many institutional devices to build governing coalitions and impose party discipline and/or when the electoral survival of legislators fundamentally depends on their personal records, especially delivering benefits to local constituencies.

Both institutional conditions seem to be present in the Brazilian political environment. On the one hand, party leaders concentrate a lot of institutional prerogatives, such as, to appoint and substitute at any time members of committees; to add in or withdraw proposals in the legislative agenda; to decide if a bill would have an urgency procedure; to indicate the position of the party regarding a bill at the floor; and fundamentally, to negotiate with the Executive individual demands of the members of his/her party. In other words, party leaders are the bridges linking individual legislators and Executive's demands (Pereira and Mueller 2003). Thus, it is not rational legislators that act individually inside Congress. On the other hand, some features such as electoral rules, a multiparty system, and federalism act to decentralise the political system providing incentives for politicians to behave individually, responding to constituents' demands. The combination of these institutional rules is the key for understanding how it is possible for weak political parties in the electoral arena to coexist with strong political parties inside Congress.

So, to what extent is the actual record of roll call voting behaviour of legislators in the Brazilian Congress consistent with a legislator's true policy preferences? Assuming that legislators sincerely exposed their true policy preferences in the seventh round of a survey conducted by Power and Zucco (2012), we could compare the degree of consistency between what they actually think and how they in fact behaved on the Congress floor.

We also reveal variations with regard to membership in the governing coalition or the opposition. The literature (Zucco 2009; Santos 2003; Figueiredo and Limongi 1999) has argued that, despite of the huge partisan fragmentation, the main political cleavage in the Brazilian politics has been between the governing coalition and the opposition.

The seventh round of the survey with Brazilian legislators specifically raised a question related to legislators' preferences of government budgetary spending in five different policy areas: public health, basic public education, high public education, infrastructure, and programmes of social assistance. The way the question was raised allowed the respondents to rank their preferences in five options: 1) increasing spending even if this requires taxes to go up; 2) increasing spending but only if no tax rise is necessary; 3) maintaining current level of spending; 4) cutting spending but keeping taxation levels the same; and 5) cutting spending to allow a reduction of taxes. The idea of this question on the survey was to capture distinct beliefs along those five different policy areas.

Based on the traditional left-right ideological continuum, the obvious expectation is the following: legislators leaning towards an economic-liberal policy preference, usually identified as right-wing, would be more inclined to vote in favour of spending fewer resources in policies advocating social protection, on the one hand, and greater tax cuts, on the other. Economic-liberal legislators would even vote for policies of social inclusion as long as they do not engender further tax increases. On the other side of the ideological spectrum, economic-conservative legislators deemed 'left-wing' would fundamentally support the intensification of policies advancing social inclusion without further concerns of increasing the tax-burden. Legislators positioned somewhere in the middle of those two extreme policy-ideological preferences would demonstrate sympathy for upholding policies of social inclusion that maintain the current level of spending.

## Competing (or Complementary) Beliefs within the Brazilian Society

Individuals have mental models or beliefs that work as cognitive maps about the functioning of a society or how the world works (North 2005; Greif 2006). Beliefs, which are not reducible to preferences or values, have the ability to affect both the formal and informal institutions of a particular society. In turn, beliefs may impact policy outcomes that are implemented by those institutions, as well as the behaviour of political actors.

Alston *et al.* (2016) claim that two dominant beliefs have emerged and have strongly impacted the set of institutional choices and policies in Brazil during the last three decades or so. The first dominant belief has been social inclusion, which arose as a reaction to the inequalities and injustices that took place during the military dictatorship. The developmentalist dominant belief during the dictatorship that economic growth should precede social inclusion started losing political support. Since the re-democratisation, there has been a drastic change in the social contract, with incremental increases in public spending and the tax burden to account for, making the provision of public services increasingly inclusive. Everything in Brazil became a matter of inclusion and politically justifiable in its name.

The second dominant belief is the need for macroeconomic equilibrium and growth, which came from the aversion to hyperinflation, resulting from the traumatic experience of consecutive years of uncontrolled prices. The period 1985–1993 witnessed several episodes of hyperinflation. The inflation increased from about 40 per cent per year to nearly 430 per cent per year in same period. The Sarney government was not able to say 'no' or deny the inclusive demands from organised groups in the society. Therefore, conceding or accepting the vast majority of these demands was the way the Sarney and opposition governors found to survive politically. This should be interpreted as the origin of hyperinflation in Brazil.

The former President, Fernando Henrique Cardoso, seized the window of opportunity, first as the finance minister and later as president, to finally put the economy in order with the Real Plan in 1994. Later, by the end of his second term, Brazilian society had adopted an anti-inflation belief, maintaining the belief in inclusion. That is, social inclusion would still be given priority as long as it was fiscally sound.

These two beliefs, seemingly contradictory, are in fact complementary. On the one hand, citizens care about inflation control, economic growth, unemployment and public accounts. On the other hand, they also want to continue sharing the powerful apparatus of social protection that has been implemented in Brazil, gaining scale and covering new areas of services and sectors in recent governments. From the combination of these two beliefs, Brazil has managed to achieve a more equal balance and greater redistribution under the dominant belief of fiscally sound social inclusion.

Together, these two separate strands form a belief of fiscally sound social inclusion that constrain and influence the choice of institutions by the dominant, thereby crucially affecting the selection of policies and the incentives influencing outcomes. The new beliefs and institutions (e.g., constitutional constraints that emerged in the 1980s and 1990s) effectively constrained political and economic elites in their interaction, thereby enabling competitive processes in the political and economic arenas. The established political institutions locked-in and reinforced the direction of change by affecting the incentives facing individuals, organisations, and politicians. The functioning of these economic and political institutions largely explains policy continuity in key areas such as macroeconomic management.

Figure 11.1 reflects well the transformation of Brazilians' beliefs both in relation to social inclusion as well as with regard to macroeconomic stability. It contains answers about who should be given the responsibility for providing the needs of individuals: the government or the individuals themselves. It also shows the variation with regard to the satisfaction of individuals about the economic system during the same period. As we can observe, Brazilian voters dramatically changed their set of beliefs during twenty-three years of democracy.

The role of the individual for their success used to be seen as predominant during the 90s. However, as democracy has evolved and has become consolidated on a very stable macroeconomic environment, the majority of Brazilian voters have consistently transferred this responsibility to the government as the source of policies capable of providing of social inclusion and protection. It is very interesting to note that the linear trend of presidential popularity is strongly correlated to the growing belief among Brazilians that the government should take greater responsibility for their wellbeing. In other words, as it is suggested in Figure 11.1, there is an association between a growing belief in favour of social inclusion and a positive assessment of governments.

Since 2013, the popularity of the President, Dilma Rousseff, has fallen despite the fact that the belief in favour of social inclusion, measured by the increasing responsibility of the government over the wellbeing of the individuals, continued to grow and her political party has been identified as the main supporter of social inclusion. The fall of Rousseff's popularity can be interpreted as a consequence of the macroeconomic mismanagement of her administration, which led to the return of high inflation and to a gloomy economic growth. Figure 11.1 clearly shows that the lack of satisfaction with the economic system, which was too high in the beginning of the 90s, substantially declined in the following years of the Real Plan.

*Figure 11.1: Belief changes in Brazilian society*

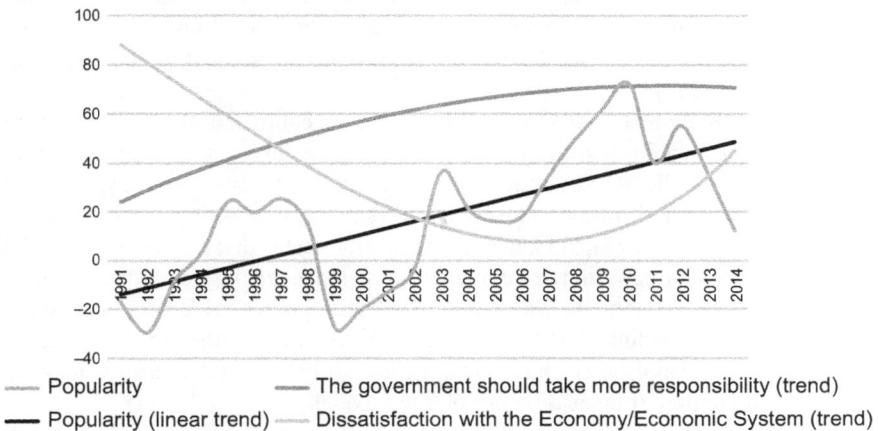

— Popularity　　　　　　—— The government should take more responsibility (trend)
—— Popularity (linear trend)　⋯ Dissatisfaction with the Economy/Economic System (trend)

*Source:* World Values Survey, Latinobarómetro and DataFolha

This trend, however, was reverted during the Rousseff's administration when the belief that something was going wrong with the economic system started rising again. This is in fact another piece of evidence, that Brazilians are intolerant to high inflation and averse to governments that do not deliver macroeconomic stability.

Although seemingly antagonistic, these two dominant beliefs are complementary in Brazil. Failure to deliver macroeconomic stability leads to the unpopularity of the president, even if the government continues to offer social inclusion. The reverse is also true. It is no longer permissible that a government capable of providing inflation control and economic growth does so at the cost of setbacks in the provision of public policies that maintain or expand the path of social inclusion.

### There are no Unbearable Costs when Social Inclusion and Fiscal Responsibility are at Stake

The most striking, but not necessarily surprising, result that came out from the seventh round of the Brazilian Legislative Survey (Power and Zucco 2012) is that a great majority of respondent legislators consistently supported the increase of spending no matter what public policy was in question. In health and basic education this dominant belief is self-evident for about 80 per cent of respondents. In fact, very few legislators were in favour of cutting spending in those policies, and in basic education, none. This result unequivocally suggests that Brazilian representatives have a very strong bias toward a belief of social inclusion and social protection. As discussed, social inclusion has been the dominant belief in the country since the re-democratisation. Everything and every policy became an issue to be included for whoever (social or political group) demands some degree of state protection. However, most of the legislators favour more public spending only if no tax rise would be necessary to carry those policies out, which also suggests legislators' concerns about the already extremely high tax burden in Brazil (see Figure 11.2). This result is evidence that the combination of social protection and inclusion with fiscal responsibility has been the dominant belief in the Brazilian society.

In the more salient issues of health and basic education about 30 per cent of respondents would even agree with tax increase in order to offer a greater supply of those policies. Nevertheless, the pattern of responses concerning basic education, health and infrastructure are very similar, supporting the increase of spending without tax expansion, which also demonstrates that fiscal responsibility matters for legislators. With regard to social assistance and higher education there are some differences though, with one third of respondents preferring to keep the current level of spending. About 8 per cent of respondents only supported cuts in spending in social assistance and about 5 per cent only in higher education in order to allow a reduction of taxes on those public policies.

When we take into account, in our descriptive analysis of the legislators' ideological preferences, the role played by the dominant belief of social inclusion becomes even more revealing. In other words, ideological differences (left-right

*Figure 11.2: Distribution of legislators' beliefs about public policies*

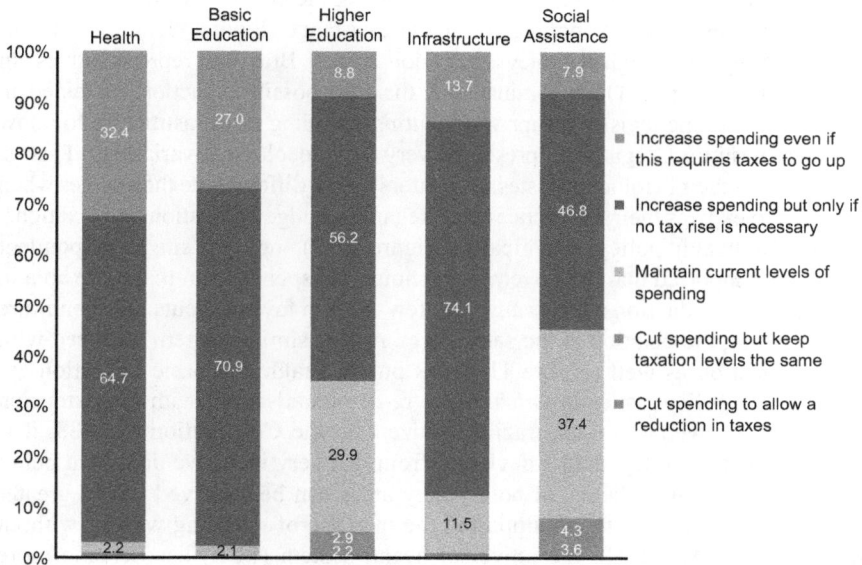

continuum) do not seem to matter to explain policy preferences among legislators. This result is somehow surprising given our original expectation stated earlier that economically conservative left-wing legislators would be more inclined to support the implementation of public policies capable of providing social inclusion even if these policies would lead to higher taxation, while economically liberal right-wing legislators would care for less social protection and inclusion and would be in favour of fewer taxes. We borrowed a measure of ideology from Power and Zucco (2012), who rescaled ideological estimates for each legislator, anchored by the entire 1990–2013 BLS time series (N=1145 responses) and estimated using the one-shot Bayesian procedure. These are rescaled and normalised estimates centred on 0 and with a SD of 1 (positive values are right of centre).

In general terms, as we can see in Figures 11.3 to 11.7, there is no direct relation between politicians' ideology (Y axis) and their policy preferences with regard to the level of spending and taxes on each of those public policies (X axis). The closer the median preference (dark line) from the zero point of ideological dimension, the smaller the ideological bias towards a specific policy area. The boxplots provide additional information concerning the size of the boxes and their respective whiskers.[1] The bigger the box and/or their whiskers, the more ideologically disperse are the survey respondents within a particular answer. Therefore, the greater the ideological dispersion in a single answer could be

---

1.   The ends of the whiskers represent here the lowest datum still within 1.5 IQR of the lower quartile, and the highest datum still within 1.5 IQR of the upper quartile.

considered as a sign of the salience of the issue area, given that there would be many ideologically divergent politicians choosing the same answer.

With the exception of policies of social assistance (Figure 11.7), there is not much left-right ideological policy dispersion among Brazilian representatives. In infrastructure (Figure 11.6), for instance, the four possible reactions obtained in the survey (no one legislator supported cutting spending in infrastructure to allow a reduction in tax), legislators presented very little ideological variations. That is, regardless of their ideological tastes, legislators do not differentiate themselves when it comes to express their preferences with regard to budget allocation and taxation.

As for health policy specifically (Figure 11.3), no one single respondent legislator supported that the government should cut spending on that issue area in order to allow reduction in taxes and very few of them favoured cuts in expenditure even keeping the taxation at the same level. A very similar pattern occurred with basic education as well (Figure 11.4). As public health and basic education are very salient policy issues in Brazil since re-democratisation, with the extension of universal coverage to all Brazilian citizens in the Constitution of 1988, it is unlikely to observe legislators deviating from this very inclusive dominant belief in the country. The salience of both policy areas can be observed with a greater dispersion of legislators that supported the increase of spending with or without tax increases. Above all, the universal health system (SUS) has become more expensive and complex overtime. Despite the considerable absolute increase in resources, the share of resources devoted to health has stagnated in the last ten years engendering, thus, great tension for increasing spending in the sector.

*Figure 11.3: Legislators' beliefs and ideology about health policy*

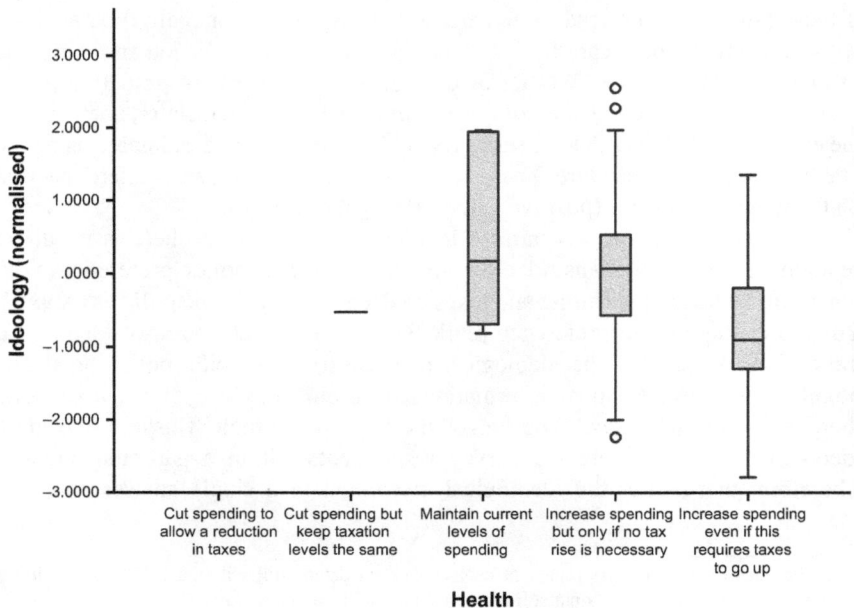

This partially reflected the fact that the spectacular expansion of conditional cash transfers has had a crowding out effect on health. Costing slightly more than 1 per cent of GDP, the *Bolsa Família* programme has absorbed part of the additional resources to universal social security. *Bolsa Família* has become the flagship programme of the Workers Party's (PT) governments (2003–present), and has certainly dwarfed the political saliency of other issue areas on the government agenda (Melo 2007, 2008). The episode involving the extinction of CPMF (the provisional 'contribution' on financial transactions) points to the fact that the tax burden has reached a plateau. At 35 per cent of GDP it is slightly lower than the OECD average. More importantly, the political feasibility of raising additional taxes in Brazil has declined rapidly. Considering that coverage has also reached a plateau of 100 million people, it means that quality improvements in SUS and in public education would have to be achieved by efficiency gains rather than by funnelling more resources to the system. That might be the reason why a minority of Brazilian legislators considers supporting greater expenditure on health and basic education with the correspondent increase in tax.

However, since 2012 and particularly following a wave of street protests in 2013, there has been strong social mobilisation for more resources to health and basic education. Although SUS continues to receive strong support as a political priority there is widespread dissatisfaction with the quality of the services it provides. This is also found in other areas including educational services. According to the CEPAL, the subjective evaluation about the quality of public expenditure in Brazil is very low: 15 per cent of respondents replied positively

*Figure 11.4: Legislators' beliefs and ideology about basic education*

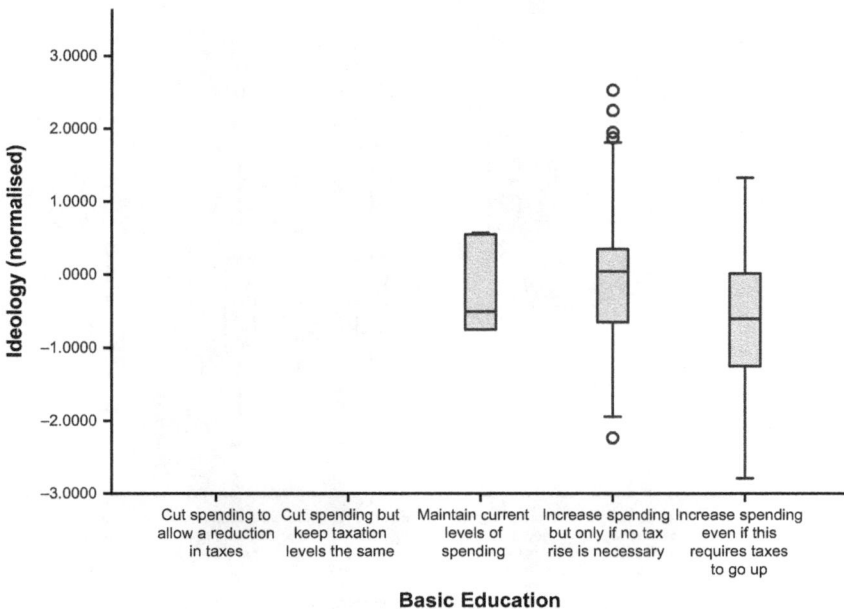

when asked in 2012 about their trust in the quality of spending, much below the Latin American average.

The issue of higher education seems to present a little more ideological variation as well as greater diversity of answers among Brazilian legislators who replied in the survey (Figure 11.5). The clear distinction has to do with the group of legislators that supported cutting spending but keeping taxation at the same level, who might be considered economically liberal representatives, and the group of legislators that are in favour of increasing spending even if this requires tax to go up, the left-wing economically conservative representatives. That is, these two groups of legislators are ideologically different and this distinction seems to matter in this particular policy area.

As mentioned earlier, legislators displayed very little ideological variation with regard to infrastructure policy (Figure 11.6). The great majority of them were in favour of increasing spending in that area of public policy. They also presented a great level of ideological dispersion in a single answer, both in terms of supporting the correspondent tax increase as well as without consequences in higher taxation. This suggests that infrastructure also became one of the most salient policy issues in the country. In fact, the lack of investments in infrastructure converted into a mantra: everyone says that infrastructure is the most important bottleneck holding back Brazilian development.

The drop in infrastructure investment as a percentage of GDP in the last decade has tracked the growing fiscal effort by the government, suggesting that infrastructure investment is in fact crowded out by the state's need to finance other

*Figure 11.5: Legislators' beliefs and ideology about higher education*

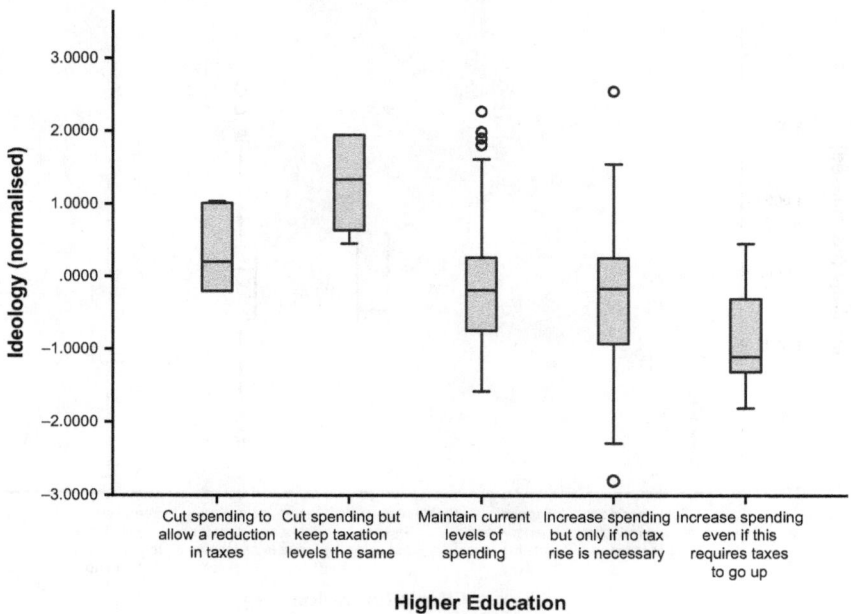

**Higher Education**

*Figure 11.6: Legislators' beliefs and ideology about infrastructure*

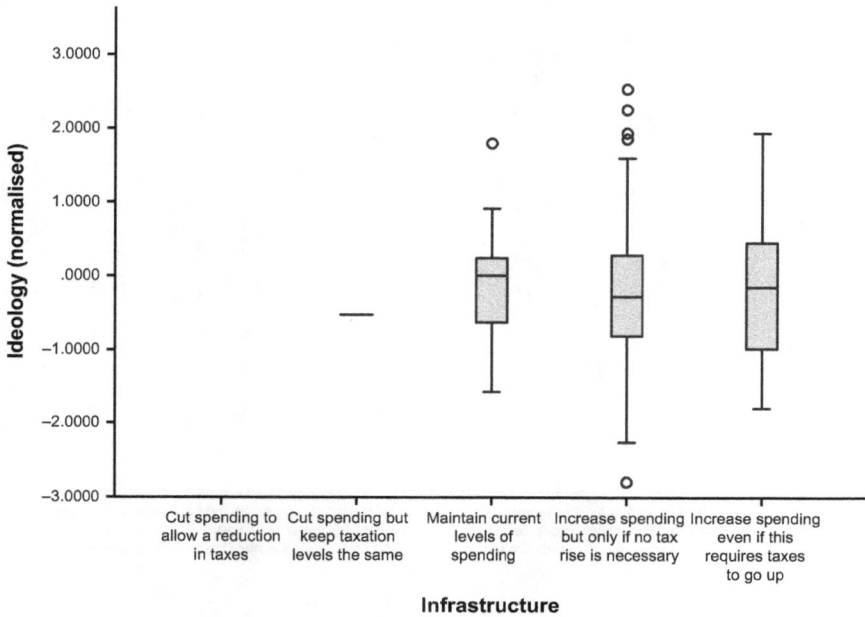

expenditures. It is important to acknowledge, however, that the decline in public investment in infrastructure is a common trend in most Latin American countries, with an average decline of about 2.27 per cent in the last decade. In some cases, notably in Chile and Colombia, this decline was caught up by a massive private investment, compensating for the lack of public investments. Although private financing of infrastructure exists in Brazil, it has been very low (about 1 per cent of GDP) and has never reached the scale of Chile and Colombia, 5.7 and 2.6 per cent of GDP respectively. Low investment returns in infrastructure are closely related to relatively high and risky opportunity costs for business in Brazil. Faced with the risk of administrative expropriation by governments, private investors have been discouraged from financing infrastructure projects.

Finally, with regard to social assistance, it is possible to identify much clear left-right ideological dispersion among Brazilian representatives (Figure 11.7). On the one extreme, a great number of legislators strongly supported cutting spending on policies of social assistance in order to reduce tax. These legislators are distinctly positioned in the right-wing of the ideological spectrum, with their median preferences located nearby at 2.0 points on the ideology scale. On the other extreme, it is also possible to identify another large group of legislators that positioned themselves in favour of increasing spending on social policies even if this requires taxes to go up. They are clearly leaning toward the left-wing in the ideological spectrum, with their median preferences just over -1.0 points. Other legislators that preferred to offer different answers to that question are positioned in the centre of the ideological scale.

*Figure 11.7: Legislators' beliefs and ideology about social assistance*

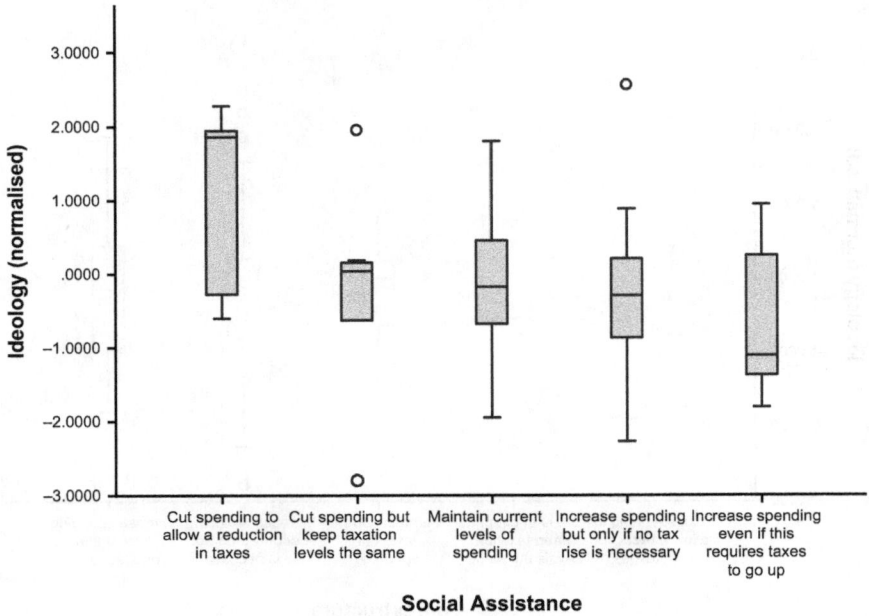

**Social Assistance**

This degree of ideological polarisation with regard to social policies might be a consequence of the Worker's Party government's direct identification with conditional cash transfer programmes like *Bolsa Família*. Although most of those programmes have started at the municipal level in the 1990s they were later transformed into national programmes. In 2003, *Bolsa Família* became the leader social programme of Lula's government. It was initially conceived as a programme to provide the poor families with incentives to send their children to school, but later included other existing incentives in a unified system of social protection and inclusion. According to Schwartzman (2013: 14–15):

the main virtue of the program is that spending actually benefits the poorest, in contrast with other policies of welfare, health and education that are regressive and benefit mostly the middle and upper sectors [...] cash transfer programs are very popular, and an important source of political allegiance bringing strong support to government candidates in elections in the poor region of the country.

In other words, policies of social assistance acquired a much politicised and ideologically driven profile under PT administrations. Even economically liberal legislators, who have played the opposition game for about ten years up to now, would agree with inclusive policies of social assistance; politically speaking it would be very difficult for them to express their support for that particular inclusive agenda. With this degree of political polarisation generated by the direct link between a government and a particular public policy, the coalitional multiparty presidential regime would rather resemble a polarised bipartisan US-like counterpart, in which its 'winner takes all' institutional design does not provide enough incentives for parties to compromise and cooperate. Consequently, political bickering and charged rhetoric become the order of the day. In this polarised environment, any potential compromise between government and opposition clearly undermines either side's electoral prospects. In this context, compromise has become a dirty word and ideological distinctions tend to become self-evident.

## Increasing Spending *but not* Taxation

As demonstrated in the previous section, the dominant preference of Brazilian legislators concerning budget allocation, regardless of the policy issue and ideological flavours, was to support the increase of public spending without further consequences to taxation. How can one reconcile those two apparent contradictory choices?

In order to address this question we rely on the concept of belief (Alston *et al.* 2016). These authors argue that one of the most important and most neglected factors that emerge during decisive moments, changing institutions and ultimately outcomes, are beliefs of how the world works. Although beliefs do appear in some treatments in the literature (in particular, North, Wallis and Weingast 2009), they are usually given a secondary role. We are not alone in giving beliefs a central role. Eggertsson (2005) and Greif (2006) both argue that beliefs are the key to understanding the institutions that those in power put in place. Eggertsson argues that Iceland was locked into 'imperfect institutions' because of a social model held by the rural elite that fishing would make the elite worse off by driving up their wage costs. For Greif, differing beliefs in Italy versus North Africa led to more open institutions in Italy while in North Africa the beliefs led to institutions fostering a closed society.

A central question in the literature on institutions has always been why all countries do not put in place good institutions given that they are widely recognised as the key to long-term growth. The standard answer is: new institutions have redistributive consequences that cannot be renegotiated due to transaction costs and commitment problems, such that those in power prefer to block the change and retain a larger expected share of a smaller pie. We agree that such social conflict issues are essential for understanding the process of development. However, this explanation requires that all economic agents can calculate, without cost or mistakes, the impact of each set of new institutions and rationally pick that which maximises the discounted present value of the inherent rental streams. In the absence of such unrealistic powers of rationality, beliefs arise out of the need to interpret the way the world works.

When assessing whether to pursue or block changes in institutions, those in power have to have a map in their heads of how each set of institutions leads to different outcomes. Beliefs are those maps. They provide an interpretation of cause and effect between how different institutions translate into economic and political outcomes. If the world was such that those maps varied little across different groups and circumstances, and that beliefs had a natural tendency to reflect reality very closely (when there even is a 'true' relationship between institutions and outcomes), then beliefs would not be very consequential. However, the diversity of human experience shows that interpretations of how the world works have varied dramatically across societies, so that understanding why particular institutions have emerged and persisted in specific countries requires careful and explicit attempts at understanding those beliefs.

In fact, the survey, which covers politicians' beliefs regarding budget and policy spending, provides two distinct dimensions in one single question/answer. One dimension is about legislators' beliefs towards taxation. The other dimension is about legislators' beliefs towards allocating greater or fewer public resources to a particular policy area. In each dimension the responses can be categorised as positive, when the incumbent reaction is congruent to the widespread belief with regard to that particular public policy; neutral – when the incumbent position matches the *status quo*; and negative, when the incumbent disagrees with the expected response or belief.

The categorisation as 'positive' can be interpreted as if the representative was fulfilling the dominant set of beliefs of a particular society and, as such, would be able to drive electoral returns from that legislative behaviour. In other words, as if the politician reacted in correspondence to what the median voter would prefer. In contrast, the 'negative' category means that a politician reacted in the opposite direction of the dominant belief of a society regarding a particular policy and, consequently, he/she would have to bear the political cost of doing so.

Consistent with Alston *et al.* (2016), we claim that the dominant belief in Brazil, since the re-democratisation, has been 'fiscally sound social inclusion'. The clearest manifestations of the belief in social inclusion is the 1988 Constitution, as Constitutions by definition are places where powerful groups delineate guiding principles, general rules and the accepted outlook on how things should be setup and operated. The fundamental spirit of the new Constitution was exactly to make a break with the past, abandoning the development-at-any-cost nature of the previous regime and embracing values of equality, social justice, human rights, inclusiveness, citizenship, and participation. These values not only oriented the content and tone of much of the text, but several were explicitly highlighted as fundamental principles.[2] The fact that the judiciary has become a major locus of policymaking in Brazil implies that the social inclusion bent of the Constitution does, in fact, have palpable consequences.

A key change that was squarely compatible with the new belief and that would corroborate the above mentioned impact of the new Constitution was the

---

2. Article 1 establishes at the outset 'citizenship', 'dignity to the human person', and 'political pluralism' as fundamental principles. Article 3 proclaims it a fundamental objective, among others, to 'build a society that is free, just and has solidarity'. Similarly, Title 5 of the Constitution, dedicated to Fundamental Rights and Guarantees has 78 items, assuring things such as the 'inviolability of the right to life, liberty, equality, security and prosperity' (Article 5).

extension of the franchise that took place with re-democratisation. Figure 11.8 shows the evolution of the proportion of the total population that effectively voted for President and Congress from 1894 to 2006. Only in 1985 did Brazil authorise the right to vote to illiterates, so the first time that a majority of the Brazilian population voted for President occurred in the 1989 election. The previous presidential election had been almost thirty years earlier and less than 20 per cent of the population voted in that election.

More than in any other time in Brazilian history, there were strong electoral incentives for policy to pursue the public good rather than private interests. The belief in social inclusion that undergirded the choice of policies was a natural reaction by the new coalition seeking to redress what it saw as the errors and injustices of the previous government. This belief led to a strong presumption that policy would thereafter be inclusive and promote social justice. The 1988 Constitution epitomised this process not only in terms of political rights, as noted above, but also by distributing economic benefits to large arrays of the population. An example of this is the extension of social security and pensions to non-contributing rural workers. This has had an important redistributive effect but at the same time added considerable pressure to the system's precarious fiscal balance. Other examples include the universal education and health benefits, and the guarantee of job stability to civil servants. Together with these social and universalistic transfers in the Constitution, interest groups also managed to embed their own particularistic transfers and so insulate them from future alterations. The result of this unmitigated inclusiveness was naturally a sharp jump in public expenditure.

Concerning taxes, the Brazilian government has achieved a manageable fiscal adjustment by a massive increase in tax revenues since the mid-1980s – during a time of already high taxes. In fact, the tax taken as per cent of GDP rose

*Figure 11.8: Per cent of total population that voted for President and Congress, 1894 – 2006*

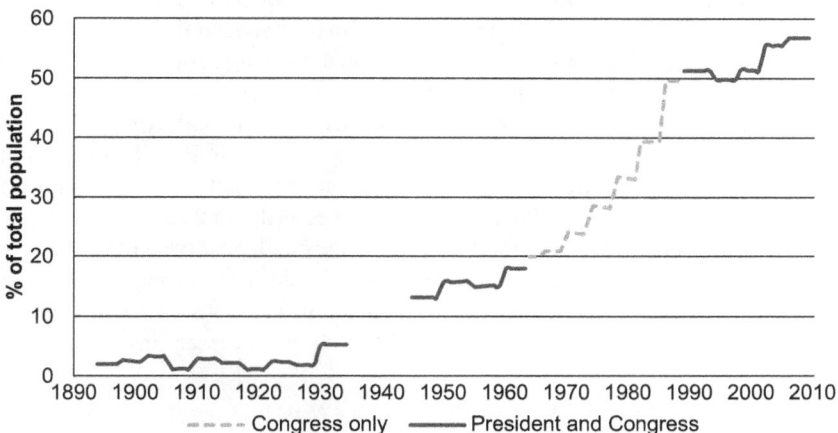

12 percentage points (from 25 to 37 per cent) between 1993 and 2005. This makes Brazil an outlier among developing countries in terms of its ability to extract resources from society (Lora 2007). Although the government's capacity to collect taxes has provided conditions for a comprehensive system of social protection, this tax burden has also generated a negative impact that affects Brazil's investment and productivity sectors. However, rather than complaining with this tremendous tax burden, the business sector appears satisfied with the status quo. In fact, the last time the business sector decisively complained against high taxes in Brazil was in December 2007 when the government proposal to extend the CPMF (the tax of financial transactions) was defeated in the Senate. Hence, although there is no great satisfaction with the current tax burden, it also seems that there is no real will within the Brazilian business leadership to mount pressure on the government to undertake a tax reform. Initiatives like 'Impostômetro', a giant tax meter or debt clock, developed by the FIESP (São Paulo's Industry Federation) fell short or found no significant echo on society claims. The private sector has enjoyed a mediocre growth and in return it has kept quiet in demanding a reform to the draconian Brazilian tax code, which is among the highest in the world (Melo *et al.* 2009). In fact, in the international ranking of better countries for doing business in, Brazil ranks among the highest in terms of costs and one of the worst in terms of its tax-collecting structure, behind countries like Eritrea and Vietnam.[3]

A closer analysis behind the Brazilian Development Bank's – BNDES massive loans for the manufacturing and infrastructure industries reveals it as a mechanism of subsidies from the national treasury that pays the difference (about $6 billion a year) between the rate the BNDES lends at (6 per cent) and the yield on the ten-year government bonds of 12 per cent. Pereira (2012), for instance, has demonstrated that there is a clear gains-from-trade mechanism by allowing the executive to have access to greater revenues via a distortionary tax system in exchange for subsidised public loans to the national business sector. Pereira shows that direct connections have existed between subsidised loans made by the BNDES and campaign donations made by firms, which receive these loans. On the one hand, this politically motivated bargain has generated a relatively high degree of satisfaction with the current level of taxes between the business sector and the government. On the other hand, there is a growing sentiment that the tax burden has reached a plateau and taxpayers are no longer willing to increase this burden, decreasing the political feasibility of raising additional taxes. As we can see in Figure 11.9, among the five possible answers offered to Brazilian legislators in the seventh round of the survey, there is a clear dominant strategy: supporting the increase of spending but only if it does not necessarily translate in tax increase. This is the only alternative that provides, on the one hand, positive electoral returns by favouring the increase of spending in public policies and consequently greater social inclusion and protection. On the other hand, this response does not generate political costs, which would occur when supporting the necessary tax increase that

---

3. According to the International Financing Corporation – World Bank (http://www.doingbusiness. org).

*Figure 11.9: Expected outcomes from politicians' responses*

| Response to survey | Position towards policy | Position towards taxation |
|---|---|---|
| Cut spending to allow a reduction in taxes | Negative (Reduce policies) | Positive (Reduce taxes) |
| Cut spending but keep taxation levels the same | Negative (Reduce policies) | Neutral |
| Maintain current levels of spending | Neutral | Neutral |
| Increase spending but only if no tax rise is necessary | Positive (Increase policies) | Neutral |
| Increase spending even if this requires taxes to go up | Positive (Increase policies) | Negative (Increase taxes) |

would be a required condition to provide a greater offer of those policies. This result is consistent with what one would expect from an environment constrained by a fiscally sound social inclusion. The other possible responses in the survey would necessarily lead to worse outcomes.

We also compared the five possible responses about budget allocation and contrasted them in two dimensions of beliefs: reduction of taxes and increase of spending in public policies. In order to do so, we recoded each variable (health, basic education, higher education, infrastructure and social assistance) in two categories: 'against taxation' (fiscally conservative) and 'pro-spending' (fiscally expansionist). We then subtracted the percentage of legislators supporting tax reduction by the percentage of legislators that either supported a tax increase or the maintenance of the same level of tax in order to create a measure named 'against taxation', which ranges from -100 to 100. Positive values mean that the legislature favours tax reduction whereas negative values mean the legislature favours the status quo or tax increase. A similar rationale was applied to a 'pro-spending' measure. To generate this variable we sum the percentages of respondents in favour of increasing spending and subtract them by the sum of legislators who are not in favour. Positive values mean a pro-spending preference. Finally, we plotted those two variables, 'against taxation' and 'pro-spending', of a left-right ideological continuum.[4]

As we can see in Figure 11.10, values of the variable 'against-taxation' are always negative in all five-policy areas. This strongly suggests that the legislature is very lenient with the high amount of taxation already imposed by the Brazilian government. Concerning the variable 'pro-spending' it is always positive in all five-policy areas. When observe the two variables together the inexistence of ideological cleavages from the more left-wing to right-wing legislators becomes

---

4. For simplicity, we assumed right-wing legislators to be the ones with values beyond zero and left-wing the ones below zero in the ideological scale.

*Figure 11.10: Against-taxation versus pro-spending and ideological preferences*

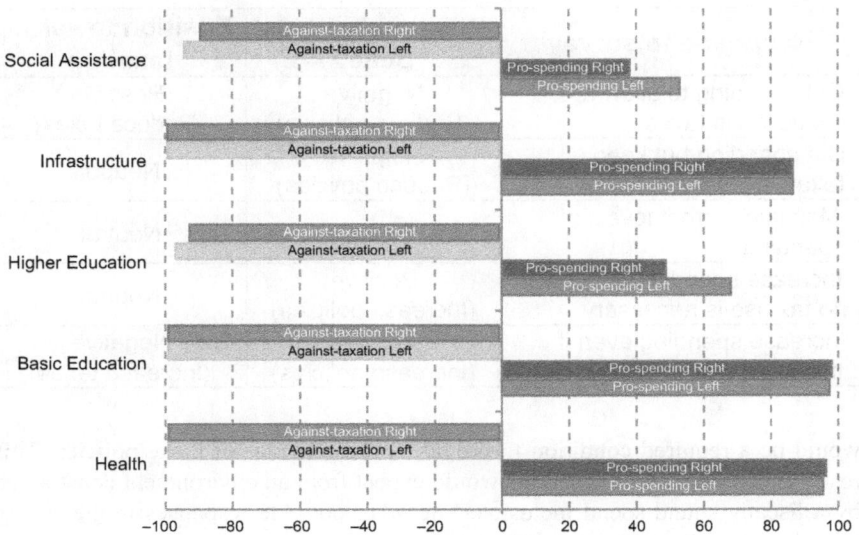

clear. As discussed before, the only significant exceptions take place with the variable 'pro-spending' in policies of social assistance and higher education in which left-wing legislators seem to be spendthrifts.

Given the dominant belief of fiscally sound social inclusion in Brazil, a less inclusive cutting spending approach to public policies seems to be very costly in political terms, since almost no one is capable of bearing the political cost of favouring a fiscally restrictive agenda of decreasing spending in any public policy. In addition, both left and right legislators want to keep taxation at the same level. Therefore, the pro-spending preference cannot be directly associated to ideological preferences. It could rather be better understood as a political reaction to the dominant belief of social inclusion that constrains representatives' ideological distinctions in public policy and tax matters.

Similar inferences can be drawn from the distribution of policy preferences among the main political parties in Brazil. In Figure 11.10, for instance, we take the two extreme alternatives of answers in the survey, *cut spending to allow a reduction in taxes* and *increase spending even if this requires taxes to go up*, as benchmarks to differentiate legislators and political parties in an ideological continuum. Whereas the former alternative of answers theoretically represents the dominant preference of contractionary (right-wing) legislators/parties, the latter represents the dominant preference of expansionary (left-wing) legislators/parties. The dots represent the mean and the lines represent the 95 per cent confidence interval, which symbolise the degree of dispersion of policy preference within a political party.

Figure 11.11 shows that there are very minor differences between political parties with regard to the five policy areas that the legislators were questioned

*Figure 11.11: Distribution of partisan preferences on public policies*

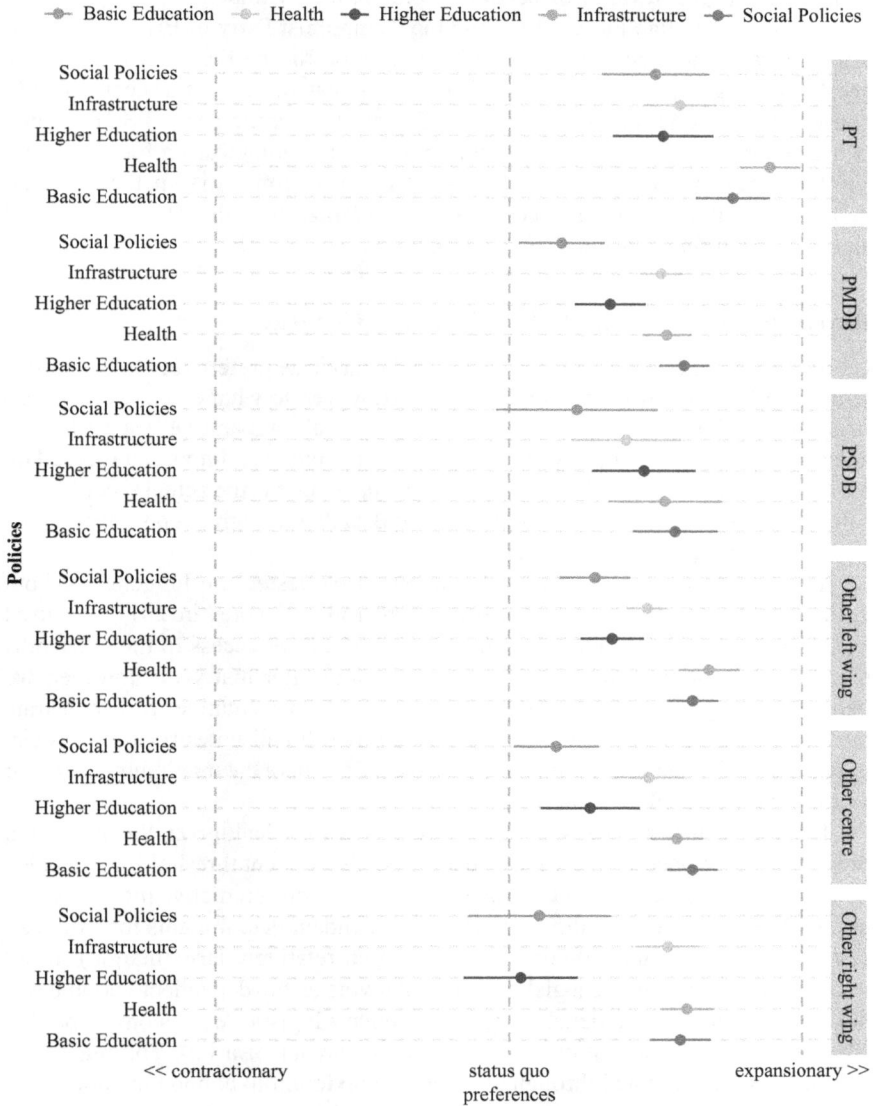

on. In fact, this exercise emphatically reveals that we do not have truly economic liberals in Brazil. Every one heavily supports social inclusion. On the one hand, health and basic education look like to be the top policy partisan priorities with regard to budget allocation. On the other hand, social assistance and higher education are the least preferred policies among political parties. Although minor, there are interesting differences and particular aspects that should be highlighted.

Again, social assistance and, to a less extent, higher education, are the policy areas that present a great level of dispersion of preferences within parties, in particular in the Social Christian Party – PSC and the Communist Party of Brazil – PCdoB. The PSC and the Democrats – DEM seem to be the parties with a relatively greater ideological dispersion. The PSOL representatives are not as economically conservative as one might expect.[5] The Social Democratic party, PSDB, which is the major opposition party in Brazil, presents an ideological profile extremely similar to the supposedly centrist PMDB's ideological profile. In sum, the dominant belief of social inclusion has been so strong in Brazil that almost all ideological and partisan differences have been fading away.

## Revealed Preferences in Roll-Call Votes in Congress

Up to now we have analysed legislators' budgetary true preferences in the survey with regard to five different public policies. However, to what extent would these 'true' revealed preferences in the survey hold in a comparative test with their actual 'strategic' behaviour by the time legislators vote in an important roll call on the floor of the Congress? In other words, to what extent is the actual record of the roll call voting behaviour of legislators in the Brazilian Congress consistent with a legislator's true policy preferences?

In order to analytically assess this question we tested the influence of both politicians' ideology and beliefs for different roll call votes in 2011. We used 2011 because of data availability, since we did not have access to the other bills organised by complete topic and voting behaviour after that year; however, we believe a one-year sample is fairly adequate and representative to demonstrate our point. We selected, within the year of 2011, roll call votes related to social issues that had some degree of controversy; that is, where the maximum margin of victory was about 30 per cent.

The selection of roll calls on social issues is self-evident, given the discussion previously developed. Concerning the arbitrary 30 per cent threshold, we decided to have at least some level of controversy; otherwise our predictive models would not be able to fit (it is very difficult to find independent determinants for a roll call that is approved by unanimous decision or by a relatively large margin). In all tested models we have the legislator's roll call vote as the dependent variable and our unit of analysis. We developed a set of binary logistic regressions to predict whether the legislator is more likely to vote in favour of a bill. The regression coefficients are estimated through an iterative maximum likelihood method.

In Model 1, the dependent variable is a dummy indicating whether the legislator voted in favour of an amendment that increased the value of the minimum wage to a higher value than the one originally proposed by the executive. The major opposition party, the PSDB, introduced this amendment. This is a typical position-taking movement from the opposition, which is very unlikely to pass under the

---

5.　As a consequence of having only one legislator in the sample the PSOL does not present ideological discrepancies in any single policy area.

overwhelming size of the legislative majority supporting the government in Congress. In Model 2 we have, as dependent variable, a dummy representing voting in favour of the urgency procedure with regard to the increase of the minimum wage. This is a very socially inclusive policy issue with the potential to have important electoral consequences for legislators in the future. The roll call analysed in Model 3 concerns the implementation of changes that goes against the executive position in the 'National Access to Technical Education and Employment Project' (Pronatec Project), which is the main Brazilian qualification project for youth.

We included three independent variables and four controls for each model. As independent variables we included a variable called 'beliefs' which means the overall support for higher expenditure in the five previously analysed public policies preferences, namely Health, Basic and Higher Education, Infrastructure and Social Assistance.

We created the variable Beliefs to function as a measure of how far one can go in the name of the expansion of public policy. For this purpose, we used the five previously explored and described different scales related to each policy issue (Health, Basic and Higher Education, Infrastructure and Social Assistance) ranging from one to five. We simply combined and rescaled the average of them for every legislator to create an additive index varying from 0 to 100, where 0 is the most contractionary congressman (therefore, opposing the expansion of public policy) and 100 is the most expansionary (therefore, favouring the expansion of public policy) following the same idea of Figure 11.11.

Our naïve expectation is that the greater the legislator's support for inclusive public policies, the higher the probability that she/he would vote in favour of both the urgency petition that would lead to an increase in the minimum wage (Model 2), the amendment initiated by the opposition (Model 1) and the expansion of the PRONATEC (Model 3). Therefore, legislators leaning towards an economic-liberal policy preference would be more inclined have a more restrictive policy agenda of social protection and therefore, vote against the increase of the minimum wage, against its urgency and against the PRONATEC expansion. On the other side of the ideological spectrum, economic-conservative legislators would fundamentally support the higher values of a minimum wage so on and so forth. In other words, we expect the legislators voting favourable for those bills to be consistent with what they declared in the survey. We expect, thus, a match between beliefs and voting behaviour.

We also included the variable ideology measured by Power and Zucco (2012), who rescaled ideological estimates for each legislator, anchored by the entire 1990–2013 BLS time series, as we used in a previous section of this paper. However, we expect that ideology will have no effect on our dependent variables. The literature offers a strong theoretical and empirical support for the idea of a non-ideological behavior by legislators in Brazil (Pereira and Mueller 2003; Zucco and Lauderdale 2011). In addition, Zucco (2009) has demonstrated that when parties take part in the governing coalition, party members tend to vote more consistently supporting the president regardless of their ideological preferences. Zucco argues that previous observations of ideological behaviour by parties were driven by the coincidence between the left-right and the government-opposition dimensions. This leads to a deceptive 'appearance of an ideologically organised legislature'. Because Cardoso's managerial strategy of how to deal with coalition partners was fundamentally based on an ideologically homogeneous coalition, the cleavage between left and right basically resembled the cleavage of the government and the opposition. With PT administrations, however, the coalition was fairly ideologically heterogeneous comprising of parties from the extreme left to the extreme right of the political spectrum, which made it clear that belonging to the governing coalition was a much stronger predictor of legislators' behaviour than ideological preferences. Notwithstanding, ideology and parties matter, but their importance is subsumed by coalition membership.

Rather than being sources of ideological aggregation, political parties in Brazil have basically been labels capable of increasing politicians' electoral survival and channels to obtaining political and monetary resources under the control and discretion of the executive.

Finally, as the key independent variable we included 'coalition membership', which corresponds to a dummy with the value of 1 if the legislator belongs to a political party that takes part of the governing coalition, and 0 otherwise. We expect that this variable will be the main explanatory variable for our three roll call logistic regression models. In a multiparty setting, in order to implement public policies and govern, the president needs to build and sustain a majority coalition. However, succeeding in Congress in such a fragmented legislature is not a trivial task given that the president's party rarely obtains the majority of seats. To solve coordination and governability problems, the Brazilian president controls several coalition tools (cabinet portfolio, pork, policy concessions, job positions in the public bureaucracy, etc.) capable of attracting different political parties to hang in with the presidential coalition. Even though this pool of resources is finite, its usage is very discretional and usually generates political and electoral benefits for their recipients. For instance, there is evidence (Pereira and Renno 2003) suggesting that the legislative's re-election rate is positively associated with access to political and monetary resources produced by a robust support for presidential initiatives and interest in Congress. Therefore, we expect that belonging to the government's coalition increases the probability of voting with the executive in Congress.

As for control variables, we included age, legislative number of terms, HDI of the legislator's State and a dummy identifying if the legislator is an evangelical. Controlling for HDI is important, since there can be a doubt if a legislator originally from a poorer state faces higher pressure by the constituents to vote more consistently in favour of inclusive public policies. We also want to show that the geographical and socioeconomic conditions do not have an impact on voting behaviour. The same rationale can be applied to religion and one could expect a bias towards piety and inclusion that would favour the approval of inclusive bills. Seniority, measured as the numbers of previous terms, which accounts for the experience in the profession and age, complete the list of controls.

Results consistently indicate that legislators neither take into account beliefs nor ideology when voting for social issues. The only variable statistically

*Figure 11.12: Selected roll calls*

| Variables | Main tests | | | Robustness tests | | | | | | |
|---|---|---|---|---|---|---|---|---|---|---|
| | Model1 Minimum wage amendment | Model2 Minimum wage | Model3 PRONATEC | Model4 High Speed tram | Model5 Itaipú treaty amendment | Model6 Itaipú treaty | Model7 Fiscal incentives to automotive industry | Model8 IRS compensation | Model9 Fiscal incentives | Model10 Fuel policies |
| (Intercept) | 3.591 | -1.222 | 11.665* | 5.578 | -3.089 | -1.337 | -4.197 | -8.829 | 2.777 | -0.288 |
| | (5.142) | (4.903) | (5.368) | (4.544) | (4.228) | (4.023) | (4.112) | (4.621) | (7.271) | (6.257) |
| Belief | 0.025 | 0.018 | -0.014 | 0.027 | -0.008 | 0.024 | 0.030 | 0.029 | -0.064 | -0.004 |
| | (0.041) | (0.036) | (0.037) | (0.033) | (0.031) | (0.030) | (0.031) | (0.033) | (0.054) | (0.046) |
| Ideology | -0.391 | 0.204 | -0.217 | 0.445 | -0.088 | -0.287 | 0.413 | 0.638 | -0.028 | -0.269 |
| | (0.357) | (0.330) | (0.379) | (0.324) | (0.289) | (0.280) | (0.292) | (0.333) | (0.492) | (0.384) |
| Government | -4.001*** | 3.088*** | -2.519** | 2.003** | 1.636** | 0.422 | -0.155 | 1.998*** | 4.713*** | 2.804*** |
| | (0.930) | (0.663) | (0.830) | (0.626) | (0.556) | (0.502) | (0.503) | (0.607) | (1.068) | (0.772) |
| Terms | 0.280 | -0.212 | 0.013 | -0.126 | -0.201 | -0.275 | -0.260 | -0.456* | 0.029 | -0.360 |
| | (0.205) | (0.198) | (0.201) | (0.172) | (0.165) | (0.158) | (0.153) | (0.181) | (0.242) | (0.225) |
| Age | -0.057 | 0.012 | 0.024 | 0.008 | -0.006 | 0.025 | 0.028 | 0.069* | 0.010 | 0.091* |
| | (0.035) | (0.030) | (0.031) | (0.027) | (0.026) | (0.025) | (0.025) | (0.029) | (0.040) | (0.038) |
| Evangelical | -2.093 | 2.147 | 0.247 | 2.522 | 1.460 | 0.146 | 0.632 | 0.806 | 1.996 | -2.235 |
| | (1.557) | (1.338) | (1.362) | (1.297) | (1.224) | (0.946) | (0.976) | (1.073) | (1.781) | (1.397) |
| HDI | -3.455 | -2.097 | -13.967* | -12.562* | 5.239 | -2.018 | 2.163 | 3.864 | -0.735 | -6.370 |
| | (6.412) | (6.075) | (7.101) | (5.665) | (5.307) | (4.891) | (4.876) | (5.289) | (9.061) | (7.623) |
| Likelihood-r | 35.532 | 37.673 | 17.591 | 24.165 | 17.527 | 8.096 | 6.414 | 22.486 | 43.965 | 32.496 |
| Nagelk.R-sq. | 0.491 | 0.480 | 0.345 | 0.334 | 0.252 | 0.123 | 0.099 | 0.314 | 0.673 | 0.516 |
| N | 85 | 85 | 60 | 84 | 84 | 84 | 84 | 84 | 63 | 67 |

significant for our three models was Coalition Membership. Although we expected that ideology was not an important predictor of legislative behaviour, the tests also suggested, in the opposite direction of our expectation that beliefs do not matter for legislators' voting decision on the floor of the Congress.

The results in fact revealed that there has existed a mismatch between legislators' true preferences (beliefs) and their actual vote behaviour in Congress. What justifies this inconsistency? It is simply too costly and many times prohibitive for members of the governing coalition to deviate from executives' policy preferences. Unfaithful coalition members have to bear the cost of being out of the spotlight and powerful hierarchical positions in committees, receiving fewer resources from the executive and, therefore, diminishing their chances of electoral survival.

As a robustness test, we ran further logit regressions (Models 4 through 10) to investigate if the same pattern would be identified in roll calls not necessarily related to social issues but that presented high degrees of controversy – in which the margin of victory was smaller than 10 per cent. We expect that the higher the controversy concerning the bill, the greater will be the importance of beliefs and ideology to legislative voting behaviour. However, the tests show once again that what really matters when deciding the vote is belonging to the governing coalition and not what legislators believe with regard to public policies.

The combination between these regression results and the previous exploratory analysis indicates incongruence between voting behaviour and legislators' beliefs. Politicians apparently want to declare their beliefs in favour of social inclusion, following their own recipes of the world and/or pleasing their constituencies. If fiscally sound social inclusion is a dominant belief, as we have argued, one should expect that society shares the same set of beliefs. However, when it comes to making the votes count, both on the social issues or any other controversial issues, neither ideology nor beliefs have any impact on their revealed preferences within Congress. At the end of the day, legislators not only care very little about ideology, but they also abandon their inclusive beliefs in order to please party leaders and uphold the government.

## Conclusion

In this paper we addressed two main complementary issues. First, we investigated how Brazilian legislators have reconciled the support for a very inclusive social agenda beyond the ideological division between left and right in an environment of macroeconomic stability and fiscal responsibility. Second, the extent to which legislators' true budgetary preferences on public policies are consistent with their actual voting behaviour was analysed.

With regard to a greater support for expenditure on social policy without further consequences on an already high tax burden, we argue that this apparent contradictory result is very consistent with the dominant belief of fiscally sound social inclusion that has evolved and dominated the country since the re-democratisation, on the one hand, and the achievement of macroeconomic stability with the Real Plan, on the other.

That is, there is a clear dominant belief among Brazilian legislators which favours an increase of spending on public policies but only if it does not necessarily generate tax increase. As emphasised, this is the only political alternative that provides positive electoral returns. This result is consistent with what one would expect from an environment constrained by a fiscally sound social inclusion. The test also demonstrated the inexistence of ideological cleavages from the more left-wing to right-wing legislators. The only significant exceptions took place with the variable 'pro-spending' in policies of social assistance and higher education in which ideology seems to play a role. Therefore, the pro-spending without tax increase preference cannot be directly associated to ideological preferences. It could, rather, be better understood as a political reaction to the dominant belief of social inclusion that constrains representatives' ideological distinctions in public policy and tax matters.

Our assessment of the survey applied by Power and Zucco with Brazilian legislators demonstrated that their ideological preferences or partisan orientations play a minor role in their preferences of how the country should allocate budgetary resources on public policies. The great majority of legislators supported the increase in social policy expenditure regardless of their ideological or political tastes.

This result confirmed our expectation that there is an important role played by the belief of social inclusion in Brazilian society. This belief frames economic and political institutions and makes them capable of enhancing cooperation towards the common goal of inclusion in Brazil. Although previous analysis using Nominate techniques (Leoni 2002) indicate two dimensions in Brazilian legislators' voting patterns, clearly distinguishing an ideological continuum of left-right, a deeper look into the micro-dynamics of legislators' voting suggests that there is an outer space for cross-ideological beliefs within these patterns between governments versus opposition. That is, whenever the social inclusion policies are at stake, legislators will consistently proclaim being in favour of greater expenditure despite of their own ideological preferences.

There is a clear mismatch, however, between legislators' true preferences revealed in the survey and their actual voting behaviour as our statistical tests suggest. Rather than beliefs, legislators take into account coalition membership when they decide their voting behaviour on substantive issues, especially on inclusive public policies. This mismatch suggests that the real source of dispute or conflict in the Brazilian legislature is the one between the government and the opposition, mainly because it provides important consequences for legislators' electoral survival. There is little doubt that the existence of government and opposition is a kind of continuous conflict in politics, even less of a doubt that this kind of democratic conflict is not exclusive to Brazil.

## References

Acemoglu, D. and Robinson, J. (2012) *Why Nations Fail: The origins of power, prosperity and poverty*, New York: Crown Publishing Group.

Acosta, A. and Coppedge, M. (2001) 'Political Determinants of Fiscal Discipline in Latin America, 1979–1998', Working paper presented at the International Congress of the LASA, Washington, DC.

Alesina, A., Hausmann, R., Hommes, R. and Stein, E. (1999) 'Budget institutions and fiscal performance in Latin America', *Journal of Development Economics* 59: 253–273.

Alesina, A. and Rosenthal, H. (1995) *Partisan Politics, Divided Government, and the Economy*, Cambridge: Cambridge University Press.

Alston, L., Melo, M., Mueller, B. and Pereira, C. (2016) *Beliefs, Leadership and Critical Transactions: Brazil 1964–2014*, Princeton: Princeton University Press.

Ames, B. (2001) *The Deadlock of Democracy in Brazil*, Ann Arbor: University of Michigan Press.

Amorim Neto, O. and Santos, F. (2001) 'A Conexão Presidencial: Frações Pró e Antigoverno e Disciplina Partidária no Brasil', *Dados* 44(2): 291–321.

Eggertsson, T. (2005) *Imperfect Institutions: Possibilities and limits of reform*, New York: Cambridge University Press.

Figueiredo, A. and Limongi, F. (1999) 'Executivo e Legislativo na nova ordem constitucional', Rio de Janeiro: FGV.

Greif, A. (2006) *Institutions and the Path to the Modern Economy: Lessons from medieval trade*, New York: Cambridge University Press.

Hallerberg, M. and Marier, P. (2004) 'Executive authority, the personal vote, and budget discipline in Latin American and Caribbean countries', *American Journal of Political Science* 48(3): 571–587.

Hallerberg, M. and Von Hagen, J. (1997) 'Electoral Institutions, Cabinet Negotiations, and Budget Deficits in the European Union', *NBER Working Papers Series*, 6341.

Hallerberg, M., Scartascini, C. and Stein, E. (2009) *Who Decides the Budget? A political economy analysis of the budget process in Latin America*, Cambridge, Mass: Harvard University Press.

Leoni, E. (2002) 'Ideologia, Democracia e Comportamento Parlamentar: A Câmara dos Deputados (1991–1998)', *Dados-Revista de Ciências Sociais* 45(3): 361–386.

Lora, E. (2007) *The State of State Reform in Latin America*, Stanford: Stanford University Press.

Melo, M. (2007) 'Political Competition can be Positive: Embedding cash transfer programs in Brazil', in A. Bebbington and W. McCourt (eds) *Statecraft in the South*, London: Palgrave, pp. 30–51.

—— (2008) 'Unexpected Successes, Unanticipated Failures: Social policy from Cardoso to Lula', in P. R. Kingstone and T. J. Power (eds) *Democratic Brazil Revisited*, Pittsburgh, PA: University of Pittsburgh Press, pp. 161–184.

Melo, M., Pereira, C. and Figueiredo, C. M. (2009) 'Political and institutional checks on corruption: explaining the performance of Brazilian audit institutions', *Comparative Political Studies* 42(9): 1217–1244.

Nicolau, J. (2012) *Eleições no Brasil: do Império aos dias atuais*, Rio de Janeiro: Zahar.

North, D. (2005) *Understanding the Process of Economic Change*, Princeton: Princeton University Press.

North, D., Wallis, J. and Weingast, B. (2009) *Violence and Social Orders: A conceptual framework for interpreting recorded human history*, New York: Cambridge University Press.

Pereira, C. (2012) 'Selecting National Champions: The Political Economy of BNDES', Unpublished manuscript presented at LASA Congress, San Francisco.

Pereira, C. and Mueller, B. (2003) 'Partidos Fracos na Arena Eleitoral e Partidos Fortes na Arena Legislativa: A Conexão Eleitoral no Brasil', *Dados* 46(4): 735–771.

Pereira, C. and Renno, L. (2003) 'Successful re-election strategies in Brazil: the electoral impact of distinct institutional incentives', *Electoral Studies* 22(3): 425–448.

Poterba, J. (1994) 'State response to fiscal crises: the effects of budgetary institutions and politics', *Journal of Political Economy* 102(4): 799–821.

Poterba, J. and Rueben, K. (2001) 'Fiscal rules, state budget rules, and tax-exempt bond yields', *Journal of Urban Economics* 50(3): 537–562.

Power, T. and Zucco, C. (2012) 'Elite preferences in a consolidating democracy: the Brazilian legislative surveys, 1990–2009', *Latin American Politics and Society* 54(4): 1–27.

Roubini, N. and Sachs, J. (1989) 'Political and economic determinants of budget deficits in industrial countries', *European Economic Review* 33: 903–938.

Santos, F. (2003) 'O Poder Legislativo no Presidencialismo de Coalizão', Belo Horizonte/Rio de Janeiro: UFMG/IUPERJ.

Scartascini, C. and Crain, W. (2001) 'The size and composition of government spending in multi-party systems', *Working paper presented at the Public Choice Society Conference*, San Antonio, Texas.

Schwartzman, S. and Campos, M. C. de (2013) 'Brazil: Democracy and inclusive growth', Working paper presented at *Democracy Works* Project seminar at Casa Das Garças, Rio de Janeiro, May 15, 2013.

Stein, E., Talvi, E. and Grisanti, A. (1998) 'Institutional Arrangements and Fiscal Performance: The Latin America experience', *NBER Working Papers Series*, 6358.

Stein, E. and Tommasi, M. (2008) *Policymaking in Latin America: How politics shapes policies*, Cambridge, Mass.: Harvard University Press.

Von Hagen, J. (1992) 'Budgeting procedures and fiscal performance in the European communities', *Economic Papers* 96.

Weingast, B. (1979) 'A rational choice perspective on congressional norms', *American Journal of Political Science* 23(2): 245–262.

Weingast, B., Shepsle, K. and Johnsen, C. (1981) 'The political economy of benefits and costs: a neoclassical approach to distributive politics', *Journal of Political Economy* 89(4): 642–664.

Zucco Jr, C. (2009) 'Ideology or what? Legislative behavior in multiparty institutional settings', *Journal of Politics* 71(3): 1076–1092.

Zucco Jr, C. and Lauderdale, B. (2011) 'Distinguishing between influences on Brazilian legislative behavior', *Legislative Studies Quarterly* 36(3): 363–396.

Chapter Twelve

# Participatory Self-governance and Conflict Intensification in Bolivarian Venezuela

*Matthew Rhodes-Purdy*

## Introduction

This book focuses on the role of institutional innovation in managing distributional and ethnic conflict. The underlying supposition is that bitter disputes over economic inequality and the marginalisation of some ethnic groups can be ameliorated by changing the rules of the political game. Given this, Bolivarian Venezuela is a fascinating case study. The regime of Hugo Chávez and his successor, Nicolás Maduro, has inaugurated a seismic shift in the mechanisms of democracy in Venezuela, moving away from party-centred representative democracy to more participatory institutions on the one hand, and to greater centralisation of authority in the hands of the President and the executive branch on the other. Contrary to the hopes outlined in the first chapter of this book, this has not tamed the furore of social conflict in Venezuela. Quite the opposite, in fact: political conflict between supporters of Chávez and his opponents has only grown more acrimonious as the Bolivarian regime has remade Venezuelan democracy.

Making this combination of institutional change and conflict intensification even more surprising is the fact that many of the newly introduced institutions are inspired by participatory democracy. Deliberative and participatory governance mechanisms are, in theory, intended to resolve (or at least overcome) deep-seated social antagonisms by allowing a space for and forging a 'common will', a political path which benefits society as a whole and transcends narrow and selfish interests (e.g. Rousseau 2002). Yet in Bolivarian Venezuela, battles over policy and politics rage on. This much is certain: in Venezuela, participatory self-governance does not and never has played the theoretical role that democratic theorists have assigned to it.

With the book's analytical framework in mind, in this case study I seek to answer this: what is the role of the form of participatory fora in managing social conflict in Bolivarian Venezuela? It seems clear, upon even a cursory glance, that such innovations have done little to tame the vitriol of either *chavista* or regime opponents. However in this chapter I will show that participatory fora in Venezuela have not simply failed to manage social conflict, but have actively contributed to its aggravation. This, despite minimal differences in the details of institutional design from similar, more successful (in terms of conflict management), instances of participatory governance in other Latin American countries, such as Brazil and Uruguay.

How can similar institutions ameliorate conflict in some countries but exacerbate it in others? The short answer is that participatory institutions do not exist in a vacuum, and their impact on social conflict is extremely sensitive to the political context in which they operate. Participatory fora shape social conflict in Bolivarian Venezuela in distinct ways because they exist within a political context defined by populism, rather than by representative democracy. Representative democracies use participatory fora to provide spaces for policy making where unmediated democracy's greater political equality can give numerical majorities a freer hand to enact egalitarian policies (Barber 1984). In representative democracies, participatory fora provide a respite from the rough and tumble of electoral politics by creating a space for discussion and consensus-building. Participatory governance in a populist system like Bolivarian Venezuela serves a fundamentally different purpose: to legitimate the rule of the populist and to reinforce the ties between the leader and the masses. And because these programmes buttress the stability of populist rule, they tend to reinforce the battle lines between 'the oligarchy' and the 'the people'.

This chapter proceeds in three sections. In the first section, I briefly review the historical development of participatory programmes in Bolivarian Venezuela. In the final sections, I focus on the *consejos comunales* (communal councils), which are the umbrella participatory organisation in a given locality. In the second section, I show that, far from alleviating conflict, participatory programmes in the Bolivarian system are primarily intended to legitimate populist hegemony at the national level by allowing confined spaces for participatory governance at the local level. In the final section, I analyse the role institutional weakness plays in allowing the theoretical role of participatory fora to be altered under populism. Specifically, the lack of clear sources of funding and organisational support make participatory programmes and the organisations which coalesce around them dependent upon the Bolivarian movement to function effectively. This contributes to both the cohesion of the *chavista* movement and the marginalisation of the political opposition, thus reinforcing the conflict-laden dynamics of Bolivarian populism. This chapter demonstrates how minor changes in institutional design can interact with major differences in political conflict to create drastic differences in the ways similar institutions shape social conflict.

## The populist roots of participatory governance in Venezuela

A thorough retelling of the history of *chavismo* is outside the scope of this chapter. However some review of these events is necessary as it is not possible to understand *chavista* participatory programmes without reviewing the historical trajectories which led to their creation. Bolivarianism in Venezuela predates Chávez's rise, if only in inchoate form (Ciccariello-Maher 2013). However it coalesced into its modern incarnation within the Venezuelan military as a reaction to the perceived corruption of the democratic state, and its inability to meet the challenges that arose during the economic crises of the early 1980s. The political system of this era (called the *Punto Fijo* system) was formally democratic, but its claim to legitimacy was based more on the regularity of competitive elections and the distribution of oil rents than on any true adherence to popular sovereignty (Hellinger 2003). Authority was tightly held by a small number of elites within the system's dominant parties (Coppedge 1994), and the mass bases of the parties had a largely subordinate role that did little to genuinely empower average citizens (Ellner 2003a, 2003b).

With the arrival of the debt crisis of the early 1980s and subsequent fluctuations in the price of oil, this system of rent distribution became unsustainable and eventually imploded. However the breakdown of representative democracy in Venezuela can be only partly attributed to the recurrent economic crises that rocked the country from 1983 through the 1990s. The inability of the political system to absorb new demands generated by these crises destroyed the legitimacy of representative institutions, leading to massive social unrest (López Maya 1999) and the eventual collapse of the party system. The behaviour of various leaders further contributed to the loss of faith in the ability of *puntofijismo* to enforce popular sovereignty. The lack of accountability and responsiveness was perhaps most clearly embodied when Carlos Andrés Pérez, a member of the centre-left and statist AD, implemented a programme of neoliberal structural adjustment shortly after running against such programmes during the election of 1988 (López Maya 1999: 212–214). This about-face was only the latest in a long line of perceived slights by *Punto Fijo* elites against popular opinion. It also signalled the beginning of the system's end; Andrés Pérez was the last President from either of the two parties that had dominated Venezuelan politics for over 40 years. Ten years later, both AD and COPEI were forced to give up any ambitions of regaining power with their own candidates, throwing their support to outsider, Henrique Salas Römer.

Hugo Chávez, who achieved political fame (or infamy, depending on one's point of view) as the leader of a failed coup, was Römer's challenger in the 1998 presidential elections. Both candidates attempted to mobilise voters around the banner of anti-elite resentment, with both running on anti-party platforms. Chávez's victory and rise to power can be attributed to two strategic sources: unwavering opposition to all elements of the partyarchy of the *Punto Fijo* era (Molina 2006: 170) and the unification of excluded sectors under a single political banner (Myers 2006: 13). In particular, his insistence on consigning not only the parties, but also the constitution which supported their dominance, to the dust bin of history, in favour of a new system based upon principles of 'participatory, protagonist democracy', aided his victory. Chávez's militant insistence on a new institutional framework resonated deeply with an electorate which had become deeply disillusioned by the ability of representative politics to bind elite decisions to the will of the people. Empowerment of the excluded is perhaps the central source of legitimacy for the Chávez regime; promises of political inclusion had to be fulfilled in order for the movement to survive. Once in power, the newly ascendant Bolivarians found, as have many politicians throughout history, that promises are far easier to make than to keep.

*Chavistas*, like many populists, viewed the political exclusion around which they coalesce not as a problem to be resolved through politics as usual, but as the result of the wicked design of an implacable elite foe determined to deprive the people of their rightful sovereignty. In other words, populists tend to adopt a Manichean view of political competition (Hawkins 2010), where all members of society are either members of 'the people', or the evil elite, with nothing in between. To the Bolivarians, steeped in resentment towards every aspect of the old regime, the 'elite' included all those actors who had any significant role in the *Punto Fijo* party system. The 'elite' or 'oligarchy', so defined, included not only the leaders of AD and COPEI, but also their largely subordinate social organisations, such as the national labour confederation. Destruction of *la oligarquía* and continuous struggle to prevent its return is seen as a necessary precondition for ending the exclusion of the masses. This theme is apparent in *chavista* rhetoric which emphasises movement unity and solidarity above all other concerns, lest the old elite take advantage of intra-factional conflict (Yepes 2006: 251).

Concerns over infighting were more than justified. The Bolivarian coalition has included a wide variety of groups and social sectors. By basing his electoral appeal on resentment towards the crumbling party system, Chávez drew significant amounts of support at different times from the urban poor, intellectuals, the military, social movements, and even the private sector (McCoy and Myers 2006: ch 2–6). Clearly, these groups have many contradictory interests and historical antagonisms, but they unified around the promise to end their political marginalisation. The cracks in this coalition became apparent shortly after Chávez took power. Populist movements are, in a sense, inherently self-defeating: victory destroys their primary point of grievance. The leftward tilt of Chávez's actual political platform immediately drove away those in the business sector and a substantial portion of the middle class that had supported the MVR movement (Corrales 2011: 75).

Latent conflicts were further exacerbated by the heavy-handed tactics seen as necessary for uprooting remaining traces of the *ancien régime*. Whatever the attitudes of its elites, grassroots *chavistas* tend to be fully committed to the principle of a direct political role for the masses (Hawkins and Hansen 2006; Ramírez 2005). The tactics required by the drive to destroy all vestiges of the old system further eroded support for Chávez among those sectors who had been co-opted under *Punto Fijo* and for whom emancipation from party dominance was an especially potent draw. Nowhere was this clearer than in the 2002 coup that briefly removed Chávez, and the subsequent general strike of 2002–2003, and recall referendum of 2004. The protests that led to Chávez's brief removal and the effort to hoist Chávez on his own constitutional petard by recalling him from office were both led by a worker-business coalition; this odd political union was forged by an attempted takeover of the national worker confederation through a reform of the national labour law and the firing of upper executives of the state oil company (Ellner 2003b: 170–173). The coalition was joined by those sections of civil society that were dissatisfied with *chavista* policy towards autonomous social movements (García-Guadilla 2003:181). A number of prominent intellectuals who had supported Chávez mostly out of antipathy towards the old oligarchy also parted company as the hegemonic tendencies of the regime became more apparent (Hillman 2006).

Although the Bolivarian movement survived all this turmoil, it did not do so unscathed. Support for Chávez had cratered, leading to significant defections of both prominent elites and large swathes of the movement's popular base. Rhetorical paeans to 'participatory protagonist democracy' became difficult to reconcile with the movement's attempts to forcefully assert its control over civil society. When a movement which promises empowerment shows more interest in establishing hegemony over every aspect of society than in actually providing a meaningful political role for its core constituency, the result is inevitable: a major crisis of legitimacy is a foregone conclusion. Survey data from the period confirms this: regime legitimacy, measured by satisfaction with the way democracy works, reached its lowest ebb in 2004 (Latinobarómetro 1998–2008).

To summarise, the Bolivarian movement's commitment to expanding the political role of its constituents exists in constant tension with its need to fortify its ramparts for battle with the oligarchy. The movement's military origins shape this dynamic: supporters are seen as soldiers who must do their duty to protect the movement from omnipresent threats, and the struggle against the enemies of the people must take precedence over proactive inclusion of the masses. Meeting commitments of popular empowerment in this context is extremely tricky. Traditional institutions, such as political parties and elections, are unattractive mechanisms because they are marred by their association with the old regime. The situation is further complicated by the need for movement unity: any devolution of political power must be done in such a way that it does not ignite latent conflicts. This dilemma was particularly acute in the specific case of Bolivarian Venezuela, where the revolution had already strained the ties that bound its coalition nearly to (and for some groups far past) the breaking point in its war with *la oligarquía*. And yet, it should be reemphasised, empowerment was not optional: the legitimacy of the Bolivarian regime, already tarnished by intense conflict and repeated power grabs, rested on it.

### *Los consejos comunales:* participatory governance under populism

The antecedents to the communal councils, in place as early as 2000, demonstrated a potential escape from this dilemma. As it waged its campaigns against the perceived enemies of the revolution at the national level, the Bolivarian movement was experimenting with a number of local level organisations aimed at deepening ties with its popular base through the provision of participatory self-management. One of the earliest and most important of these were the Bolivarian Circles, which were formed in small cells of up to eleven individuals sworn to defend the Bolivarian Constitution and its principles, as well as serve their communities (Hawkins and Hansen 2006: 102–103). In 2002, Chávez issued a decree (in response to an earlier opposition demand for land titles for *barrio* residents) to form Urban Land Committees (CTUs) in groups of 100–200 families in the vast *barrios* of the country's cities, where (as in most large Latin American cities) self-help housing is the rule and many residents lack any legal rights to their property (Holland 2006). The CTUs were organised as self-managed organisations responsible for drawing up maps of their communities to be submitted to the government, at which time individual families would be granted titles to their land. The CTUs also had broad discretion to address issues of community identity, strategies for improvement and other community issues (García-Guadilla 2011: 104). Other organisations, such as rural equivalents of the CTUs, Water Roundtables, and legally recognised cooperative associations were also established during Chávez's first term (López Maya and Lander 2011).

The potential of these organisations to reinforce the faltering Bolivarian movement became apparent during the response to the 2002 coup and the recall election of 2004. The Bolivarian Circles played a key role in organising the protests that returned Chávez to power after his brief removal (Hawkins and Hansen 2006: 102). The Circles, CTUs and other organisations were extremely effective in mobilising support for Chávez during the recall elections (García-Guadilla 2011: 94–98). These institutions proved capable of organising large numbers of citizens from the popular groups which the movement relied upon for support, even when the Bolivarian elite was in total disarray, as it was during the coup. That these organisations could be re-directed towards defence of the revolution at times of extreme threat was no less important: as will be shown later, citizens involved in these organisations who might otherwise have preferred to maintain a focus on community issues felt compelled, either by a sense of duty or direct pressure from *chavista* elites, to do their part in defending the revolution in a time of peril.

Throughout the tumultuous period between the passage of the Bolivarian constitution and the movement's multiple existential crises throughout 2004, the drive to expand participation was undeniable, but was almost entirely reserved for the community level. This was no accident: devolution of power to local-level self-management organisations was a uniquely attractive tactic because it avoided many of the inherent risks that populist movements face when devolving power to their bases. Participatory organisations would concern themselves primarily with basic issues of community development, decided among groups of individuals with common social status and backgrounds. This left thorny policy questions that might cross the social cleavage lines that constantly threaten to become active fault lines within the *chavista* coalition in the hands of Chávez himself, relying on his personal charisma to settle disputes and adjudicate conflicts in a controlled manner. However the patchwork of multiple programmes, often with overlapping mandates and goals, prevented them from fulfilling their full potential, both for deepening local democracy and defending the national movement.

Clearly the historical context which gave rise to the communal councils and other participatory fora in Bolivarian Venezuela differs significantly from cases like Uruguay and Brazil, wherein such programmes were grafted on to representative democracies. In that context, participatory governance was intended to produce more egalitarian policy outcomes and train citizens to participate more effectively when engaging with representative institutions (Biaocchi 2001). Under populism, such programmes serve a different role, although some similarities do exist. Both representative democracy and charismatic populism share an inherent contradiction. Both legitimate themselves by claiming to embody popular sovereignty. Representativists and populists alike claim the right to rule because they are chosen by the people. And yet both allow the people only indirect exercise of that sovereignty. Participatory programmes allow for a relatively unmediated exercise of self-governance, helping to ease any discontent which arises from this contradiction.

Quantitative analysis supports this interpretation of the role of communal councils in Venezuela. To show this, I use data from the 2010 and 2012 waves of the LAPOP survey in Venezuela. LAPOP is one of the most frequently used and highly respected regional public opinion survey projects.

## Dependent variable

The theory presented here is that communal councils (as a stand-in for all participatory fora) increase support for the *chavista* regime. I use three questions to measure regime support: respect for political institutions (b2), pride in the political system (b4) and systemic support (b6). These indicators are recommended as measures of regime support by the creators of the LAPOP survey who have also demonstrated their validity as indicators of the concept (Booth and Seligson 2009). Results from the measurement portion of the model indicate that these indicators are appropriate measures of the latent concept; the results are presented in Table 12.1.

## Independent variables

Participation in the communal councils is measured via a four-point scale of frequency of participation (cp15). The last of the substantively interesting variables, participatory preference, is measured via a seven point scale question which asked respondents if they agreed that the people should govern directly (pop107). In addition to these, I include a number of standard demographic control

*Table 12.1: Measurement model estimation results*

| Loadings for regime support | Est. | SE | P-value |
| --- | --- | --- | --- |
| Pride in political system (b2) | *1.000* | – | – |
| Respect for institutions (b4) | .717 | .021 | .000 |
| Systemic support (b6) | .938 | .020 | .000 |

| Error Variance | Est. | SE | P-value |
| --- | --- | --- | --- |
| Pride in political system (b2) | .277 | .012 | .000 |
| Respect for institutions (b4) | .627 | .018 | .000 |
| Systemic support (b6) | .358 | .013 | .000 |

variables: support for Chávez, income, education, ideology, sex, race (a dummy coded 0 for white respondents and 1 for all others), urban/rural, and a dummy variable for survey year.

## Estimation

Estimation of model parameters was conducted using MPLUS version 7.2 (data and code are available on request), using Maximum Likelihood with missing values (MLMV). MLMV builds the likelihood function one observation at a time, using whatever information is available for each observation, without requiring the specification of a measurement model (Allison 2012).

Because communal council participation is likely to be predicted in part by systemic support and *chavismo*, I allow participation to be endogenous in order to avoid bias. This requires treating the council participation variable as continuous, which is risky given its four-point scale; treating it as ordinal using a WLS estimator did not substantially alter the results. The measurement model is identified via the three factor rule. By excluding the 'urban' dummy variable from the equation for support and including it in the equation for council participation, the structural portion of the model is identified via the rank and order conditions (Bollen 1989). Since efficacy is not impacted by support, I conducted analysis of that model separately. This allowed the inclusion of all relevant control variables without concerns over identification issues. Results of the structural component of analysis are presented in Table 12.2.

Council participation has a substantial positive impact on support, but only among those with strong participatory preferences. Among those who do not prefer direct participation (standardised value of -2), the effect is actually negative (-1.30), which may reflect dissatisfaction with some of the operational problems that impact many councils. However among those with strong participatory preferences (standardised value of 2), the impact of council participation rivals that of *chavismo* (.577 compared to .653), which is remarkable given the overwhelming dominance of Hugo Chávez in the Venezuelan political system.

In sum, these analyses demonstrate that the councils allow the Bolivarian movement to convince its militants that its most important promise is being kept: that those who were long excluded from democracy, as practiced during the *Punto Fijo* era, finally be allowed to exercise power directly and collectively within their communities to solve social problems. They further show the importance of this promise to the legitimation of a regime which might otherwise have alienated its base with its authoritarian practices.

This does not, however, qualitatively demonstrate that the councils serve a different function than participatory budgeting does in Brazil, for example. There is no reason why we should not expect participants in a programme which becomes popular to increase their support for the political actor or regime which sponsors that programme. However, in the following sections I demonstrate that the actual practices of the councils do mark them as significantly different from similar programmes in representative systems.

*Table 12.2: SEM analysis of communal council participation (YX standardised)*

| | Regime Support (n=2,986) | | | Council Participation (n=2,986) | | |
|---|---|---|---|---|---|---|
| | Estimate | SE | p-value | Estimate | SE | p-value |
| Council participation | −.359 | .099 | .000 | − | − | − |
| Participatory preference | −.287 | .079 | .000 | − | − | − |
| Interaction (CP*PP) | .468 | .116 | .000 | − | − | − |
| External efficacy | .218 | .017 | .000 | − | − | − |
| Chavismo | .653 | .018 | .000 | −.019 | .071 | .786 |
| Regime support | − | − | − | .316 | .088 | .000 |
| Income | −.011 | .017 | .538 | −.012 | .020 | .557 |
| Education | −.005 | .016 | .763 | − | − | − |
| Female | −.050 | .014 | .000 | − | − | − |
| Age | .039 | .015 | .010 | − | − | − |
| Urban | − | − | − | −.068 | .019 | .000 |
| Ideology | −.073 | .017 | .000 | − | − | − |
| Race | .022 | .014 | .119 | − | − | − |
| 2012 wave dummy | .017 | .016 | .281 | −.066 | .012 | .000 |

| | Regime Support | |
|---|---|---|
| Goodness of Fit Statistics | Statistic | P-value |
| Chi-Square (REF) | 433.9 | .000 |
| RMSEA | .046 | |
| CFI | .957 | |
| SRMR | .034 | |

## Legitimating populism: participatory governance and regime support

Before investigating the councils' practices, a clear standard for evaluating their participatory *bona fides* must be put forward, and potential violations of that standard posited. The central argument of this chapter is that participatory fora can have radically different effects on social conflict in different contexts; if programmes like the communal councils are not truly participatory that argument cannot be sustained. Participation is an extremely broad term that can include anything from signing a petition to running for office, depending on how the concept is defined. Many populist movements involve a substantial degree of mobilisation, although this often takes the form of predominantly symbolic activities (such as rally attendance). This is a critically important distinction for the theory presented herein, as I will argue that the communal councils provide much more genuine participatory opportunities than other 'mobilised' variants of authoritarian politics, such as communism or electoral authoritarianism. Given the importance of genuine empowerment to my argument, a stricter standard is necessary here, one wherein the political action of common citizens has a meaningful and relatively direct effect on governance. I borrow a concept from participatory economics to serve as this standard: the concept of self-management, which requires that decisions be made by those who are governed by those decisions (Albert and Hanhel 1991). This concept overlaps a great deal with the top three rungs of Sherry Armstein's 'ladder of participation', especially 'delegation of power' (1969: 219–223). More specifically applied to the councils, policies and projects decided upon must be made by the assembly of citizens (wherein the citizenry as a whole has final authority), without undue interference from outside actors. Potential violations of this standard include higher-level government organisations dictating policy to the councils (which would then be reduced to little more than a rubber stamp), or the hijacking of council governance by their administrative personnel.

The legal framework that establishes the councils is clear: the assembly of citizens in the council is the 'highest instance of deliberation and decision making for the exercise of community power'. Decisions in this body must be made by majority vote of at least 20 per cent of community members to have legal force ('Ley Orgánica de los Consejos Comunales' 2009: art. 20–22). The councils determine community development priorities, and may implement projects based on those priorities using resources transferred from municipal or regional governments, or from funds (such as *Fundacomunal*) managed by the central government. Often projects involve working with other Bolivarian organisations, such as the social mission for housing or the *chavista* union for construction workers, especially for major projects such as housing construction (Caripa 2012). Types of projects include housing, organising sports teams, developing basic infrastructure such as electricity and water.

The rules of procedure set out by law, supported by evidence from survey data, are sufficient to dismiss concerns that *voceros* may exercise undue dominance in their councils. As José Machado of *Centro Gumilla* points out, *voceros* are subject to recall at any point; those who usurp the assembly's authority can be easily dismissed (Machado 2009: 17). An analysis which relied on extensive interviews with council leaders found that the election of *voceros* was not a significant problem (Triviño Salazar 2013). Concerns over hijacking of the councils by their administrative personnel seem unfounded. The importance of funding from the central government is a more serious potential violation and thus requires closer analysis.

Although funds for council projects can, by law, come from a number of sources (including municipal and regional governments), in practice most of the funds for projects come from the national government, especially in poor communities where municipalities lack resources (Briceño 2012; Liendro 2012a). This dependence on external funding raises the questions of whether the funding decisions of the central government reflect stated community priorities or unilateral impositions. If national elites ignore or pre-shape the will of the community, participation cannot be considered genuine. Deepening this concern, the ministries often submit project proposals to the councils. For example, two *voceros* whom I interviewed mentioned that their councils were currently working on projects proposed by the central government (Liendro 2012b; Ripley 2012).

Although these objections are serious, neither proves common enough to abrogate the authority of the councils to make decisions for themselves. Both the *voceros* who mentioned government-proposed projects (one of whom is an opposition supporter) denied that there was any undue pressure to accept the government proposals. Relations between the councils and the central government were not always cordial, often due to conflict with the ministries over funding delays and a lack of transparency. Nevertheless, a survey of 1,000 council members collected by *Centro Gumilla* (Machado 2009: 29) indicate that 71 per cent of respondents felt that the community as a whole consented to all council projects in their community; only 7 per cent felt that 'official entities' (i.e. the central government) had the last word in council decisions. The ministries may not be entirely responsive to the stated priorities of the communities, but violations seem to be the exception rather than the rule. This undermines the suggestion that the existence of government proposals represent violations of participation. In the normal course of things, the assemblies appear to work largely as intended, at least in the planning phase: they set community priorities, and create proposals for development projects based on participatory decision making.

The design of the councils in law clearly establishes them as participatory organisations, and no compelling evidence exists in either qualitative or public opinion data that the state or political actors intervene in the councils' business in a manner sufficiently systematic to represent a violation of participatory norms. This is not to say that the councils function exactly as designed. Like everything else in Venezuela, serious problems of corruption, inefficiency and outright incompetence create all manner of problems for the day to day functioning of the councils. Whether or not the participatory opportunities provided by the councils are also democratic is another question entirely.

### *¿Quiénes son el pueblo?* Participation and democracy in the communal councils

Participatory the communal councils may be, but they do not contribute to the deepening of democracy in Venezuela. The concepts of institutional strength and weakness, outlined in the introductory chapters of this book, shed light on why, although in a somewhat complex manner. The introductory chapter emphasises the shortcomings of strong institutions (where powerful actors can use rigid institutional rules to reinforce their authority), and the promise of weak institutions (which allow for innovation). The councils have elements of both strong and weak institutions. They are strong because their existence is encoded in law, as are many of the details of their praxis; they are weak because necessary elements of financial and organisational support are not sufficiently institutionalised.

In this section I argue that the role the councils (and similar participatory fora) play in reinforcing populist social conflict is not a straightforward result of either strength or weakness, but rather of an interaction between the two. Various legal formalities, especially the requirement that the councils be registered with the central bureaucracy and the availability of government funding, channel the energies of civil society into these institutions, even if activists would rather remain independent. This draws social organisations into the Bolivarian orbit, perhaps against the better judgment of civil society actors. This would not necessarily exacerbate social conflict, were participatory institutions even stronger in specific ways (if they had guaranteed funding streams, as participatory budgeting programmes often do).

It is here where institutional weakness comes into play. The councils suffer from what might be called 'strategic weakness'. That is, that various aspects of their design and praxis are informal in a way that benefits the Bolivarian movement. It is perhaps impossible to know if this fortuity was intentional or merely a happy (from the *chavista* perspective) accident, given the impenetrability of the Bolivarian elite. What matters is that two areas of institutional weakness have allowed the *chavista* movement to penetrate and politicise these organisations in a way which is clearly outside the bounds of participatory democracy. First, the dependence of the councils on funding from the central government, and the lack of transparent and predictable mechanisms for distribution of resources, makes good relations with the Bolivarian movement an important element in a council's success. Ties to the Bolivarian elite help cut through the red tape of the central ministries, ensuring that programmes get funded. Second, the councils require a considerable amount of operational knowledge and organisational skill on the part of their members, many of whom have never actively engaged in politics under the oligarchic *Punto Fijo* regime. This leads to a situation wherein the councils require outside organisational support, which is not provided by law. This creates a gap which the Bolivarian movement has been quick to fill, to its advantage.

**Funding the Councils**

As mentioned before, the dependence of the councils on state funding raises the real possibility of deliberate politicisation, wherein government allies may be given unfair access to resources. This dependence ties the effectiveness of councils to the central government, reinforcing delegative tendencies of the political system (Lovera 2008). With few safeguards for ensuring that funding decisions are apolitical, serious potential for abuse exists (Álvarez and García-Guadilla 2011: 177). There is further cause for concern because not all projects are funded, although ministry personnel involved in funding decisions claim that sufficient resources are available to fund major priorities for all councils (Araujo 2012). *Centro Gumilla* found that only 57 per cent of councils had their projects funded, and of those 47 per cent experienced significant delays in funding (Machado 2008: 37–38). *Centro Gumilla* further found that a plurality of individuals, dissatisfied with their council, cite the fact that the councils do not function at all, and this tendency is especially marked among opposition councils (Machado 2009: 16). These findings concur with other studies of other *chavista* programmes, such as the social missions (Hawkins 2010; Hawkins, Rosas and Johnson 2011). Nor is deliberate, top-down bias the most important source of exclusion from the communal councils.

## Bolivarian Culture and the Politicisation of Participatory Opportunities

The ambiguity of evidence for direct discrimination in terms of funding is far from sufficient to support the Bolivarian movement's democratic *bona fides*. While direct and intentional violations of democratic norms are difficult to conclusively show given available data, there is considerable evidence for another form of discrimination, more nebulous but nonetheless crucial. This violation of universality follows directly from the Bolivarian worldview, wherein political power is the sole right of 'the people', membership in which is synonymous with membership in the movement and support of its revolution. This close identification of political access and movement loyalty was written into law in 2009, wherein the purpose of the councils was rewritten to include 'the construction of a [...] socialist society' (*Ley Orgánica de los consejos Comunales 2009*, art. 2). The inclusion of the term 'socialist', which occurs throughout the document, sends a clear message: the councils and other participatory forums do not represent universal democratic rights, but are tightly intertwined with the struggle against those whom the Bolivarians view as enemies of the people.

This association between the councils and *chavismo* has become so close that in some circumstances the distinction disappears entirely. One professor, trying to get a list of council participants in a given municipality was directed by the mayor's office to another location where the list was available; the location turned out to be local headquarters for PSUV (García-Guadilla 2013). Occasionally the lack of distinction between these programmes and their political creators leads lower level functionaries to engage in demonstrably undemocratic activity. An employee in the complaints department of *Fundacomunal* reported, shortly after the new organic law for the councils was enacted (which required all councils to re-register and demonstrate their compliance with the new laws) that a local official was refusing to certify the founding documents of councils whose *voceros* were not PSUV members (Bowman 2013).

This partiality manifests itself not so much in what the state provides but in what it fails to provide: political education and organisational support for citizens, many of whom are new to political participation of any kind, much less direct deliberative participation. One ministry employee cited the lack of organisation as the reason why opposition councils have trouble gaining funding; these councils often submit dozens of contradictory, underdeveloped proposals that require months of revision with ministry technical teams to become ready for action. *Chavista* councils, by contrast, tend to be high functioning, submitting proposals that demonstrate feasibility of the work proposed and have clear priorities already in place when they arrive at the ministries (Araujo 2012).

The reason that *chavista* councils are so much better organised is not entirely clear. Within the councils, the result is that many citizens who would prefer to focus on community priorities exclusively feel compelled to take a more active role in *chavista* politics in order to get the support their councils need. Many *voceros* reported feeling compelled to join PSUV in order to 'be heard' (Álvarez and García-Guadilla 2011: 199–200; García-Guadilla 2008: 139). Even if there is no deliberate discrimination at the ministerial level, the crippling inefficiency of the central government means that a strong connection within the PSUV is a considerable advantage in getting through administrative bottlenecks.

This would mirror the experience of other participatory programmes, where active work in *chavista* campaigns is expected of participants in government-sponsored participatory programmes, especially when the revolution was seen as facing an existential threat (García-Guadilla 2011). In times of great need, the Bolivarian elite has on occasion thrown out all pretence of impartiality and demanded that the councils fulfil their 'duties' to the movement. In 2009, the Minister of Participation directly ordered the councils to campaign for the *chavista* side in the constitutional referendum (López Maya and Panzarelli 2013: 257).

To summarise, discrimination against opposition councils is likely to be a mixture of direction from upper leadership, sporadic acts by individual *chavistas*, and unconscious adherence to a populist view of opponents as enemies. Whatever the relative proportions of each, the councils clearly fail to meet the standard of universality which should be required to consider them truly democratic. Instead the councils are an instance of what one author who conducted extensive interviews with council participants called 'conditioned participation' (Triviño Salazar 2013). Self-governance in local matters is a real aspect of the councils, but it is granted in such a way that it encourages movement unity and allows the councils to be turned towards defence of the regime when the need arises.

It should be re-emphasised that this does *not* cast any doubt on the reality of participatory governance within the councils; discrimination can be thought of as unacceptable restrictions on democratic citizenship, which is an entirely separate issue from the *content* of rights conferred by that citizenship upon those who possess it. This distinction is important, because it further supports the view of Bolivarianism as an instance of participatory populism. Partiality in the provision of access to functioning councils is clear, but that partiality does not extend to the principles of participatory decision making within the councils. This combination fits poorly within a framework influenced by *caudillismo* or participatory democracy, but is entirely consistent within a worldview that sees direct participation, and the empowerment it brings, as essential political rights, but which reserves political rights for those who prove themselves worthy through support of the struggle against an oligarchical class constantly scheming to usurp the authority of the people.

## Conclusion

This chapter demonstrates the importance of analysing institutions with the institutional ecology in which they operate firmly in mind. Crude attempts to divine patterns of association between institutional types and political outcomes are likely to be doomed to fail in many circumstances because assumptions of unit homogeneity are invalid. Brazil and Uruguay are not the same as Venezuela. Although one can observe participatory fora in each, the underlying purpose of these programmes, and the other institutions with which they interact, are so fundamentally different that it would approach foolishness to assume that they would have similar impacts on social conflict.

The Venezuelan case, in particular, raises some interesting (and troubling) questions about the role of participatory institutions in modern politics. Bolivarian initiatives like the communal councils demonstrate that genuine participatory institutions need not be democratic in a meaningful sense. Many students of participatory democracy experiments hope that such organisations can improve the quality of democracy (Biaocchi 2001). Following Rousseau (2002) and others, advocates argued that micro-level participation could train citizens to become more assertive and active in the political process at higher levels, challenging entrenched power-holders and thereby enhancing representative institutions (Avritzer 2002; Barber 1984; Pateman 1970).

This analysis shows the necessity of an important caveat: that participatory governance can exist outside a democratic framework. In the Venezuelan case, participatory governance actually serves to reinforce the ties between the masses and a hegemonic leader (Lovera 2008); local participation supports national subservience. Nor is democracy, depending on how one defines the concept, a necessary precondition for meaningful participation in all circumstances. In certain contexts, especially those wherein empowerment is viewed as desirable or necessary but notions of universality and fair competition are held in contempt, participatory access can become a benefit to be given only to supporters of an elite faction. The interaction between the effects of participation and the dynamics of national politics can produce strange outcomes. In the Venezuelan case, participatory access serves as another mechanism for binding together a weak coalition that might otherwise fracture.

The implications for conflict management are fairly clear. Populism is an ideology that thrives on conflict (Madrid, Hunter and Weyland 2010); it views politics not as a competitive sport but a permanent war between the people and an evil elite which has usurped its sovereignty (Hawkins 2010). Waging that war requires organisation of 'the people'; militants must be formed into units capable of concerted action (particularly during elections), and wavering supporters must be wooed (or coerced) back into the fold.

In representative democracies, parties (such as the PT in Brazil or the FA in Uruguay) certainly hope that grateful participants in participatory fora they sponsor will reward their beneficence on election day. Under populism, that hope becomes an existential imperative. As such, the ties that bind participants to elites are tighter, and the hand that forges those ties heavier. The preferential granting of organisational support, and the need to tow the party line in order to dislodge projects from the central bureaucracy produce overbearing pressures that improperly politicise such programmes. The end result is perverse: programmes which theoretically should usher in a more consensual, harmonious mode of politics instead push citizens more firmly into warring camps of elites and masses, populists and oligarchs.

## References

Albert, M. and Hanhel, R. (1991) *The Political Economy of Participatory Economics*, Princeton, NJ: Princeton University Press.

Allison, P. (2012) 'Handling Missing Data by Maximum Likelihood', *SAS Global Forum 2012*. http://www.statisticalhorizons.com/wp-content/uploads/MissingDataByML.pdf (accessed 6 February 2017)

Álvarez, R. and García-Guadilla, M. (2011) 'Contraloría social y clientelismo: la praxis de los consejos comunales en Venezuela', *Politeia*, 34(46): 175–207.

Araujo, K. (2012) Telephone interview by author with Fondacomunal employee.

Armstein, S. (1969) 'A ladder of participation', *Journal of the American Institute of Planners*, 35(4): 216–224.

Avritzer, L. (2002) *Democracy in the Public Space in Latin America*, Princeton, NJ: Princeton University Press.

Barber, B. (1984) *Strong Democracy: Participatory politics for a new age*, Berkeley, CA: University of California Press.

Biaocchi, G. (2001) 'Participation, activism, and politics: the Porto Alegre experiment and deliberative democratic theory', *Politics and Society*, 29(1): 43–72.

Bollen, K. (1989) *Structural Equations with Latent Variables*, New York: Wiley.

Booth, J. and Seligson, M. (2009) *The Legitimacy Puzzle: Political support and democracy in eight nations*, Cambridge: Cambridge University Press.

Bowman, Q. (2013) Interview with Fondacomunal employee.

Briceño, H. (2012) Interview by author with UCV-CENDES Professor.

Caripa, B. (2012) 'Constructores trabajarán con consejos comunales: proyectan hacer un centro de convenciones en La Carlota', *Últimas Noticias*, 11 October 2012. Retrieved from http://www.ultimasnoticias.com.ve/noticias/actualidad/economia/constructores-trabajaran-con-consejos-comunales.aspx (accessed 13 October 2012).

Ciccariello-Maher, G. (2013) *We Created Chávez*, Durham, NC: Duke University Press.

Coppedge, D. (1994) *Strong Parties and Lame Ducks: Presidential partyarchy and factionalism in Venezuela*, Stanford, CA: Stanford University Press.

Corrales, J. (2011) 'Why Polarize? Advantages and disadvantages of a rational-choice analysis of government-opposition relations under Hugo Chávez', in T. Ponniah and J. Eastwood (eds) *The Revolution in Venezuela: Social and political change under Chávez*, Cambridge, MA: Harvard University Press, pp. 67–98.

Ellner, S. (2003a) 'Introduction: A search for explanations', in S. Ellner and D. Hellinger (eds) *Venezuelan Politics in the Chávez Era: Class, polarization and conflict*, Boulder, CO: Lynne Rienner Publishers, pp. 7–26.

—— (2003b) 'Organized Labor and the Challenge of Chavismo', in S. Ellner and D. Hellinger (eds) *Venezuelan Politics in the Chávez Era: Class, polarization and conflict*, Boulder, CO: Lynne Rienner Publishers, pp. 161–78.

García-Guadilla, M. P. (2003) 'Civil Society: Institutionalization, fragmentation, autonomy', in S. Ellner and D. Hellinger (eds) *Venezuelan Politics in the Chávez Era: Class, polarization, and conflict*, Boulder, CO: Lynne Rienner Publishers, pp. 179–96.

—— (2008) 'La praxis de los consejos comunales en Venezuela: ¿Poder popular o instancia clientelar?', *Revista Venezolana de Economía y Ciencias Sociales*, 14(1): 125–151.

—— (2011) 'Urban Land Committees: Co-optation, autonomy and protagonism', in D. Smilde and D. Hellinger (eds) *Venezuela's Bolivarian Democracy*, Durham, NC: Duke University Press, pp. 80–103.

—— (2013) E-mail interview by author with Universidad de Simón Bolivar professor.

Hawkins, K. (2010) *Venezuela's Chavismo and Populism in Comparative Perspective*, Cambridge: Cambridge University Press.

Hawkins, K. and Hansen, D. (2006) 'Dependent civil society: the Circulos Bolivarianos in Venezuela', *Latin American Research Review*, 41(1): 102–132.

Hawkins, K., Rosas, G. and Johnson, M. (2011) 'The Misiones of the Chávez Government', in D. Smilde and D. Hellinger (eds) *Venezuela's Bolivarian Democracy: Participation, politics and culture under Chávez*, Durham, NC: Duke University Press, pp. 186–218.

Hellinger, D. (2003) 'Political Overview: The breakdown of *Puntofijismo* and the rise of *Chavismo*', in S. Ellner and D. Hellinger (eds) *Venezuelan Politics in the Chávez Era: Class, polarization, and conflict*, Boulder, CO: Lynne Rienner Publishers, pp. 27–54.

Hillman, R. (2006) 'Intellectuals: An elite divided', in J. McCoy and D. Myers (eds) *The Unraveling of Representative Democracy in Venezuela*, Baltimore, MD: Johns Hopkins University Press, pp. 115–29.

Holland, A. (2006) 'Venezuela's Urban Land Committees and Participatory Democracy', *Venezuelanalysis.com*. http://venezuelanalysis.com/analysis/1611 (accessed 6 February 2017).

Ley Orgánica de los Consejos Comunales (2009) No. 751. Retrieved from http://www.mp.gob.ve/c/document_library/get_file?uuid=cc72df08-0593-422e-a70b-0e884f7cd59a&groupId=10136 (accessed 6 February 2017).

Liendro, F. (2012a) E-mail communication by author with comite de viviende de Francisco de Miranda member (22/10/2012).

—— (2012b) Interview by author with member of el comite de viviende de Francisco de Miranda (27/10/2012).

López Maya, M. (1999) 'La protesta venezolana entre 1989 y 1993 (en un umbral del neolibralismo)', in M. López Maya (ed.) *Lucha popular, democracia, neoliberalismo: protesta popular en América Latina en los años de ajuste*, Caracas: Editorial Nueva Sociedad, pp. 211–38.

López Maya, M. and Lander, L. (2011) 'Participatory Democracy in Venezuela: Origins, ideas, and implementation', in D. Hellinger and D. Smilde (eds) *Venezuela's Bolivarian Democracy: Participation, politics, and culture Under Chávez*, Durham, NC: Duke University Press, pp. 58–79.

López Maya, M. and Panzarelli, A. (2013) 'Populism, Renterism and Socialism in Twenty-First-Century Venezuela' in C. de la Torre and C. J. Arnson (eds) *Latin American Populism in the Twenty-First Century*, Washington, D.C.: Johns Hopkins University Press, pp. 239–68.

Lovera, A. (2008) 'Los consejos comunales en Venezuela: ¿Democracia participativa o delegativa?', *Revista Venezolana de Economía y Ciencias Sociales*, 14(1), Retrieved from Scientific Electronic Library Online website: http://www.scielo.org.ve/scielo.php?pid=S1315-64112008000100008&script=sci_arttext (accessed 6 February 2017).

Machado, J. E. (2008) 'Estudio de los Consejos Comunales en Venezuela', Retrieved from http://gumilla.org/files/documents/Estudio-Consejos-Comunales01.pdf. (accessed 6 February 2017).

—— (2009) Estudio cuantitativo de opinión sobre los Consejos Comunales. Retrieved from http://www.civilisac.org/civilis/wp-content/uploads/estudio-cualitativo-de-consejoscomunales-gumilla-2009-1.pdf. (accessed 6 February 2017).

McCoy, J. and Myers, D. (eds) (2006) *The Unravelling of Representative Democracy in Venezuela*, Baltimore, MD: Johns Hopkins University Press.

Madrid, R., Hunter, W. and Weyland, K. (2010) 'The Policies and Performance of the Contestory and Moderate Left', in K. Weyland, R. Madrid and W. Hunter (eds) *Leftist Governments in Latin America: Successes and shortcomings*, Cambridge: Cambridge University Press, pp. 140–80.

Molina, J. (2006) 'The Unraveling of Venezuela's Party System: From party rule to personalistic politics and deinstitutionalization', in J. McCoy and D. Myers (eds) *The Unraveling of Representative Democracy in Venezuela*, Baltimore, MD: Johns Hopkins University Press, pp. 152–80.

Myers, D. (2006) 'The Normalization of Punto Fijo Democracy', in J. McCoy and D. Myers (eds) *The Unraveling of Representative Democracy in Venezuela*, Baltimore, MD: Johns Hopkins University Press, pp. 11–32.

Pateman, C. (1970) *Participation and Democratic Theory*, New York, NY: Cambridge University Press.

Ramírez, C. V. (2005) 'Venezuela's Bolivarian revolution: who are the Chavistas?', *Latin American Perspectives*, 32(3): 79–97.

Ripley, G. (2012) Interview by author with *vocero from El Valle (comuna Galipan)*.

Rousseau, J. (2002) 'The Social Contract', in S. Dunn (ed.) *The Social Contract and the First and Second Discourses*, New Haven, CT: Yale University Press, pp. 149–256.

Triviño Salazar, J. (2013) 'The promise of transformation through participation: an analysis of Communal Councils in Caracas, Venezuela', Retrieved from http://repub.eur.nl/pub/39829 (accessed 6 February 2017).

Yepes, J. (2006) 'Public Opinion, Political Socialization, and Regime Stabilization', in J. McCoy and D. Myers (eds) *The Unraveling of Representative Democracy in Venezuela*, Baltimore, MD: Johns Hopkins University Press, pp. 231–262.

# Index

Numbers in *italics* refer to Tables and Figures

www.ingramcontent.com/pod-product-compliance
Lightning Source LLC
Chambersburg PA
CBHW021808270326
41932CB00007B/103